Chinese American Death Rituals

Chinese American Death Rituals

Respecting the Ancestors

Edited by
Sue Fawn Chung and
Priscilla Wegars

ALTAMIRA
PRESS

A DIVISION OF
ROWMAN & LITTLEFIELD PUBLISHERS, INC.
Lanham • *New York* • *Toronto* • *Oxford*

ALTAMIRA PRESS
A division of Rowman & Littlefield Publishers, Inc.
A wholly owned subsidiary of The Rowman & Littlefield Publishing Group, Inc.
4501 Forbes Boulevard, Suite 200
Lanham, MD 20706
www.altamirapress.com

PO Box 317, Oxford, OX2 9RU, UK

British Library Cataloguing in Publication Information Available

Library of Congress Cataloging-in-Publication Data

Chinese American death rituals : respecting the ancestors / edited by Sue Fawn Chung
and Priscilla Wegars.
   p. cm.
  Includes bibliographical references (p.) and index.
  ISBN 0-7591-0733-5 (alk. paper) — ISBN 0-7591-0734-3 (pbk. : alk. paper)
  1. Chinese Americans—Funeral rites and ceremonies. I. Chung, Sue Fawn, 1944–
II. Wegars, Priscilla.

E184.C5C4757 2005
393'.089'951073—dc22

2004014825

Printed in the United States of America

∞™ The paper used in this publication meets the minimum requirements of American
National Standard for Information Sciences—Permanence of Paper for Printed Library
Materials, ANSI/NISO Z39.48-1992.

Contents

Acknowledgments

We are pleased to acknowledge a number of people for their help in making this book a reality. Our greatest thanks are reserved for Claire and Lennard Chin and family, Gail DeSantis, Walter and Dora Mih, Darby Stapp and Julie Longenecker, Alison Stenger, Brenda von Wandruszka, Lily and Chien Wai, Gloria and Bruce Wong, and an anonymous donor, who all generously contributed toward a publication subvention. We are particularly grateful to them for their continuing support of research on Chinese Americans in the West. Special thanks to Grace Ebron and our two anonymous readers and especially to all the contributors, who endured several revisions without complaint and who agreed that all authors' royalties will benefit the University of Idaho's Asian American Comparative Collection.

—Sue Fawn Chung and Priscilla Wegars

Introduction: The editors acknowledge, with thanks, assistance from Terry Abraham, Alan Solomon, and Emma Woo Louie.

Chapter 1: This chapter was completed primarily under the direction and guidance of Jerald Johnson, who encouraged me to pursue my research interests. Special thanks to Priscilla Wegars, Sue Fawn Chung, Philomene Smith, Joan Neide, and Wil Jorae for their editorial assistance on this project.

—Wendy L. Rouse

Chapter 2: The members and friends of the Bok Kai Temple and the City of Marysville have assisted in this project. Special thanks to my wife and assistant, Phyllis Chace.

—Paul G. Chace

Chapter 3: This work was completed primarily through the fieldwork of Jerald J. Johnson and Melissa K. Farncomb, who devoted many years to the study of the Chinese at Virginiatown. The semesters of fieldwork would not have been possible without the hard work and physical labor of the many CSUS volunteers and students. Special recognition to Philomene Smith, Dan Patrick, Betty and Jim Falltrick, Theresa Lechner, and Linda Sandelin for their archaeological expertise. Thanks to Hiroshi Matsuda and the Engellener family for their generosity and support throughout the project. Thanks to Jerald Johnson, Priscilla Wegars, Sue Fawn Chung, Joan Neide, and Philomene Smith for their editorial advice. Also thanks to Linda Crowder, Fred Blake, Paul Chace, Roberta Greenwood, Terry Abraham, Mary Maniery, Cindy Baker, and Sylvia Sun Minnick for sharing their research and professional knowledge. Thanks to Sunshine Psota, Lynn Downey, Thomas Rost, Margie Akin, Glenn Farris, Maggie Craw, Jenny Gao, Xiao Yun Yao, Emma Woo Louie, and Samantha Hens for their assistance in the artifact-analysis phase of the project. This chapter is dedicated to the memory of all the Chinese miners who lived and died in the gold towns of California.

—Wendy L. Rouse

Chapter 4: We gratefully acknowledge the assistance of staff members of the U.S. Forest Service, Humboldt-Toiyabe National Forest; Bureau of Land Management, Elko District; Nevada Humanities; Elko County Commission; Northeastern Nevada Museum; Elko County Chapter of the Nevada Archaeological Association; University of Nevada, Las Vegas; staff members at the Office of Vital Statistics in Carson City; and Engel Brothers Media for *National Geographic*. Excavation was made possible with permission from the landowners Cammy and Randy Meierhoff and Michael Tangreen, whose families assisted in the archaeological project. Others who assisted us in various ways were Mary Wammack; LuAnn Caressi; Sondra Cosgrove; Ralph Giles; Gerhard Grytz; Donna L. Murphy; Alan M. Solomon; Mary and Elmer Rusco; David Valentine; Neil Thomsen, now retired, of the National Archives and Records Administration; Jeffrey Kintop and other staff members of the Nevada State Archives; Judy Swett of the Elko County Genealogy Society; Phillip Earl, formerly of the Nevada Historical Society, Reno; and Amy Dansie, formerly of the Nevada State Museum.

—Sue Fawn Chung, Fred P. Frampton, and Timothy W. Murphy

Chapter 5: Thanks to Peter Bell, Randall Bloch, Tim Marsh, Trelle Morrow, Gertrude Perkins, and DeAnn Scrabeck for sharing hard-to-find articles; to Charles L. Belanger for a lengthy telephone interview; to Emma Woo Louie for clarification of Chinese names; and to Jennifer O'Laughlin and the staff of the Interlibrary Loan Department, University of Idaho Library, for their assistance.

—Terry Abraham and Priscilla Wegars

Chapter 6: We gratefully acknowledge the assistance of Fred Blake, Mr. and Mrs. George C. K. Young, Alan M. Solomon, Mary Wammack, Gertrude Ceballos, David Chang, Roland Chang, Bobby Motooka, Richard Tam Sing, Alice Tihada, and Anthony Vierra.

—Sue Fawn Chung and Reiko Neizman

Chapter 7: This article would not have been possible without the help and support of Clifford Yee, former manager of the Green Street Mortuary, and his staff. In addition, historian Him Mark Lai; Lisa Pollard of the Green Street Brass Band; Wilson Wong, formerly of the Cathay Club Band; and Larry Chan of the Nam Hoy Association have provided invaluable assistance and data. I thank all my sources and friends for their patience and trust. In particular I would like to acknowledge Lily Tsui, Bill Steiner, and Bernard Wong, PhD.

—Linda Sun Crowder

Chapter 8: The author is very grateful to Judith Rasson, PhD, for the sensitive interviews, and to all those who contributed their information and insights.

—Roberta S. Greenwood

Introduction

Sue Fawn Chung and Priscilla Wegars

Death is a topic that has fascinated people for centuries. In the English-speaking world, eulogies in poetic form can be traced back to the 1640s, but gained prominence with the "graveyard school" of poets in the eighteenth century often stressing the finality of death. Thomas Parnell's "Night-Piece on Death" (1722), Robert Blair's "The Grave" (1743), and Thomas Gray's "Elegy in a Country Churchyard" (1751) are a few examples of this.[1] Within the last fifty-plus years, popular books, such as Evelyn Waugh's *The Loved One* (1948) and Jessica Mitford's *The American Way of Death* (1963), have fed this interest. More recently, semiautobiographical and biographical works about Chinese Americans and their concern for ancestors and spirits have enjoyed critical and popular acclaim, most notably Maxine Hong Kingston's *The Woman Warrior* (1976) and *China Men* (1980), Amy Tan's *The Joy Luck Club* (1989) and *The Kitchen God's Wife* (1991), and Lisa See's *On Gold Mountain* (1995).

This book will survey Chinese American funerary rituals and cemeteries from the late nineteenth century until the present in order to understand the importance of Chinese funerary rites and their transformation through time. Asian ethnic expressions regarding death differ from Western traditions. Until recently, little has been known about Chinese American funerary rituals and practices that illustrate the weltanschauung of the people. The authors in this volume examine the meaning of funerary rituals and their normative dimension and the social practices that have been influenced by tradition. Shaped by individual beliefs, customs, religion, and environment, Chinese Americans have resolved the tensions between assimilation into the mainstream culture and their strong Chinese heritage in a variety of ways. The authors have demonstrated this in their studies. The purpose of this work is to describe and analyze cultural retention and transformation in rituals after death.

When the Chinese immigrants first arrived in large numbers on the West Coast in the mid-nineteenth century, the nation was segmented into racial and ethnic groups. By the mid- to late nineteenth century, the influx of large numbers of "different-looking" immigrants from Asia and southern and central Europe prompted an American nativist reaction. In the late nineteenth century through the early twentieth century, Americanization and assimilation were major national issues, but according to most Euro-Americans, the Chinese stood out as a group that clung to traditional ways and could not assimilate. Shipments of bodies or exhumed bones for reburial in China ("returning to their roots"), so that their spirits could rest in peace at home, reinforced the American belief that the Chinese were sojourners, not immigrants. As is evident throughout this book, frontier newsmen often made derogatory comments about Chinese funerary practices, viewing them as being radically different from Western customs. In the eyes of anti-Chinese advocates, these rituals were another concrete example of the inability of the Chinese to assimilate into the American culture. These opinions helped to justify anti-Chinese movements that culminated in the first national ethnic exclusion act of 1882.

However, like many immigrant groups and their descendants, the Chinese began the processes of adaptation, acculturation, and assimilation while preserving aspects of their cultural heritage that they considered important. Chinese immigrants had a more difficult time than other newcomers did because American immigration laws essentially had created a "bachelor" society. The 1875 Page Law discouraged Chinese women from entering. The 1882 Chinese Exclusion Act prohibited the admission of laborers and the wives of laborers.[2] Because parents, wives, and children often remained in China, the family-oriented Chinese men maintained ties to the land of their birth. The shortage of women led to the practice of marrying a woman in China and hoping to return to join her in later years. If a wife was able to immigrate, she acted as a cultural preserver and drew on her knowledge of Chinese customs to bury her husband and friends. Those immigrants who had families made the transition to mainstream culture faster because of the educational programs in the public schools and the need to interact with the larger community. As American-born second-generation men and women began to come of age in the early twentieth century, the transplantation of Chinese cultural institutions weakened. Over the succeeding decades, Chinese Americans continually modified their customs and beliefs, adjusting them to American traditions while perpetuating certain Chinese cultural aspects. Adapting to the local frontier environment and adopting Christianity were two important factors contributing to changes. Unfortunately there was no uniformity in decisions about what Chinese beliefs and practices should be preserved. The results were many variations with some common traditional foundations. This is most evident in Chinese American funerary rituals and cemeteries. Chinese American customs trace their traditions to ancient China. Birth and death are two important events in the life cycle of the Chinese. Recently uncovered Neolithic graves dating back to the eighth through second millennium B.C. demonstrate the early concern for the afterworld.[3] Burials for the ruling class became very elaborate, but the city-states of the Shang dynasty (1600–1050 B.C.) differed from one region to another. By the succeeding Zhou dynasty (1050–256 B.C.), ritual specialists systematized the earlier ritual procedures and institutions in the *Three Ritual Canons* (*Sanli*: *Liji* [Book of Rites], *Yili* [Ceremonies and Rites], and *Zhouli* [rites of Zhou]). Minute details such as dressing the corpse, placing food and treasures (coins) into the mouth and onto the eyes, and preparing items to accompany the deceased were detailed for future generations. The process, so different from Western practices, fascinated nineteenth-century English anthropologists. J. J. M. de Groot based his six-volume study, *The Religious System of China*, on observations of funerals in Xiamen (Amoy), the same place that anthropologist W. Eatwell wrote about in the summer of 1842.[4] This became the Western standard interpretation of Chinese funerals, but actually described the rituals in Fujian province and nearby Taiwan.

It is important to understand the historical background to traditional practices and their links to Chinese America. The Chinese believe that living people have two souls: the *hun* (an emanation of the *yang*, the light, male, active principle), which gives people their intelligence or spark of life, and the *po* (derived from the *yin*, the dark, female, passive principle), which animates the body, and in death these become the *shen* (the spirit that ascends to heaven) and the *gui* (the spirit that returns to or remains on earth).[5] The living had to pay reverence to the deceased in order to attain good fortune for themselves and their descendants. These ideas were incorporated into the Confucian reverence for ancestors. Thus King Xing of Zhou had engraved on a set of bronze bells an acknowledgment that the venerable ancestors looked sternly upon him, and beseeched, "May they let me be rich and prosperous, forever [enjoying] . . . good fortune."[6] These same words were echoed by later generations to their august ancestors. If the living performed their obligations, then the spirits of the deceased would grant favors to present and future generations. A person of higher status and wealth was buried with greater pomp and circumstance than ordinary men. Age, manner of death, status and position in society, and marital status determined the elaborateness of the funeral.

Much of this has been detailed in recent monographs of Chinese views of death and burial practices. Most notably, these have included *The Cult of the*

Dead in a Chinese Village, by Emily M. Ahern; *Religion and Ritual in Chinese Society*, edited by Arthur P. Wolf; *Chinese Ideas of Life and Death*, by Michael Loewe; *To the Yellow Springs: The Chinese View of Death*, by T. C. Lai; *Worshipping the Ancestors: Chinese Commemorative Portraits*, by Jan Stuart and Evelyn S. Rawski; and *Death Ritual in Late Imperial and Modern China*, edited by James L. Watson and Evelyn S. Rawski.[7]

Other relevant monographs are William R. Jankowiak, *Sex, Death, and Hierarchy in a Chinese City*; Joseph P. McDermott, *State and Court Ritual in China*; Norman A. Kutcher, *Mourning in Late Imperial China*; Patricia Buckley Ebrey, *Confucianism and Family Rituals in Imperial China*; and Tianlong Jiao, "Gender Studies in Chinese Neolithic Archaeology."[8] These authors reveal the complexities and differences of Chinese death rituals as well as the regional and class variations of practices and beliefs.

Local or regional studies of Chinese funeral and burial customs have included Leon Comber's *Chinese Ancestor Worship in Malaya*, which traces burial practices there, while Vivian Lim Tsui Shan's article "Specializing in Death: The Case of the Chinese in Singapore" details the role of funeral specialists in the Cantonese tradition.[9] Chee-Kiong Tong's doctoral dissertation, "Dangerous Blood, Refined Souls: Death Rituals among the Chinese in Singapore," and Gang Chen's doctoral dissertation, "Death Rituals in a Chinese Village: An Old Tradition in Contemporary Social Context," further expanded our knowledge of the practices.[10] Preservation of tradition was more likely in Singapore because of its proximity to Guangdong (Kwangtung) Province and the ability of families to live together. Goran Aijmer studies the Hakkas in his book *Burial, Ancestors, and Geomancy among the Ma On Shan Hakka, New Territories of Hong Kong*.[11] In addition, a website, www.missouri.edu/~religpc/bibliography_CPR.html, contains a comprehensive list of recent articles in the field.

These publications all discuss funeral rites and burial customs in China and its environs. In comparison, except for Wallace R. Hagaman's brief *A Short History of the Chinese Cemetery at Nevada City, California, and Chinese Burial Customs during the Gold Rush*,[12] to date there has been no comparable body of work that reviews Chinese *American* funerary rituals and cemeteries. The present volume will both fill that void and stimulate additional scholarship in this emerging field of inquiry.

With the passage of time in both China and America, the precise customs and rituals became modified. The Confucian reverence for ancestors merged with a concern for the siting of the burial grounds.[13] Known as *fengshui* (literally "wind and water," or geomancy), the Daoist concern for Nature became an integral part of the funerary rituals, as explained in chapter 1 and seen in succeeding chapters. From the Sui dynasty (581–618 A.D.) to the

Song dynasty (960–1279 A.D.), people wishing to properly site their loved ones' graves turned to the geomancer—a specialist who was regarded as a scientist rather than a religious person. The geomancer worked with the Daoist and/or Buddhist priests.[14]

Although *fengshui* was not universally accepted, it was important in Guangdong Province, the region producing over 90 percent of the early Chinese immigrants to the United States. People in neighboring provinces also utilized *fengshui*. For example, in 1841 the British heedlessly began to develop their business quarter in Happy Valley, Hong Kong, a site of malicious *fengshui*. When they encountered construction difficulties, Chinese geomancers blamed the problems on the builders' ignorance of geomancy.[15]

Immigrants to early Chinese America included geomancers. An 1878 "Forest of Clouds" (Yunlin) advertisement, offering Daoist geomantic services,[16] provides additional evidence for their presence. Chinese communities in many places established Daoist temples in the late nineteenth century. The Chinese cemeteries described in subsequent chapters in this book all indicate the use of *fengshui* in the siting of graves.

Various superstitions played a role in funeral customs. Fear of malevolent spirits led to the practice, during the funeral procession, of scattering off-white paper containing numerous holes. Because evil spirits had to pass through all the holes before continuing, they became confused and distracted and were unable to learn where the deceased was to be buried. Music also was a means of distracting evil spirits, and if a Chinese band could not be found, American musicians could be substituted. The recognition of the need to transmit wealth to the other world led to the burning of symbolic money for the celestial bank[17] and, in more recent times, to the burning of symbolic paper items, such as houses, televisions, watches, computers, cell phones, and cars. Personal effects and clothing might also be burned. These items were placed in pits or furnaces, such as the two twelve-foot-high burners at the Evergreen Cemetery in Los Angeles that were built in 1888.[18] Thus the ascending *shen* spirit and the earth-bound *gui* spirit would both be appeased.

With the advent of Buddhism after the first century A.D. and especially in the Six Dynasties (420–589 A.D.), Buddhist concepts of afterlife and karmic retribution greatly influenced Chinese funerary practices.[19] Buddhist practices were combined with Confucian ones in the eclecticism of Zhu Xi (Chu Hsi, 1130–1200 A.D.) of the Song dynasty. High culture, dominated by the Confucianists, favored the neo-Confucian rituals laid out by Zhu Xi, but popular culture preferred Buddhist funerals, so the two were combined. His set of rules became the foundation of Chinese funerary rituals through the twentieth century. Patricia Buckley Ebrey's translation and annotation of *Chu Hsi's Family Rituals: A Twelfth Century Chinese Manual for the Performance of Cappings, Weddings, Funerals, and Ancestral Rites* reveals the complexities and differences in the rituals.[20] In his study of funerary rituals in Guangdong province, historian Timothy Brook shows that both Confucian and Buddhist rituals are used.[21] In Chinese America popular folk beliefs were transformed further—sometimes to the point of not being recognizable as Confucian, Daoist, or Buddhist.

The Daoists were concerned with the forces of Nature, the Confucianists with the community and family, and the Buddhists with the afterlife. In the United States, several late nineteenth-century Chinese American community leaders had both Daoist and Buddhist priests at their elaborate funerals, which were based on Confucian customs. When Tom Kim Yung (1858–1903), a military attaché to the Chinese legation in the United States, committed suicide in San Francisco in September 1903, the elaborate funeral procession of hundreds of people included fifteen Buddhist monks and fifteen Daoist priests as well as policemen, relatives, friends, and representatives of the Chinese Consolidated Benevolent Association (Chinese Six Companies). Thomas A. Edison, Inc., captured the colorful event in a brief black-and-white film that has been preserved in the Library of Congress and can be viewed online.[22]

For those Chinese who went abroad seeking adventure and fortune, the specter of death was never far from their minds. In a strange country, far from their birthplace and natal family, the Chinese turned to district or family associations to take care of their burials. The earliest shipment of bones from San Francisco to Hong Kong was in 1855.[23] In September 1868, several Chinese American organizations reported to the American government the number of their members who had arrived in and departed from the United States as well as the thirty-six hundred who had died.[24] An 1873 report on the one hundred forty thousand Chinese sailing to Cuba listed more than sixteen thousand who died en route from sickness, hunger, thirst, suicide, and mistreatment by those in charge of the ships.[25] Death occurred during the trip and in the new country. This highlighted the need for some systematic way to care for the sick and dying, thus giving rise to more mutual aid and protection organizations in Chinese America. As early as the 1850s district associations (*huiguan*) promised to assist their members in matters such as burials, exhumations, and repatriation of bones.

By the 1880s, with the Chinese population near its peak, cemeteries became extremely important. Since no single individual could afford to buy burial grounds, specialized associations connected with a *huiguan* or *tang* (*tong*, organization), through membership dues, purchased cemeteries. Huang Tsun-hsien (Huang Gongdu; pinyin, Huang Zunxian, 1848–1909), the Cantonese Chinese Consul General of San Francisco from 1882 to 1885, noted to Cheng Tsao-ju (pinyin, Zheng Caoru, Zheng Yuxuan, 1824–1894), the Chinese ambassador to the United States, that each *huiguan* imposed an exit fee on its members who returned to China.[26] Half of the $3 to $6 fee was used to bury fellow members and later send their bones to Hong Kong for final reburial. The *huiguan* often organized a *shantang* (charity hall) that sent bone collectors to various burial sites throughout the American West. American mortuary practices required separate burial facilities for "Mongolians," as the Chinese were racially categorized, and, in the case of Los Angeles in the late nineteenth century, the city or county government collected a fee from the organization at the time of each burial.[27] If one did not belong to a district or family association, then the only other alternative was to join a fraternal or secret society organization that had no birthplace requirements. In the absence of family members, the organizations took over the duties of funerary rituals and burials. A basic premise of all of these traditional organizations was the perpetuation of cultural traditions that were very different from those prevalent in the United States.

The main practice that offended the American observers was the shipping of bodies or exhumed bones back to China, where relatives buried them and tended the graves. In 1863 the Panyu district charity house connected with the Sanyi (Three Districts) *huiguan* spent $20,500 to send the remains of 258 people back to the county of Panyu, Guangdong Province.[28] The largest single shipment, of over twenty thousand pounds, was made in 1870 when the remains of twelve hundred Chinese Central Pacific Railroad workers were repatriated through Hong Kong to their native places.[29] Several chapters discuss these customs, and historical records confirm them.

Exhumation, shipping, and reburial in China were expensive. In 1875 the Guangzhou (Canton) *huiguan* alone shipped the bones of 1,002 members to Guangdong Province.[30] In some cases, the state, county, or city government charged a $10-per-grave public health fee for the exhumation.[31] Other fees might include the $5 shipment fee per box (holding the bones), handling fees, a reburial fee of $7 per grave in China, the cost of the plot and reburial in the home village, and the expenses involved in the first and second funeral services, in addition to miscellaneous costs.[32] Relatives often had to collect the metal box or ceramic jar of bones in Hong Kong, usually at the Tung Wah Hospital from 1869, when it was established, through the early twentieth century.[33]

Not all exhumations were voluntary. In 1928 the Chinese in St. Louis, Missouri, had to ship about a hundred deceased Chinese to China because the land on which their cemetery stood was to be reused by the local government.[34] Return to China hopefully ensured that the deceased would be remembered, but in reality these overseas Chinese were forgotten in their birthplace because of the passage of time since they had lived in their home village. What many Chinese feared might happen to their graves in the United

States became a reality in the twentieth century, as Chinese American cemeteries were forgotten and became empty lots or sites of parks, schools, private homes, parking lots, and office buildings. For example, in 1996 two homes were built on the Carlin, Nevada, Chinese American cemetery.

Various parts of China have different customs, and even within Guangdong Province, the ancestral home of most Chinese Americans, there are several distinct mortuary practices. During the twentieth century fewer Chinese bones were shipped back to China. In the Reno, Nevada, area, the Ross-Burke Funeral Home records of 1904–1919 and the O'Brien Rogers Funeral Home records of 1911–1939 contradict the popular stereotype that the Chinese in death returned to their native place.[35] Of the seventeen deceased Chinese who were born in China and handled by Ross-Burke, fourteen were buried in the Reno area, one coffin was shipped to China, one was sent to Sacramento, and one was disinterred and sent to China via San Francisco. Of the thirty-three dead Chinese handled by O'Brien Rogers, nine were buried in Reno's Chinese Cemetery, seventeen were interred in Reno's Mountain View Cemetery, two were placed in other local cemeteries, three were disinterred and returned to China, and two were buried in California. After Japan took control of Canton during the Sino-Japanese War of 1937–1945 and the establishment of the People's Republic of China, beginning in 1949, shipments of bones drastically decreased or ceased altogether.

At first, Chinese Americans tried to preserve as much of their traditional funerary practices as possible, but by the late nineteenth century, they had adopted a combination of Chinese and American rituals for funeral processions and burials. When the laundryman Sam Sing of Nevada City died of tuberculosis, his partner had funeral bills printed announcing the services on March 1, 1874.[36] The partner then posted the notices on the doors of the home and businesses of the deceased, in typical Euro-American fashion. Because of the small number of religious leaders who immigrated, the Chinese turned to Christian ministers for funerary services. Thus Wong You, who died in St. Louis, Missouri, was buried in a Christian service in 1879.[37] By the turn of the twentieth century there were more Christian burials among Chinese Americans because the federal government, in the 1892 extension of the 1882 Chinese Exclusion Act, reclassified Chinese priests and religious leaders, including Christian ministers, as "laborers," thus making them ineligible for immigration into the United States. Traditional Chinese increasingly had to rely on lay people rather than on specialists for burial services. The elders of the community had to instruct those in mourning about the proper steps to take.

Grave markers also demonstrated a transition in burial practices. At first, headstones were written in a traditional Chinese fashion. If all the information was known, the inscription, in Chinese, contained the place and date of birth, the name of the deceased, and the place and date of death. Identification brick inscriptions are similar to the writings on headstones. At the Chinese cemeteries in and around Colma, California (a suburb of San Francisco), engraved stone or marble markers abound, but one cemetery near Skyline Boulevard includes wooden markers. Most headstones are upright, and, when a man had two wives, the grave site contains three coffins duly noted.[38]

Later headstones contained the information in a combination of Chinese and English. The English headstone might be inscribed with "Jue" in capitals at the top; then the two individuals, "Paul, 1890–1959" and "Lum Shee, 1890–1967"; followed by the Chinese giving birthplace and date, name, and death dates.[39] C. Fred Blake, in his study of the Chinese markers in Valhalla Cemetery of St. Louis, Missouri, asserts that the combination of Chinese and American writing was an effort to preserve Chinese tradition and accommodate American culture at the same time.[40] Stones engraved after the 1930s often had inscriptions just in English.[41] Only the wealthy could afford substantial headstones, so at first many of the markers were written on wood. Stone markers required engraving, and only a few non-Asian stonecutters were able to perform the task of copying Chinese inscriptions. Tombstone size and shape varied greatly as well. One unique type was the "omega-style" tombstone, shaped like the last letter of the Greek alphabet, Ω. This allowed the spirit to observe this world in a relaxed, seated position. Omega-style tombstones could be found throughout the twentieth century and were indicators of wealthy families.

The Qingming festival, remembering the dead in a celebration of life and renewal, continued to be observed by many California Chinese Americans who cleaned their ancestors' graves or paid homage to them in ancestral halls or family shrines in the home, regardless of the type of religious ceremony performed at the funeral. Every April, in Colma, California (burial grounds for San Francisco and Bay Area Chinese), the cemeteries with a Chinese section hold an elaborate Qingming observance, complete with free lunches, Buddhist religious personnel, and music. Elsewhere in the United States, there are some exceptions to this California practice. Fenggang Yang's study of Chinese Christians (often post-1975 immigrants) indicates that the Washington, DC, Chinese Christians do not observe Qingming but do celebrate the Lunar New Year and the Mid-Autumn Moon Festival.[42] This probably was the result of the fact that in the People's Republic of China, funerary rituals were discouraged because they were "superstitious," and it is only in the early 1980s that a simplified version of funerary practices was revived.

Practical issues also arose that led to modifications in tradition. For almost all Chinese Americans, for example, it was impractical and impossible to adhere to the Mahayana Buddhist tradition of forty-nine days for a funeral ceremony, or even the shortened form of three to seven days.[43] The prayer ceremony, held every ten days for a total of forty days, was especially important to ensure that the departed would have a favorable rebirth in the next life, but few hardworking Chinese Americans could afford the time required. The expense for an elaborate Buddhist funeral, "dictated by . . . fear," was greater than that for a simpler neo-Confucian funeral, "dictated by grief."[44]

In general, women, children, and those who died a violent death were buried with less fanfare. There were exceptions. For example, China Mary, a resident of Tombstone, Arizona, from 1880 until her death in 1906, had a very elaborate funeral.[45] Her body lay in state at her home with offerings of a whole pig, chickens, and ducks—all roasted and surrounded by fruits and vegetables. The funeral procession featured Chinese music, six professional mourners in white sackcloth, scattered white paper with holes, and a wagon of ritual foodstuffs. China Mary was an exception because of her prominence in the community as a labor contractor, opium dealer, brothel operator, restaurant owner, and well-known caregiver to both the Euro-American and Chinese communities. In 1921 the death of Loy Lee Ford of Tonopah, Nevada, was announced in the local newspaper because of the prominence of her husband, Billy Min Chung Ford.[46] Billy was popular in both the Euro-American and Chinese communities of Tonopah and Reno, and the couple knew many of the political leaders of Nevada. The deaths of most Chinese American women and children, however, went unnoticed by local newspapermen.

Around the turn of the twentieth century, Chinese Americans adopted a combination of Chinese and American rituals for funeral processions and burials, but always held as most important those rites that reaffirmed the family identity and adhered to the belief that the dead affect the lives of those left behind. For example, when Hoy Chong Gar, a Chinese doctor and owner of the Wing Wo Chinese Medicine Company in Spokane, Washington, died in 1926, over one thousand people attended his funeral.[47] Reverend Louis Magin of St. Paul's Methodist Church officiated, the band played Chopin's funeral march, and the widow wore black instead of white, the Chinese traditional mourning color for immediate relatives. However, Dr. Gar's nephew wrapped white crepe bands around his head and arm and held a picture of his uncle during the funeral procession, while other mourners scattered perforated white paper along the route, thus maintaining Chinese customs. At the cemetery, Chinese burial practices were followed. Two years later, despite the fact that Dr. Gar had lived in Spokane for twenty years and was an American citizen, his family chose to have his remains reburied in China, where another elaborate funeral service was conducted. Having performed her duties faithfully, the young widow returned to the United States and settled in Seattle. However, contrary to Confucian principles of loyalty to one husband, she remarried. She lived into her nineties; her first husband apparently was satisfied with the rites that had taken place, since malevolent spirits did not bother the former Mrs. Gar.

Scholars studying overseas Chinese have begun to focus on the transplantation and modification of this important aspect of Chinese cultural heritage. The discovery and uncovering of Chinese cemeteries, particularly in the western United States by archaeologists, have resulted in the need for more information on this heretofore little-known subject. And, as they became more knowledgeable, scholars posed research questions. What aspects of the funerary rites were strictly southern Chinese (Punti) as opposed to Hakka or even northern Chinese? Were there practices followed by the Siyi (Four Districts) Chinese immigrants that differed from those of the Chinese of other localities? Why were some people exhumed and reburied in the land of their birth and others not? At what point did the Chinese in the United States become content to remain buried in the United States instead of having their bones exhumed? When did the trend reverse itself, so that bones buried in Guangdong Province were exhumed and reburied in the United States? Since we feel that the term "ancestor reverence" more closely approximates the entire activity, we have not used the more common terminology, "ancestor worship."

In recent decades efforts have been made to preserve Chinese American cemeteries, most notably in Los Angeles, California; Virginia City, Nevada; and Boston, Massachusetts—to name just a few. Moreover, as Chinese traditions have yielded to the incorporation of more American rituals, the younger generations have forgotten about the older customs and their meaning. Consequently this pioneering study attempts to provide some answers to the research questions stated earlier, using comparative examples of the transplantation and modification of Chinese funerary practices.

In chapter 1, Wendy L. Rouse presents an overview of the death rituals in China and California. *Fengshui* was important in locating auspicious grave sites, and postfuneral ceremonies kept the memory of the deceased alive. However, when the Chinese in California wanted to continue the practice of exhumation and the shipping of bones back to China, they encountered legal problems. In 1878, for example, the California legislature passed a law requiring a permit prior to the exhumation of the bodies. Other western states followed suit. Thereafter, other laws were enacted to discourage this and other traditional Chinese funerary practices.

In chapter 2, Paul G. Chace examines death and burial practices in the California mining city of Marysville. Most of the Chinese immigrants came from Siyi, and their funerary practices were different from those in Fujian-Taiwan and Hong Kong. Two major district associations and the Gee Hing Tong (Zhigong-tang) were in charge of the funerals and jointly held title to the community's Bok

Kai (Daoist) Temple, founded in 1852. From the 1870s until the present, the temple's activities have included two traditional funerary celebrations: the Qingming (Pure Brightness) festival to commemorate the deceased and clean the graves in the spring, usually in early April, and the Yulanpen (Hungry Ghosts) festival in the fall, around September or October, to pacify those spirits who were restless because they had not had a proper burial. Although Daoist priests sometimes were present, religious personnel were not required for funerals. Marysville had its own Chinese specialist who disinterred the bones and prepared them for shipment to China. In the 1870s and 1880s, when Marysville's Chinese population numbered one thousand or more, the Chinese rituals addressing death and ghost-spirits were very elaborate, but in the decades following World War I, when the Chinese population had dropped to five hundred, or about 2 percent of the town's population, Chinese traditions diminished and funerary practices became more Americanized.

In chapter 3, Wendy Rouse compares two Chinese cemeteries in Virginiatown, California, a mining town that prospered between 1850 and 1890. Both sites followed *fengshui* principles and were located on gently sloping hills, with the Auburn Ravine running in a westerly flow south of the cemeteries. All of the bodies were disinterred. An extensive study of the nails found allowed the relative dating of the two cemeteries. Grave goods such as a Chinese lock and key, an inkwell, eyeglasses, and rice "liquor" jars were found and indicated that the bone collector was not careful to include all burial objects with the deceased's bones. Identification bricks also were left at one of the sites. A third cemetery, for Chinese women, and probably children, could not be examined because of prior destruction. Normally women were buried next to their husbands, and the separation by sex of the Virginiatown cemeteries yielded some interesting information.

In chapter 4, Sue Fawn Chung, Fred Frampton, and Timothy Murphy scrutinize the situation in Carlin, Nevada, a railroad and mining town where thirteen coffins were uncovered in a long-forgotten Chinese cemetery. Unlike the other cemeteries discussed in this book, Carlin's cemetery still contained bodies that were buried prior to 1924. The natural environment mummified one of these thirteen early burials as well as body parts of others. Three identification bricks contributed to the probable identification of three of the thirteen. From newspaper articles, census records, local and federal government documents, vital statistics, and business records, some information emerged about the lives of these men and about the causes of their deaths.

In chapter 5, Terry Abraham and Priscilla Wegars look at late nineteenth-century Chinese activities in the Pacific Northwest, focusing on Chinese cemeteries in Idaho and Oregon. In 1870 the Chinese constituted 28.5 percent of the population of Idaho and had a different experience than did the Chinese in Nevada. In the Pacific Northwest cemeteries, pits were clearly visible where bodies were exhumed, but there are also sites with undisturbed graves. By the 1890s the Chinese could be buried in Christian cemeteries. Archival documentation gave information about some of the people buried and the organizations that had leased the burial grounds. Several of the sites had structures where paper goods could be burned to accompany the deceased into the next world. One famous Chinese American woman, Polly Bemis, buried her Euro-American husband in accordance with aspects of Chinese tradition, while she was buried according to American tradition.

In chapter 6, Sue Fawn Chung and Reiko Neizman trace the varied practices of remembering ancestors in Hawai'i. They look at the Manoa Chinese Cemetery on Oahu, the largest Chinese American cemetery in Hawai'i. Chartered in 1889, the Lin Yee Chung Association maintained this magnificent memorial park primarily for Chinese immigrants from Zhongshan District and their descendants. Maui's numerous smaller Chinese cemeteries, by contrast, illustrate burial practices in more-rural areas. These can suffer from development; in one case, a mall surrounds a single grave. Grave markers in Hawai'i vary in size, shape, and inscription, and Qingming is still celebrated.

In chapter 7, Linda Sun Crowder focuses on more recent mortuary practices as seen in San Francisco's Chinatown. The colorful funeral processions combine Chinese and American traditions and demonstrate the constraints of American government, the endurance of Chinese culture, and the demographics and political-social mechanism of Chinatown. Beginning in 1851 Chinese district associations owned their own cemeteries. Later, other cemeteries established a "Chinese section." Chinese mortuaries handled the arrangements, and, with the passage of time, both Chinese and American funerary rituals could be observed. The history and roles of the Cathay Band and the Green Street Brass Band indicate one of the major adaptations made in this urban setting, the unofficial capital of Chinese America. With the influx of new immigrants after 1965, the funerary practices became more varied because the new immigrants came from many parts of China, as well as from Hong Kong, Taiwan, Southeast Asia, and the interior of the mainland. By the 1980s five mortuaries offered traditional Chinese funerals, but only Cathay Mortuary on the corner of Jackson and Powell Streets had been in existence since the 1930s and was centrally located in Chinatown. In 1989 Cathay Mortuary was forced to relocate so that its site could become a park.[48] City politics, global marketing and capital, immigration, tourism, and special interest groups have influenced funerary processions in Chinatown and modified the inhabitants' expression of their cultural heritage.

Finally, in chapter 8, Roberta Greenwood explores the recent, and continuing, phenomenon of the reburial of bones in the United States. Post-1950 Chinese

Americans, mindful of the traditions connected with Qingming and realizing that having access to gravesites in China is impossible or difficult, have chosen to bring back the bones of ancestors for another reburial in the United States. This evolving custom makes it easier for descendants to perform their required filial duties without suffering the time and expense of going abroad.

Remembering the dead brings unity to the Chinese Americans, as the past becomes an integral part of the present and future. In this multicultural United States of America, it is important that people respect and appreciate a wide variety of ethnic customs. These chapters will provide both Chinese and non-Chinese Americans with a better understanding of Chinese funerary rituals, beliefs, and practices as we question what happens after death.

A NOTE ON ROMANIZATION

Names of places, organizations, and festivals have been romanized using the pinyin system in accordance with the *Chicago Manual of Style*. For example, we use the pinyin system "Zhigongtang" (Chinese Freemasons or Chinese Masons) instead of the older Western romanization of "Chee Kung Tong," "Gee Hing Tong," and so forth. Chinese tradition gives a person's last name first, then first name. Names of individuals are in the pinyin system unless the American spelling of the person's name is known from commonly used English-language sources. The Americanized names usually capitalize the last and the first name that has two components.

NOTES

1. Stanley French, "The Cemetery as Cultural Institution: The Establishment of Mount Auburn and the 'Rural Cemetery' Movement," *American Quarterly* 26, no. 1 (March 1974): 40.

2. The 1882 Chinese Exclusion Act prohibited the immigration of any newly arrived laborers. Although it did not specifically mention women, wives of laborers had the same occupational classification as their husbands. Therefore, they were forbidden entry as new laborers.

3. Albert E. Dien, "Chinese Beliefs in the Afterworld," and Robert L. Thorp, "The Qin and Han Imperial Tombs and the Development of Mortuary Architecture," in *The Quest for Eternity: Chinese Ceramic Sculptures from the People's Republic of China*, ed. Susan Caroselli (San Francisco: Chronicle Books for the Los Angeles County Museum of Art, 1987), 1–15, 16–37.

4. J. J. M. de Groot, *The Religious System of China*, 6 vols. (Leiden, Netherlands: Brill, 1892–1910); W. Eatwell, "On Chinese Burials," *Journal of the Anthropological Institute of Great Britain and Ireland* 1 (1872): 207–208.

5. Eatwell, "On Chinese Burials."

6. Wu Hung, *Monumentality in Early Chinese Art and Architecture* (Stanford, CA: Stanford University Press, 1995), 97.

7. Emily M. Ahern, *The Cult of the Dead in a Chinese Village* (Stanford, CA: Stanford University Press, 1973); Arthur P. Wolf, ed., *Religion and Ritual in Chinese Society* (Stanford, CA: Stanford University Press, 1974); Michael Loewe, *Chinese Ideas of Life and Death: Faith, Myth, and Reason in the Han Period (202 B.C.–220 A.D)* (London: Allen and Unwin, 1982); T. C. Lai, *To the Yellow Springs: The Chinese View of Death* (Hong Kong: Joint Publishing, 1983); Jan Stuart, and Evelyn S. Rawski, *Worshipping the Ancestors: Chinese Commemorative Portraits* (Washington, DC: Freer Gallery of Art, 2001); and James L. Watson and Evelyn S. Rawski, eds., *Death Ritual in Late Imperial and Modern China* (Berkeley: University of California Press, 1988).

8. William R. Jankowiak, *Sex, Death, and Hierarchy in a Chinese City: An Anthropological Account* (New York: Columbia University Press, 1993); Joseph P. McDermott, *State and Court Ritual in China* (Cambridge: Cambridge University Press, 1999); Norman A. Kutcher, *Mourning in Late Imperial China* (Cambridge: Cambridge University Press, 1999); Patricia Buckley Ebrey, *Confucianism and Family Rituals in Imperial China: A Social History of Writing about Rites* (Princeton, NJ: Princeton University Press, 1991); and Tianlong Jiao, "Gender Studies in Chinese Neolithic Archaeology," in *Gender and the Archaeology of Death*, ed. Bettina Arnold and Nancy L. Wicker (Walnut Creek, CA: AltaMira, 2001), 51–64.

9. Leon Comber, *Chinese Ancestor Worship in Malaya* (Singapore: Eastern Universities Press, 1963); Vivian Lim Tsui Shan, "Specializing in Death: The Case of the Chinese in Singapore," *Southeast Asian Journal of Social Science* 23, no. 2 (October 1995): 63–88.

10. Chee-Kiong Tong, "Dangerous Blood, Refined Souls: Death Rituals among the Chinese in Singapore" (PhD diss., Cornell University, 1987); Gang Chen, "Death Rituals in a Chinese Village: An Old Tradition in Contemporary Social Context" PhD diss., Ohio State University, 2000.

11. Goran Aijmer, *Burial, Ancestors, and Geomancy among the Ma On Shan Hakka, New Territories of Hong Kong* ([Göteborg], Sweden: IASSA, Göteborgs Universitet, 1993).

12. Wallace R. Hagaman, *A Short History of the Chinese Cemetery at Nevada City, California, and Chinese Burial Customs during the Gold Rush* (Nevada City: Cowboy Press, 2001).

13. This is explained in detail by Andrew L. March, "An Appreciation of Chinese Geomancy," *Journal of Asia Studies* 27, no. 2 (February 1968): 253–267.

14. Maurice Freedman, "Geomancy," *Proceedings of the Royal Anthropological Institute of Great Britain and Ireland 1968* (London: The Institute, 1968), 5–15.

15. Chuen-Yan David Lai, "A Feng Shui Model as a Location Index," *Annals of the Association of American Geographers* 64, no. 4 (December 1974): 510–511.

16. This advertisement is now in the collection of the Nevada State Museum.

17. Hill Gates, "Money for the Gods," *Modern China* 13, no. 3 (July 1987): 259–277, explains that this practice has capitalistic overtones.

18. See Chinese Historical Society of Southern California, "19th Century Chinese Memorial Shrine Preservation Project," at www.chssc.org/shrinefull.html (accessed November 16, 2003).

19. Robert F. Campany, "Return-from-Death Narratives in Early Medieval China," *Journal of Chinese Religions* 18 (Fall 1990): 122.

20. Chu Hsi, *Chu Hsi's Family Rituals: A Twelfth Century Chinese Manual for the Performance of Cappings, Weddings, Funerals, and Ancestral Rites,* trans. Patricia Buckley Ebrey (Princeton, NJ: Princeton University Press, 1991).

21. Timothy Brook, "Funerary Ritual and the Building of Lineages in Late Imperial China," *Harvard Journal of Asiatic Studies* 49, no. 2 (December 1989): 465–499.

22. See Library of Congress, "San Francisco Chinese Funeral," in *Library of Congress, American Memory: Historical Collections for the National Digital Library*, at www.sfmuseum.org/loc/chinfuner.htm (accessed November 16, 2003).

23. William Speer, *The Oldest and the Newest Empire: China and the United States*, vol. 2 (Cincinnati, OH: National, 1870), 614–615.

24. United States Navy, Twelfth Naval District Commandant's Office, General Correspondence, Intelligence Office, 1945, formerly classified. NND Project 868156, RG 181, Folder A8-5, National Archives, San Bruno, California, containing a detailed account, dated September 1868, of the histories, functions, and officers of the Chinese Six Companies.

25. *The Cuba Commission Report: A Hidden History of the Chinese in Cuba*, introduction by Denise Helly (Baltimore: Johns Hopkins University Press, 1993), 42, reprint of original English language text of 1876.

26. Marlon K. Hom, "Fallen Leaves' Homecoming: Notes on the 1893 Gold Mountain Charity Cemetery in Xinhui," in *Chinese America: History and Perspectives 2002*, ed. Colleen Fong and others (San Francisco: Chinese Historical Society of America, 2002), 39.

27. Chinese Historical Society of Southern California, "19th Century."

28. Yong Chen, *Chinese San Francisco, 1850–1943: A Trans-Pacific Community* (Stanford, CA: Stanford University Press, 2000), 105.

29. *Sacramento (CA) Reporter*, June 30, 1870. William F. Chew provided this information.

30. Jack Chen, *The Chinese of America* (San Francisco: Harper and Row, 1980), 20.

31. Judy Nelson, "The Final Journey Home: Chinese Burial Practices in Spokane," *Pacific Northwest Forum*, 2nd ser., 6, no. 1 (Winter–Spring 1993): 70–76. The public health fee was charged in Washington, as this article indicates, and neighboring states, including Nevada and Idaho.

32. Nelson, "Final Journey Home."

33. Elizabeth Sinn, "Moving Bones: Hong Kong's Role as an 'In-between Place' in the Chinese Diaspora" (paper presented at the Association for Asian Studies Conference, Washington, DC, 2002).

34. *St. Louis (MO) Post-Dispatch*, November 17, 1928, details the shipment of bones to be sent to China because the Wesleyan Cemetery was to be leveled, leaving the Valhalla Cemetery for burials.

35. The records of both of these funeral homes are found in the Family History Library, Salt Lake City, Utah.

36. Hagaman, *Short History*, n.p.

37. C. Fred Blake, "The Chinese of Valhalla: Adaptation and Identity in a Midwestern American Cemetery," in *Markers X: Journal of the Association for Gravestone Studies*, ed. Richard E. Meyer (Worcester, MA: Association for Gravestone Studies, 1993), 53.

38. This is exemplified in the case of Edwin Owyang, whose first and second wives are buried with him in Greenlawn Cemetery, Colma, California.

39. The Jue family gravestone is illustrated in Blake, "Chinese of Valhalla," 55.

40. Blake, "Chinese of Valhalla," 56, 79.

41. See Blake, "Chinese of Valhalla," 53–90, for a detailed account of Chinese grave markers.

42. Fenggang Yang, "Religious Conversions and Identity Construction: A Study of a Chinese Christian Church in the United States" (PhD diss., Catholic University of America, 1997), 218–219.

43. Brook, "Funerary Ritual," 481.

44. *Jingzhou fuzhi (Jingzhou Gazetteer)*, 1757, 18.3b–4a, quoted in Brook, "Funerary Ritual," 482.

45. China Mary was a common name given to Chinese women throughout the West. This China Mary was married to Ah Lum, one of the owners of the famous Can Can Restaurant in Tombstone. She died at the age of sixty-seven. See *Tombstone (AZ) Epitaph*, December 18, 1906, and Ben Traywick, "Tombstone's Dragon Lady," *True West* 46, no. 5 (May 1999): 26–31 for more information. Her grave in the Chinese section of Boot Hill remains in good condition.

46. For more details, see Sue Fawn Chung, "Ah Cum Kee and Loy Lee Ford: Between Two Worlds," in *Ordinary Women, Extraordinary Lives: Women in American History*, ed. Kriste Lindenmeyer (Wilmington, DE: Scholarly Resources, 2000), 185–194. Loy Lee Ford's obituary was published in the *Tonopah (NV) Bonanza*, February 1, 1921.

47. This event is described in detail by Nelson, "Final Journey Home," 70–76.

48. *Cathay Mortuary, Inc. v. San Francisco Planning Commission* (207 Cal.App.3d 275), No. AO39937, January 20, 1989. The Court of Appeals ruled against Cathay Mortuary's efforts to remain in the original location, thus reaffirming the lower court's decision.

1

"What We Didn't Understand": A History of Chinese Death Ritual in China and California

Wendy L. Rouse

Shelves of historical documentation and boxes of archaeological remains attest to the success of the Chinese in retaining their distinct culture in the nineteenth-century American West. Chinese miners carried their food, clothing, religion, and family traditions with them into the gold mines of the mother lode. The Chinese, however, were not a static people. As countless scholars have demonstrated, Chinese individuals adapted and met the challenges of this and other foreign lands. Nevertheless, an obvious gap still exists in the story of the overseas Chinese. Just as the modern American approach to death avoids discussion of funeral and burial customs, similar aspects of Chinese American culture have so far evaded analytical scrutiny. This examination of the Chinese approach to death will reveal the underlying motivations influencing Chinese individuals to retain their elaborate rituals so far from home.

Since the Chinese believed that the dead could influence the lives of the living, customs centuries old decreed reverence for the deceased. Proper ritual following the death of a relative or friend was essential not only to the soul of the departed but also to the happiness, harmony, and well-being of those left behind. Elaborate ceremonies awakened onlookers of both worlds to the tragic event that had occurred. From the moment of death and for generations afterward the deceased were remembered in annual ceremonies performed religiously by their descendants. Thousands of miles of ocean and residence in a strange land modified, but failed to break, the continuity of these traditions (fig. 1.1).

This two-part study first presents a historical overview of evolving death ritual in China to provide the reader with a broader understanding of the culture brought to California by the Chinese. Modern scholarly research projects

Figure 1.1. The funeral of Li Po Tal. *Morning Call,* March 23, 1893.

and primary accounts of visitors to China underlie most of this analysis. Next, a discussion of death practices and beliefs in nineteenth-century California examines primary source accounts depicting the elaborate death rituals of the California Chinese.

DEATH IN CHINA

Since the history of Chinese funeral customs and burial practices extends far beyond human memory, the exact origins of modern customs cannot be definitively linked with a specific date. However, the concept of providing for the material comfort of the deceased existed at least as early as the Shang dynasty (1600–1050 B.C.). Both real and symbolic gifts of elaborate burial goods, human sacrifices, and offerings of food and clothing provided the deceased with the comforts of life.[1]

During the Zhou dynasty (c. 1050–256 B.C.) there emerged three classical texts—the *Yili*, the *Zhouli*, and the *Liji*—outlining specific ceremonies and rituals that pertained to appeasing the spirits of the ancestors. These ancient texts prescribed ritual wailing, fasting, and the burning of symbolic sacrifices of food and clothing as a means of providing for the deceased. The use of the "spirit tablet" as a material house for the dead also emerged at this time. The family cared for the ancestor by chanting prayers and sacrificing food to the tablet placed in the family shrine.[2]

Confucianism embraced the concept of *li*, or ritual, and reinforced the importance of rites connected with ancestor reverence, including the observance of a number of holidays to honor the dead. According to Confucianism, an individual fulfills certain obligatory roles throughout his life. The five basic relationships are (1) ruler to subject, (2) father to son, (3) husband to wife, (4) elder brother to younger brother, (5) friend to friend.[3] These relationships create an orderly society in which the individual experiences no confusion about his moral obligations. Thus, the proper performance of burial rituals, especially those involving parents, reinforced the necessity of ancestor reverence and filial piety.

One of the most spectacular discoveries demonstrating the importance of burial practices in China was the 1974 excavation of the tomb of Qin Shihuangdi, first emperor of the Qin dynasty (221–207 B.C.). At this site in Xi'an, amazed excavators discovered over 124 pottery horses, eighteen wooden chariots, nine thousand weapons, and eight hundred life-size terra cotta soldiers arranged in battle formation around the tomb.[4] These statues were to protect the emperor in his afterlife. The use of statues ended the earlier practice of human sacrifices until the Mongols' Yuan dynasty (A.D. 1270–1368). In Mongol tradition, human sacrifice reemerged briefly, but it never fully regained its earlier prominence.[5] Funerals and burials continued to grow in extravagance despite attempts during the Han dynasty (206 B.C.–A.D. 220) to regulate their size and elaborateness.[6] The upper class sought to emulate imperial burials on a smaller scale in succeeding dynasties.

The development of the three major religions of China, Confucianism, Daoism, and Buddhism, significantly influenced the evolution of Chinese death rituals and beliefs. Over the years these philosophies became so intertwined that it is now difficult to determine which religion influenced what death ritual. However, the contribution of each may be considered in very general terms. Confucianism, concerned with promoting social harmony through structure, emphasized the importance of specific death rituals in reinforcing filial piety and ancestor reverence. Daoism, with its emphasis on harmony and balance in the universe, influenced the development of *fengshui* (geomancy), the orientation of graves and residences in a manner favorable to maintaining a balance of *qi*, energy. Daoist philosophy evolved to include belief in a number of deities and adherence to certain rituals in hopes of achieving immortality. With the development of Daoism and the numerous sects of Buddhism there emerged a variety of concepts of paradise, purgatory, and reincarnation. Buddhism and Daoism appealed to the supernatural aspects of Chinese belief, while Confucianism provided a structural organization to these beliefs.

Buddhist and Daoist philosophers grappled with concepts of the human soul. The Daoist philosopher Zhuangzi emphasized the desire to prolong the life of the flesh on earth as long as possible. Popular Daoist sects adopted alchemy and a variety of ritual and meditative techniques for achieving long life.[7] Buddhists added the belief in the afterlife or otherworld.

Desire for the preservation of the body is also related to the popular Chinese idea of the two elements of the soul: the *hun* and the *po*. This concept of the duality of the human soul existed in China as early as the sixth century B.C., although it was later embraced and adapted by Confucianist, Daoist, and Buddhist philosophers. The *hun* embodies the spiritual and intellectual energy of the individual while the *po* enables physical action. At death the *hun* separates from the body and ascends to the realm of immortal beings, *xian* (*hsien*), while the *po* remains with the body.[8] Mourners provided the *po* with all the necessary comforts of human life, including material possessions.

Archaeologists excavating Han-era tombs have discovered food vessels, clothing, wash basins, incense burners, and other artifacts of home life deposited with the dead. Since the preservation of the body was essential to the well-being of the *po*, this concern manifested itself in the form of jade suits and other means of dressing the deceased. Jade, silver, gold, or pearls were placed in the mouth of the deceased in the belief that they could impart preservative qualities.[9]

The living also performed certain rituals to ensure the comfort of the *hun*. Immediately after death, Buddhist or Daoist officials chose from a number of ceremonies designed to encourage the *hun* to return to the body. Such ceremonies included the Ritual of Fu, or "The Summons of the Soul," in which a family member carried the robe of the deceased to the roof of the house and attempted to call the deceased's soul back to the body. When such attempts to revive the dead person failed, priests and relatives performed certain rites to guide the *hun* into the other world.[10] The Ritual of Fu existed as early as Han times, and anthropologists have observed similar ceremonies in modern China. In *The Cult of the Dead in a Chinese Village*, Emily Ahern describes a 1960s-era ceremony in which a paper effigy of the deceased is symbolically guided safely through the underworld. In this manner, living family members actively assist the *hun* soul in its journey.[11] The *hun* soul was also invited to inhabit the ancestral tablet. The spirit tablet allowed the living to mourn and commemorate their deceased relatives. The eldest male descendant held the responsibility of keeping the ancestors informed of family affairs. In this manner, the deceased maintained a continuous presence in the lives of the living.[12]

Although notions of the netherworld had existed since the Shang era, the concepts of paradise and purgatory evolved with the growth of the various forms of Daoism and Buddhism in China. Buddhist and Daoist priests presided over the funeral ceremony, performing the necessary rites to ensure the ancestor's comforts. They often called on the deities to guide the *hun* through the spirit realm and on into the next incarnation. The death would first be announced to an authority in the underworld. This authority might be any one of the following three deities believed to guard the gates into the underworld: Tudi (T'u-ti, the earth god), Chenghuang (Ch'eng-huang, the city god), or Wudao (Wu-tao, the god of five roads).[13] Upon arrival in the underworld, the soul of the deceased must visit purgatory to be judged by the authorities of the ten kingdoms of purgatory. The individual would then receive either punishments or rewards for his deeds. Punishments might include perpetual deprivation of food and water, confinement in chains, boiling in oil, disembowelment, or being eaten alive by wild animals. After a long period of suffering the convicted could return to the earth in the form of some lower animal such as a dog or a cat.[14] Virtuous souls, on the other hand, would be rewarded for their deeds and returned to earth in a higher form.[15] The righteous few whom the deities deemed worthy could pass on to enjoy the pleasures of heaven.[16] The living could help relieve the suffering of the deceased through chanting incantations and burning offerings of food, money, and clothing.[17] Once the deities of the netherworld received these appeals, the deceased could be granted a reprieve through rebirth.[18]

The growth of Buddhism and Daoism may have also contributed to the development of certain superstitions surrounding the deceased that persist to the modern day. The descendants considered the comfort of the deceased ancestor of utmost importance. If the *po* soul remained comfortable in the grave, the living would reap the blessings of their contented ancestor. Failure to provide for the deceased could result in punishment in the form of bad health, poor harvests, or a variety of calamities.[19] Mourners thus took the necessary precautions to ensure their own safety should the discontented ancestor return to earth in the form of a *gui* (*kuei*, demon or ghost).[20] A mid-twentieth-century custom insisted that "before being put into the coffin, the corpse was always placed with its feet facing the door, so that should it rise as a vampire it would walk straight out the door instead of doing harm in the house."[21] Diviners carefully selected the date and place of burial to avoid the presence of such evil spirits. Individuals whose birthday fell on the dates selected by the geomancer were encouraged to stay away from the burial ground on the day of the funeral. To appease any wandering spirits, relatives provided offerings of food and mock paper money at the ceremonies. Food offered to supernatural beings was often dry or uncooked to distinguish it from food for humans.[22]

Contact with the dead, though inevitable, was undesirable. People believed that after an individual had touched seven corpses, he could no longer be made clean again and might contract diseases such as leprosy and syphilis. There existed, therefore, disdain for professional corpse handlers. James L. Watson's 1970s-era study of two Chinese villages reveals that the southern Chinese believed that at death the corpse released "killing airs" that contaminated everything and everyone around. Men were especially susceptible to this pollution since it attacked their *yang*, or masculine, essence. Women, then, were more likely to attend the funeral as representatives of the family. All those present at the funeral assumed the responsibility of absorbing some of this pollution. Sometimes relatives hired a professional to divert the contamination from them.[23]

Emily Ahern observed a unique ceremony in a twentieth-century Taiwanese village. The rite was designed to free family and friends from their connection with the deceased. All present lined up next to the coffin while an assistant priest brought out a length of string, which he tied to the wrist of the corpse and fed out so that it passed through the hands of everyone in the line. Next he gave each mourner a stick of incense and a slip of the mock paper money ordinarily burned at funerals. Each person folded the paper money and held it in one hand so the string passed through the fold and did not touch his hands. The incense was held with the money. While everyone stood there silently except for several women who continued to wail, a Daoist priest faced the corpse, banging together two cleavers and reciting incantations. After a time he moved down the line of people followed by his assistant. Stopping in front of each person, he cut the string, leaving everyone holding a separate piece. This they then placed, along with the paper money and incense stick, in a basket held by the priest's assistant. Finally, when all the pieces of string were in the basket, it was taken away and burned to ashes.[24]

FENGSHUI

Fengshui, literally translated as "wind" and "water," refers to the positioning of graves and residences in a harmonious position with the elements of nature. The ultimate goal of *fengshui*, or geomancy as it is called in the West, is to please the deceased ancestor with a comfortable resting place where a balance of *qi*, vital energy, can be found. Families often hire professional geomancers to determine the time of burial and to site the grave. *Fengshui* is related to the early philosophy of *yin* and *yang* and its concern with balance in the universe, but historians cannot determine the exact origins of its creation. *Fengshui* evolved along different paths in China. Historians credit Guan Lo (A.D. 210–256) as the first famous prophet of geomancy, although Guo Pu (A.D. 276–324) is often credited as the patriarch of *fengshui*.[25] Known throughout the Six Dynasties (A.D. 420–589) as an important soothsayer and geomancer, Guo Pu was acknowledged as the author of the *Zangshu*, the Book of Burial.[26] Individuals sought the guidance of Guo Pu in siting the graves of their deceased relatives because a man buried in a properly sited grave will grant prosperity to all descendants.[27] By the end of the Song dynasty (A.D. 960–1279) two distinct schools of *fengshui* had emerged.[28] The first, often called the "Ancestral Hall" or "Forms" school, popular in Fujian Province, emphasized the direction of the graves determined by the use of a magnetic compass, the planets, and the trigrams system.[29] The specially designed compass determined the most auspicious site for burial.[30] The specific alignment of the grave may depend on the hour, day, and year of birth and death of the deceased.[31] The second school originated in Jiangxi Province and is called the "Shapes" school.[32] This school also used the magnetic compass but placed great importance on landforms and terrains, especially the mutual appropriateness of dragons, eminences, and water, to name a few aspects. A simplified formula was mountains at the back and water at the front of cemeteries. As *fengshui* grew in popularity, each school borrowed heavily from the other in order to meet the demands of the consumer.[33] The result differed depending on the school or combination of schools employed for the burial site.

Despite the popular growth of *fengshui*, not all accepted its precepts unquestioningly. By 1082, laws had emerged in opposition to certain rituals associated with *fengshui*. Criminal punishment awaited those who failed to immediately bury the dead while seeking an auspicious date.[34] During the Song dynasty the famous philosopher and statesman Sima Guang (Ssu-ma Kuang, 1019–1086) began to write against *fengshui*:

> The people nowadays do not bury the dead more luxuriously than they did anciently, but the importance attached to the prohibitions created by the Yin-and-Yang system has become much greater! The treatises on burial now in circulation investigate the influences of the forms of mountains and water-courses, rocks and fields; they examine the [Earthly] Branches and [Celestial Stems] which indicate the years, months, days and hours, considering the low or high rank of the offspring in the social scale, their wealth and poverty, late or early death, intelligence or stupidity to be entirely bound up with those factors, so that burials cannot be performed unless in such-and-such grounds and at such-and-such times. The whole nation is bewildered by these theories and places belief

therein, in consequence of which it frequently occurs that those who lose their parents postpone their burial for a considerable time.[35]

Nevertheless, proper care of an ancestor provided hope for improving the living descendants' present status. A story from the third century A.D. illustrates this point:

When Ch'ing [Qing], the great-grandfather of (Chang) [Zhang] Yu, had to bury his father, Kwoh Poh [Guo Bo] drew prognostics about some spots, and said: "If you bury him in this place, you will live to be over a hundred years of age and attain one of the three highest official dignities, but you will then not have numerous offspring. And if you inter him in that spot, your lifetime will only be half as long and your official career will be cut off on having attained the dignity of Director of a Court, but your issue [will] be honoured and illustrious for a series of generations." Ch'ing [Qing] performed the burial in the weaker spot, and thus he became Director of the Court of Imperial Entertainment and died at the age of sixty-four; but his children and grandchildren had a glorious career.[36]

Proper orientation of the grave coupled with appropriate graveside rituals offered a means through which the individual could improve his social status. In this manner the individual became an active participant in determining his destiny.

The popular growth of geomancy may be attributed to Daoist philosophy. Daoist concerns with harmony and balance in the universe carried over into beliefs about the resting place of the dead. Hills and mountains provided a barrier to dangerous winds that might carry evil spirits while allowing beneficial winds to pass.[37] Water balanced the *yang* influence of the mountains and carried along *yin* energy with it. However, even these two elements, if improperly oriented, could bring bad luck to the family. People generally believed that evil spirits traveled in straight lines; therefore, a watercourse could not run straight to a grave or dwelling lest evil accumulate on that spot. The water must pass alongside the grave, allowing negative energy to meander by while dispersing good *qi* along the way.[38]

The family considered the shape of the grave to be as important as the location itself. Sometimes artificial ridges were built along the back and sides of the graves to allow rainwater and negative energy to flow away from the grave. An omega-shaped grave, with the person's head buried up against the slope of a hill, afforded this type of protection around the tomb.[39]

In the Guangzhou (Canton) region, where some of the people practiced secondary burial, gravediggers buried the body in a shallow pit to allow the flesh to decompose before the pit was opened again and the bones removed. Several years after death the descendants returned to scrape the flesh from the bones and then rebury the bones in urns. This practice reflected different views toward the corpse than were held in other regions of China. The "burial of the body in a coffin . . . followed by a later unearthing, scraping of the bones, temporary storage of the bones in an urn, and later reburial of the urn in a geomantically suited setting . . . is related to ideas about the power of bones and the dangers of the flesh."[40] Since bone preservation was of utmost importance for its benefit to the ancestor, the urn supposedly prevented further decomposition of the bones.[41] Geomancy proved just as important in secondary burial, since reburial of the urn in a geomantically suitable setting completed the process.[42]

FUNERALS IN NINETEENTH AND TWENTIETH CENTURY CHINA

By the nineteenth century, funerals had become a means through which families demonstrated their position in society. Sons were expected to uphold the family honor by planning an elaborate ceremony on behalf of their deceased parents. A typical ceremony included a funeral procession to the cemetery, the performance of rites at the grave, and a memorial service several days later. Music was also important.

The funeral procession often received the most attention, as it constituted a public display of wealth and prestige. Decorative paper banners, hung from bamboo sticks and carried by family and friends, proclaimed the solemnity of the occasion. Since the people believed that music would guide the deceased in his journey, bands hired for the occasion included musicians playing gongs, drums, cymbals, wind instruments, and stringed instruments.[43] Buddhist and Daoist priests chanted incantations while family members, and sometimes hired professionals, wailed loudly to demonstrate their grief. The children of the deceased exhibited the most grief, and were often seen in a state of extreme mourning that required the support of one or two friends. The mourners wore white, the color of death, and scattered perforated white paper money along the way. The money was intended to distract evil spirits as well as to provide a trail for the deceased's soul back to the house after the funeral. Sometimes an image of the deceased would precede the coffin. After the turn of the century, a green sedan chair in the procession symbolized the presence of the soul of the deceased.[44]

"The degree of elaborateness of mortuary rites was based upon the status of the deceased in the family."[45] The men of the family, especially the heads of household, received the most ceremony at their death. This practice represents a further extension of the patrilineal nature of Confucianist doctrine. Unmarried adults and young children received little, if any, attention.[46] A person without descendants was simply placed into a plain wooden coffin and buried anywhere a grave site could be obtained.[47] Criminal offenders likewise received very few rites upon their death. Graves of convicts were dug in straight rows with no attention to the positioning of the graves according to the principles of *fengshui*.[48] The elaborateness of the ceremony also varied according to the economic status of the family. However, rich and poor alike struggled to provide their beloved deceased with the most ostentatious ceremony they could afford.

The excessive elaborateness of these ceremonies, and the burden they placed on the poor, did not go unnoticed by contemporaries. The poor often transcended their financial means in order to provide for the future welfare of the deceased. "Though the poorer classes cannot, of course, afford great outlays for their dead, yet they seldom neglect consulting a Fung-Shui [*fengshui*] expert when they have to bury their father or mother."[49] Individuals believed that such measures not only benefited the deceased but also ensured a shower of blessings from the contented ancestor on the descendants. In 1924, historian Gu Jiegang (Wade-Giles, Ku Chieh-kang) protested the excessiveness of funerals in China. Criticizing the funeral ceremony of his own grandmother, Gu explained that four to five hundred dollars was spent on horses, six horn players, nine musicians, nine Daoist priests, floats, a ten-man orchestra, nine Chan (Ch'an) monks, string musicians, brass players, and so on. He claimed, "If the arrangements are too simple, older relatives will make critical remarks, and sons will be accused of unfilial behavior and face the disapproval of society."[50] Clearly, the public also expected the family to "put on a good show." This attitude became the norm.

Ceremonies at the grave were often no less dramatic. The personal belongings of the deceased were burned in the cemetery to accompany him, or her, into the afterlife. Paper representations of money, clothing, houses, and servants were likewise burned.[51] Various types of food offerings, including pork, fish, chicken, rice, liquor, and tea, were brought to the cemetery to be consumed first by the dead and later by the living. The coffin, often made of China fir or cypress, depending on the wealth of the mourners, was then lowered into the grave pit.[52] Relatives placed some personal items inside the coffin along with symbolic gifts to aid the deceased in his or her journey. Nails, coins, and grains were often placed inside the coffin or distributed to mourners as symbols of hope for male offspring, wealth, and good crops for the descendants.[53] Sometimes coins or strips of red paper were placed in the four corners of the coffin to keep away evil spirits; the deceased may also have been provided with mirrors and paper money to serve a similar purpose. In some cases the edges of the coffin lid were sealed with mortar or putty to keep the coffin airtight.[54] "At the time of burial, the foot-end of the coffin has holes drilled in it, or may even be smashed open, to let out the *ch'i* [*qi*], everyone is forewarned to stand clear."[55]

POST-FUNERAL CEREMONIES IN CHINA

Every seventh day for seven weeks after the individual's death, certain ceremonies, designed to guide the ancestor into heaven, were performed. Some of these rites included reenactments of significant events in the deceased's journey. Priests and family members participated in ceremonies designed to guide the soul across bridges and through the gates of the underworld. One ceremony involved burning a paper house to represent the moving of the ancestor into his new house in the underworld, and another service helped guide the individual through the ten kingdoms of purgatory. Descendants wailed and made pleas on behalf of the deceased in hopes of convincing the gods of the deceased's worthiness in life. Paper money and other belongings were also burned throughout this period to accompany the deceased into his or her new life.[56]

The living also continued to honor the deceased through the ancestral tablet. Shortly after death, a temporary tablet made of paper was placed in the community ancestral hall. Within a year the family destroyed the paper tablet and held a ceremony to replace it with a permanent one. The permanent tablet was usually made of wood and displayed the full name, rank, and title of the deceased. The right to have a tablet placed in the ancestral hall depended on the contribution of property or members to the lineage and the possession of the lineage surname. The tablets were venerated for several generations by the descendants, who provided offerings of food and incense to the memory of the deceased.[57]

The dead were further remembered in certain annual ceremonies. During Qingming (Ch'ing-ming), the spring Pure Brightness festival, families visited graves and carefully tended them. A family elder swept the grave clean with a willow branch believed to repel evil spirits. Families presented offerings of food and liquor while burning paper money and incense to provide for the needs of the deceased.[58] Similar sacrifices were made during Yulanpen, the Hungry Ghosts festival, usually in mid-August. Offerings were again given at the Chinese New Year.

REGIONAL AND ETHNIC VARIATIONS

It is important to recognize the diversity of customs, reflecting various beliefs, that existed throughout China. Nearly every province, village, and family unit, as well as ethnic minorities, had their own beliefs regarding death and the afterlife. As mentioned earlier, the three philosophies of China each viewed death in very distinct terms. No single belief dominated Chinese thinking. Although individual beliefs varied, according to scholar James Watson, a uniform structure of funerary rites emerged in late imperial China. The uniformity of funerary ritual allowed for variation in burial practices.[59] The intent here is simply to identify a "typical" funeral and burial in order to help better explain the variation of practices observed in the nineteenth-century American West. As individual Chinese moved to the West, they brought with them their own unique ideas and beliefs and often modified them to suit the needs of their strange new environment.

THE CHINESE IN CALIFORNIA

The Euro-Americans seemed enthralled by the "peculiar" funerary traditions of their Chinese neighbors: "The death of Chin Quong Wee, which occurred two days ago, was the first that had taken place among his people here for a long time, and in consequence the burial yesterday excited so much attention and curiosity that a very large number of persons, probably 500, assembled to witness it."[60]

Newspaper articles and diaries attest to this curiosity. Unfortunately, the majority of available primary accounts were written by Euro-Americans who, characteristic of their time, used such events as examples of Chinese "inferiority." As such ignorance spread, so too did discriminatory practices against California's Chinese population.

Funeral practices no doubt served many purposes to Chinese individuals and society in nineteenth-century California. Emigrating from their homeland in a time of internal strife and famine, the Chinese sought their fortune in the Gold Mountain. At first they met with relative success. Caught in a wave of gold rush excitement, the immigrants mined for the precious metal that would provide for their families back home. Many more subsequently found employment building the railroads that would connect western America to the East Coast. In the boomtowns of California, these original immigrants found a means of providing for their families at home in China. However, boom soon gave way to bust. About twenty years after their arrival in the new land, the Chinese met the hostility of their jealous Euro-American neighbors as the two groups increasingly competed for work. Discriminatory legislation prevented new Chinese immigrants from entering the United States. Those who were already here endured prejudice, as towns all across the state adopted policies that forcibly segregated the Chinese from their Euro-American neighbors. Yet the

Chinese remained, continuing to mine for the dwindling supplies of gold in the hills of California or working in other types of jobs. Discrimination and financial hardships no doubt had the effect of bonding the Chinese community closer together. Historians and archaeologists have proven that communities worked hard to retain the culture of their homeland. Food preparation remained relatively unchanged. Recreational practices, such as music performances, opium smoking, storytelling, and gambling, continued. The existence of "joss houses" (temples) attests to the importance of religious observances. Numerous primary source accounts describe elaborate ceremonies for various religious holidays and festivals. Ceremonies for the dead were no exception.

The highly ritualized Chinese funeral ceremonies represented a means by which individuals found comfort in the community during a time of despair. Far from the security of family and home, individuals sought reassurance in the familiar ceremonies of their homeland. Orientation of the graves according to the principles of *fengshui* served the function of alleviating many of the fears associated with death. By properly burying the deceased in a manner that provided a harmonious balance with the environmental elements, individuals could hope to reap the blessings of the departed relative. Fear of unhappy relatives was foremost on their minds. Because reburial of the individual in China would definitely ensure that the ancestor rested well, mourners paid special attention to the process of unearthing the bones and returning them to China. In death, the individual far from his native land could be guaranteed a connection to home and family.

For the society as a whole the ceremonies helped reinforce the importance of filial piety. Centuries of ancestor reverence continued unabated. Ceremonies for the dead confirmed Confucianist doctrines emphasizing patriarchal authority and respect for ancestors. The chief mourner, usually the eldest son, held primary responsibility for ensuring that the burial of his parents was handled properly. If an individual was the only direct descendant or the most obligated descendant he might be required to assume primary responsibility of caring for the deceased.[61] Since most of the immigrants were in the United States without their wives and children, a relative, clansman, or close friend filled the role of the eldest son. This system of obligatory duty helped to ensure the survival of ancient practices of ancestor reverence, as well as "reaffirming the cohesion and solidarity of the family group."[62] Similarly, other social structures also benefited from the continued practice of *fengshui* in California. The establishment of Chinese cemeteries and the exhumation of bodies for reburial in China remained an important function of the Chinese associations in California. These associations played a large role in organizing Chinese communities in towns throughout the state. Because individuals relied heavily on their services, death practices helped to maintain the authority of these institutions far from home.

FUNERALS

The California Chinese retained most of their religious beliefs and practices, as well as their customs regarding death. The souls of the deceased were cared for through the proper ceremonies at the appropriate times of the year. Sacrifices of food, money, and clothing accompanied the deceased into the next life. Various means of distraction repelled evil spirits. Guests received gifts of candy and money to sweeten the bitterness of the occasion. Images of heaven and hell remained relatively the same. Accounts of funeral ceremonies describe this continuity of religious beliefs as embraced by the Chinese in California.

Primary accounts of Chinese funeral ceremonies in California are abundant due to the curious interest of Euro-American spectators. The elaborateness of these ceremonies often drew the attention of townsfolk regardless of age or race. Curious young boys in the town of Chinese Camp did not miss the opportunities provided by such events: "Every American attending the funeral was given a ten-cent piece and some incense for good luck. Boys old enough to know better would line up in the procession, get their ten cents, then crawl through the fence and get at the end of the procession again and receive another dime. Some of them got thirty cents before they were caught."[63]

Yet, the Euro-Americans attending Chinese ceremonies understood very little of the symbolism involved. In 1876, the editors of Dutch Flat's newspaper admitted, "We attended a big celebration at Chinatown last Sunday. . . . What we didn't understand about the ceremonies would make a very large book."[64]

Although the funerals of early Chinese pioneers were simple, they were not lacking in symbolism and ritual:

> One Euro-American miner working in the Folsom region observed that after a Chinese miner drowned on the North Fork of the American River in 1850, his countrymen put gold dust in his mouth and hands and buried him. Four weeks after the burial the remaining members of the dead man's company [association or *huiguan*] came down to the grave, bringing boiled beef, pork, a dozen oranges, raisins and some brandy. They placed the food on the grave, burned cakes beside it, and shared the brandy with the Euro-American on-lookers.[65]

The first dead among the San Francisco Chinese received simple funerals involving the beating of gongs, explosion of firecrackers, and scattering of perforated white paper.[66] Similar processions occurred in Chinese communities throughout the state. As communities grew, ceremonies became more traditional, and many became more elaborate as the wealth of Chinese families increased (fig. 1.2).

When a death occurred, a relative or friend announced it by posting a white paper with Chinese calligraphy on the deceased's door. Another relative announced the individual's death to the gods at the temple. Obituary notices informed friends of the death. Next the body was laid out in the house near a table with various types of food offerings. The family offered several types of cooked and uncooked meats, vegetables, fruits, liquor, and tea to the spirits. A geomancer might then be called in to determine the time of burial. Relatives dressed the deceased in his or her best clothes and prepared for the funeral procession.[67]

Elmer Wok Wai remembered his mother's funeral in San Francisco: "In the morning my sister and I were dressed by the women in white mourning garments and burlap bands were put around our heads. They took off our felt slippers and tied yellow mat sandals on our feet."[68] In a typical procession, mourners wore white and blue, the colors of death. The chief mourner usually led the procession, visibly expressing his grief while supported on either side by friends. Wailing relatives announced, through "a mixture of sobbing, of eulogies of the dead, and of regrets for the bereavement," the death of an important family member.[69] Large silken banners recounted the life story of the deceased while a riderless horse symbolically carried the soul to its final destination.[70] Family and friends threw perforated white paper along the street to confuse any lurking spirits.[71]

Figure 1.2.   Chinese funeral procession in California, 1887. Negative #6207. Courtesy California State Library, California History Room.

Priests, bands, and professional wailers were often hired to accompany family and friends throughout the streets. The reporters of the *San Francisco Call* described the elaborate funeral of Low Yet in 1888:

> The procession was headed by an advance guard carrying banners, then came the carriages of the distinguished Chinamen, followed by members of the Chee Keong Tong [Zhigongtang, or Chinese Freemasons]. Next, came the hearse, drawn by four black horses, and a wagon bearing a picture of the deceased. These were followed by the hired mourners . . . followed by a company of soldiers armed with rifles, and another company with cutlasses and shields. Then came a heterogeneous collection of express wagons, buggies and old vehicles of all patterns and stages of decrepitude, each loaded to its utmost capacity. Bands of music were located at intervals along the line, dispensing discord without stint. One feature of the procession was a led horse saddled and bridled.[72]

Buddhist and Daoist priests accompanied the procession, chanting various incantations and performing burial rites. Hired to announce the tragedy of the occasion and to frighten away evil spirits, the sounds of Chinese bands and wailers often drew criticism from observers. In 1876 a Mendocino newspaper explained, "When the mourners get off an unusual piercing shriek or wail, the clarinets, gongs and one-stringed fiddles in the hands of the musicians clang louder and more furiously than ever, and the very pavement seems to shake beneath us."[73]

A wagon carrying all of the belongings of the deceased arrived at the cemetery with the procession. The items in the wagon, including clothing, bedding, and other belongings, were burned near the cemetery. Symbolic money and other worldly possessions were also burned at the cemetery. Some California Chinese built specialized ovens (burners) in their cemeteries for the burning ceremony. Mourners wept and knelt at the grave, kowtowing and singing. Relatives placed offerings of food and liquor before the grave. Whole roast pigs, chicken, soup, rice, cakes, and other food and drink items remained at the grave site until evening for the spirits' delight.[74]

The individual was often buried with his possessions and symbolic gifts. Mourners cast coins, both American and Chinese, into the coffin or placed them in the mouth, ears, and hands of the deceased.[75] In some cases, the family tossed handfuls of popcorn and sand into the coffin.[76] Individuals were occasionally buried with bricks or bottles containing information about their identity and home village for later identification at exhumation. Wooden markers at the head of the grave served a similar purpose.[77] The coffins were usually very simple and composed of pine or redwood. Buried in shallow pits to enhance decomposition of the flesh, they often were not more than six inches below the surface. One firsthand account from Oroville in 1862 claimed that in some cases the tops of the coffins were exposed to view.[78]

Few Euro-Americans watched these proceedings with quiet respect; indeed, some individuals even became violent. In Nevada County the funeral of Jim Yet Wah nearly ended in disaster:

> For some reason or other a handful of nickels and dimes was showered over the remains. *That* nearly wrecked the works. We white urchins viewing the proceedings made one wild dive and scramble. For a few moments it was nip and tuck as to whether Old Jim was to remain in state on the saw-horses or was to be cast upon the ground. Precariously the coffin tilted on one saw-horse and then upon the other, the coffin jigging meantime. After much "ki-yi-ing" and uproar the young ruffians were scattered and order restored.[79]

Even the funerals of prominent Chinese were not immune from harassment by Euro-Americans. At the 1897 funeral of Chinese gangster Little Pete, in San Francisco (fig. 1.3), spectators suddenly turned violent:

> Men and women fought for sticks of incense, bits of paper, flowers, ribbons — anything for a souvenir of "Little Pete." They knocked the roast meats and fowls into the sand. One man grasped a chicken and carried it away. A big, red-faced citizen swabbed a piece of pork in the sand and shouted for joy as he held aloft this trophy. . . . And in this fashion and worse 3000 white people of a civilized and Christian race and country gave a lesson in manners to 600 of their pagan brothers.[80]

Food left at the graves as a sacrifice to the deceased often became the meal of inconsiderate witnesses.[81]

In many cases, local authorities determined the Chinese a health hazard and barred them from burying their dead in existing cemeteries.[82] This ban resulted in the development of exclusively Chinese cemeteries throughout the state and may have inadvertently served to foster traditional burial practices. Most Chinese cemeteries in California are located very near the Euro-American burying grounds. They were usually maintained by the appropriate branch of a district association; these organizations assumed the responsibility of the family in caring for the dead. Mourners continued to consider the principles of geomancy in siting graves, while still observing traditional holidays and ceremonial practices for the dead. After several years, the associations hired men to exhume the bones and ship them to China.

GEOMANCY

The ancient practice of *fengshui* followed the Chinese to the New World. The Chinese in California consulted diviners to determine appropriate days for

Figure 1.3.   Funeral procession for "Little Pete." *San Francisco Call,* January 27, 1897.

services and burials.[83] After death, the family may have consulted a geomancer to forecast the precise time at which the spirit would leave the body. The family would not want to be present at such a time since the potential for danger at that point was high.[84] Folk stories recorded in the 1930s by the Works Projects Administration seem to confirm that *fengshui* continued to be an important part of life and death to the California Chinese. One such story recounted the calamities faced by a family shortly after the burial of the father. After the son in a sick delirium repeated the phrase, "Coffin to the west!" the mother consulted an expert to examine the father's grave. The expert concluded the husband was inappropriately buried facing west, thereby causing discomfort for the deceased. At the expert's command the family dug up the coffin and reburied it in the right position, thus freeing the family from all misfortune.[85]

In his study of the Riverside, California, Chinese settlement, Fred W. Mueller Jr. examines the application of *fengshui* to dwellings in overseas Chinatowns. Mueller concludes that several Chinatowns appeared to be appropriately oriented in compliance with the principles of *fengshui*.[86] In a similar manner, the location and orientation of some California Chinese cemeteries may have been determined by these same principles (see chapter 3). In selecting a grave site, the Chinese ideally considered the direction and location of geographical features such as trees, water, and hills; practically, though, financial constraints probably prevented most immigrants from siting individual graves.

In some cases, the deceased may have been buried with his or her head facing west toward China. The presence of a hill usually resulted in burials with the heads toward the hill. Mountains to the north and water to the south provided a very auspicious grave site. In many cases, however, when the Euro-American community dictated the location of the cemetery, the Chinese may have had very little control over the landscape.[87]

In recent times, *fengshui* experts have helped to site some modern California Chinese cemeteries. The local Chinese community hired a geomancer to help reconstruct Cypress Lawn Cemetery in Colma, California. The cemetery has been oriented so that the dead face the sun in the morning, have water at their feet, and have mountains on their side or front. Generally, heads face southeast or northeast depending on the desires of the family and the geomancer.[88] Individuals are usually buried with family groups. "If the woman is married, she should be buried on the right hand side from her husband. If the children [are] buried within the family garden, the children should be buried lower than the parents."[89] The ancient art of *fengshui* continues to influence modern Chinese American burial practices.

EXHUMATION

The practice of secondary burial took on a new meaning to the overseas Chinese. Belief in the dangers of the flesh, and the desire to rest in native soil, led to exhumation practices (see also chapter 7). Two to ten years after a death, community members, or hired exhumers appointed by the proper district association, excavated the bones from the local cemetery and shipped them back to China.[90] The exhumers removed the remaining flesh from the bones by either boiling or scraping it off prior to transporting the bodies to San Francisco for shipment. Costs for these services varied; one researcher found that shipping the bones cost five dollars while reburial in China cost seven dollars.[91] The bodies were returned to China in either metal boxes or barrel-shaped ceramic jars.[92] A label posted on the outside of the box or jar identified the individual.[93] The Donghua (Tung Wah) Hospital in Hong Kong received the bones and returned them to the appropriate village for reburial.[94]

Differing accounts exist about the exact handling of the bones. In many cases, the reporters describe the exhumers as meticulous and credit them for their exactness in locating every bone. The following excerpt describes the thorough exhumation process practiced in Chico in 1897:

> The "official bone digger" tears off the lid of the coffin, and commencing at the foot carefully sifts all the earth that has gotten into the coffin and not a piece of bone is allowed to escape. . . . After the bones are removed from the ground,

they are sorted over. All the bones of the right side of the body are placed in one pile and all those of the left side another. They are then placed in the sun to dry, after which they are placed in a tin box.[95]

Police officials in 1885 San Francisco were surprised to encounter a basement full of bodies prepared for shipment to China. An article in the *Sacramento Union* for September 16, 1885, described how the larger bones were carefully wrapped in oiled cloth while the smaller bones were wrapped separately and placed within the larger box.[96] Sylvia Sun Minnick, in *Samfow*, explains, "An account was made of every bone. Should one be missing, care was taken to resift the loose dirt until it was located. The carpal, metacarpal and phalanges of each hand were placed in a small bag, and the bones of the feet were similarly separated and bagged."[97]

Other primary source accounts tell a different story. In 1897, the Chinese in Shasta reportedly

drag their diseased dead from their foul graves and make a charnel house in town where these defunct heathen breed in the heat of germs of all diseases that cause their deaths. . . . They bury their dead in shallow graves, and flies and ants can be seen swarming in and out of the exposed coffins. They leave their fowl [*sic*] clothes and remains of the decayed corpses around the graveyard where children or persons are apt to wander and contract diseases.[98]

Although this account is perhaps as exaggerated as it is biased by the prejudices of the time, it may reveal some truth of the consequences of hasty exhumation procedures. In 1862, the grand jury of Butte County reported that in Oroville, "they divest the bones of flesh, and leave the latter, with their grave clothes, in all stages of decomposition, scattered on the ground, creating a stench and endangering the health of the adjacent inhabitants."[99] Angry Euro-Americans across the state began a call for action.

At the height of discriminatory practices against the Chinese, Californians began adopting laws designed to further restrict traditional burial practices. Calling the Chinese hazardous to public health, many towns forced them to bury their dead away from the common burying ground. In 1878 California passed "An Act to Protect Public Health from Infection Caused by Exhumation and Removal of the Remains of Deceased Persons." Exhumers were thereafter required to get permits from county health officials prior to removal. The permit fee was ten dollars for each grave exhumed. Nevertheless, exhumations continued. In Watsonville, 108 bodies were returned to China between 1902 and 1913. By the 1930s, however, this practice had waned as more Chinese permanently made their home in California.[100]

POST-FUNERAL CEREMONIES IN CALIFORNIA

Services for the dead did not end with the funeral. Three days afterward, sacrifices of food and paper money were again offered at the grave. "The mourners take with them two cakes of white flour. They divide the cake in half and lay it on either side of the head of the coffin. Invisibly the wood of the coffin underneath will likewise crack in two and release three spirits."[101] Similar activities occurred every other week for a couple of months.

Unlike in China, most individuals in California had no families to care for them after death. The associations adopted this task and made caring for graves a community affair.[102] At appropriate times of year, the associations organized trips to the local cemeteries to offer sacrifices and repair graves as families did in China. On April 3, 1887, the San Francisco Chinese gathered at the Point Lobos Road Cemetery at 7:00 a.m. to celebrate Qingming. Euro-American witnesses described carts of "barbecued hogs, chickens, rice puddings, cakes and shamshoo [Chinese liquor]" being carted to the cemetery for consumption by the spirits (fig. 1.4). After a brief ceremony, firecrackers were set off and offerings made. "Three or four would assemble round a headstone and spread out the eatables. The next thing to be done was to light a bunch of joss-sticks and stick them in the ground all around." Then a speech was made to the deceased and liquor poured on the ground. The reporter sarcastically insisted, "There is no deception about your Chinaman. He does not make pretense of offering up the good comestibles and then sending them off home to enjoy them. No; he casts good liquor to the four winds of heaven."[103]

Figure 1.4.   Chinese funeral feast in California, 1887. Courtesy California State Library, California History Room.

As in China, similar offerings occurred at the August Hungry Ghosts festival, when, Daoists believe, the dead return to earth in search of food and other necessities.[104]

Rather than the ancestral halls used in China, California's Chinese reserved special rooms in temples and company houses devoted to the dead. These rooms housed the ancestral tablets and became the place of reverence for the deceased. A common tablet on which names of the recently deceased were added replaced individual tablets that would have been constructed in China.[105] This was another American adaptation of Chinese tradition.

WESTERNIZATION AND MODERNIZATION

As more and more Chinese made their homes in California, they began to adapt to a Western way of life. Often, customs and practices changed or completely disappeared. As many Chinese converted to Christianity, traditional ceremonies were likewise abandoned. Not so surprisingly, however, many traditions continued unchanged. The funeral procession through the streets, the sacrifices of food, the dispersal of spirit money, and the burning of symbolic representations of material possessions can be seen in modern Chinatowns (see chapter 7). Modern adaptations replaced the wagon with the hearse. Paper cars, computers, and jet airplanes are now burned along with symbolic money and food. Some families mix Christian and Chinese traditions at funeral ceremonies.[106] Certain practices, including exhumation and reburial in China, have disappeared almost completely in California as practicality provides other alternatives. In a reversal of the old custom, some families are even bringing the remains of their ancestors to the United States for reburial (see chapter 8).

Although time passed and their culture changed, the Chinese American community adapted to the circumstances of Westernization and modernization by incorporating its own traditions. Even in death, the California Chinese struggled in the face of adversity to retain the customs that bound them to their homeland. Many Euro-Americans, in their ignorance of Chinese customs, chose to mock them. Others, however, struggled to understand. An oft-repeated anecdote of a Chinese and a Caucasian man in a cemetery illustrates this point:

> The Caucasian placed a bouquet of flowers before the grave and stood for a moment in silent meditation. Then he watched the Chinese man go through the motions of offering wine, food, and money.
>
> "Come now," he jested, "Do you really think your ancestors can eat the food, drink the wine, and spend the money?"
>
> "As much as your ancestors can sniff your flowers," replied the Chinese.[107]

This story, recorded over a century ago, suggests that the gap of ignorance between the cultures is slowly closing.

NOTES

1. Te-Kun Cheng, *Archaeology in China*, vol. 2, *Shang China* (Toronto: University of Toronto Press, 1960), 78–79.

2. James Legge, trans., *Li Chi Book of Rites*, vol. 1 (New Hyde Park, NY: University Books, 1967), introduction; Leon Comber, *Chinese Ancestor Worship in Malaya* (Singapore: Donald Moore, 1957), 1–2; John Steele, trans., *The I-Li, or Book of Etiquette and Ceremonial*, vol. 2 (London: Probsthain, 1917), introduction.

3. Wei-ming Tu, *Confucian Thought: Selfhood as Creative Transformation* (Albany: State University of New York Press, 1985), 138.

4. Institute of Archaeology, Academy of Social Sciences, People's Republic of China, *Recent Archaeological Discoveries in the People's Republic of China* (Tokyo: Center for East Asian Cultural Studies, 1984), 65. More recently, additional archaeological discoveries have been made at the site, increasing both the number of objects and the significance of the tomb.

5. Charles Caldwell Dobie, *San Francisco's Chinatown* (New York: D. Appleton-Century, 1936), 66.

6. Howard J. Wechsler, *Offerings of Jade and Silk: Ritual and Symbol in the Legitimization of the T'ang Dynasty* (New Haven, CT: Yale University Press, 1985), 142–144.

7. Niels C. Nielsen Jr. and others, *Religions of the World*, 3rd ed. (New York: St. Martin's, 1993), 241.

8. Judith A. Berling, "Death and Afterlife in Chinese Religions," in *Death and Afterlife: Perspectives of World Religions*, ed. Hiroshi Obayashi (New York: Greenwood, 1992), 183; Ying-Shih Yu, "'O Soul, Come Back!' A Study in the Changing Conceptions of the Soul and Afterlife in Pre-Buddhist China," *Harvard Journal of Asiatic Studies* 47, no. 2 (December 1987): 370–395.

9. Comber, *Chinese Ancestor Worship*, 11; Michael Loewe, *Chinese Ideas of Life and Death: Faith, Myth, and Reason in the Han Period (202 BC–AD 220)* (London: George Allen and Unwin, 1982), 117–121; C. K. Yang, *Religion in Chinese Society: A Study of Contemporary Social Functions of Religion and Some of Their Historical Factors* (Berkeley: University of California Press, 1961), 31.

10. Loewe, *Chinese Ideas*, 114–115; Yu, "O Soul," 369.

11. Emily M. Ahern, *The Cult of the Dead in a Chinese Village* (Stanford, CA: Stanford University Press, 1973), 222–224.

12. Berling, "Death," 183.

13. Yang, *Religion*, 31; Susan Naquin, "Funerals in North China: Uniformity and Variation," in *Death Ritual in Late Imperial and Modern China*, ed. James L. Watson and Evelyn S. Rawski (Berkeley: University of California Press, 1988), 61. Pinyin romanization is used with the familiar Wade-Giles system or Americanized Chinese romanization throughout.

14. Alexander McLeod, *Pigtails and Gold Dust* (Caldwell, ID: Caxton, 1948), 289–291.

15. McLeod, *Pigtails and Gold Dust*; Ahern, *Cult*, 220–221.

16. Ahern, *Cult*, 220–221.

17. Ahern, *Cult*.

18. Berling, "Death," 182–188.

19. Ahern, *Cult*, 180; Berling, "Death," 182–183.

20. Berling, "Death," 182–183.

21. Yang, *Religion*, 33.

22. Ahern, *Cult*, 164–167.

23. James L. Watson, "Funeral Specialists in Cantonese Society: Pollution, Performance, and Social Hierarchy," in *Death Ritual in Late Imperial and Modern China*, ed. James L. Watson and Evelyn S. Rawski (Berkeley: University of California Press, 1988), 112–114.

24. Ahern, *Cult*, 172.

25. J. J. M. de Groot, *The Religious System of China*, vol. 3 (1897; reprint, Taiwan: Ch'eng Wen, 1969), 1000–1001.

26. De Groot, *Religious System*, 1004.

27. De Groot, *Religious System*, 1000.

28. Sang Hae Lee, "Feng Shui: Its Context and Meaning" (PhD diss., Cornell University, 1986), 99, 158; Sarah Rossbach, *Feng Shui: The Chinese Art of Placement* (New York: E. P. Dutton, 1983), 12.

29. Andrew L. March, "An Appreciation of Chinese Geomancy," *Journal of Asian Studies* 27, no. 2 (February 1968): 255–261.

30. Fred W. Mueller Jr., "Feng-Shui: Archaeological Evidence for Geomancy in Overseas Chinese Settlements," in *Wong Ho Leun, An American Chinatown*, vol. 2, *Archaeology* (San Diego: Great Basin Foundation, 1987), 4.

31. Comber, *Chinese Ancestor Worship*, 23; Cornelius Osgood, *Village Life in Old China: A Community Study of Kao Yao, Yunnan* (New York: Ronald, 1963), 296.

32. Comber, *Chinese Ancestor Worship*, 23.

33. De Groot, *Religious System*, 1008.

34. De Groot, *Religious System*, 1027.

35. Sima Guang, quoted in de Groot, *Religious System*, 1022.

36. De Groot, *Religious System*, 1002–1003.

37. Comber, *Chinese Ancestor Worship*, 24; de Groot, *Religious System*, 940.

38. Rossbach, *Feng Shui*, 38.

39. De Groot, *Religious System*, 941–942; Maurice Freedman, *The Study of Chinese Society: Essays by Maurice Freedman*, ed. G. William Skinner (Stanford, CA: Stanford University Press, 1979), 196; Stuart E. Thompson, "Death, Food, and Fertility," in *Death Ritual in Late Imperial and Modern China*, ed. James L. Watson and Evelyn S. Rawski (Berkeley: University of California Press, 1988), 104.

40. Naquin, "Funerals," 58.

41. Ahern, *Cult*, 204.

42. Freedman, *Study*, 196; Naquin, "Funerals," 58; Thompson, "Death," 104.

43. Watson, "Funeral Specialists," 123.

44. Comber, *Chinese Ancestor Worship*, 15–30; Patricia Buckley Ebrey, ed., *Chinese Civilization and Society* (New York: Free Press, 1981), 289–293; Osgood, *Village Life*, 297.

45. Yang, *Religion*, 47.

46. Yang, *Religion*, 47.

47. Osgood, *Village Life*, 299.

48. De Groot, *Religious System*, 1076; Loewe, *Chinese Ideas*, 125.

49. De Groot, *Religious System*, 1034.

50. Gu Jiegang, quoted in Ebrey, *Chinese Civilization*, 290–291.

51. Naquin, "Funerals," 61; Yang, *Religion*, 32.

52. Osgood, *Village Life*, 291.

53. Comber, *Chinese Ancestor Worship*, 31; Thompson, "Death," 105; Ahern, *Cult*, 179.

54. Comber, *Chinese Ancestor Worship*, 14, 31; Rossbach, *Feng Shui*, 68.

55. Thompson, "Death," 105.

56. Ahern, *Cult*, 222–227; Comber, *Chinese Ancestor Worship*, 17–18; Yang, *Religion*, 32–33.

57. Ahern, *Cult*, 92–121; Comber, *Chinese Ancestor Worship*, 14, 31; Rossbach, *Feng Shui*, 18–22.

58. Thomas W. Chinn, H. Mark Lai, and Philip P. Choy, eds., *A History of the Chinese in California: A Syllabus* (San Francisco: Chinese Historical Society of America, 1969), 76; Comber, *Chinese Ancestor Worship*, 35; Osgood, *Village Life*, 898.

59. James L. Watson, "The Structure of Chinese Funerary Rites: Elementary Forms, Ritual Sequences, and the Primacy of Perormance," in *Death Ritual in Late Imperial and Modern China*, ed. James L. Watson and Evelyn S. Rawski (Berkeley: University of California Press, 1988), 3–4.

60. Harry W. Lawton, "Selected Newspaper Accounts of Riverside's Chinese Settlers," in *Wong Ho Leun, An American Chinatown*, vol. 1, *History* (San Diego: Great Basin Foundation, 1987), 275.

61. Ahern, *Cult*, 149.

62. Yang, *Religion*, 34.

63. Irene D. Paden and Margaret E. Schlichtmann, *The Big Oak Flat Road: An Account of Freighting from Stockton to Yosemite Valley* (Oakland, CA: Holmes Book, 1959), 137.

64. *Dutch Flat Forum*, 1876, cited in Russell Towle, ed., *Artifacts from the Dutch Flat Forum, 1875–1878*, 3rd ed. (Dutch Flat, CA: Giant Gap, 1993), 40.

65. Cindy L. Baker and Mary L. Maniery, *Historical Summary of Chinese Cemeteries in Folsom, Sacramento County, California: Final Report* (Sacramento, CA: PAR Environmental Services, 1995), 15.

66. Dobie, *San Francisco's Chinatown*, 63.

67. Marla McBride, "Chinese Funerals," in *Chinese Argonauts: An Anthology of the Chinese Contributions to the Historical Development of Santa Clara County*, ed. Gloria Sun Hom (Los Altos, CA: Foothill Community College, 1971), 63–64; Sylvia Sun Minnick, *Samfow: The San Joaquin Chinese Legacy* (Fresno, CA: Panorama West, 1988), 288–289; "Chinese 'Funeral Baked Meats,'" *Overland Monthly* 3 (July 1869): 23–24.

68. Veta Griggs, *Chinaman's Chance: The Life Story of Elmer Wok Wai* (New York: Exposition, 1969), 14.

69. "Chinese 'Funeral Baked Meats'"; *San Francisco Call*, January 27, 1897; November 10, 1889.

70. *San Francisco Chronicle*, September 24, 1903.

71. *San Francisco Call*, January 20, 1883.

72. *San Francisco Call*, March 21, 1888.

73. *Mendocino Democrat*, 1876, cited in Ronald Riddle, *Flying Dragons, Flowing Streams: Music in the Life of San Francisco's Chinese* (Westport, CT: Greenwood, 1983).

74. Minnick, *Samfow*, 288; Joseph A. McGowan, *History of the Sacramento Valley*, vol. 1 (New York: Lewis Historical, 1961), 330; *San Francisco Chronicle*, March 14, 1903.

75. *The Journals of Alfred Doten, 1849–1903*, vol. 2, ed. Walter Van Tilburg Clark (Reno: University of Nevada Press, 1973), 1484; W. W. Kallenberger and R. M. Kallenberger, *Memories of a Gold Digger* (Garden Grove, CA: R. M. Kallenberger, 1980), 55; Lawton, "Selected Newspaper Accounts," 276.

76. *San Francisco Call*, March 21, 1888.

77. Lawton, "Selected Newspaper Accounts," 132; Baker and Maniery, *Historical Summary*, 2.

78. George C. Mansfield, *History of Butte County* (Los Angeles: Historic Record, 1918), 252.

79. Kallenberger and Kallenberger, *Memories*, 55.

80. *San Francisco Chronicle*, January 27, 1897; *San Francisco Call*, January 27, 1897; Laverne Mau Dicker, *The Chinese in San Francisco: A Pictorial History* (New York: Dover, 1979), 83.

81. Vern Richards, "Boyhood Recollections of the Silver Creek Chinese," *Plumas Memories* 25 (June 4, 1967): 9.

82. Dicker, *Chinese*, 83.

83. Sandy Lydon, *Chinese Gold: The Chinese in the Monterey Bay Region* (Capitola, CA: Capitola Book Company, 1985), 262.

84. McBride, "Chinese Funerals," 62.

85. Paul Radin, ed., *The Golden Mountain: Chinese Tales Told in California* (Formosa [Taiwan]: Orient Cultural Service, 1971), 33.

86. Mueller, "Feng-Shui," 9–20.

87. Herman Lopez, interview by author, Cyprus Lawn Cemetery, Colma, CA, September 26, 1996; Sylvia Sun Minnick, interview by author, September 25, 1996; Dale Seuss, interview by author, September 25, 1996; Priscilla Wegars, interview by author, October 12, 1996.

88. Lopez, interview.

89. Edgar Sung (*fengshui* master), interview by author, October 24, 1996.

90. *San Francisco Alta*, January 19, 1858; *Sacramento (CA) Union*, January 21, 1858.

91. Minnick, *Samfow*, 291.

92. *Sacramento (CA) Union*, January 21, 1858; Jeannie K. Yang and Virginia R. Hellmann, "What's in the Pot? An Emic Perspective on Chinese Brown Glazed

Stoneware" (paper presented at the twenty-ninth Conference on Historical and Underwater Archaeology, Cincinnati, OH, January 1996), 7.

93. *Sacramento (CA) Union*, September 16, 1885.

94. Minnick, *Samfow*, 292.

95. *Shasta Courier*, 1897, cited in Dottie Smith, *The History of the Chinese in Shasta County* (Redding, CA: CT Publishing, 1995), 63.

96. *Sacramento (CA) Union*, September 16, 1885.

97. Minnick, *Samfow*, 292.

98. Smith, *History*, 63.

99. Mansfield, *History of Butte County*, 252.

100. Lydon, *Chinese Gold*, 133; Minnick, *Samfow*, 291.

101. McBride, "Chinese Funerals," 66–67.

102. Lydon, *Chinese Gold*, 265.

103. *San Francisco Call*, April 4, 1887.

104. Chinn, Lai, and Choi, *History*, 76–77; Comber, *Chinese Ancestor Worship*, 38.

105. "Chinese Funeral Baked Meats," 28.

106. Linda Sun Crowder, "Mortuary Rituals and the Public Identity of San Francisco Chinatown" (paper presented at the Hawai'i/Pacific and Pacific Northwest Asian American Studies Joint Regional Conference, Honolulu, HI, March 1996), 1–7; Jessie Wong Lee, *Rites of Passage in Death and Dying in the Chinese American Culture* (master's thesis, California State University, Sacramento, 1975), 9.

107. Betty Lee Sung, *The Chinese in America* (New York: Macmillan, 1972), 8.

2

On Dying American: Cantonese Rites for Death and Ghost-Spirits in an American City

Paul G. Chace

Death and ghost-spirits are very serious concerns in Chinese folk religion and philosophic thinking. Death creates ghost-spirits. Ghost-spirits remain and affect the living community.[1] In funeral rites, but also in many other rites conducted throughout the year, ghost-spirits can be placated, to the benefit of the people living in the community. If not satisfied by rites with proper offerings, unhappy and malevolent ghost-spirits may cause earthly disharmony and bad fortune. As summarized by James Watson,

> A preoccupation with controlling, managing, and placating the dangerous aspects of the spirit of the deceased, . . . the ritual at funerals is aimed specifically at settling the volatile and disoriented spirit of the recently dead. There is, in other words, a need for social control in the nether world. . . . To bury a person without proper attention to ritual details is to create a hungry ghost who will return to plague the living. . . . A central feature of Chinese funerals and postburial mortuary practices is the transfer of food, money, and goods to the deceased. . . . In return the living expect to receive certain material benefits, including luck, wealth, and progeny.[2]

This descriptive study addresses Cantonese death and ghost-spirit rites in an American city, Marysville, California. Marysville boomed with California's 1849 gold rush, and Cantonese people from the Siyi (Four Districts) regions around Guangzhou (Canton) have made up a significant portion of the community throughout its history. These pioneering Chinese immigrants in America had to address the inevitability of death. They had to adapt their rites for ghost-spirit propitiation within the diverse community of a new American city, without the close support of their family lineage and comforting home-village traditional ritual practices. For the Chinese in Marysville, the complexities of social relations included both (1) their own diverse origins from many different home villages, mostly in the rural Siyi region; and (2) a new urban community dominated by Euro-American society, with a different language, a different worldview, and a dominant Christian religious perspective. This study hypothesizes that new and syncretic ghost-spirit rites were evolved to reflect this new social community.[3]

Marysville, as a locale for the study of Chinese rites, religion, and social relations, is rather special. The Chinese contributed approximately one-quarter of the city's economy throughout its first half century, beginning with the gold rush in 1849. This city's entire population remained around five thousand for a century, until World War II. Almost everyone probably knew everyone else. Unlike in many other California urban localities, interethnic relations were generally positive. The Euro-American majority population was generally tolerant and even supportive of the local Chinese. Similarly, the ethnic Chinese advanced and maintained good relations with the Euro-American population. The local Chinese purposely involved Euro-American residents in the celebrations of Chinese New Year and in the annual Chinese temple festivals.[4] Notably, the Chinese leaders within Marysville invited the local English-language newspaper editors and their reporters to participate in the celebrations of many Chinese public rituals and festivities. Consequently the newspapers are an unusually rich source of primary historical information on Chinese rites.

Private or household rituals for ghost-spirits have not been rigorously addressed in any local studies. No historical sources on such personal rites have been noted, and few inquiries have been made about private rites. Prior studies simply have not inquired about ancestors' birthdays, death days, or altar tablets, or about any other private household customs for ghost-spirits. This chapter does not address private rites.

There can be little question that the early Chinese of Marysville considered that a multitude of ghost-spirits probably lingered in and around this American community. The voluminous historic records about local ghost-spirit rites are very detailed. On the other hand, the local folks of Chinese ancestry now are quietly quizzical and uncertain about the nature of the ghostly souls, particularly those of deceased Euro-Americans or those of other local non-Chinese peoples, and, apparently, even those of Chinese Americans. Nowadays, various ghost-spirit rites continue but are more modestly pursued than before. There does not seem to be expressed the traditional Chinese distinction between gods, ghosts, and ancestors.[5] Indeed, recent Chinese studies have demonstrated that such conceptual categories are not absolute but are socially malleable and can merge.[6]

This descriptive study of ghost-spirit rites is presented in five major divisions: (1) the ghost-spirit rites noted at the earliest company shrines, (2) the rites conducted at *tong* lodges, (3) public funeral and burial rites, (4) rites conducted by the community temple association, and (5) calendrical rites for ghost-spirits. A brief description of the historic origins of the Marysville community provides the context. In Marysville the rites have changed over time, reflecting changing social relations. This study concludes that the described rites evolved through three general eras: an initial pioneering period that was indicative of a community in flux, a second era with emerging community organizations and flourishing rites, and a third long-tapering period of diminishing concerns and practices. In this way the local Chinese death and ghost-spirits rites became transformed—into a way of dying American.

HISTORIC MARYSVILLE AND ITS CHINESE

Historically, the city of Marysville developed on the north bank of the Yuba River during the gold rush. Riverboats could bring passengers and cargoes up the river from Sacramento and from the big port city of San Francisco, 45 miles and 125 miles away respectively, to this northern region of the vast California Central Valley. The foothills and steep Sierra Nevadas began about 15 miles to the east. When the gold rush began in 1848, these mountains became the northern mother lode. Almost instantly, this river transportation terminus became the jumping-off center for multitudes of gold seekers, and Marysville quickly became a bustling urban trade center and the county seat. By the 1860s, Marysville was the third-largest city in California in terms of taxable property. A quarter century later this urban center claimed one courthouse, three banks, nine Christian churches, and thirty-four saloons—without counting the Chinese establishments.[7]

The number of Chinese business establishments in Marysville is challenging to determine. Although certainly not comprehensive, seven Chinese-language directories listing local Chinese merchant houses, published between 1878 and 1952, are the best historical sources. These directories demonstrate that the Chinese maintained a major sector among the business enterprises of this American city. There were twenty-four Marysville Chinese businesses listed for 1878, forty-two for 1882, thirty-five for 1892, seventeen for 1900, forty-five in 1913, thirty-one in 1946, and forty in 1952.[8] The Chinese represented about one-fourth of the population of the city of Marysville throughout most of the nineteenth century, roughly one thousand in the city's total population of about four thousand, according to federal census figures.[9] Through the twentieth century, the local Chinese population gradually has declined to just under 2 percent, while the city's total population has tripled.

The Chinese ritual traditions of Marysville were brought by immigrants who originated predominantly in the rural Siyi region of Guangdong (Kwangtung) Province, near Hong Kong. This was evident in the local social organizations that coalesced within the local Chinese community, reflecting social relations among the Chinese themselves. Rival Chinese home-district associations, or *huiguan*, were the initial organizational institutions of the 1850s to 1860s. People from the Siyi region formed the major local association, the Siyi *huiguan* (Four Districts Association), and they constituted at least three-fourths of Marysville's Chinese population. A separate and rival district association was the Sanyi *huiguan* (Three Districts Association). By the 1860s this rival district *huiguan* also had created a local temple and boarding facility.[10] A single historical source suggests a third such district association also was established in Marysville.[11] The Yanghe *huiguan* (Young Wo Association) represented people from the more urban and wealthier Zhongshan district. However, these last two *huiguan* only "compose[d] together two or three hundred,"[12] or less than a fourth of the local urban Chinese population. Each of these *huiguan* represented home-district immigrant organizations, each group having its own distinctive regional speech dialect and cultural practices.

Approximately three-fourths of Marysville's early Chinese population came from rural Siyi.[13] Hong Woo and Company, the largest and wealthiest business house in Marysville, was a Siyi enterprise. Its proprietor was the leader of the Siyi *huiguan*.[14] The Siyi merchants were major stockholders in Marysville's big woolen mill of the 1870s and 1880s and supplied the Chinese laborers there.[15] This organization maintained a two-story lodge tenement. Nearby, in 1854, the Siyi people built the first Chinese shrine in the city—a small temple.[16] Subsequently, the wealthy Siyi *huiguan* secured a lease on a brick building alongside the river bridge at the very entrance of the city, reconstructed it, and dedicated it as a major Chinese temple with a great public demonstration in 1869.[17] A grand expansion of this temple occurred in 1880.[18] This time, the dominant Siyi leadership in the town apparently permitted a newly formed all-inclusive Chinese community association to manage and own this newly rededicated "community" temple. However, the principal Siyi business house, Hong Woo and Company, continued for years to be the principal financier and supplier to this community temple.[19] Overall, it is clear that the Chinese ritual traditions of nineteenth-century Marysville originated predominantly with Siyi region people from Guangdong Province.

EARLY COMPANY SHRINES AND GHOST-SPIRIT RITES

In early Marysville, within each *huiguan* and each business house, there was typically an altar or small shrine where deceased brethren, saintly Chinese deities, and ghost-spirits could be worshiped and appeased ritually with offerings. Newspaper reporters making the rounds during the Chinese New Year celebrations in early Marysville observed many such shrines with burning joss sticks, smoldering incense, and sweetmeats.[20] In the late 1860s, these business and *huiguan* shrines were described in more elaborate terms:

> Yesterday was spent among the "upper crust" in paying and receiving calls. Though the Chinese have no great Josh [*sic*] house here, many of the storekeepers and washhouse proprietors improvised little Joshes [*sic*], which were decorated in the usual . . . style—red paper and tinsel.[21]
>
> If our citizens enter a Chinese store tomorrow they will see pictures of the *deceased friends* suspended over shrines whereon tapers and joss sticks burn. Before these the [Chinese] will bow and do honor to the *memory of the dead* [emphasis added].[22]

In the 1880s, such *huiguan* and business shrines, with their pictures and statuettes, were evidenced when the wealthy merchants escorted their altar deity figures to the community temple rites during the annual temple festivals. The existence of similar shrines, even within Marysville laundries, certainly is implied by the use of deity umbrellas in the laundrymen's processions to the temple.[23]

The tradition of private shrines within the Chinese business houses of Marysville persisted well into the twentieth century. The bomb prizes from the annual community temple festivals were carefully maintained on such private shines in many businesses for private religious rites.[24] In a few cases, shrines still are present in local businesses.

TONG LODGES AND RITES

The local Chinese community through the 1870s was reorganized by a series of Triad lodge brotherhoods, or secret societies, which competed for members with the district associations. These *tong* (in pinyin, *tang*) lodges became very prominent in the social relations within the local Chinese community. Members sponsored prospective members into the brotherhood. Having a particular birthplace or surname was not required for membership. The lodges sponsored three types of traditional Chinese rites for members: birth rites, elaborate marriage rites (beyond the scope of this chapter), and funeral rites. Two of these rites are described in detail below. These rituals addressed ancestral ghost-spirits. Whenever necessary a volley of firecrackers spurred malevolent ghost-spirits from these occasions.

The first Triad lodge, the Gee Hong Tong (a branch of the Zhigongtang, or Chinese Freemasons), originated in San Francisco in the 1850s.[25] Probably in about 1860, this group secured a prime lot in Marysville and soon built a large hall there with a shrine.[26] Other splinter lodges of the Triad organization soon emerged, and three of these other Triad groups formed branch lodges in Marysville: the Suey Sing Tong,[27] the Hop Sing Tong,[28] and the Hip Yee Tong.[29] It was said that the local members of the Suey Sing Tong were "mostly merchants in this city."[30] The leadership of this group originated within the local Siyi *huiguan*.[31] The rival Hip Yee Tong, formed by Sanyi people, occupied the same building for their Marysville branch lodge as the earlier local Sanyi *huiguan*. The difference was that these *tongs* could include members from other localities.

By the late 1870s the Triad lodges in Marysville completely dominated the structure of Marysville's Chinese community. They had subsumed completely the earlier *huiguan* structure. The four local lodges controlled the community for the next half century. When a Chinese community conference in 1914 was convened with all the principal societies, the major local organizations were the Gee Hong Tong, the Hop Sing Tong, the Suey Sing Tong, and the Hip Yee Tong.[32] In the years following, however, the local lodges of the Gee Hong Tong and the Hip Yee Tong disappeared or were disbanded. Family surname associations did not develop in Marysville as they had in many other Chinese communities in the 1880s because no one clan had enough representatives.[33]

Since the 1920s, two social institutions have persisted and dominated the organization of the local Chinese community, the Hop Sing Tong and the Suey Sing Tong. Within Marysville, these two groups essentially serve as benevolent associations for their members, who represent a grouping of different clans. The Chan, Lam, Wong, and Hom/Tom families dominate the Suey Sing Tong.[34] The local Hop Sing Tong is composed primarily of families with the surnames of Ng, Chow/Joe/Jew, Choy, Yung, and Tso.[35] These united clans can be found in other overseas Chinese communities where no single lineage was strong enough to create the usual clan association. The lodge members form two groups of sworn brotherhoods, and sons become members of their father's lodge.[36] The Hip Yee Tong seems to have been formed by Yue clan members, often locally spelled as Yee/Fee.[37] Thus the local Triad lodges formed in the 1870s played a major role in the development of the Chinese community in Marysville.

Each of the two surviving *tong* halls still has a large altar or a dedicated room with an elaborate altar, where Guan Gong is the central deity figure. Because these *tongs* are not based on lineages, ancestral tablets of the deceased are not placed on the altars there. Elder informants confirmed this.[38] Similarly, birth registers are not maintained for the clans in these two local lodge organizations.[39] On the other hand, large framed photographic portraits of prominent local leaders, most wearing twentieth-century business suits, hang on the lodge walls.

BIRTH RITES

In Marysville, the birth of a baby boy was celebrated with a coming-out rite when the son was a month old. These glad occasions usually were held before the altar in the father's *tong* hall, as though that altar served as a local clan or lineage shrine where ancestral clan spirits could be addressed. This pattern is recounted in a family story about the birth of a boy in 1900:

> It was the custom to take cooked chicken with whiskey or gin to the Suey Sing Building and present it to the deities in honor of the deceased when important events took place. . . . My father and his friends were so happy and made so much noise when I was born that a Chinese interpreter who had been waiting in the next room for the Portland train to San Francisco asked what the occasion was. My father said, "I have a baby boy." "The spirits were happy for you," the interpreter said.[40]

These personal rites, following the birth of a son, were rarely mentioned in newspapers but were privately celebrated in front of the altar, sometimes with accompanying firecrackers.[41] However, the birth of a Chinese boy child was proudly talked about, and such happy news might even be covered in early Marysville's English-language newspapers.[42] Later, in the twentieth century, when a baby was a month old, the family typically held a coming-out dinner with their new son at their *tong* or, alternatively, if they could afford it, at a notable restaurant.

MARRIAGE RITES

Sometimes, for important large marriage ceremonies, the rites and major meal were held at the groom's *tong*. The details of marriage ceremonies are beyond the scope of this chapter. The only rites mentioned that might be considered to address ghost-spirits—to scare them away from happy marriage occasions—were firecrackers and loud music. These noisy moments sometimes were reported when the bride arrived and when the feasting occurred.[43]

FUNERAL AND BURIAL RITES FOR THE DECEASED

Funeral and death rites among the Chinese in Marysville always were somewhat diverse. The Euro-American undertaker interred many deceased Chinese without any reported ceremony. Funerals for other Chinese were conducted with quiet but substantial rites. Major Chinese funerals for prominent individuals were organized with elaborate presentations; with extensive rites, sometimes at the deceased's *tong*; and with lengthy processions. By the 1910s a variety of American customs were being adapted into Chinese funerals.

Accidental deaths in the river were considered to be particularly terrible tragedies, because the deaths were untimely and the deceased persons' ghost-spirits were unattended. Substantial rewards were offered to recover the bodies (and, thus, the spirits) of men who drowned in the river. It was considered important to recover the body and to be able to conduct proper funeral and burial ceremonies.[44]

Deceased Chinese in the 1850s were buried in the "citizens grounds" along with all the others that died in the new town. However, in 1862 the Chinese, undoubtedly the Siyi *huiguan*, secured a burial area along the northern side of the Marysville city cemetery. The city council contracted to have the previous Chinese interments removed to the new area. At some point, a still-surviving shrine was constructed in this cemetery and dedicated to the "good Chinese friends," brothers without recorded names, with a platform for making presentations. A simple brick oven was added for burning offerings, and in 1889 a handsome new brick oven of ornate Victorian design was constructed.[45] In 1896 a separate Chinese association or the Siyi *huiguan* sought another cemetery site on the western side of town because it had superior locational qualities, but the city council denied the petition.[46] Through most of the twentieth century the Chinese and everyone else in Marysville used the area's Sierra View Memorial Park to inter their deceased. There is no burner for special offerings there.

Some interments in the Chinese section of the city cemetery occurred without any mention of ceremonies. An undertaker or coroner simply buried the body of the deceased. Those individuals interred without any rites noted in the records apparently lacked local family, supportive friends, or any assets. One was a convicted Chinese murderer; after his hanging, the coroner buried his body.[47] In another case, the "absence of a 'distributor'" in the undertaker's hearse was noted; presumably this refers to the agent who often distributed perforated prayer papers to waylay malevolent spirits.[48] These secular interments occurred just before the formation of the temple community association in 1880 and again after 1900.

In handling the body of the deceased, Marysville's official coroner seems, in essence, to have served neatly in the place of the ritually paid Chinese "corpse handler," as described for a rural village near Hong Kong. There, the dangerous tasks of washing, dressing, and arranging the corpse, and then carrying the casket and digging the grave, were considered so polluting as to situate the corpse handler beyond the pale of any other normal social inter-changes.[49] Further, from the earliest years, the descriptions of elaborate Chinese funerals in Marysville indicate that the Chinese regularly employed a Euro-American undertaker, with his elaborate hearse and dark horses in the funeral processions.

Some Chinese funerals, for reasons that are not apparent, were expressly conducted "in as quiet a manner as possible" and without an accompanying Chinese band. These might be small or fairly large services. Mention is made of the hearse and, sometimes, relatives in white mourning clothes. One large procession even included "two hacks and three express wagons."[50] There may have been numerous such quiet and unassuming funerals that occurred with little public notice. In official records eleven Chinese deaths occurred in Marysville in 1892, but no notice appeared in the newspapers about any funeral events.[51]

Major funeral ceremonies involved elaborate preparations and wide participation. The area in front of the deceased's *tong* or his business house usually was covered with mats, and the coffin was placed there in the street. Sometimes a canopy was erected overhead. Presented near the coffin were one or more roasted pigs, a sheep or a goat, other foods, candles, and offerings. Mourners appeared, women dressed in white sackcloth with their heads covered with a garment resembling a pillowcase. Occasionally several women were paid to serve as mourners. Wailing and mourning rites were conducted in the public street. For major funerals, the procession to the cemetery typically was headed by a Chinese band in a wagon and might include many carriages, hacks, and express wagons. The Euro-American undertaker's elegant hearse with the casket, drawn by dark horses, almost always came at the rear of the procession. Perforated prayer papers were dropped along the route. The body was buried with rites, and offerings were left at the grave. A coin and a piece of sweet candy often were given to all those present.[52]

The funerals for prominent members of the Gee Hong Tong, the Chinese Freemasons, were particularly elaborate. Each lodge brother wore a red rosette on his good business suit, and only the immediate relatives wore white mourning clothes. The Masonic funeral processions sometimes marched up the main street with tall banners, with the pallbearers in long gray dusters bearing the casket. After passing through the main part of the city, the casket was placed in the hearse, and everyone mounted carriages to ride to the cemetery.[53]

The wearing of red rosettes, mentioned specifically in accounts of Chinese Masonic funerals, was in keeping with the organization's colors and served as protection from the unsettled ghost-spirit of the recently deceased "brother." Elsewhere, the wearing of a bit of red during Chinese funerals was also considered as protection from the unsettled ghost-spirit of the recently deceased.[54]

Interestingly, only two local funeral accounts, from 1893 and 1901, actually mention observing Chinese funeral priests who might have been directing the rites and the mourners' ritual actions. Both were very large funerals for extremely important men who were members of the Gee Hong Tong, and the newspaper coverage was unusually detailed.[55] Most Chinese funerals in Marysville seemingly did not require a priest to provide formal direction.[56] It can be inferred from mentions of the typical Chinese band leading many formal Chinese funeral processions that there was some muted local manner of ritual funeral guidance. The Euro-American coroner or undertaker, without any guided public funeral or burial rites worthy of mention, conducted other Chinese burials quite simply. In the twentieth century, a professional Euro-American undertaker sometimes handled the funeral rites for deceased local Chinese partly within the undertaker's own Marysville chapel.

Special rites existed for collecting and sending off the bones for secondary reburial back in China. Marysville had a Chinese resident who served as a "bone digger." He exhumed the bones from the Chinese section of the cemetery, conducted special rites, and carefully packed the bones for shipment back to families in China for reburial there. The boxes were stored with a local Euro-American undertaker until shipment could be arranged.[57]

In the early twentieth century, both a local funeral service and a major burial ceremony in China might be conducted. Obviously, such double services reflected considerable prestige and wealth. The Marysville rites began inside the lodge and continued with a formal procession to the cemetery with the hearse, mourners, and a Chinese band. Roast pig and other edibles were deposited at the cemetery with the coffin, and then the party returned to town. Later, the Euro-American undertaker returned the coffin and corpse to town, and the body was further prepared for travel. The corpse was placed on the train to San Francisco and then shipped on to China, where it was to "be buried with . . . pomp and ceremony." Shipment of the prepared body became a standard practice.[58]

Certain American customs were adapted into local Chinese funerals beginning in the 1910s. The first Marysville report of cremation for the corpse of a local Chinese man was in 1915.[59] Also beginning in that decade, the funeral processions of prominent local Chinese men employed the Marysville Brass Band as well as a Chinese band. The Euro-American musicians loudly played their own popular tunes.[60] Interestingly, beginning about twenty years later, brass bands playing American tunes began to be incorporated into rural Cantonese funeral rites around Hong Kong.[61]

THE "CHUNG WAH" ASSOCIATION AND
COMMUNITY TEMPLE RITES FOR GHOST-SPIRITS

Around 1880 a community-wide organization formed to include all the local Chinese people, referred to as Marysville's "Chung Wah" (Zhonghua) Association. This was seen in the form of deeds transferring the temple property at the entrance to the city to four named trustees of the Bok Kai Temple.[62] These four trustees probably headed the four Chinese *tong*s in Marysville. Through the previous decade, this temple operated essentially for the people of the Siyi *huiguan*. In 1880 a grand temple expansion occurred.[63] The renovated temple-building complex included a large side room marked by an old sign over the door, *gong so* or "community council room," a meeting hall "for everyone in the community." The variety of community activities conducted through the new temple establishment was delineated in the temple's account books for the 1880s to 1890s.[64] Thus, the expanded Bok Kai Temple[65] was transformed into the hall of the entire Chinese community (fig. 2.1). However, this all-inclusive Chinese community association apparently waned in the years between the 1910s and the 1930s. Following World War II, a temple restoration effort began.[66] Subsequently, late in 1949 the "Marysville Chinese Community, Incorporated" formally reorganized as a nonprofit California corporation to work on the preservation of the temple (figs. 2.2 and 2.3).[67] While this association still holds title to the Bok Kai Temple (as well as to a school hall, a hospital/*daibingwu* [old age house], and some other properties), in recent decades this "Chung Wah" Association has had less organizational dominion than the two local *tong* lodges.

TEMPLE REDEDICATION AND *JIAO*
(UNIVERSAL WORLD RENEWAL RITUAL)

For the ritual rededication of the renovated Bok Kai Temple in 1880, the community raised the funds to have Daoist priests, along with their retinue of musicians, from San Francisco[68] attend and officiate. They performed a three-day *jiao* of rededication, the Universal World Renewal Ritual. This ritual involved calling all the gods and other ghost-spirits to earth, making appropriate offerings, and reestablishing these ghost-spirits in their proper orderly universe.[69] Local newspapers described the Daoist priests' formal *jiao* rites of the first day in considerable detail, if not with a deep understanding of the incredible religious rites being performed.[70] Unfortunately, it started raining thereafter and the subsequent coverage was abbreviated. The rites depicted in the English-language newspaper obviously included the Daoist priests' three initial ritual

Figure 2.1.   Bok Kai Temple in 1900. Courtesy Wallace (Cowboy Wally) Hagaman. The Daoist Bok Kai Temple was built on this site in 1880 and was the entranceway to Marysville.

audiences calling down the gods and calling forth all ghost-spirits in order to renew the proper spiritual order of the entire universe. Briefly extracted, the available English-language account of the second audience and its grand procession underlines the importance of food offerings to attract and to appease the deities and the ghost-spirits:

> The Boc ky [*sic*] Church, or Chinese Temple, recently erected on D and Front streets, in this city, was dedicated on Sunday with much pomp, noise, and enthusiasm. . . . At an early hour on the morning of the 21st instant, a regular bombardment of the Yuba [River] commenced with bombs and firecrackers, and by daylight the Temple was in order for formal dedication. . . . At 10 o'clock A.M. another procession formed on First street at the foot of C, and moved under the inspiring music of the "brass band" [sarcasm] to the Temple. The line was headed by a Chinaman with a string of burning firecrackers hanging eight or ten feet from the end of a pole. Following were roasted and decorated pigs, sheep and other toothsome looking edibles, which were set upon trays having four shoulder handles, and each was packed by four Celestials. This was designated the "offering train," and one to be sacrificed upon the altar of the new Temple. Ten Priests, decorated in large black robes and cocked hats with red crowns, closed up this formidable procession.[71]

Figure 2.2. **Bok Kai Temple main entrance. Photograph by Helen Martin in 1999. The temple has three main rooms: a community meeting room, the main temple, and a complex that includes a kitchen, housing, and recreational area.**

No other available historical accounts suggest that the important *jiao* rites occurred in other years in Marysville, although the Daoist priests from San Francisco also were present for some public rites in the 1870s and 1880s.[72]

ANNUAL TEMPLE FESTIVAL RITES, "BOMB DAY"

Marysville's annual temple festival clearly is a traditional community-oriented celebration, with the rites focused on supplicating the Chinese deity, Bok Kai,

Figure 2.3. Interior of main altar space from entrance doorway of the Bok Kai Temple showing intricately carved gilt altar tables. Photograph by Alexander M. Solomon in 2001.

the adopted spiritual protector of the town.[73] This has been an annual festive ritual since the temple was founded and still occurs. In recent years, this celebration has sometimes been referred to as the "birthday" of Bok Kai, but locally it usually is called "Bomb Day." During the loud, dazzling, brilliant, spectacular celebration rites focused in and around the community temple, the worshippers address the spirit of Bok Kai, and all the other saintly ones represented on the altars, as well as the ghost-spirits of others who may need to be considered. Multitudes of noisy firecrackers are employed throughout various portions of the celebration to scare off all angry ghost-spirits. Formal processions to the temple, in years past as well as now, involve musicians with gongs and drums (and, in the past, horns), as well as exploding firecrackers, standard rites for ridding the roadway of any lurking ghost-spirits.

Clearly, during this major temple festival, individual worshippers can make personal prayers, make personal inquiries with oracle rites, and make their own personal offerings with burning incense, fine food, paper money, and so on—to the gods, to their own ancestors, or to ghost-spirits. To the individual worshippers, the temple caretaker sells prebundled offering supplies, each bundle containing many incense sticks, two candles, imprinted offering papers, and both gold and silver paper money. Elsewhere, the silver paper money is said to be specifically for ancestors and ghosts.[74] There is nothing to preclude worshippers from sending off some of their money, as well as incense, various foods, and other offerings, for the ghost-spirits of their own deceased ancestors. Clearly, observations in recent years suggest personal ritual behaviors that are directed to ancestral ghost-spirits are being pursued during the loud temple festival, which would attract and make present the spiritual essences of all the efficacious Chinese saints, and even the ghost-spirits of all past deceased. Examples of such recent individual behaviors toward personal ghost-spirits during temple festivals have included offerings of commercially printed paper clothing and personal accoutrements for the deceased, commercially printed "hell banknote" paper currency, and offerings of cartons of special-order Chinese take-out food, favored dishes of the recently deceased, undoubtedly.[75]

Additionally, during the festivals, numerous family groups each bring a roasted pig, or small amounts of golden-roasted pork, set it before the temple altars, and then remove it to take home for a grand family-clan feast. Sometimes a roasted pig is presented with a carving knife stuck handily into the shoulders. It can be inferred that the ghost-spirits of deceased ancestors slice and partake of this ritual pork presentation. Elsewhere, it has been noted that while the roasted pig meat is on display, the ghost-spirits of deceased ancestors can instill the essences of good influences into the meat for the family's consumption.[76] Further, the two local *tong*s bring several roast pigs to the temple in separate loud formal processions, set them before the temple altar, and then retrieve them; the pork later is served to all those feasting together at the lodge banquets.

At various junctures in the Bomb Day rites at the temple, multiple packets of exploding firecrackers are tossed out the front door of the temple. Traditionally, these loud firecrackers frighten off any malevolent ghost-spirits lingering in the area that might disrupt affairs. Interestingly, any Euro-American anthropologist or observer (considered probably to be a *guilo*, or "foreign ghost-spirit fellow") standing nearby on the temple's front porch is likely to have a packet of firecrackers thrown very near his feet. This is an intentional and recurring ritual act, presumably to cleanse the very spirit of a too-friendly "stranger" or someone who innocently might have some bad ghost-spirit attached.

THE BOMB RITE, AND CLEANSING THE BOMB RITE AREA (BATTLING AWAY GHOST-SPIRITS RITE)

The ultimate activity in the temple's annual festival rites is the exciting competition for the temple's lucky bombs. In this rite, which is sponsored by the temple, individual giant firecrackers are exploded that hurl a lucky red ring high into the sky. Whoever catches such a ring and is able to keep it in the skirmish that follows is considered to be blessed with good fortune for the year. The very first lucky Bomb Rites in Marysville were organized in 1873 and 1874, separately arranged by different worshipful *huiguan*,[77] and these rites have been a recurring element in the community's worshipful festivals ever since.

Daoist priests sometimes led the Bomb Rite in the 1870s and early 1880s. At the same time they conducted traditional and recognized Daoist rituals.[78] To initiate the Bomb Rites, these Daoist priests first ritually cleansed the open ground, the bomb-firing site, of potentially present malevolent ghost-spirits. Variously described, their ritual efforts involved: sword work,[79] an empty-handed "pantomime . . . sword exercise . . . also . . . a lance exercise,"[80] a bell,[81] spreading incense,[82] or sprinkling water.[83] These variations in noted ritual techniques suggest that different priests of various orders were employed in battling away ghost-spirits.[84] Further, following the Bomb Rite, the priests might stand chanting as the lucky bomb prizes were awarded back at the temple.[85] Earlier in the ceremonies, these same priests sometimes were noted as leading the temple services in invoking the deities and spirits with chants and offerings at the temple.[86] Interestingly, after the middle 1880s, the presence of any Daoist priests with their specialized rites went unmentioned. Their specialized rites cannot even be inferred from the descriptions of subsequent temple festival celebrations. This probably was the result of the 1892 renewal of the 1882 Chinese Exclusion Act, which reclassified Chinese religious persons as laborers and therefore subject to the Chinese exclusion acts.

In recent years, the lucky Bomb Rite has been held in the street intersection nearest the two association halls. The city ropes off the intersection, and a temporary altar table is established. Immediately before the competition begins, to cleanse the area of ghost-spirits, tumultuous fusillades occur with multiple packets of firecrackers thrown into the intersection. Thereafter, after each skirmish to capture a lucky bomb ring, additional packets of firecrackers are thrown near to, or even amid, the battling competitors. These additional firecrackers help scare any lingering ghost-spirits, and they help curtail the continuing melees that sometimes develop between overheated and spiteful earthly competitors. Nowadays, the throwing of firecrackers directly amid combating competitors also might be viewed as an intentional ritual act to cleanse the very spirits of these too-violent "warriors-strangers."

UNIVERSAL SALVATION RITE (PUDU)

Sometimes, in the earliest public temple annual festivities at the cemetery, rituals similar to the Qingming rites in the spring and Hungry Ghosts (Yulanpen) rites in the fall were included to acknowledge the ghost-spirits of deceased ancestors and other unknown "good brothers." At least a few times, on the day after the big public temple celebration, a delegation went out to the cemetery with large firecrackers and festive food offerings. This suppliant Daoist ritual occurred at least twice in the middle 1880s.[87]

A shrine for the souls of unknown brothers, ghost-spirits in hell, was located at the Marysville city cemetery, so this suppliant rite probably may have been the rite of Pudu (Universal Salvation), or an equivalent.[88] Since the actual presence of any Daoist priests went unmentioned in the newspapers, priests may not have been necessary. This cemetery-offering rite did not become a traditional annual element of subsequent temple festivals.

CALENDRICAL RITES BY INDIVIDUALS FOR GHOST-SPIRITS

The members of the Chinese community in Marysville, more or less individually, have personally conducted a series of special calendrical rites to regularly address ghost-spirits throughout each year. In the early 1860s they conducted such calendrical rituals, particularly the spring rite of Qingming at the cemetery. Historic descriptions of these calendrical rites are quite limited, and these rites probably were conducted more often than available historic sources suggest. Apart from those marking New Year and Qingming, many calendrical rites probably were pursued quietly and modestly, even individually, such that newspapers rarely described these rites. Elder informants in the Chinese community have mentioned, and, in some cases, still pursue, some of these calendrical rites for ghost-spirits.

Interviews regarding household rites and forms of private worship, including calendrical rites for addressing ghost-spirits by individuals, have not been pursued in Marysville with any rigor. No inquiries have been made about private rites for ancestor's birthdays, death days, or altar tablets; about household offerings to ghost-spirits on the first or fifteenth of the month; about stove-gods; about rites of health or exorcism; or about any other private household customs. In retrospect, one can presume that a wide variety of such personal and household rites previously were pursued, although it probably would have been challenging in recent years to know or to reconstruct the extent of such personal ritual practices conducted within the private space of households.

FIRST MONTH, FIRST DAY, CHINESE NEW YEAR

Chinese New Year always has been one of the major traditional rituals in Chinese communities inside and outside of China. Public celebrations within the Marysville Chinese community began in the middle 1850s. The initial accounts mention firecrackers, parading, "considerable jollity," a general work holiday, feasting, rejoicing, and hosting special interethnic dinners. Euro-Americans and all others who made calls to the Chinese business houses were greeted with prodigality and lavished with dainties and delectables. Chinese brandy was much in evidence, as were firecrackers and burning joss sticks. The "outside barbarians" went about "greedily devouring the hospitable Chinamen's sweetmeats and drinking their strong water."[89] Later accounts, in the 1890s, are equally elaborate about these happy festivities, with displays of local interethnic community goodwill.[90]

The explosion of nearly a "million" firecrackers sometimes created political problems, but the custom prevailed.[91] On the eve of the New Year, to ensure the harmonious renewal of life and prosperity, hundreds of thousands of firecrackers were exploded. Firecrackers call happy attention to the moment and also frighten away all evil ghost-spirits, which are abroad at the passing of the year.[92] Thus, exploding firecrackers constitute a rite for ridding a locale of ghost-spirits, while also creating happiness.

With the Chinese revolution of 1911 the traditions of the Chinese New Year became somewhat subdued in favor of celebrating the western New Year. In Marysville, however, the Chinese New Year again was widely celebrated privately by the mid-1920s, and a few public festivities were noted. In 1925, on the fourth evening, a special private dinner party was reported; a prominent Chinese invited fifteen of his American friends to his home for an eight-course Chinese feast. The Hop Sing Tong held a banquet on the opening night of the New Year, and the Suey Sing Tong held their banquet the sixth night. On the seventh evening, the last fusillade of firecrackers was heard. The next year more than five hundred Chinese celebrated in town for the week. There were lots of firecrackers the first night, and the Suey Sing Tong held a banquet.[93]

In the twentieth century, many people in Marysville considered the community temple "Bomb Day" festival to be the culmination of the Chinese New Year celebration. As local activities marking the beginning of the Chinese New Year waned, the big temple festival became the grand celebration, coming just a month into the new Chinese calendar year. The belief that the temple festival was part of the New Year celebrations appeared around 1905, and the idea has been widely accepted in recent decades.

LION DANCING

During the New Year season, lion dance rites with bold and scary pantomime performances by vigorously dancing lion figures are sponsored at the front of many shops, at each of the major Chinese association halls, and at the community temple. The lion dance rites remove all potential bad ghost-spirits from the premises in order to ensure good fortune for the coming year.[94] The lion dancers are accompanied by multitudes of exploding firecrackers and a troupe of rhythmic drummers and loud gong players. In Marysville, troupes of lion dancers became a regular ritual performance element of the community's "Bomb Day" rites beginning only in 1925, but they have since remained as a colorful part of the ritual celebrations for the New Year.[95]

PURE BRIGHTNESS FESTIVAL (QINGMING)

By the early 1860s the local Chinese community actively observed the annual spring Qingming rite, involving visitations to the graves of relatives. Groups journeyed together out to the city cemetery to address the ghost-spirits there, often hiring most of the available express wagons:

Yesterday the Chinese residents . . . proceeded to the burial ground in a long train of express wagons to have their stated ceremony of "feeding the dead." . . . They took along a hog roasted whole, some strong waters [liquors], cakes, and divers heathen inventions, and had their pagan rites . . . in their allotted corner of the city cemetery, where they howled, eat [*sic*] pig and burnt toy-paper to their heart's content. After depositing a homeopathic dose of "grub" on each grave and going through their peculiar [bowing or prayerful] motions they came back to town, bringing the major part of their hog's flesh with them. An intelligent Chinaman says that the food left on the graves is to feed the spirits of the departed and comfort their souls withal on their way to "lam-shi," which is their Happy Land, Elysium or Celestial Paradise.[96]

Similarly, in other years, the long train of express wagons was observed in the procession out to the burial ground. In the 1870s the rite was noted most years but with few details. Sometimes these observances occurred over several days, and it may be that different companies or parties went to the cemetery on successive days.[97]

The rite of Qingming continues to be recognized within the Marysville community. In recent decades a small committee from the Chung Wah organization collected subscriptions and purchased a whole roast pig, chickens, apples and other fruits, whiskey, and incense to take out as offerings. These offerings were presented at the graves in the local cemeteries. The food was then brought back to town and distributed among subscribers to take home to eat.

FIFTH MONTH, FIFTH DAY: CHU YUAN FESTIVAL

This annual festival near the summer solstice was associated in the Daoist view with water-oriented ghost-spirits, the maturation of crops, and *yang* reaching its zenith. Among the California Chinese, the popular view seemed to have focused more on revering Confucian honor for Chu Yuan (332–296 B.C.), an ancient statesman-poet.[98] The fabled Chu Yuan, rather than compromise his personal principles, drowned himself in a river, thus creating an enduring water-oriented ghost-spirit.[99] Rice filled with meats, an egg yolk, and perhaps nuts are wrapped in a type of dried leaves, resembling the Mexican tamale, and offered to Chu Yuan during this celebration. Boat races also occur in some communities.

During the late nineteenth century, the Marysville community organized an annual remembrance ceremony for Chu Yuan within the community temple, supported by solicited subscriptions.[100] Food offerings of the Chinese "tamale" for ghost-spirits were made, but the rites went unnoticed in early newspapers, so no particularly conspicuous activities presumably ever were conducted in public or on the river.

Some senior Marysville individuals remember these ceremonial rites. In their youth, offerings of special rice tamales were made into the local river for ghost-spirits. A few local families still observe this festival by preparing and eating the rice tamales and other special foods linked with this date. No one recalled that dragon boat races ever were part of any local observations, as they have been elsewhere.[101]

SEVENTH MONTH, FIFTEENTH DAY, HUNGRY GHOSTS FESTIVAL (YULANPEN)

In the Daoist tradition, each year on the fifteenth day of the seventh month all orphaned souls in the underworld are released to roam the earth, and they must be fed or they will seek revenge on those who wronged them during their lives. This is also the date when the chief judge of the deathly underworld comes forth and is feted.[102]

The Bok Kai Temple organized the rites during the seventh month with support from community-wide subscriptions. In some years, the rites of "feeding" the souls of the dead were conducted at the cemetery for several days just before midmonth, with additional rites occurring at the end of the month with firecrackers. The local newspaper published a sympathetic account of the ceremony as it was conducted in early twentieth-century China, undoubtedly in recognition of the paper's multicultural readership within the Marysville community.[103] A half century ago, some elders recall, this festival was widely recognized in Marysville, with special offerings presented at the temple. Even now, some local individuals and households still set out food for the hungry ghosts.

TENTH MONTH, FIFTEENTH DAY, OR ADAPTING AMERICAN THANKSGIVING

In the Daoist view, at this time of year the spirits of the water and underworld begin their rule, and temples sponsor banquets to release souls in the water regions.[104] As noted in various years, near this beginning of the winter season, a "religious observation" with noisy firecrackers was held at the Bok Kai Temple. On the Chinese calendar, these local rites seemingly occurred on various dates in the latter half of the tenth month.[105]

In Marysville's Chinese American community, by the 1880s and possibly earlier, the local celebrations apparently were adjusted from the fifteenth day of the tenth month by a few days so that the observations coincided with the American Thanksgiving feast day. Thanksgiving for Americans, a community harvest festival for bounties received, has been celebrated since the early 1600s and became an annual national holiday beginning in 1863. Based on the calendrical adjustment for rites in Marysville, the local Chinese might have presumed that the ghost-spirits of those Chinese dying in America were able to read, learn, feast—and fully appreciate the very nature of the American calendar.

CONCLUSIONS

Historically, the evolving forms of the Chinese rites addressing death and ghost-spirits in Marysville fall into three general eras: a brief period of transient pioneering; a second period of florescence as the community became settled and emergent social relations developed; and a third long-tapering period of diminishing concerns and practices.

During the initial quarter century of settlement, when the new immigrant population was barely formulating any cohesive community social organizations, the paucity of historical accounts and their brevity suggest that the rites for Chinese death and ghost-spirits were not particularly elaborate. The rare occurrence of such rites, as reflected in early historical documentation, probably is valid.

As a hypothesis, it can be posited for the early pioneering era that: (1) lacking local sons and family to follow traditional home-village ancestral practices, (2) lacking their own established death ritual specialists, and (3) with the expediencies of pioneering economic endeavors, traditional Chinese rites for death and ghost-spirits were often minimally performed, improperly practiced, or even omitted. For this reason many of the Chinese ghost-spirits were unfulfilled. Further, three-fourths of the pioneers in Marysville were not even Chinese. Therefore, from the perspective of the Chinese folk religion, these other peoples followed distinctly nonorthodox funeral practices, which doubtlessly created multitudes of malevolent ghost-spirits. If so, there would have been greatly heightened psychological uncertainty and concern to placate ghost-spirits, of both Chinese and non-Chinese forms, and, thereby, to enhance human fate in this new and uncertain land.

Local Euro-American coroners and undertakers from the beginning conducted the actual handling of dead bodies. These same Euro-American specialists also were called on to handle much of the secular practice that the Chinese population required for the abhorred handling of their own Chinese corpses. These local Euro-American specialists were of critical importance, but they could remain truly marginal persons to the structure of the Chinese community. In contrast, the often-noted band or Chinese piper playing at funerals indicated a strong traditional concern about having funeral specialists and, by implication, about obtaining proper guidance for funerary rituals. In Marysville, however, the direction for funerary rituals usually did not observably reside with formally robed priests; evidently, unnoticed lay leaders within the community provided the direction.

Actual Chinese religious rites addressing death and ghost-spirits become elaborately evident in the second era, through the 1870s and 1880s, as the immigrant population stabilized and various new social organizations were created within the Chinese community. Initially, the *huiguan* or home-district associations structured Chinese affairs, but within Marysville these district associations soon waned. With their Chinese populations drawn from diverse home villages, the dominant social organizations in Marysville were the emergent united clan brotherhoods of *tong*s and a more inclusive Chung Wah organization. The Chinese built lodge halls with altars and eventually constructed a very elaborate community temple, called the Bok Kai Temple. At the city cemetery they built a shrine and made improvements such as a burner for ghost-spirit offerings. In this second era, they conducted more elaborate rites for local deaths and ghost-spirits. These organizations provided the class structure and leadership for the Chinese community in Marysville. A flourishing of rites can be noted from the 1890s through the 1910s.

In the third era, beginning particularly with the decades following World War I, the local Chinese became more Americanized. A long-tapering period of diminishing traditional ritual practices addressing ghost-spirits seems evident. Over time, the rites became more Americanized and more involved with Euro-American social institutions, reflecting social relations with members of the Euro-American community. Ultimately, in this third era the rituals for death and dying—and the rites for any perceived ghost-spirits—were rarely noteworthy in local newspaper coverage. The Chinese rites were becoming American. Further, it has been noted that American life is free and easy, "a world without ghosts."[106] Concerns about traditional Chinese rites to address ghost-spirits simply diminished in this American city, and fewer folks within the community considered ghost-spirit rites as necessary and important. The local Chinese themselves were becoming American Chinese.

The American Chinese patterns in locally observed, syncretic funeral rites, along with the broad concerns about ghost-spirits that evolved in Marysville, are in sharp contrast to those that James Watson observed in Hong Kong. Watson concludes:

> I would contend that is not possible for people who conceive of themselves as "Chinese" to hold what amounts to a do-it-yourself funeral, with untrained and unpaid personnel performing the rites. Among the rural Cantonese a *minimal ritual set* of four specialists is essential for the proper conduct of a funeral. This set includes a priest, a piper, and two corpse handlers. Anyone, it was explained to me, who attempts to bury a family member without the services of these four specialists would be risking serious consequences, namely the possibility of creating a dangerous ghost and disrupting the entire community.[107]

In Marysville historically there emerged a broad Chinese concern with ghost-spirits as the lodges attempted to preserve Chinese traditional beliefs and practices. From the perspective of Chinese folk religion, the foreigners of the California gold rush and, later, all those who settled in Marysville, and even before them the local Native Americans who had died locally, all with their own secular and potential unorthodox funeral and burial rites, may have inadvertently created a land full of ghost-spirits.

The religious ritual practices addressing ghost-spirits often caught the eyes, the ears, and the notice of English-language newspaper reporters because Chinese funerals and other rites for ghost-spirits were unusual and newsworthy in early Marysville. Following the first half century, however, even these rites were becoming more Americanized, employing American brass bands and held in the local undertaker's chapel. As these funeral rites became ever more adapted to local American social relations, these rites became less and less Chinese. Many of the older practices were no longer followed, or they were not conducted publicly in earnest. The very subject of the original rites, Chinese death and ghost-spirits, had been transformed—into dying American.

NOTES

1. On Chinese ghost-spirits or souls, broadly considered, see Arthur P. Wolf, "Gods, Ghosts, and Ancestors," in *Religion and Ritual in Chinese Society*, ed. Arthur P. Wolf (Stanford, CA: Stanford University Press, 1974); Stevan Harrell, "When a Ghost Becomes a God," in *Religion and Ritual in Chinese Society*, ed. Arthur P. Wolf (Stanford, CA: Stanford University Press, 1974), and his "The Concept of Soul in Chinese Folk Religion," *Journal of Asian Studies* 38 (1979); Robert P. Weller, "Bandits, Beggars, and Ghosts: The Failure of State Control over Religious Interpretation in Taiwan," *American Ethnologist* 12, no. 1 (1985), and his *Unities and Diversities in Chinese Religion* (Seattle: University of Washington Press, 1987); Myron L. Cohen, "Souls and Salvation: Conflicting Themes in Chinese Popular Religion," in *Death Ritual in Late Imperial and Modern China*, ed. James L. Watson and Evelyn S. Rawski (Berkeley: University of California Press, 1988); and Kristofer Schipper, *The Taoist Body* (Berkeley: University of California Press, 1993), 35–38.

2. James L. Watson, "The Structure of Chinese Funerary Rites: Elementary Forms, Ritual Sequence, and the Primacy of Performance," in *Death Ritual in Late Imperial and Modern China*, ed. James L. Watson and Evelyn S. Rawski (Berkeley: University of California Press, 1988), 9.

3. This theoretical perspective, that distinctive social relations generate different religious beliefs and practices, is informed principally by Weller, *Unities*, but see also Michael W. Hughey, *Civil Religion and Moral Order, Theoretical and Historical Dimensions* (Westport, CT: Greenwood, 1983). This descriptive study of ghost-spirit rites stretches to include Chinese practices in America within the ongoing debate about "diversity within the unity" of Chinese popular religion, as does Paul G. Chace, "Interpretive Restraint and Ritual Tradition: Marysville's Festival of Bok Kai," *Journal of Contemporary Ethnography* 21, no. 2 (1992); "Returning Thanks: Chinese Rites in an American Community" (PhD diss., University of California, Riverside, 1992); and "Dancing with the Dragon: A Study of Ritual and Inter-Ethnic Community Relations," in *Origins and Destinations, 41 Essays on Chinese America* (Los Angeles: Chinese Historical Society of Southern California and UCLA Asian American Studies Center, 1994). This scholarly debate about perspectives began in 1971 (in California, no less!), with Arthur P. Wolf, ed., *Religion and Ritual in Chinese Society* (Stanford, CA: Stanford University Press, 1974), and it is formally continued by James L. Watson and Evelyn S. Rawski, eds., *Death Ritual in Late Imperial and Modern China* (Berkeley: University of California Press, 1988), and by Meir Shahar and Robert P. Weller, eds, *Unruly Gods, Divinity and Society in China* (Honolulu: University of Hawai'i Press, 1996).

4. Chace, "Interpretive Restraint," "Returning Thanks," "Dancing," and his *The Bok Kai Festival of 1931 in Historic Marysville: Creating a California Community* (Yuba City, CA: River City Printing, 1994) and *A History of Marysville's Bok Kai Temple* ([n.p.: privately printed for a temple benefit by the Marysville-Peikang Sister City Association], 1999); Reuben Ibanez, ed., *Historical Bok Kai Temple in Old Marysville, California* (Marysville, CA: Marysville Chinese Community [Inc.], 1967); and Clark A. Buschmann, ed. *Third City* ([Marysville, CA]: Yuba Sutter Arts Council, 1991).

5. E.g., Wolf, "Gods"; Weller, *Unities*, 22–59; and David K. Jordan, *Gods, Ghosts, and Ancestors: Folk Religion in a Taiwanese Village* (Berkeley: University of California Press, 1972).

6. See Harrell, "When a Ghost" and "Concept"; Paul Katz, "Demon or Deities? The Wangye of Taiwan," *Asian Folklore Studies* 46 (1987); Weller, "Bandits," and *Unities*; Cohen, "Souls"; Yu Kuang-hong, "Making a Malefactor a Benefactor: Ghost Worship in Taiwan," *Bulletin of the Institute of Ethnology Academia Sinica* 70 (1990); and Meir Shahar and Robert P. Weller, "Introduction: Gods and Society in China," in *Unruly Gods, Divinity and Society in China*, ed. Meir Shahar and Robert P. Weller (Honolulu: University of Hawai'i Press, 1996), 11–12.

7. Earl Ramey, *The Beginnings of Marysville* (San Francisco: Lawton R. Kennedy, 1936); M. Belinda Desmond, "The History of the City of Marysville, California, 1852–1859" (master's thesis, Catholic University of America, 1962); Thompson and West, *History of Yuba County, California* (Oakland, CA: Thompson and West, 1879); Sucheng Chan, "Chinese Livelihood in Rural California: The Impact of Economic Change, 1860–1880," *Pacific Historical Review* 53, no. 3 (1984): 294–296, and *This Bittersweet Soil: The Chinese in California Agriculture, 1860–1910* (Berkeley: University of California Press, 1986), 97–101, 256–258; Caroline M. Olney, "Mountains and Valleys of Yuba County," *Overland Monthly* 40 (December 1902); T. J. Sherwood, *The Resources of Yuba County, the Garden Spot of California* (Marysville: Democrat Publishing, 1894); *Marysville (CA) Daily Appeal*, January 27, 1865; March 13, 1874; January 1, 1893; *San Francisco Alta*, January 18, 1867; February 25, 1867; March 8, 1867; *San Francisco Post*, September 21, 28, 1877; *Sacramento (CA) Daily Record Union*, January 1, 1878; *San Francisco Bulletin*, July 2, 1879; and *Oroville (CA) Mercury*, August 3, 1912.

8. Wells Fargo, *Wells Fargo and Co.'s Express Directory of Chinese Business Houses, San Francisco, Sacramento, Marysville, Portland, Stockton, San Jose [and] Virginia City, Nev.* (San Francisco: Wells Fargo, 1878), and *Directory of Principal Chinese Business Firms in San Francisco [Oakland, Sacramento, San Jose, Stockton, Marysville, Los Angeles, Portland, Virginia City, Victoria]* (San Francisco: Wells Fargo, 1882); A. R. Dunbar, *A. R. Dunbar's Chinese Directory of the United States, British Columbia, Canada, and Honolulu, H. I.* (Portland, OR: A. R. Dunbar, 1892), and *A. R. Dunbar's United States Chinese Directory, 1900, including Hong Kong, Canada, and Hawaiian Islands* (San Francisco: A. R. Dunbar, 1900); [Wong Kin, ed.], *International Chinese Business Directory of the World for the Year 1913* (San Francisco: International Chinese Business Directory, 1913); N. C. Chan, *Handbook of Chinese in America* (New York: People's Foreign Relations Association of China, 1946);

Chinese Directory Service, *Chinese Business Directory, Sacramento–Marysville and Vicinity* (San Francisco: Chinese Directory Service, 1952). The annual Marysville city directories published after 1920 list some Chinese businesses but are inconsistent. The four major early merchant houses were Hong Woo, Ti Wa, Tuck Chung, and Wing Wa; see *Marysville (CA) Daily Appeal*, February 19, 1863; January 27, 1865. There are fifty-one files with business partner lists for separately named Chinese firms in Marysville covering the years 1893 through the 1920s; see United States Immigration and Naturalization Service, Chinese Partnership Lists, San Francisco District, record group 85, boxes 58 and 59, folders 13525/1 through 13525/51, National Archives, Pacific Sierra Region, San Bruno, CA. This total appears generally consistent with the numbers enumerated in the 1892 and 1913 directories.

    9. See below.

Table 2.1.   Population Figures, from Government Census Reports

Year	City of Marysville		All of Yuba County		Sutter County[a]
	Chinese	Total	Chinese	Total	Chinese
1850	??	8,000 est.	2,100 est.	9,673	0?
1852	??	??	??	19,758	0?
1860	(228)[b]	4,740	1,781	13,668	2
1870	1,417	4,738	2,337	10,851	208
1880	1,040	4,321	2,146	11,284	266
1890	478	3,991	974	9,636	327
1900	483	3,497	719	8,620	226
1910	687[c]	5,430	493	10,042	79
1920	502[c]	5,461	359	10,375	42
1930	779[c]	5,763	259	11,331	13
1940	666[c]	6,646	344	17,034	25
1950	401[c]	7,826	302	24,420	38
1960	472[c]	9,553	303	33,859	141
1970	149	9,353	329	44,736	187
1980	114	9,898	128	49,735	176
1990	128	12,324	167	58,228	246

Source: Numbers are from United States Census, California, Yuba County, Marysville, 1850, 1852, 1860, 1870, 1880, 1890, 1900, 1910, 1920, 1930, 1940, 1950, 1960, 1970, 1980, 1990.
[a]Sutter County is directly across the Feather River, but the Chinese there associate with urban Marysville in Yuba County.
[b]The number of Chinese in Marysville for 1860 is taken from Sucheng Chan's recount of the original manuscript census; Chan, "Chinese Livelihood," 300.
[c]These figures include Japanese, Asians from India, and other races with the Chinese; but the figures reported for the county are Chinese only, and most are from Marysville.

    10. *Marysville (CA) Daily Appeal*, February 10, 1872; March 18, 19, 1874; February 1, 1878; March 7, 1914; Sanborn Map Company, *Map of the City of Marysville, Yuba County, California*, 1909, 1921, copies at Paul G. Chace and Associates, Escondido, CA; L. Eve Armentrout Ma, "Urban Chinese at the Sinitic Frontier: Social Organizations in United States Chinatowns, 1849–1898," *Modern Asian Studies* 17,

no. 1 (1983): 111; City of Marysville, "Assessor's Plat Book," History Room, Yuba County Library, Marysville, CA.

11. *Marysville (CA) Daily Appeal*, March 14, 1873.

12. *Marysville (CA) Daily Appeal*, March 14, 1873.

13. *Marysville (CA) Daily Appeal*, March 14, 1873; Him Mark Lai, "Historical Development of the Chinese Consolidated Benevolent Association/Huiguan System," in *Chinese America: History and Perspectives 1987* [ed. Him Mark Lai, Ruthanne Lum McCunn, and Judy Yung] (San Francisco: Chinese Historical Society of America, 1987).

14. *Marysville (CA) Daily Appeal*, February 10, 1872; March 4, 14, 1873.

15. *Marysville (CA) Daily Appeal*, February 10, 1872; March 14, 27, 1873; February 17, 20, 1874; March 6, 1874; April 15, 1875; January 19, 1877; February 14, 1877; February 1, 1878; February 17, 18, 1887. Even earlier, in the 1860s, Chinese leaders were investing in woolen mill businesses in various locales; see *Sacramento (CA) Bee*, July 16, 18, 19, 21, 1862.

16. Chace, "Interpretive Restraint," 71–72; Marysville City Council, "Minutes," May 31, 1875, 41, History Room, Yuba County Library, Marysville, CA.

17. Chace, *History*; *Marysville (CA) Daily Appeal*, March 23, 1869; April 21, 1869; May 7, 15, 1869; also in *Marysville (CA) Weekly Appeal*, March 27, 1869; April 24, 1869; May 15, 22, 1869; *Yuba City (CA) Weekly Sutter Banner*, April 24, 1869; City of Marysville, "Assessor's Plat Book," 1876. See also *Sacramento (CA) Bee*, February 27, 1966. The newspaper reports that the Chinese purchased this property in 1869 are not accurate.

18. Chace, *History*; *Marysville (CA) Daily Appeal*, January 30, 1880; March 3, 6, 9, 17, 20, 21, 1880; *Marysville (CA) Weekly Appeal*, February 6, 1880.

19. Wolfram Eberhard, "Economic Activities of a Chinese Temple in California," in *Settlement and Social Change in Asia by Wolfram Eberhard, Collected Papers*, vol. 1 (Hong Kong: Hong Kong University Press, 1967).

20. *Marysville (CA) Daily Appeal*, February 10, 1861; January 29, 30, 1862; February 9, 1864; *Marysville (CA) North Californian*, February 5, 1867.

21. *Marysville (CA) Daily Appeal*, February 5, 1867.

22. *Marysville (CA) Daily Appeal*, January 23, 1868.

23. *Marysville (CA) Daily Appeal*, March 7, 1883; February 27, 1884. Special tall silken deity umbrellas, typically with elaborate embroidery and fringe, traditionally are used to shade and protect altar figures during outdoor processions. Sometimes such an umbrella is symbolically utilized to mark the protected sacred space even if an actual figure is not being carried beneath the umbrella in a community procession. For a photograph of such a "company" shrine within a laundry, in early Philadelphia, see Stewart Culin, *The Religious Ceremonies of the Chinese in the Eastern Cities of the United States* (Philadelphia: privately printed, 1887), [1].

24. Chace, "Returning Thanks."

25. Ma, "Urban Chinese," 119, and her "The Social Organization of Chinatowns in North America and Hawaii in the 1890s," in *Early Chinese Immigrant Societies: Case Studies from North America and British Southeast Asia*, ed. Lee Lai Top (Singapore: Heinemann Publishers Asia, 1988), 178.

26. San Francisco attorneys for the Chinese held this property title in their names through the 1860s and 1870s. In later Marysville plat and tax records, this society's name was variously rendered: Hong Son Tong in 1882, Hong Sang Tong in 1888 (both inversions of Sam Hop Tong), and later Hong Gee Tong, Gee Hong Tong, and Gee Kong Tong. The name was rendered as Gee Gung Hong in a local 1890 court case.

27. Ma, "Urban Chinese," 118, 121; Eng Ying Gong and Bruce Grant, *Tong War!* (New York: Nicholas L. Brown, 1930), 31.

28. Ma, "Urban Chinese," 118, 121; Gong and Grant, *Tong War!* 36; *Marysville (CA) Appeal-Democrat*, March 8, 1972.

29. Ma, "Urban Chinese," 111; City of Marysville. "Assessor's Plat Book"; Sanborn Map Company, *Map of the City of Marysville*, 1909, 1921; [Wong Kin, ed.], *International Chinese Business Directory*, lists this facility as the "Chung Gee Tong Society" (Devoted to Justice Society). Mention of the Hip Yee Tong appears in *Marysville (CA) Daily Appeal*, March 7, 1914.

30. The earliest local reference encountered for this *tong* is *Marysville (CA) Daily Appeal*, March 10, 1883. Other mentions are in *Marysville (CA) Evening Democrat*, February 14, 1912; February 15, 1915; March 1, 2, 1915; February 27, 1922; *Marysville (CA) Appeal*, March 4, 1927; and *Marysville (CA) Appeal-Democrat*, March 13, 1929. Veta Griggs, *Chinaman's Chance: The Life Story of Elmer Wok Wai* (New York: Exposition, 1969), 133, tells of a Marysville Suey Sing Tong man.

31. Eberhard, "Economic Activities," 265, 274.

32. *Marysville (CA) Appeal*, March 7, 1914.

33. Ma, "Social Organization," 171–173. These locally formed associations of Marysville were somewhat distinct from those in other California communities of Chinese Americans. See also Lai, "Historical Development"; Stanford Morris Lyman, "Strangers in the Cities: The Chinese on the Urban Frontier," in *Ethnic Conflict in California History*, ed. C. Wollenberg (Los Angeles: Tinnon-Brown, 1970); and his *Chinese Americans* (New York: Random House, 1974); Sylvia Sun Minnick, *Samfow: The San Joaquin Chinese Legacy* (Fresno, CA: Panorama West, 1988); and Melford Weiss, *Valley City: A Chinese Community in America* (Cambridge, MA: Schenkman, 1974).

34. Eberhard, "Economic Activities," 265, 274.

35. Eberhard, "Economic Activities," 265, 274.

36. "Bok Kai Supplement," *Marysville (CA) Appeal-Democrat*, 1985, 10–11, 27.

37. Eberhard, "Economic Activities," 265, 274. The principal leader probably was Ah Fee, who died in 1912; see *Marysville (CA) Appeal*, September 19, 24, 1912; *Marysville (CA) Evening Democrat*, September 23, 1912. Subsequently, most of the Yue clan apparently left the community; in later years, remnant Yue clan members in town may have been joined into the Hop Sing Tong.

38. Ancestral tablets possibly may have been brought to the 1880 Bok Kai Temple rededication for the *jiao* rites that year, but the newspaper rhetoric is equivocal; see *Marysville (CA) Daily Appeal*, March 23, 1880.

39. For a few people in Marysville at least, their local births were recorded in their lineage home villages in Guangdong Province. For some who have made visits to

their family's home village in recent decades, their identities and relations were already widely recognized within the village, somewhat to their own surprise.

40. Sally Herr, "Bok Kai Temple Prayer Director Combines Religion and Philosophy in His Preaching," *Yuba-Sutter Business* 3, no. 3 (1984): 6.

41. *Marysville (CA) Daily Appeal*, February 26, 1869, citing the *Nevada City (CA) Gazette* for February 24, 1869; repeated in *Marysville (CA) Weekly Appeal*, March 6, 1869.

42. *Marysville (CA) Daily Appeal*, March 14, 1899; April 10, 1910; *Marysville (CA) Appeal-Democrat*, February 17, 1930. The first birth of a baby boy to Chinese parents in Marysville reportedly occurred in 1855; see *Marysville (CA) Appeal-Democrat*, January 30, 1930. The first birth of a Chinese baby girl in Marysville reportedly was in 1860; see *Marysville (CA) Daily Appeal*, November 13, 1885; *Sacramento (CA) Daily Bee*, November 13, 1885.

43. *Marysville (CA) Daily Appeal*, December 31, 1893; *Marysville (CA) Daily Democrat*, December 30, 1893; *Marysville (CA) Appeal*, December 27, 1911; *Marysville (CA) Evening Democrat*, December 27, 1911; *Marysville (CA) Appeal*, December 29, 1923, January 1, 1924; *Sacramento (CA) Bee*, December 28, 1923.

44. *Marysville (CA) Daily Appeal*, March 13, 1867; April 9, 1867.

45. Marysville City Council, "Minutes," April 22, 1851, 17; May 5, 1862, 512; June 3, 1889, 680; *Marysville (CA) Daily Appeal*, June 11, 1876; *Marysville (CA) Appeal-Democrat*, July 10, 1956, October 3, 1991; *Sacramento (CA) Bee*, March 19, 1960; *Yuba City (CA) Independent-Herald*, June 14, 1951; Buschmann, *Third City*, 23; Ibanez, *Historical*, 16.

46. Marysville City Council, "Minutes," August 3, 1896, 424.

47. *Marysville (CA) Daily Appeal*, March 24, 1877; February 8, 1879; March 13, 15, 16, 1879; May 17, 1879; March 14, 1903; October 12, 1910; March 4, 1919; *Marysville (CA) Daily Democrat*, March 13, 1903; February 16, 1906; *Marysville (CA) Times of Yuba-Sutter*, May 10, 1996, describing a 1926 funeral.

48. *Marysville (CA) Daily Appeal*, February 20, 1879.

49. James L. Watson, "Of Flesh and Bones: The Management of Death Pollution in Cantonese Society," in *Death and the Regeneration of Life*, ed. Maurice Bloch and Jonathan Parry (Cambridge: Cambridge University Press, 1982), 155–186, and his "Funeral Specialists in Cantonese Society: Pollution, Performance, and Social Hierarchy," in *Death Ritual in Late Imperial and Modern China*, ed. James L. Watson and Evelyn S. Rawski (Berkeley: University of California Press, 1988), 109–110, 114, 118.

50. *Marysville (CA) Daily Appeal*, May 25, 1875; January 12, 1887; *Marysville (CA) Weekly Appeal*, February 15, 1895.

51. *Marysville (CA) Daily Appeal*, January 1, 1893. Only a few Chinese funerals are listed in the local library's Ramey index of the Marysville newspapers. No effort has been made to locate any private records of local funeral home businesses.

52. *Marysville (CA) Daily Appeal*, December 17, 1869; March 23, 1875; May 12, 1876; October 24, 1876; July 9, 1878; August 30, 1878; November 20, 1883; January 6, 12, 1887; May 11, 1893; November 16, 1909; September 24, 1912. *Marysville (CA) Weekly Appeal*, March 26, 1875; *Marysville (CA) Daily Democrat*, May 9, 10,

1893; September 24, 1912; *Marysville (CA) Appeal-Democrat*, February 17, 1930. Anita Laney, "The Chinese in Our Area," *Yuba County–Sutter County Regional Arts Council [Newsletter]*, February–March 1987, describes a 1913 funeral.

53. *Marysville (CA) Appeal*, May 11, 1893; May 16, 1901; *Marysville (CA) Weekly Appeal*, February 22, 1895; *Marysville (CA) Daily Democrat*, May 10, 1893.

54. Watson, "Of Flesh," 167–168; and Arthur P. Wolf, "Chinese Kinship and Mourning Dress," in *Family and Kinship in Chinese Society*, ed. Maurice Freedman (Stanford, CA: Stanford University Press, 1970), 192–195.

55. *Marysville (CA) Daily Appeal*, May 16, 1901; and *Marysville (CA) Daily Democrat*, May 10, 1893. The latter newspaper wrote, "This funeral differed materially from any that has been held in Chinatown." It is difficult to account for the fact that Daoist priests, with their ritual directives, were not more prominently noted in local funeral accounts, considering their so obvious funeral roles in rural Cantonese villages near Hong Kong; see Watson, "Funeral Specialists," 117–122. Funeral priests sometimes were noted in San Francisco—as reprinted in *Marysville (CA) Daily Appeal*, February 23, 1868—and in Los Angeles—see Nellie May Young, *William Stewart Young, 1859–1937, Builder of California Institutions, An Intimate Biography* (Glendale, CA: Arthur H. Clark, 1967), 52.

56. William L. Parish and Martin King Whyte, *Village and Family in Contemporary China* (Chicago: University of Chicago Press, 1978), 261–262, 266, similarly report a recent trend for families, rather than ritual specialists, to officiate in rural Cantonese villages.

57. *Marysville (CA) Daily Appeal*, June 11, 1872; and *Marysville (CA) Appeal*, September 17, 1908, November 15, 1910; May 17, 1913. See also *Sacramento (CA) Daily Record-Union*, February 24, 1877. These accounts make no reference to any local municipal codes or restrictions on such customary bone exhumation. See also Marlon K. Hom, "Fallen Leaves' Homecoming: Notes on the 1893 Gold Mountain Charity Cemetery in Xinhui," *Chinese America: History and Perspectives 2002*, ed. Colleen Fong and others (San Francisco: Chinese Historical Society of America, 2002), 36–50.

58. *Marysville (CA) Daily Appeal*, January 10, 11, 1908; February 9, 1908; March 3, 1908; September 17, 1908; September 24, 1912.

59. *Marysville (CA) Appeal*, January 30, 1915. This man was a noteworthy local Chinese pioneer whose family is associated closely with the (Daoist) Bok Kai Temple. Almost certainly this individual was not a Buddhist, since Buddhists do follow cremation practices.

60. *Marysville (CA) Appeal*, September 24, 1912; January 30, 1915; *Marysville (CA) Evening Democrat*, September 23, 1912; February 1, 1915; *Marysville (CA) Appeal-Democrat*, February 17, 1930.

61. Watson, "Funeral Specialists," 123–124.

62. Yuba County Deeds, "Deed Book," 29, 336–337, Thomas Seward, deceased, to Chow You and Yee Wat Chung, February 4, 1880, Office of the Yuba County Recorder, Marysville, CA; Yuba County Deeds, "Deed Book," 372–373, Chow You and Yee Wot Chung to Trustees of Bok Ky Church, April 12, 1880. See also City of Marysville, "Assessor's Plat Book." Chace, *History*, provides a comprehensive and updated history of the Bok Kai Temple.

63. *Marysville (CA) Daily Appeal*, January 30, 1880; March 3, 6, 9, 17, 20, 21, 1880; *Marysville (CA) Weekly Appeal*, February 6, 1880.

64. Eberhard, "Economic Activities."

65. The old carved inscription over the temple doors simply reads "Bok Ch'i Miu" (in Cantonese, or "Bei Chi Miao" in Mandarin). This would translate as "North Riverbank Temple," although the temple is referred to locally as the Bok Kai Temple. Any distinction between the temple's sign name and its central deity is no longer considered significant within the community; see Eberhard, "Economic Activities," 265, 277, and as cited in Mariann Kaye Wells, *Chinese Temples in California* (San Francisco: R and E Research Associates, 1971), 98, who also recognizes that this was not a "Pei-Ti" (Beidi) temple. Eberhard reflects that the main deity should be the local "God of the Yuba or Feather River and not necessarily identical with Pei-Ti"; Eberhard, cited in Wells, *Chinese Temples*, 98. My own supposition is that Bok-Ch'i, now locally spoken of as Bok Kai, was originally a regional Earth God or Tudi here, possibly even the "Earth Spirit for the Riverbank Lands of the Northern Rivers (of California)"; Paul G. Chace, "The Oldest Chinese Temples in California, A Landmarks Tour," *Gum Saan Journal* 14, no. 1 (1991): 4–5, "Interpretive Restraint," 249–250, "Returning Thanks," 110, and *History*, 10. My numerous inquiries with local Chinese community seniors, however, have provided no recognition that either the temple or its central deity ever was referred to in this manner.

66. *Marysville (CA) Appeal-Democrat*, March 4, 1949.

67. March Fong Eu, secretary of state for California, gives the date as December 12, 1949; letter to Paul G. Chace, March 27, 1992.

68. *Marysville (CA) Daily Appeal*, March 17, 23, 1880.

69. John Lagerwey, *Taoist Ritual in Chinese Society and History* (New York: Macmillan, 1987); Michael R. Saso, *Taoism and the Rite of Cosmic Renewal*, 2nd ed. (Pullman: Washington State University Press, 1990), and his *Blue Dragon White Tiger*, *Taoist Rites of Passage* (Washington, DC: Taoist Center, 1990). Historical documentation has been found of Daoist *jiao* rites in San Francisco, Sacramento, San Jose, Los Angeles, and some other California localities; see Paul G. Chace, "The Turtle Dove Messenger, A Trait of the Early Los Angeles *Chiao* Ceremony," *Gum Saan Journal* 12, no. 2 (1989), and his "*Jiao* Rites in Chinese California" (working paper, n.d.).

70. Chace, "Returning Thanks," 156–161.

71. *Marysville (CA) Daily Appeal*, March 23, 1880.

72. *Marysville (CA) Daily Appeal*, March 14, 1873; March 19, 1874; February 26, 1876; March 21, 1882; March 10, 1883; *Marysville (CA) Daily Democrat*, March 17, 1885.

73. Chace, "Oldest," "Interpretive Restraint," "Returning Thanks," *Bok Kai*, "Dancing," *History*; and Ibanez, *Historical*.

74. Silver spirit money is for propitiating ancestors and ghost-spirits, while gold spirit money is burned to honor the gods. See Wolf, "Gods," 180–181; Harrell, "When a Ghost"; Stephen Feuchtwang, "Domestic and Communal Worship in Taiwan," in *Religion and Ritual in Chinese Society*, ed. Arthur Wolf (Stanford, CA: Stanford University Press, 1974), 107; Weller, "Bandits," 49, and *Unities*, 267–272; and Hill Gates, "Money for the Gods," *Modern China* 13, no. 3 (1987): 267–272.

75. Wolf, "Gods," 177.

76. Watson, "Of Flesh," 181.

77. Chace, "Returning Thanks," 119–121, 131–134, 140–148.

78. Chace, "Returning Thanks," 129; Lagerwey, *Taoist Ritual*; Saso, *Taoism, Blue Dragon*, his "Orthodoxy and Heterodoxy in Taoist Ritual," in *Religion and Ritual in Chinese Society*, ed. Arthur P. Wolf (Stanford, CA: Stanford University Press, 1974), and his *The Teachings of Taoist Master Chuang* (New Haven, CT: Yale University Press, 1978); Schipper, *The Taoist Body*.

79. *Marysville (CA) Daily Appeal*, March 14, 1873.

80. *Marysville (CA) Daily Appeal*, March 10, 1883.

81. *Marysville (CA) Daily Appeal*, March 19, 1874; *Marysville (CA) Weekly Appeal*, March 21, 1874.

82. *Marysville (CA) Daily Democrat*, March 17, 1885; and this very same account is duplicated on March 13, 1888.

83. *Marysville (CA) Daily Appeal*, March 21, 1882.

84. The ritual variations noted, with the various theatrics, possibly represent Poyu, the Daoist exorcistic rite termed "The Attack on Hell"; Lagerwey, *Taoist Ritual*, 216–237.

85. *Marysville (CA) Daily Appeal*, February 26, 1876; also *Marysville (CA) Weekly Appeal*, March 3, 1876.

86. *Marysville (CA) Daily Appeal*, February 26, 1876; also *Marysville (CA) Weekly Appeal*, March 3, 1876.

87. *Marysville (CA) Daily Democrat*, March 17, 1885; *Marysville (CA) Daily Appeal*, February 26, 1887; Chace, "Returning Thanks," 126–127.

88. The rite for souls in hell, Pudu or Universal Salvation, is offered "towards the end of every major temple festival" according to Lagerwey, *Taoist Ritual*, 21, and also near the end of the *jiao* festival of renewal; see Duane Pang, "The P'u-tu Ritual: A Celebration of the Chinese Community in Honolulu," in *Buddhist and Taoist Studies I*, ed. Michael Saso and David W. Chappell, Asia Studies at Hawai'i 18 (Honolulu: University Press of Hawai'i, 1977), 97. See also Weller, "Bandits," and *Unities*.

89. The newspapers of 1852 to 1854 do not survive, but no mention of Chinese New Year was made in the 1851 and 1855 newspapers. *Marysville (CA) Daily Herald*, February 6, 1856; January 29, 1857; *Marysville Daily California Express*, February 13, 1858; January 23, 1860; February 11, 1861; *Marysville (CA) Daily National Democrat*, February 2, 1859; *Marysville (CA) Daily Appeal*, January 24, 31, 1860; February 9, 10, 12, 1861; January 29, 30, 1862; February 1, 1862; February 19, 1863; February 5, 1864; January 24, 26, 27, 28, 1865; February 14, 16, 1866; February 3, 5, 6, 7, 1867; *Marysville (CA) North Californian*, February 5, 1867. For banquets, see *Marysville (CA) Daily Appeal*, February 10, 1863. See also *Marysville (CA) Daily Appeal*, January 1, 1887.

90. *Marysville (CA) Daily Appeal*, January 24, 1890; February 17, 1893.

91. *Marysville (CA) North Californian*, February 5, 1867; *Marysville (CA) Daily Appeal*, January 28, 31, 1865; February 1, 4, 1865; February 3, 5, 1867; January 23, 24, 25, 26, 28, 1868; February 7, 11, 12, 13, 14, 1869; January 20, 22, 23, 25, 28, 1887.

92. Barbara E. Ward and Joan Law, *Chinese Festivals in Hong Kong*, 3rd ed. ([Hong Kong]: Guidebook, 1995), 23; William Hoy, "Native Festivals of the California Chinese," *Western Folklore* 7, no. 3 (1948): 243.

93. *Marysville (CA) Appeal*, January 22, 29, 30, 31, 1925; February 13, 1926.

94. Hoy, "Native Festivals," 245.

95. Chace, "Interpretive Restraint," 229–230, 336, 414.

96. *Marysville (CA) Daily Appeal*, April 5, 1862.

97. *Marysville (CA) Daily Appeal*, April 3, 1867; April 5, 1868; April 6, 1870; April 5, 1871; April 5, 1873; April 5, 1874; April 1, 5, 1879. For nearby Oroville and Sacramento there are detailed descriptions of early Qingming rites in the *Butte (CA) Record*, quoted in the *San Francisco Herald*, April 9, 1858; and the *Sacramento (CA) Standard*, quoted in the *San Francisco Herald*, April 5, 1860.

98. Hoy, "Native Festivals," 247; Laurence A. Schneider, *A Madman of Ch'u: The Chinese Myth of Loyalty and Dissent* (Berkeley: University of California Press, 1980); Saso, *Taoism*, 34.

99. Schneider, *Madman*.

100. Eberhard, "Economic Activities," 272, 277.

101. The Chinese staged an exceptional regatta with four or more competitively paddled dragon boats on the slough in Sacramento in 1857, on the Chinese calendar date of Third Month, Third Day; *Sacramento (CA) Bee*, March 28, 29, 1857.

102. Saso, *Taoism*, 35–36; Ward and Law, *Chinese Festivals*, 59–67; Weller, "Bandits"; and Hoy, "Native Festivals," 247.

103. Eberhard, "Economic Activities," 272, 277; *Marysville (CA) Daily Appeal*, August 21, 1888; February 21, 1911.

104. Saso, *Taoism*, 38.

105. *Marysville (CA) Daily Appeal*, December 1, 1883; November 26, 1896; November 29, 1913.

106. R. David Arkush and Leo O. Lee, trans. and eds., *Land without Ghosts: Chinese Impressions of America from the Mid-Nineteenth Century to the Present* (Berkeley: University of California Press, 1989), 181, as noted in the 1940s by anthropologist Fei Xiaotong.

107. Watson, "Funeral Specialists," 133. However, Martin K. Whyte, "Death in the People's Republic of China," in *Death Ritual in Late Imperial and Modern China*, ed. James L. Watson and Evelyn S. Rawski (Berkeley: University of California Press, 1988), 313–314, notes a different pattern of reformed customs within post-1949 urban communities in China.

3

Archaeological Excavations at Virginiatown's Chinese Cemeteries

Wendy L. Rouse

Virginiatown, located in western Placer County, was established as a mining camp shortly after the discovery of gold in California in 1848. Situated just north of the Auburn Ravine, Virginiatown attracted a variety of Chinese and Euro-American prospectors. At its peak in the 1880s, the town boasted a population of over 1,220. As in so many other towns in California in the mid-nineteenth century, the Euro-American population of Virginiatown quickly began to resent their Chinese neighbors and forced them to move outside the boundaries of the town. A separate Chinatown thus emerged on the western outskirts of the Euro-American section of Virginiatown. The Chinatown served as a hub for the local Chinese population from the mid- to late nineteenth century. As the placer deposits dwindled, the miners left to seek their fortunes elsewhere. In 1906 the few remaining Chinese also left Virginiatown.

Archaeological excavations at the site of Virginiatown began in 1992. Under the direction of Dr. Jerald J. Johnson and Melissa K. Farncomb, the archaeological field class from California State University, Sacramento (CSUS), spent six years conducting a nearly complete excavation of several features of the community's historic Chinatown. These investigations have produced a wealth of information about the Chinese in gold rush California. CSUS excavated a variety of archaeological features including basements, wells, trash deposits, ovens, stores, houses, and two cemeteries. Although the processing of the artifacts will take several more years of laboratory analysis, the preliminary results of the excavations have been documented in various master's theses available through CSUS.

The initial 1992 surveys of the Virginiatown area confirmed the location of at least three Chinese cemeteries. One of the landowners recalled that at least twenty-three grave pits associated with Cemetery 2 were filled in during the construction of a home on the property in the 1960s. Archaeological testing of the Cemetery 2 area revealed two empty grave pits that do not appear to have been associated with the Chinese. Unfortunately construction activities may have destroyed the integrity of any remaining deposits in this cemetery, although the contents of the pits may still exist.

The purpose of this chapter is to document the excavation of Virginiatown's two remaining Chinese cemeteries (Cemeteries 1 and 3). Located just outside of the central portion of town, these remote vestiges of the past reveal striking information about the beliefs of the overseas Chinese. Although the bodies of the deceased Chinese have been long since exhumed, there remained much to be learned from the material culture they left behind. Many scholars have recognized the potential of mortuary studies in affording glimpses into the minds of past peoples. In no other context can we so graphically visualize the ideological traditions of a community. The Chinese at Virginiatown maintained very specific beliefs about death and the afterlife. Rituals accompanying the funeral, burial, and exhumation processes reflect these beliefs, and evidence of these traditions has been preserved in the archaeological record. The location of the cemeteries on private property in rural Placer County essentially protected them from threats of vandalism, "pot-hunting" (illegal excavation), or construction activities. CSUS archaeologists truly had a unique opportunity to extract valuable information from these sites.

The excavation of Cemeteries 1 and 3 began in spring 1996. CSUS excavated a sample of eighteen graves in Cemetery 1 and nineteen graves in Cemetery 3. Excavations at Virginiatown temporarily ceased for the next year and a half. In August 1998, the CSUS field crew returned to complete the sampling of Cemetery 1. CSUS conducted a nearly complete excavation of all of the Chinese exhumation pits in Cemetery 1.

The excavation of cemeteries is a serious issue, not to be taken lightly. The discovery of human remains understandably sparks intense emotion in many people. In most cultures, reverence for the dead maintains a long tradition. Prior to the excavation of the cemeteries at Virginiatown, CSUS archaeologists had many ethical issues to consider. Although historical records and ground surveys suggested that the deceased Chinese were exhumed in the earlier part of the century, there remained the possibility of the discovery of human remains. We determined that should our excavators unearth an in-situ Chinese burial, local Chinese historical societies would be immediately consulted to determine the appropriate course of action. Fortunately, no such consultation was necessary. However, our excavations did reveal at least two in-situ Euro-American burials on the western edge of Cemetery 1. Further surveys indicated the possibility of at least fifteen additional Euro-American burials in that location. After consulting the appropriate authorities, CSUS archaeologists determined to record the likely locations of these burials and to leave the individuals undisturbed.

Prior to the start of excavation, the following broad questions were composed to guide our research:

1. Is there evidence for a deliberate orientation of the cemetery or individual graves according to the principles of *fengshui*?
2. Why were there three Chinese cemeteries at Virginiatown? Does this segregation represent various socioeconomic levels, temporal distinctions, or association with different family, district, or *tang* (*tong*) associations?
3. Is there material evidence of distinct beliefs in an afterlife?
4. How "Chinese" were the funerals? Were the Chinese in California adhering strictly to Chinese tradition regarding burial customs? How much influence did Euro-American burial practices have on the Chinese at Virginiatown?
5. What was the process involved in the original excavation and burial of the individuals?
6. Can examples of regional variation as demonstrated in China be seen in the assemblage at Virginiatown?
7. What was the process involved in the exhumation of the bodies? How "neat and meticulous" were the exhumers? Who were they? When did the exhumations occur?
8. How much of the site has been disturbed by contemporary observers, subsequent landowners, construction activities, and earlier archaeological investigations?

With these research questions in mind, the CSUS archaeologists began an intensive archival and archaeological investigation of the Virginiatown cemeteries. A few points regarding potential research biases had to be considered. Although the site had not been recently disturbed, it is likely that many of the items originally placed with the deceased were removed or destroyed during or following the exhumation process. The graves were left open for over one hundred years prior to the arrival of the CSUS archaeologists, and it is very likely that some items were damaged or lost over the years. These facts may bias any attempt to simply offer a quantitative interpretation of the data. For this reason, the present study makes little attempt to compare the frequency and percentage of material type of the two cemeteries. Instead, this report is concerned solely with the presence of the material itself. In addition, the interpretation of the symbolic meaning of burial goods may vary from observer to observer. The intent here is not to assert that the Chinese individuals at Virginiatown strictly adhered to a set of beliefs but, rather, to suggest a variety of interpretations that may explain the presence of certain material goods within the Chinese cemeteries.

SPATIAL ORGANIZATION/*FENGSHUI*

The Chinese concept of *fengshui* often figured prominently into the positioning of graves and houses in China. Recent studies of nineteenth-century Chinese communities in California have suggested that this practice was applied to the establishment of several Chinatowns in gold rush communities.[1] It is logical then to assume that Chinese individuals also applied the principles of *fengshui* to burials (see chapter 1 for a discussion of the history of *fengshui*). The continuity of traditional funeral rituals confirms that individuals sought to retain Chinese customs in California whenever possible.

The exhumation pits at Cemetery 1 contour around the eastern side of a small hill (fig. 3.1). The Auburn Ravine flows along the southeastern side of the hill. The location of buttons, clothing, burial markers, and personal goods indicates that the heads of the deceased individuals were positioned on the uphill slope. This unique orientation of individual burials stands in stark contrast to the Euro-American burials discovered on the western side of the cemetery. These burials, all located near the top of the hill, were aligned with the heads pointed toward the west in the typical Christian fashion. Euro-American burials are also typically oriented in rows with walkways at the head and foot of the graves. Unlike the Chinese, the Euro-Americans seemed more concerned with cardinal direction than orientation in accordance with specific geographical features such as hills or watercourses.

The segregation of the Chinese and Euro-American burials at Cemetery 1 also mirrors the inherent conflicts existing between the two groups in life. The Chinese at Virginiatown, and all across California, were not well received by their non-Chinese neighbors. The "peculiar" life ways of the Chinese miners bewildered and frightened onlookers. Ignorance and fear eventually led to distrust, discrimination, and, in some cases, violence. In 1860, the Euro-Americans at Virginiatown voted to forcibly segregate the Chinese population from the rest of the community.[2] Declaring them a fire hazard, the town agreed that the Chinese should live outside the main part of Virginiatown. The segregation of the races at Cemetery 1 seems to represent an extension even unto death of the hostilities that existed between the Chinese and Euro-Americans at Virginiatown.

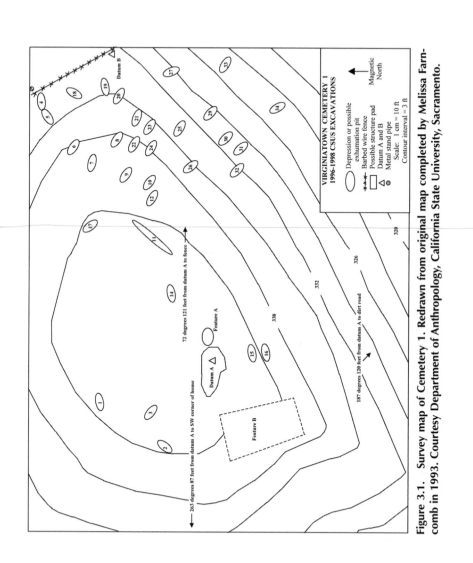

VIRGINIATOWN CEMETERY 1
1996-1998 CSUS EXCAVATIONS

◯ Depression or possible exhumation pit
×-×-× Barbed wire fence
▭ Possible structure pad
△ Datum A and B
⊚ Metal stand pipe
Scale: 1 cm = 10 ft
Contour interval = 3 ft

← Magnetic North

Datum B

Datum A △

Feature A

Feature B

72 degrees 121 feet from datum A to fence

263 degrees 87 feet from datum A to SW corner of house

187 degrees 120 feet from datum A to dirt road

320

326

332

338

Figure 3.1. Survey map of Cemetery 1. Redrawn from original map completed by Melissa Farncomb in 1993. Courtesy Department of Anthropology, California State University, Sacramento.

Cemetery 3 is located on a small knoll just south of the central portion of the Chinatown. Most of the exhumation pits contour around the southern and western sides of the hill (fig. 3.2). The Auburn Ravine is located just south of the cemetery. The discovery of in-situ bones, clothing, burial markers, and personal goods again confirmed that the deceased were positioned with their heads pointed toward the uphill slope.

The two cemeteries at Virginiatown were ideally situated according to the basic principles of *fengshui*. The Virginiatown Chinese seem to have deliberately oriented the graves in relationship to local geographical features. Hills and mountains, while allowing beneficial winds to pass, were believed to provide a barrier against dangerous winds that may carry evil spirits. The shape of the grave itself was also important. An omega-shaped grave (Ω), with the head up against the slope of a hill, afforded protection around the burial. The burials in both cemeteries were oriented with the heads pointed toward the hill in this manner. Likewise, the location of the Auburn Ravine, just south (or to the feet) of the deceased, was ideal since it was believed that water passing alongside the grave dispersed the *yang* energy of the mountains while allowing *yin* energy to flow with it (fig. 3.3).[3]

ARCHAEOLOGICAL EVIDENCE OF CHINESE DEATH RITUAL

The examination of primary source material coupled with the interpretation of the archaeological data has allowed us to begin to understand the funeral, burial, and exhumation rituals of the Chinese in California. In several instances the archaeological evidence seems to confirm early newspaper accounts describing traditional Chinese death rituals. In other cases primary accounts conflict with the archaeological data. This section considers how the archaeological assemblages of the two Virginiatown cemeteries compare with historical data regarding Chinese funeral, burial, and exhumation rituals. For the sake of this report these terms have been adopted to more clearly define three distinct stages of death ritual. "Funeral" refers to the procession from the deceased's home to the cemetery. "Burial" refers to the ceremonies surrounding the interment of the deceased at the cemetery. Finally, "exhumation" refers to the process of the removal of the bones and preparation for their shipment to China.

The Funeral

As described in detail in chapter 1, a typical Chinese burial included an elaborate funeral procession to the cemetery. Mourners exhibited public displays of

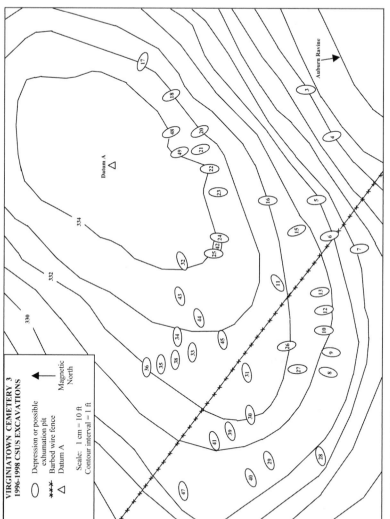

Figure 3.2. Initial CSUS survey map of Cemetery 3. Courtesy Department of Anthropology, California State University, Sacramento.

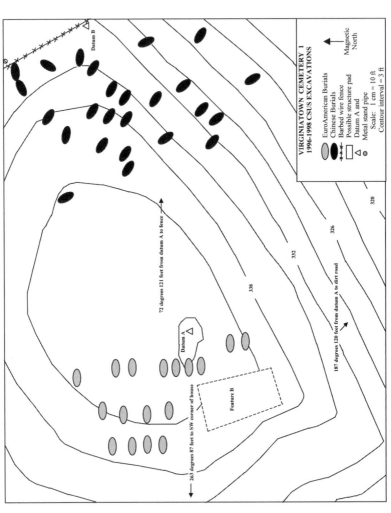

Figure 3.3. Chinese exhumation pits and Euro-American burials discovered at Cemetery 1. Courtesy Department of Anthropology, California State University, Sacramento.

grief through the wearing of white, ritual wailing, and the carrying of banners announcing the solemn occasion. The scattering of symbolic paper money, the beating of gongs, and the explosion of firecrackers helped to frighten away any lingering evil spirits. Upon arrival at the cemetery, symbolic or real clothing, money, and other personal goods were burned in a specially constructed burner to ensure that the deceased had access to these items in the afterlife. Family and priests said prayers over the deceased prior to final burial. Various types of food offerings were also left at the grave for the deceased.[4]

To date, archaeological evidence of funeral rituals is limited. Although many Chinese in northern California communities such as Dutch Flat, Nevada City, Auburn, Wheatland, and Folsom are known to have constructed burners for the burning of clothing and symbolic gifts, no reliable evidence for such a feature could be found at Virginiatown. Pit #14 at first demonstrated similar characteristics. The pit consisted of a small burn area measuring some two by two feet. A large sheet-metal fragment resembling a stovepipe was recovered from within the pit. However, the complete lack of artifacts (including buttons and pieces of cloth), the absence of any associated architectural features, and the unusual dimensions of the deposit seem to discount its association with Chinese funeral ritual.

Scattered fragments of large stoneware vessels were recovered near Trench 11 in Cemetery 1. Similarly, fragments of porcelain bowls and small stoneware vessels have been recovered adjacent to graves in both cemeteries. These findings seem to support descriptions of food offerings left in jars around the graves during funeral rituals.[5] Such jars, if not quickly retrieved, would soon fall victim to careless thieves or vandals.[6] It is also possible that the scattered artifacts represent the remains of burial goods placed inside the grave of the deceased during the funeral and later removed and discarded during the exhumation process.

The Burial

Perhaps the most telling evidence of Chinese death ritual may be found in the archaeological assemblages of the burials themselves. Primary source accounts describing burials are not as common as descriptions of funeral ceremonies. This is due in part to the higher visibility of the funeral processions compared to the more private burial process. Euro-Americans rarely observed the preparation of the body for burial, nor were they often present at the cemetery during the interment. The archaeological evidence, however, provides insight into these customs.

The graves themselves typically were shallow, not more than about three feet deep. The majority of the thirty-seven exhumation pits excavated were dug less than two feet below ground surface. Generally the tops of the burial containers were located less than one foot below the ground surface. The shallowness of these graves would have assisted in the rapid decomposition of the flesh while making the exhumation process slightly less exhausting. The practice of digging such shallow graves, however, proved controversial in nineteenth-century California. As early newspaper articles suggest, the sights and smells of the cemetery could not have been pleasant.

A careful examination of the coffin and casket architecture has revealed some information about the consumer practices of the Chinese at Virginiatown. Excavators collected samples of wood from all exhumation pits where it was encountered. With the help of Dr. Thomas Rost of the Biology Department at the University of California, Davis, samples of the wood were identified microscopically. Due to limited resources, the entire collection of wood samples could not be analyzed. However, one sample from each of the cemeteries was examined, and both were identified as Douglas fir, a conifer common to western Placer County. The Chinese at Virginiatown apparently were purchasing their coffins and caskets from a local carpenter or undertaker who relied predominantly on local sources for his wood supply.

The construction of the burial containers varied slightly. Cemetery 3 included only rectangular-shaped caskets, while Cemetery 1 included both rectangular caskets and hexagonal coffins. Four of the eighteen exhumation pits were hexagonal, while the other fourteen were rectangular. Although the graves varied in size, the caskets averaged six feet in length and two feet in width. The hexagonal coffins typically averaged six feet in length, two feet in width at the shoulders, tapering to one foot in width at the foot end of the coffin. The length of the coffins and caskets may have been necessary to allow sufficient space for food vessels and other burial goods interred with the individual. The burial containers appeared to stand approximately one foot tall. The boxes were made of one-inch-thick rough-cut lumber that measured one foot wide. The bottom of the burial boxes consisted of two boards, while the sides were constructed with one board. Excavators observed two general construction methods for the containers. In some cases, the bottoms were placed inside the box and nailed from the side, creating an interior dimension of two feet in width. In other cases, the sideboards were nailed to the base of the box, creating an interior dimension of twenty-two inches (figs. 3.4 and 3.5).

One of the most obvious differences between the two cemeteries is found in the hardware used in the construction of the burial containers. The caskets in Cemetery 3 were constructed entirely from square (cut) nails with no exceptions. Cemetery 1, on the other hand, included both cut and wire nails. Within the eighteen grave pits, eight burial containers were constructed with cut nails, while nine boxes contained both cut and wire nails. The one in Pit #22 was built

Figure 3.4. Casket remains discovered in Pit #10 in Cemetery 1. Courtesy Department of Anthropology, California State University, Sacramento.

entirely with wire nails. Also in contrast to Cemetery 3, excavators in Cemetery 1 recovered an assortment of coffin and casket hardware. The assemblage from Cemetery 1 consisted of a variety of handles, thumbscrews, escutcheons, and caplifters. At least three grave pits (#4, #31, and #34) included swing bail shipping box handles. These types of handles were typically used on the outside of shipping boxes for the interstate transportation of bodies. Shipping box handles were also found on outer boxes, which were designed as additional protection for the burial. The coffin or casket was lowered into the ground and laid to rest inside the outer box.[7] However, at Virginiatown these handles may have been used as less expensive coffin or casket handles. Pit #4 included four in-situ shipping box handles attached to the exterior of a hexagonal coffin.

Figure 3.5. Coffin discovered in Pit #4 in Cemetery 1. Flagging denotes the location of four in-situ swing bail coffin handles. Courtesy Department of Anthropology, California State University, Sacramento.

More elaborate handles were also recovered in Cemetery 1. The assemblage from Pit #26 consisted of six in-situ swing bail coffin handles. These handles consisted of an intricate acorn and oak-leaf design with silver-colored plating. A variant of this oak-leaf and acorn design was recovered from Pits #20 and #27. Although only one handle was recovered from each of these pits, the design of these two handles and the serial number on the back (2770) match exactly. It is probable that these two handles were originally from Pit #20 and one was removed to Pit #27 during the exhumation process.

The grave goods also provided information about the burial process. Of the thirty-seven graves excavated in the two cemeteries, twenty-one contained fragments of some type of food vessel. Whole vessels included three "Double Happiness" pattern rice bowls, one porcelain "Four Seasons" pattern liquor cup, one stoneware medium wide-mouthed food jar, one white earthenware plate, and one stoneware spouted jar that probably had contained soy sauce. Two whole cans were also recovered from the burial pits. The majority of the recovered artifacts consisted of small fragments of porcelain or stoneware representing the previous existence of a complete vessel within the grave pit. The presence of these artifacts seems to support contemporary accounts describing the placement of various food offerings within the grave.[8] These offerings provided the deceased with necessary sustenance in the afterlife and were also used to satisfy the appetites of any lingering evil spirits (fig. 3.6).

In addition to the ceramic remains, the bones of a gray fox, an unidentified rodent, two jackrabbits, a cat, two owls, an unidentified bird, and a chicken were discovered in seven of the grave pits. It remains uncertain whether these animals represented food offerings that accompanied the deceased or were the result of a naturally occurring deposition. With the exception of the chicken, these animals generally do not represent typical Chinese food items. However, archaeological excavations of Chinese sites in Tucson, Arizona, and Lovelock, Nevada, recovered small samples of butchered cat and rabbit bones.[9] In Chinese burials several types of cooked and uncooked foods were often deposited with the deceased. The Virginiatown Cemetery 1 bones exhibited no evidence of butchering and cannot therefore be definitively identified as food items.

The discovery of a variety of both Chinese and Euro-American buttons seems to indicate that the Chinese were burying their dead in both traditional and nontraditional clothing. At least seven graves exhibited use of traditional clothing through the presence of Chinese brass buttons. Jean rivets and ceramic, metal, and bone buttons indicate a more Euro-American style of dress. Eight rivets recovered from Pit #27 bore the inscription "L. S. & Co. SF." Levi Strauss Company historian Lynn Downey analyzed the Virginiatown rivets and concluded that the rivets were manufactured sometime after 1891 but before

Figure 3.6. Double Happiness pattern rice bowl and Four Seasons pattern liquor cup discovered in-situ in Pit #48 in Cemetery 3. Remnants of the wooden casket remain visible in the grave pit. Courtesy Department of Anthropology, California State University, Sacramento.

the early 1910s. The presence of buttons may also reveal the history of a modern Chinese burial custom. Pit #20 contained several Euro-American and Chinese buttons tied together on a leather string. Anthropologist Linda Sun Crowder has noted a similar custom among modern Chinese Americans in San Francisco. The buttons are believed to bind the soul to the earth. The removal of these buttons allows the soul to enter the other world.[10] It is possible that the Chinese at Virginiatown were practicing a similar custom.

Chinese and U.S. coins were recovered from six exhumation pits, sometimes in situ in differing locations. For example, Pit #36 in Cemetery 3 contained four Chinese coins, each carefully positioned in the four corners of the grave. At least one account claims that the purpose of these coins would have been to ward off evil spirits.[11] Similarly, coins tied together as a pendant were often worn or carried as a symbol of prosperity or to repel evil.[12] Pit #17 contained six Chinese coins tied together with a string and may demonstrate an adherence to this belief. Historical research revealed that coins were often placed in the mouth, ears, hands, or eyes of the deceased as a symbol of fertility or wealth for future generations.[13] Although it is possible that the coins served a talismanic or symbolic purpose, their actual significance to the Virginiatown Chinese may remain unknown.

Excavators also recovered shovel heads from two grave pits (Pit #27 in Cemetery 1 and Pit #22 in Cemetery 3). Apparently the shovels were broken and the handles discarded during the burial or exhumation process. At least one source described a similar practice at a Chinese cemetery in Plumas County, California. The exhumers would "see to it that the shovel that had dug up the body was smashed on the anvil and returned to the empty grave, just as at the burial ceremony seven years before."[14] This source seems to strengthen the argument that the Chinese at Virginiatown also practiced this symbolic practice as a part of the burial or exhumation rituals. It is also possible, however, that the shovels were merely discarded in the burial pits after they ceased to be functional.

At least four burial bricks were located in the Virginiatown Chinese graves. Three of these were inscribed with information about the deceased, including his name and home village. The Nevada City, Folsom, and Auburn Chinese cemeteries also included several graves marked by burial bricks. Stones, bottles, or wood were also used as grave markers at these cemeteries, although there was little evidence of this at Virginiatown. Many early graves may have been simply unmarked. However, by the twentieth century, as more Chinese families chose to remain in California, more-permanent granite and marble grave markers were adopted. Only brick burial markers were recovered at Virginiatown (fig. 3.7).

Excavators also discovered a number of personal items in the exhumation pits. Because many of these items came from the secondary deposit of Pit #27 in Cemetery 1, their primary context remains unknown. Pit #27 included two eyeglass lenses, a paintbrush, a fan, a Chinese Freemason's badge, a pencil, a whistle, an opium pipe bowl, a Chinese brass lock, a pipe stem, a mirror, and an inkwell. The majority of the exhumation pits contained few if any personal belongings. The items recovered from Pit #27 probably represent the personal remains of a number of individuals from Cemetery 1 whose

Figure 3.7. Burial brick recovered from Cemetery 1 by Sierra College excavators. Inscription reads, in pinyin, "Liao Tong Shing was from the village of Wai Ba." Translated by Xiao Yun Yao at the University of Idaho's Asian American Comparative Collection. Courtesy Department of Anthropology, California State University, Sacramento.

bones were removed to this area for cleaning and shipping. The exhumers apparently used Pit #27 as a dumping area for grave goods recovered from multiple burials. Our discussion here, then, is more concerned with the types of artifacts recovered than with the details of their context.

The only obvious reference to opium smoking was found in Pit #27 in Cemetery 1. Excavators recovered a whole light gray opium pipe bowl from the exhumation pit. The bowl's design consisted of a circular smoking surface and elaborately decorative side. A metal connector was attached to the flange where the stem had apparently worn away. Jenny Gao, a translator for the Asian American Comparative Collection at the University of Idaho, translated the negative stamp on the bowl's base as Ma Huasheng, an individual's family and first name. A Euro-American style tobacco pipe stem was also recovered from Pit #27.

Two examples of an unidentified artifact type were recovered from both cemeteries. Pit #22 in Cemetery 1 and Pit #4 in Cemetery 3 each contained an object that bears resemblance to a nineteenth-century ear cleaner. The item in Pit #4 included an 1841 dime attached by a small silver chain to a scoop. On the opposite side of the coin another chain is attached to a small, brass, cone-shaped pendant that has several raised convex circles on its flat base. The scoop end is composed of a type of nonferrous metal such as brass or copper. The artifact in Cemetery 1 is composed of a similar material, although no pendant, chain, or coin was found in association with the artifact. This artifact appears to have once included a mechanism to allow the scoop to retract into a hollow tube. The opposite end of the object includes a retractable tool resembling a small toothpick.

A number of hardware items were also recovered in the exhumation pits. Their significance to the Chinese in the burial context remains unknown. Pit #17 in Cemetery 3 contained an iron skeleton key. In addition, a Chinese brass lock and key were recovered from Pit #27 in Cemetery 1. To the excavator's surprise the lock was still functional. Translator Jenny Gao interpreted an inscription on the lock as "Chang Xue." The exact meaning of the phrase is unclear, although Gao speculated that the inscription might be an individual's first name or an official title.

Writing implements were recovered from a number of exhumation pits. Pit #27 included pencil, pen, and paintbrush fragments as well as a glass inkwell. The inkwell was apparently created using a two-part mold, while the lip was applied separately. The neck of the inkwell was corked. The artifact bore the inscription "SMCO" on the base. Fragments of a paintbrush or fountain pen were also recovered from Pit #22. These types of artifacts may provide clues to the individual's occupation or hobbies in life.

Exhumation

The exhumation process is perhaps the most visible event in the archaeological and historical record. Contemporary Euro-American observers seemed at once intrigued and horrified by the exhumation activities. Usually hired by the appropriate district association, professional exhumers arrived in the cemetery after several years to remove the remains. Exhumers often used a small washbasin to clean the bones before packing them for the return trip to China. No archaeological evidence for such a feature could be located at the Virginiatown cemeteries. Pit #27 in Cemetery 1, however, contained an unusual amount of material remains, including fifty Chinese and Euro-American buttons. It is possible that this pit may have served as a repository for miscellaneous clothing and burial goods during the exhumation process. This theory is further substantiated by the recovery of a blue bottle fragment in Pit #19 that corresponds to a blue bottle fragment in Pit #27. In addition, Pit #27 contained a coffin or casket handle identical to the handle recovered in Pit #20. This evidence strongly supports the use of Pit #27 as a processing and/or sorting area, as suggested earlier.

Obviously, local accounts of the exhumation process varied. In many instances Euro-Americans denounced the activity as a health hazard. Indeed, it appears that the exhumation procedure at Virginiatown was not as "neat and meticulous" as has been described in modern studies. At Virginiatown, coffin and casket lids were removed and left strewn about the cemetery. The bones were gathered from the grave and presumably cleaned, and prepared for shipment. Of the thirty-seven exhumation pits excavated by CSUS, however, sixteen contained at least one human bone. Typically, the forgotten bones consisted of carpals, metacarpals, tarsals, metatarsals, phalanges, or other small bone fragments.

Although it remains unknown who was responsible for the exhumation of the two cemeteries, it seems likely that this was a continuing process completed by a variety of individuals over the course of fifty or more years. The landowner recalled hearing that the Works Projects Administration (WPA) came to Virginiatown in the 1930s to exhume the remaining burials. According to the landowner, the WPA apparently set fire to the pits after the bodies had been exhumed. Fourteen burial pits in Cemetery 1 and thirteen burial pits in Cemetery 3 exhibited signs of post-exhumation burning. The burning was likely associated with the exhumation process but not necessarily with the WPA. Concern with disease may have prompted this more hygienic response to the exhumation procedure.

Secondary burial was a common practice in nineteenth-century southern China. There is some evidence that the Chinese in California retained this tradition. The Chinese residents of Wheatland apparently reinterred the decomposed remains of the deceased in stoneware barrel jars before reburying the jars in the ground. Little evidence of this practice was observed at Virginiatown. Trench #11, however, contained fragments of a stoneware barrel jar. In addition, several barrel jar fragments were recovered from the surface of Cemetery 1 and from Cemetery 3. While it is probable that these jars contained food offerings left for the deceased, it is also possible that these jars indicate the practice of secondary burial. The jars may have served as temporary repositories for the bones until the remains could be returned to China.

THREE VIRGINIATOWN CEMETERIES?

The three distinct Virginiatown cemeteries at first presented CSUS archaeologists with a variety of possibilities. We postulated that the segregation of the cemeteries indicated an association with different district, family, or *tong* associations, a distinction between socioeconomic levels, or a temporal segregation. Unfortunately, for reasons discussed earlier, data from Cemetery 2 are unavailable. However, the archaeological assemblages of Cemeteries 1 and 3 provided many clues.

District/Family/*Tang* Associations

Inquiry into the nature of the segregation of the cemeteries suggested an affiliation with different family or district associations. This has proven to be the case in other mining camps in California. Folsom, for example, had three distinct Chinese cemeteries operated by three different district associations. It seems likely and probable that this was also the case at Virginiatown. No evidence could be found in the historical or archaeological records to support this claim, although it remains a viable possibility.

It is also possible that *tong* associations organized the cemeteries. The discovery of a Masonic pin in Pit #27 in Cemetery 1 suggests that the deceased individual may have been a member of the Chinese Masonic Lodge or the Zhigongtang (Chinese Freemasons, also known as Chee Kung Tong), then popular throughout California and the West. The pin included the inscription "CFM," which may have been the acronym for the Chinese Free Masons. The Zhigongtang served as a strong political force in many nineteenth-century California Chinese communities. Branches of the order existed in large cities such as San Francisco and Los Angeles, as well as smaller outlying communities like Marysville and Santa Cruz. The Chinese Freemasons in nineteenth-century Santa Cruz adopted the Free Mason symbol, and its members wore Masonic pins with the square and compass design on their lapels. The Chinese Masonic Lodge in Marysville organized particularly elaborate funeral ceremonies for its deceased members. Mourners wore red rosettes on their lapels to signify membership in the lodge.[15] No archival evidence for the existence of a Zhigongtang lodge in Virginiatown has yet been discovered. However, the Masonic pin recovered from Cemetery 1 seems to indicate their presence in the community. It is even possible that Cemetery 1 served as a burial ground for the Chinese Masonic Lodge, although this seems like a dramatic assumption to make from the discovery of a single pin.

Socioeconomic Status

The discovery of seven graves with hardware and both coffins and caskets in Cemetery 1 at first suggested a higher socioeconomic status than for those individuals interred in Cemetery 3. Grave #26 in Cemetery 1 contained six in-situ, elaborately decorated, oak-leaf-design coffin handles. However, a 1990 study by Edward L. Bell warns archaeologists to beware of haphazardly associating ornate coffin hardware with socioeconomic status.[16] The author's excavation of a nineteenth-century pauper's cemetery in Uxbridge, Massachusetts, confirmed that despite the status of the deceased, a few individuals were provided with elaborately decorated coffins and caskets popular throughout the late Victorian period. Bell suggests that the Victorian ideology and its romanticization of death are reflected in the elaborate hardware. This hardware was mass produced and available even to the lowliest of Boston's citizens. Most of the Uxbridge coffins, however, were afforded little decoration, and Bell recognizes that the quantity and quality of hardware may differ according to socioeconomic status.

Debi Hacker-Norton and Michael Trinkley identify an association between elaborate hardware and social status in their South Carolina study of hardware recovered from a pre-1926 general merchandising store. However, the authors also warn archaeologists to beware of the difference between "real" and "apparent" status. Hacker-Norton and Trinkley argue that socioeconomic status may be inferred from the amount and type of hardware found in association with each coffin or casket. Metal short bar handles, caplifters, and coffin plates are rather expensive items that tend to suggest the "real" economic status of the deceased's family. On the contrary, steel short bar, cast swing bail handles, and a variety of decorative elements, including white metal screws and tacks, may indicate an "apparent" status suggesting the desire of the family to imply a higher-than-actual socioeconomic level.[17]

The hardware recovered from the Virginiatown cemeteries represents a range of costs. The shipping box handles, constructed of a poor-quality ferrous metal, represent the bottom of the price scale, while the silver-plated white metal handles indicate a medium price range. Pit #26 included six coffin handles, whereas four may have been used if price was an issue. It is likely that the variation of hardware within Cemetery 1 indicates some socioeconomic stratification. However, as demonstrated by primary source documentation, Chinese families often went beyond their financial means to provide the best funeral for the deceased that money could buy. Thus, the existence of more elaborate styles of burial hardware in Cemetery 1 may merely reflect the family's desire to create the illusion of wealth or "apparent" status (figs. 3.8 and 3.9).

The complete lack of hardware in Cemetery 3 at first glance may indicate a status difference between the two cemeteries. However, knowing the importance of "apparent" status to the nineteenth-century Chinese, it seems likely that the families would have purchased any hardware available to them in an attempt to reflect this status. The elaborate hardware recovered from Cemetery 1 suggests access to a greater assortment of burial hardware than was available to the individuals of Cemetery 3. The lack of hardware in Cemetery 3 may be better explained by a temporal difference between the two cemeteries.

Figure 3.8. One of six silver-colored white metal coffin handles recovered from Pit #26 in Cemetery 1. Courtesy Department of Anthropology, California State University, Sacramento.

Temporal Variation

The evidence for a temporal distinction between the two cemeteries is more convincing. Here again we return to the discussion regarding coffin and casket hardware. While the style of hardware recovered from Cemetery 1 was popular in the mid-nineteenth century, Hacker-Norton and Trinkley warn archaeologists to beware of the pitfalls of dating coffin hardware. In their study, the authors determine that there was a general shift in popularity from

Figure 3.9. Swing bail iron coffin handle recovered from Cemetery 1. Courtesy Department of Anthropology, California State University, Sacramento.

the swing bail to the two-lug short bar handle style beginning around 1880. These data suggest that the assemblage from Virginiatown Cemetery 1 represents a pre-1880 deposit. However, Hacker-Norton and Trinkley conclude that other factors—such as local popularity, availability, expense, and wholesale purchasing habits—may have also influenced the style of hardware available in local communities. For example, they observe that rural communities often suffered from a "stylistic lag" of up to twenty years. Their study of an 1896-to-1926 merchandising store assemblage in rural South Carolina demonstrates this stylistic lag. The collection included several outmoded styles clearly not representative of the popular styles of the early twentieth century.[18] This hardware was similar in design to the types recovered from the Virginiatown cemeteries. In addition, the excavation of late nineteenth-century and early twentieth-century burials in an African American cemetery in Arkansas revealed hardware stylistically similar to that recovered from the Virginiatown cemeteries.[19] It therefore seems probable that the Chinese at Virginiatown may have also suffered from a stylistic lag in coffin and casket hardware availability.

Comparative data from the South Carolina and Arkansas assemblages suggest that hardware has only limited potential in establishing a definitive date for the Cemetery 1 assemblage. However, the obvious prevalence of elaborate hardware in Cemetery 1, while not specifically datable, may indicate access to a broader assortment of material goods than at first available to the inhabitants of Cemetery 3. Such access would have been limited for rural Virginiatown during the early years of the gold rush, prior to the arrival of the railroad in the 1860s. The conspicuous lack of casket hardware and the simpler construction methods of the caskets from Cemetery 3 seem to indicate that Cemetery 3 is older than Cemetery 1.

Ceramics can also serve as a useful dating tool. It is interesting to note the predominance of Double Happiness pattern rice bowls in Cemetery 3. Archaeologists have long recognized that the Double Happiness pattern tends to dominate overseas Chinese sites that date prior to 1870. However, after 1870, Double Happiness occurs only rarely, while the Bamboo pattern gradually replaces it in popularity.[20] Although it is possible that the porcelain patterns may provide a time frame for the two cemeteries at Virginiatown, the unique nature of this particular data set must be fully understood. It is likely that some of the original porcelain was lost or destroyed during the exhumation process, skewing any type of accurate quantitative analysis. In addition, it remains uncertain whether the Chinese at Virginiatown provided a bowl owned by the deceased in life or buried the deceased with a new bowl at the time of death. Although the ceramic data tend to suggest that Cemetery 3 was in use earlier than Cemetery 1, for the reasons discussed above we must be careful of drawing this conclusion based solely on the ceramic evidence.

Further evidence for a temporal distinction between the two cemeteries may be found in the number of wire versus cut nails. Cemetery 3 revealed sixteen caskets constructed solely with cut nails. The remaining exhumation pits contained no nails. Only eight burial containers in Cemetery 1, however, were constructed solely from cut nails. Nine containers were constructed from both wire and cut nails, while Pit #22 contained only wire nails. Common knowledge indicates that wire nails gradually replaced square nails in predominance beginning after 1890. Thus the nail evidence seems to strongly suggest that Cemetery 1 is more recent than Cemetery 3.

In addition to hardware, ceramics, and nails, a number of other types of artifacts suggest a post-1880 date for Cemetery 1. Eight rivets discovered in Pit #27 bear the inscription of Levi Strauss and Company and were manufactured between 1891 and the early 1910s, suggesting a late nineteenth-century burial in Cemetery 1. Coins also suggest a late nineteenth- to early twentieth-century burial date. Excavators recovered two U.S. coins from Cemetery 1 Pits #27 and #4 dated, respectively, 1883 and 1904. In contrast, an 1841 U.S. coin was recovered from Pit #4 in Cemetery 3. A Chinese coin recovered from Pit #27 in Cemetery 1 was minted between 1906 and 1908. Two freshwater shell buttons recovered from Pits #4 and #6 suggest a post-1891 deposit. Solarized amethyst glass recovered from Pits #8 and #17 dates after 1880 and prior to 1916.

The excavation of Cemeteries 1 and 3 has provided some clues about the purpose of the three distinct Chinese cemeteries in Virginiatown. Comparative studies on similar overseas Chinese sites, such as Folsom, suggest that Chinese cemeteries were generally organized according to family or district associations. It remains probable that this was also the situation at Virginiatown. However, no historical documentation has yet been found to support this theory. It seems unlikely that the cemeteries were organized according to socioeconomic status, although this still remains a slim possibility. The strongest evidence supports a temporal distinction between the two cemeteries. The excavation data suggest that Cemetery 1 was in use much later than Cemetery 3. The Chinese coin in Pit #27 indicates that Cemetery 1 was in use as late as 1906. Oral history suggests that the few remaining Chinese were forcibly evicted from Virginiatown in 1906. While it is possible that both cemeteries existed simultaneously and were operated by different associations, the nail data suggest that Cemetery 3 appears to have fallen out of use by the 1890s. Cemetery 1, however, served as the final resting place for the few remaining Chinese inhabitants at Virginiatown after the turn of the century.

CONCLUSIONS

The CSUS excavations of the Virginiatown Chinese Cemetery revealed several important clues about the death rituals of the Chinese in California. First, the archaeological and historical evidence demonstrates the importance of funeral, burial, and exhumation rituals to the overseas Chinese in helping to maintain a connection to home. In some cases this connection was merely symbolic, as in the placement of traditional Chinese coins or food vessels in the grave with the deceased. In other cases the connection with home became very real, as with the removal and shipment of the bones back to China. Chinese death rituals helped keep the immigrants connected to the practices and beliefs of their homeland and reminded them of their familial obligations.

As evidenced by the segregated Euro-American and Chinese cemetery at Virginiatown, the Chinese immigrants continued to face racial discrimination even into death. Despite the hostility of their Euro-American neighbors, the Chinese miners practiced as closely as possible their traditional death rituals in this foreign land. Second, our findings revealed that the California Chinese were flexible and adaptive even in death. The adoption of Euro-American clothes, burial hardware, and personal goods suggests that the Chinese were able and willing to adjust somewhat to the practices of their neighbors. These individuals even adapted the foreign landscape for the purpose of making the deceased more comfortable according to the principles of *fengshui*. This is especially important if we are to recognize that no people, no matter how traditional, ever remain culturally static. The purpose of this study was not only to add to our knowledge of the historical past but also to help to humanize it. Too often, archaeological and historical studies become concerned with numbers or dates that, when inappropriately interpreted, only obscure our vision of the past. The present study has enabled us to more fully understand the mind-set of the California Chinese in both life and death. It is exactly this understanding that will help eliminate many of the misconceptions and biases that have haunted us in the past.

NOTES

1. Fred W. Mueller Jr., "Feng-Shui: Archaeological Evidence for Geomancy in Overseas Chinese Settlements," in *Wong Ho Leun, An American Chinatown*, vol. 2, *Archaeology* (San Diego: Great Basin Foundation, 1987), 1.

2. Melissa K. Farncomb, "Historical and Archaeological Investigations at Virginiatown: Features 2 and 4" (master's thesis, California State University, Sacramento, 1994), 49.

3. Leon Comber, *Chinese Ancestor Worship in Malaya* (Singapore: Donald Moore, 1957), 24; J. J. M. de Groot, *The Religious System of China*, vol. 3 (Leiden, Netherlands: E. J. Brill, 1897; reprint, Taiwan: Ch'eng Wen, 1969), 21–22; Maurice Freedman, *The Study of Chinese Society: Essays by Maurice Freedman*, ed. G. William Skinner (Stanford, CA: Stanford University Press, 1979), 196; Stuart E. Thompson, "Death, Food, and Fertility," in *Death Ritual in Late Imperial and Modern China*, ed. James L. Watson and Evelyn S. Rawski (Berkeley: University of California Press, 1988), 104.

4. *The Journals of Alfred Doten, 1849–1903*, vol. 2, ed. Walter Van Tilburg Clark (Reno: University of Nevada Press, 1973), 1484; Joseph A. McGowan, *History of the Sacramento Valley*, vol. 1 (New York: Lewis Historical Publishing, 1961), 330; Sylvia Sun Minnick, *Samfow: The San Joaquin Chinese Legacy* (Fresno, CA: Panorama West, 1988), 288; Ronald Riddle, *Flying Dragons, Flowing Streams: Music in the Life of San Francisco's Chinese* (Westport, CT: Greenwood, 1983), 121.

5. Minnick, *Samfow*, 288.

6. Laverne Mau Dicker, *The Chinese in San Francisco: A Pictorial History* (New York: Dover, 1979), 83.

7. Debi Hacker-Norton and Michael Trinkley, *Remember Man Thou Art Dust*, Research Series 2 (Columbia, SC: Chicora Foundation, 1984), 10.

8. Emily M. Ahern, *The Cult of the Dead in a Chinese Village* (Stanford, CA: Stanford University Press, 1973), 167; Charles Caldwell Dobie, *San Francisco's Chinatown* (New York: D. Appleton-Century, 1936), 66.

9. Sherri M. Gust, "Animal Bones from Historic Urban Chinese Sites: A Comparison of Sacramento, Woodland, Tucson, Ventura, and Lovelock," in *Hidden Heritage: Historical Archaeology of the Overseas Chinese*, ed. Priscilla Wegars (Amityville, NY: Baywood, 1993), 183.

10. Linda Sun Crowder, interview by author, October 23, 1998.

11. Comber, *Chinese Ancestor Worship*, 31.

12. Charles A. S. Williams, *Encyclopedia of Chinese Symbolism and Art Motives* (New York: Julian, 1960), 71.

13. Ahern, *Cult*, 167; *Journals of Alfred Doten*, 1484; Harry W. Lawton, "Selected Newspaper Accounts of Riverside's Chinese Settlers," in *Wong Ho Leun, An American Chinatown*, vol. 1, *History* (San Diego: Great Basin Foundation, 1987), 275; Thompson, "Death," 105.

14. Mary E. Phelps Dunn, "The Chinese in California," *Plumas Memories* 25 (June 4, 1967): 6, Plumas County Historical Society.

15. Paul Chace, "On Becoming American: Chinese Rites for Death and Ghost-Spirits in an Urban American City" (Escondido, CA: Paul G. Chace and Associates, 1998), 23; Roberta Greenwood, *Down by the Station: Los Angeles Chinatown, 1880–1933* (Los Angeles: Institute of Archaeology, University of California, Los Angeles, 1996), 21–22; Sandy Lydon, *Chinese Gold: The Chinese in the Monterey Bay Region* (Capitola, CA: Capitola Book, 1985), 268.

16. Edward L. Bell, "The Historical Archaeology of Mortuary Behavior: Coffin Hardware from Uxbridge, Massachusetts," *Historical Archaeology* 24, no. 3 (1990): 54–78.

    17. Hacker-Norton and Trinkley, *Remember*.

    18. Hacker-Norton and Trinkley, *Remember*.

    19. Jerome C. Rose, ed., *Gone to a Better Land: A Biohistory of a Rural Black Cemetery in the Post-Reconstruction South*, Arkansas Archeological Survey Research Series 25 (Fayetteville: Arkansas Archeological Survey, 1985).

    20. Greenwood, *Down*, 70; Ruth Ann Sando and David L. Felton, "Inventory Records of Ceramics and Opium from a Nineteenth Century Chinese Store in California," in *Hidden Heritage: Historical Archaeology of the Overseas Chinese*, ed. Priscilla Wegars (Amityville, NY: Baywood, 1993), 160.

4

Venerate These Bones: Chinese American Funerary and Burial Practices as Seen in Carlin, Elko County, Nevada

Sue Fawn Chung, Fred P. Frampton, and Timothy W. Murphy

In November 1996, while leveling the land for his new home, a resident of Carlin, Nevada, uncovered a coffin.[1] In compliance with the law, he notified the Elko County Sheriff's Office, and with the assistance of a sheriff's office detective, removed the deceased individual to the Burns Funeral Home in nearby Elko. They and others recognized the burial as Chinese because of the items that accompanied it, particularly a queue, a carved smoking pipe, and Chinese clothing. The landowner, Randy Meierhoff, believing the burial to be isolated, returned to his work, but quickly encountered four more coffins.

Upon hearing of this discovery from Dr. Eugene Hattori of the Nevada State Museum, USDA Forest Service archaeologist Fred Frampton offered his services. Since the burials were on private land, Frampton, Bureau of Land Management archaeologist Timothy Murphy, the Elko County Chapter of the Nevada Archaeological Association, and numerous others volunteered their personal time to work on the site, which encompassed not only Meierhoff's property but also that of his neighbor, Michael Tangreen. Mrs. Chin, co-owner of a Carlin Chinese restaurant, performed traditional graveside rituals, including the burning of incense and offering of food and liquor, in order to pacify the spirits of the long-forgotten departed.[2] Thus tradition was observed for the exhumation and eventual reburial in the Carlin public cemetery.

The Carlin Chinese Cemetery was located two blocks to the east of Carlin's primary public cemetery. The discovery of these graves, thirteen in all, presents several interesting questions to historians and archaeologists: how and why did the Chinese migrate to Nevada; who were the Chinese living in Carlin; how did they live and die; what kind of funerary practices might have existed among the Chinese in Nevada; and could individuals in this small cemetery be identified based on newspaper reports, obituaries, census information, coroner reports, and county death certificates? For centuries the Chinese have regarded funerals and burials as important rituals. The transition from traditional rituals to the inclusion of American practices among the Chinese in the American West demonstrated how strong traditional attitudes and beliefs were. In Carlin the graves also showed how and when traditions had to be modified. The excavation of this cemetery, and the subsequent study of the Chinese buried in the small railroad and mining community of Carlin, Elko County, provided a rare opportunity to understand something about the lives of these thirteen men and to observe and compare the physical properties of Chinese burial practices at this site with those elsewhere. It was also possible to examine the persistence of, and changes in, traditional Chinese funerary and burial practices in the American West.

PLACING CARLIN'S CHINESE CEMETERY INTO ITS HISTORICAL CONTEXT

Some historical background helps give context to the discovery of this site. In 1849 the Chinese learned about the discovery of gold in California, and thousands immigrated to the western United States. From the placer mines in California in the 1850s, they traveled eastward into Nevada in search of employment and new sources of wealth. According to the reminiscences of several older residents of Virginia City, "[The] Chinese worked where Gold Hill now is in 1853 and 1854 with long-toms and rockers."[3] The discovery of the famous Comstock Lode in 1859 brought more Chinese to western Nevada. While some searched for the elusive gold throughout Nevada, others found occupations in lumbering, the service industry, and the laundry and restaurant businesses.

The construction of the Central Pacific Railroad (CPRR) beginning in 1868 brought even more Chinese.[4] From an original crew of possibly ten to twelve thousand Chinese, approximately five thousand were employed by the railroad as tracks were laid across northern Nevada. An "advance team" of Chinese scouts discovered the natural irrigation and fertile land in "Chinese Gardens," later renamed Carlin, as the construction headed eastward toward Utah. Upon completion of the transcontinental railroad in May 1869 the majority of these five thousand workers were released. Many returned to California or worked on the construction of numerous other rail lines in neighboring states, but a considerable number remained in Nevada as railroad maintenance men and construction workers for intrastate lines.

Some Chinese railroad workers settled in Carlin because it was the CPRR's district terminus, with a roundhouse, machine and car shops, a freight depot, and, later, a refrigeration center along the transcontinental route. A few settled there because of its agricultural potential. CPRR executives decided that Carlin could serve as a connection point to the newly discovered riches of the mining communities of Tuscarora, Columbia, Mountain City, and Island Mountain in the northeast, as well as Elko and Salt Lake City to the east, and Winnemucca and Lovelock to the west. The latter three were primarily railroad towns. Shortly after 1900 the Western Pacific Railroad was completed, paralleling the CPRR (later, Southern Pacific Railroad) line through Carlin. By the late nineteenth century Carlin also became a major supplier of ice for refrigerating products being transported on the trains. In 1882, for example, C. Derby paid several thousand dollars in order to ship beef in the refrigerated cars to the western part of Nevada.[5] This practice continued through the early twentieth century.

The CPRR opened other opportunities. A few Chinese remembered the fertile soil and became "gardeners," or small land farmers. The railroad company had a policy of subsidizing restaurants along the line that would feed its workers twenty-four hours a day, and the Chinese took advantage of this opportunity, often getting fresh produce from Chinese gardeners.[6] Some Chinese went into laundry work, boardinghouse operations, housework, road construction, irrigation construction, farming, and wood chopping. The transcontinental route also opened new mining prospects. From the 1870s through the 1890s the nearby boomtowns of Tuscarora, Mountain City, and Island Mountain had sizable Chinese populations. The railroad was important in shipping supplies to the new mining towns and ores from the towns. Railroad work and mining required strenuous physical labor and accounted for some of the physical features of the deceased Chinese in Carlin.

Like many of the northern Nevada railroad communities, Carlin had a Chinatown along the railroad tracks. Chinese merchants provided goods and services to their own people and to the larger community. Chinatowns also had herbal medicines and traditional medical care, boardinghouses, religious centers, and recreational facilities, including opium-smoking dens.[7] Chain migration, the movement of people who were related or were from the same locality in China, was an integral part of frontier American life. Brothers, cousins, fellow villagers, and people from the same district banded together because of their unfamiliarity with the territory and the need for mutual aid and protection. Consequently, relatives dominated a Chinatown or merchandising businesses or a type of occupation in a given region.[8] In Carlin, for example, the Yee (Cantonese; Yu in pinyin) and Ng or Ung or Ong (Wu in pinyin), discussed below, dominated the merchandising businesses around the turn of the twentieth century. These merchant-community leaders, in cooperation with Chinese district associations (*huiguan*) and their funeral societies, probably assumed the responsibility for arranging funerals, burials, and, whenever required, exhumation of bodies and preparation for their transportation to San Francisco and China.[9] They hired the corpse handlers, gravediggers, and exhumation specialists, whose profession was specialized and regarded as lowly. They paid the exhumation fees to the county commissioners, as required by the Statutes of Nevada (1879).[10] Being outside of China, they fulfilled the role of the nuclear Chinese family; this was one of the most important changes from traditional Chinese practices.

Some of the Chinese in Nevada had no intention of returning to China alive or dead. Several historians have convincingly shown that the Chinese included immigrants who were not sojourners, but who spent the rest of their lives in their adopted homeland.[11] Some cemeteries in Nevada contain the remains of Chinese who had immigrated in the 1850s and 1860s. Two of the numerous examples are merchant and vegetable farmer Chung Kee (1847–1909), who was buried in Hawthorne, Nevada, and borax labor supervisor and cook Billy Min Chung Ford (1850–1922), who was buried in Tonopah, Nevada. Both of these men had families who remained in Nevada, and both were buried near kinsmen and friends. Chinese cemeteries or the Chinese section of cemeteries in Elko, Carlin, Winnemucca, Carson City, Virginia City, and Gold Creek have burials that were not exhumed and perhaps were never intended to be exhumed, suggesting a desire to remain in the United States. This was in sharp contrast to the traditional belief expressed in the popular Cantonese saying, "Falling leaves return to their roots (*luo ye gui gen*)."

The remains of some Chinese who died in Nevada were eventually shipped to either California, Utah, or China. Some Chinese deceased, such as all those in Tuscarora, the largest Chinese cemetery in Elko County, appear to have been exhumed and shipped out of state.[12] Some, such as a few in the Elko public cemetery, were exhumed and boxed in specially made, tightly sealed metal containers in order to "return to their roots." However, because of the political conditions in China, they never were shipped and remained in a wooden shed in the Chinese section of the cemetery.[13] What happened to these containers in the early twentieth century is unknown. The remains of other Chinese, upon death, were immediately shipped to San Francisco, Salt Lake City, or elsewhere for burial.[14] In all probability, those with wives and/or children living in China wanted their bones to be exhumed and shipped back to their families in China. Most of those not exhumed for reburial, as discussed below, were probably either unmarried, had relatives living in Nevada, or were too poor to participate in the family or district funerary fund that provided exhumation. Other explanations were that they died a violent death or chose to remain in Nevada. With the passage of time, especially after 1940, fewer and fewer bodies were returned to China. In recent years some ancestors have been returned to be reburied for a third time in the United States so that families can care for their spirits without going to China (see chapter 8).

Time, neglect, natural disasters, vandalism, construction needs, and other forces have eradicated and/or obscured many Chinese cemeteries throughout Nevada. For example, 1977 photographs of the Chinese cemetery in Lovelock taken by archaeologist Mary Rusco show an aging cemetery of wooden fences and wooden markers.[15] Fifteen years later, when a group of scholars visited the site, nothing but weather-beaten wood scattered on the ground could be seen.[16] Other Chinese cemeteries in Nevada are now under a high school, public park, road, medical building, or private homes, or have been relocated in a haphazard manner.

CHINESE AMERICAN FUNERARY PRACTICES IN NEVADA

Funerary rituals were very important, and this importance did not diminish for the Chinese who went abroad. In the United States the customs basically followed traditional practices with several major modifications. First, countrymen—often distant relatives or people from the same district—replaced the immediate family members as the main figures in the funerary process. They arranged for the cemetery plot, funeral services, and funeral procession. With the help of the local village leader, the last ritual before the actual burial was the reading of the sacrificial essay that told the deceased what was being offered to him and which was among the documents buried with him.[17] The personal touches that would have been provided by the immediate family members were missing in the American West.

The most active organizations concerned with funerary rituals were the family and district associations (*huiguan*), which often fell under the umbrella of the Chinese Consolidated Benevolent Association (Zhonghua *huiguan*, better known as the Chinese Six Companies) and the anti-Manchu political Zhigongtang (Chinese Freemasons, often called the Chee Kung Tong, a secret fraternal order connected to the Heaven and Earth Society [Tiandihui] and Hung Society [Hongmen] in South China). In rural America, and especially Nevada, the Zhigongtang was the most powerful and influential. The leaders of the organization often were merchants, physicians, or prominent laundrymen who acted as intermediaries between the Chinese and Euro-American communities. Therefore, when they died, they had elaborate funerals that often were reported in the local newspapers—usually inaccurately. This would not have been the case in Qing China, where Zhigongtang leaders were regarded as bandits. Claiming to be part of the international Freemasons, they attained power in local Caucasian communities. This added to their prestige in the Chinese American communities as well, and was another change from Chinese tradition.

Larger Chinese American communities always had a literate man who was knowledgeable about the traditional funerary rituals and who gave advice on the funeral and burial process. Urban centers like San Francisco and Los Angeles had Chinese priests who might travel to rural Chinatowns for important funerals. In the United States, because of local and state laws in the late nineteenth century, Euro-American morticians handled the deceased. Lowly corpse handlers performed this task in China. Finally, another new practice arose because the 1892 renewal of the 1882 Chinese Exclusion Act included Chinese religious persons in the excluded category with laborers. Consequently Chinese Americans turned to American clergymen to perform services, as evident in several cases found in the Elko County Recorder's Office records in the early twentieth century. Since many of the death certificates were not completely filled out, it is impossible to determine how many Chinese employed the services of American ministers.

The scarcity of qualified Chinese burial personnel may have accounted for the fact that the Chinese cemetery in Carlin did not adhere strictly to *fengshui* (geomancy) principles in regard to positioning the head of the corpse to the north and feet to the south. Another possibility was that the relatives of the deceased agreed with critics of geomancy, as expressed by the scholar-official Lu Cai (d. A.D. 655) and later writers, who believed that "ignorant people all believe the geomancy books."[18]

Unlike in some parts of China, where burials might occur weeks after death, in the United States the deceased were buried shortly after death. In Elko County, of the thirty-five Chinese individuals whose death and burial dates were recorded after 1899, nineteen (54 percent) were buried one day after death, while eleven (31 percent) were buried within two days.[19] One was buried on the third day and one on the fourth day. Only three individuals were sent out of state to California or China for burial. Therefore, among the local Chinese burials, 94 percent were buried within two days.

The deceased probably lay in state at home, in an association headquarters (often called a "joss house"),[20] in a Chinese store, or in an American funeral parlor for a few hours; the amount of time varied only with local conditions, the weather, and different situations related by friends and family. By the 1880s the Euro-American undertaker was often replacing the Chinese specialist in preparing the corpse for burial. The deceased was dressed in his best or favorite clothing. In Carlin, at least five of the thirteen had American clothing of some type, such as belts, Levi's pants, and cuff links. A temporary ancestral tablet (about a foot tall, made of paper, and identifying the deceased and the date of death in Chinese) might have been established to facilitate prayers and offerings for the soul of the deceased.[21] Guests visited the deceased and presented gifts of incense, spirit money, and messages written on white paper. Gifts of funerary money in white envelopes were not given to help the family pay for the funerary expenses, as was done in China. Instead, the deceased and his fellow countrymen (*tongxiang*), often through dues to the family or district association, paid the funeral expenses.

Many of the rituals were traditional. Although there were no records of this for Carlin, Chinese in other towns in Nevada followed these rituals. At the head of the coffin there was an altar decorated with flowers and metal incense burners, and at the foot of the coffin there was a low table with food and drink offerings. Visitors bowed three times as a sign of respect for the deceased. In the case of prominent individuals, other ancient traditions were followed. For example, the deceased was wrapped in four blankets or thin cloths, which represented the four seasons and which his spirit could use in the afterworld. In Carlin one coffin was lined with cloth that might have symbolized the four seasons. Traditionally the face was covered with a cloth. In two coffins in Carlin well-preserved silk scarves over the face were found. Usually the head rested on a pillow of straw, porcelain, or wood, but this was not evident in Carlin. More commonly, a testimonial banner was folded on top of the body inside the coffin, but none of the deceased in Carlin had this.[22] A banner should have been placed in the coffins of wealthy or prominent merchants.

In China the eldest son led the procession of mourners, but in the United States, few men had elder sons living with or near them, so close friends or relatives usually assumed the role. Mourners followed the coffin to the cemetery, often making a brief stop at the deceased's place of employment, home, or favorite site. They scattered mock paper money or small circular papers in the shape of Chinese coins in order to bribe the evil spirits not to harm the deceased.[23] Papers with holes were tossed along the processional route because the Chinese believed that evil spirits moved only in straight lines and would be confused by the holes. Often clan, district, or fraternal organizations provided the Chinese musicians for the funeral procession. Tradition dictated that music and firecrackers were needed to frighten the evil spirits so that they would not follow the entourage. Women, dressed in white, the color of mourning, wept loudly as prescribed by the official rituals. In China the women would have been relatives, but in the United States, many of them were professional mourners hired for the occasion. Banners, flags, paper lanterns with the person's status in the community written on them, and a photograph or drawing of the deceased also might be a part of the entourage.

Wagons carried the symbolic foods, incense, paper offerings, flowers, and some of the personal belongings of the deceased to the cemetery. Chicken and pork were considered ritual meats and usually were included in the food offerings. These were placed on an altar. Although Carlin's cemetery had no indication of an altar, the Chinese cemetery in nearby Tuscarora had a large wooden altar.[24] Sometimes the burning of the belongings and paper offerings took place in a finely built brick oven with or without a steel door, while at other times there was just a large depression in the ground.[25] Unfortunately the ground of the Carlin cemetery had been bladed over, and no depression could be discerned.

Most grave markers were made from a wooden board or, in the case of permanent burials, marble or stone. Chinese characters, written in an oil-based Chinese black ink or engraved by a wood or stone carver, gave the place (district and village) and perhaps date of birth on the right, formal and/or familiar name in large characters in the center, and date and time of death on the left. Usually if the deceased was to be shipped back to China, an identification brick or a bottle with the same information was buried with the corpse.

After the funeral, the mourners received gifts of candy or cubes of Chinese brown sugar and money or a small pouch of gold dust to buy some small token in remembrance of the deceased to offset the bitterness of the occasion.[26] With the promise of such customary gifts at Chinese funerals, many Euro-Americans made it a point to participate in Chinese funeral processions. Occasionally a newspaper reporter detailed the funeral. After the graveside ceremony, the family, relatives, or the association gave a dinner to thank participants for their kindness and to close the public mourning.

Because of the absence of nuclear family members, extended family members or friends performed the postburial rituals dictated by tradition. One—called "thanking the earth"—involved scattering grains, small nails, and coins. Others included grave visitations every seventh day for forty-nine days to give offerings of food and drink, the cleaning of the graves and lighting of incense and candles at the graves during the Qingming (Pure Brightness) festival in the third lunar month, and the feeding of the dead during the Yulanpen (Hungry Ghosts) festival, held on the fourteenth or fifteenth day of the seventh lunar month, when mock paper money and clothing were burned for the use of the deceased.[27] In the United States, friends and relatives who worked long hours probably had little or no free time to strictly observe the customs.

More American aspects were added to the rituals as the decades passed. By 1916 Christian ministers were burying the Chinese members of their congregations. In Reno, Washoe County, Nevada, Go Bin, who died in December 1916, is believed to have been the first in the state buried in this manner.[28] Another example of the merging of Eastern and Western funeral traditions, taken from an Elko County coroner's inquest, was seen in the case of How Yi Get.[29] In July 1921, How Yi Get, a cook at Spanish Ranch, fell off the chuck wagon, which then ran over his chest, crushing him to death.[30] Reverend Mitchell officiated at his service. Afterward the Chinese conducted their customary ceremonies, which included placing candles and a roasted chicken by the grave and offering crackers to the assembled mourners. When Louie Pole, a popular old Chinese resident of nearby Winnemucca, died in February 1924, Reverend Fred M. Clay, pastor of the Baptist church, officiated and paid tribute to the deceased both at the Butler Funeral Parlor and at the graveside in the Chinese cemetery. Once he had completed his duties, the Chinese performed their burial rites, which included a display of flags, the burning of incense and paper images, incantations, and the placement of a roasted chicken, rice, sweetmeats, and drink beside the grave.[31] These modifications to the traditional Chinese burial practices indicate increasing adaptation and acculturation in one of the most important rituals for the Chinese.

RESEARCHING CARLIN'S CHINESE RESIDENTS

Even after extensive research, little is known about the Chinese residents of Carlin. Frontier newspapers often distorted reports on the Chinese, so even these cannot be regarded as reliable sources of information. Most news pertaining to Carlin came from nonlocal sources. The three attempts at starting a local paper, all in the early twentieth century, failed after short runs. One of the three extant local early twentieth-century newspapers, the *Carlin Commonwealth*, dates from 1910 to 1914, and carried only one advertisement and two articles pertaining to Carlin's Chinese residents.[32]

For the most part Carlin residents relied on the newspapers from nearby Elko, Nevada, for news. The Elko newspapers published sporadic stories about the Chinese in Carlin and generally carried the only local news about Carlin. The closeness between the Chinese in Carlin and Elko was exemplified in a February 25, 1907, story in the *Elko Daily Independent*, which reported that the Chinese from Carlin traveled to Elko in order to celebrate Chinese New Year's in style.[33]

Some stories were exaggerated or sensationalized and demonstrated the general community's fascination with *tong* wars. For example, the *Daily Elko Independent* of March 26, 1870, bemoaned the existence of two rival Chinese associations and their *tong* (*tang*, associations) wars.[34] In one of its rare stories about the Chinese in Carlin, the *Winnemucca (NV) Daily Silver State*, June 8, 1878, reported that the train conductor had found the remains of two Chinese near Carlin who probably had been murdered by a rival *tong* over the owner-ship of a Chinese prostitute.[35] The *Weekly Elko Independent*, June 16, 1878, re-ported that the two bodies were tied together by their queues and were dis-covered in the river three miles from Carlin. Local Euro-American officials attributed their murder to tramps. The anti-Chinese editor commented that this was a way the tramps had helped to solve the Chinese problem.[36]

Most Nevada newspaper reports regarding the deaths of Chinese never mentioned their names or identified them unless there was something unusual about the individual or he had been well known to the larger Euro-American community. One of the earliest identified deaths was that of Cheong Kee, who, while traveling by train from Chicago to San Francisco in 1877, died of tuberculosis between Carlin and Winnemucca.[37] The reporter noted that Cheong Kee did not have a queue and mistakenly interpreted this to mean that he had renounced idolatry. What it really meant was that he supported the anti-Manchu movement and had no intention of returning to China, where any male caught without the mandatory Manchu hairstyle was subject to im-mediate execution.

The newspapers reported a few other deaths of Chinese men. On May 8, 1905, the *Weekly Elko Independent* and the *Elko Daily Independent* carried the story of Gow Hong, who shot himself in the abdomen in Carlin and was taken to Elko's Chinatown for surgery and recovery. Gow Hong had spent the day in Carlin and was en route from Lovelock, Nevada, to Ogden, Utah, by train.[38] Gow Hong was a transient, like many of the Chinese who passed through Carlin. He eventually died from his wound, but the newspaper did not report what became of his body, and there was no death certificate or coroner's report on him.

Occasionally the Chinese in Carlin made statewide news. On August 1, 1930, the *Winnemucca (NV) Humboldt Star* and the *Reno Nevada State Jour-nal* both carried a story about Carlin's *tong* war.[39] According to the accounts, the ownership of the Overland Café in Carlin was under dispute. The three partners in the restaurant, Henry Leong, Ng Wim, and Ng Win (the latter was in China at the time) agreed to sell their shares to Leo Lim for $485. Lim gave the money to his sixty-year-old father, Leo Chang (also known as Lee She-ung), a cook at the Overland Cafe, who in turn gave it to Ng Wim. Ng Wim lost the money gambling then refused to give up his share in the business. Members of the Hip Sing Tong (a secret brotherhood) of Reno went to Elko to search for the American-born Henry Leong, who hid in the Elko "joss house," while Leo Lim, a member of a different *tong* (*tang*, association), went to Ogden to consult with his *tong* leaders. In the end San Francisco–born Leo Chang committed suicide in an effort to end the impending *tong* war and pro-tect his son's honor. He was buried in Salt Lake City, Utah, on August 5,

1930.[40] He was not buried in Nevada probably because the Chinese cemeteries in eastern Nevada (Elko and Carlin, for example) had fallen into disrepair by 1930.

Local presses seldom included obituaries of the Chinese residents. When the wealthy and longtime Carlin Chinese merchant Sing Lee died of influenza and was buried in Carlin on November 10, 1918,[41] wartime news and influenza-caused deaths of Euro-Americans filled the pages of the newspaper, leaving no room for his insignificant obituary.

The newspaper reports presented above are typical of the limited knowledge available regarding the Chinese residents of the area. Therefore, information about the Carlin Chinese must be obtained from other sources, most notably memoirs, census data, Sanborn fire insurance maps, and government documents.

When China's first minister to the United States, Chen Lanbin, was en route to Washington, DC, in 1878, he passed through Carlin and observed three hundred or more Chinese in the town, including wives and families.[42] The census records do not show this figure, but undoubtedly many of the Chinese had come from neighboring mining communities to catch a glimpse of this high-ranking Chinese official and his entourage.

Census records of the Chinese were notoriously inaccurate; in China many villagers avoided being counted, since various taxes were based on the census. In the United States, census enumerators were paid two to four cents per name in cities and three to six dollars per day in the rural areas.[43] However, they probably found Chinese names too difficult to collect and may only have asked a Chinese community leader to enumerate the residents. Finally, the Chinese believed in avoiding any American government officials who might be collecting the four-dollar statewide poll tax or other such taxes levied on them.[44] These three factors contributed to the undercounting of the Chinese (see table 4.1).

The 1870 U.S. census manuscript listed forty-nine Chinese in Carlin, six of whom were women (occupations unknown).[45] The forty-three men included fourteen railroad workers, eight cooks, two merchants (Sing Car, age thirty, and Loy Joy, age forty), seven laundrymen, eight laborers, and four miners.[46] The census taker often gave the Chinese familiar nomenclature "Ah" as the first name and illogical names for some of the others, so it was impossible to determine the family names of the Carlin Chinese residents to show "chain migration," or the immigration of relatives from China to Carlin, in this early census.

A decade later the number had dropped to forty-six Chinese, including two railroad workers, thirty-six laborers, two clerks, two servants, two laundrymen, one boardinghouse operator, and one prostitute, but no merchants.[47]

Table 4.1.   **Population of Chinese in the United States and Nevada, 1860–1920**

Year	Total population in Nevada	Total Chinese population in U.S.	Chinese population in Nevada	Percent of Chinese in Nevada	Chinese males in Nevada	Chinese females in Nevada	Ratio of Chinese males to females
1860	6,057	34,933	23	0.3	—	—	—
1870	42,491	63,199	3,162	7.4	2,817	306	1 : 9
1880	62,266	105,465	5,416	8.7	5,102	314	1 : 16
1890	47,355	107,488	2,833	6.0	2,749	84	1 : 33
1900	42,335	89,863	1,352	3.2	1,283	69	1 : 19
1910	81,875	71,531	927	1.1	876	51	1 : 17
1920	77,407	61,639	689	0.9	630	59	1 : 11

Source: United States Bureau of the Census, 1860–1920, Characteristics of the Population (title varies).

However, when the Bureau of Immigration surveyed Chinese businesses in major centers in the 1890s, the partnership records of Quong Wing and Company and Sing Lee and Company were filed, and both indicate that they had been in existence for at least a decade.[48] The 1890 census manuscript was lost in a fire.

In comparison, by 1900 the Chinese population had dropped to thirteen: five cooks, four laborers, two laundrymen, one merchant, and one woman, the wife of a cook. In 1910 Carlin's Chinese population rose to twenty-six, because of the increased opportunities created by the newly constructed Western Pacific Railroad. This number included eight railroad workers for the Western Pacific; five for the Southern Pacific (successor to the CPRR); five cooks, including a woman whose husband worked as a railroad sweeper; four merchants; two laundrymen; one servant; and one laborer. In 1920 the number of Carlin Chinese dropped to twenty-two. There were twelve cooks, several of whom worked for the railroad; eight railroad workers; one waiter; and one laundryman.[49] Consequently, railroad employment was a major factor in the lives of the Chinese in Carlin through the early twentieth century.

These figures do not take into account individuals who lived in two places or who moved around. Wing Tang (c. 1860–1941) is one of several examples of a man who lived in Carlin and then settled in Reno.[50] Since he had been an important intermediary between the Chinese and Euro-American community in Reno, one can assume that he played the same role during his stay in Elko County.

Whether through Chinese custom or because of anti-Chinese United States laws, most wives of Carlin Chinese men remained in China. In 1880 nine of the forty-five Chinese men identified by the census were married but living separately from their wives. In 1900 one couple lived in the Chinese community of five married men and six single men. In 1910 six of the twenty-six men were married, and in 1920 one couple lived among fifteen married men, four single men, and one widower. According to prevailing beliefs, married men were more stable workers, so by 1920 the Chinese community had probably taken on a less transient character.

In Carlin in the 1880s some Chinese lived interspersed in the community, while others lived clustered together in Chinatown. Based on a January 1885 Sanborn fire insurance map, Chinatown was located near the railroad tracks, bordered by Eighth, Main, and Camp streets. Only a vacant lot on Main Street separated Chinatown from the noise of the train tracks. Undoubtedly the land and buildings occupied by the Chinese were leased from the CPRR, which was typical of CPRR railroad towns along the line.[51] Carlin's Chinatown consisted of eight wooden frame buildings that were typical of housing structures at that time. According to the 1910 Sanborn map of Carlin, Chinese Alley, as the site became known, had seven buildings occupied by twenty-two Chinese males.[52] Two of these buildings were boardinghouses, one with five men and the other with eight men. Living near the railroad station allowed the men to travel to and from California with relative ease.

In the late nineteenth century the Chinese provided the Euro-American community with much-needed services such as laundry and cooking. One laundry company was prosperous enough to establish a more substantial building of brick or adobe on Main Street, directly across from the CPRR freight depot and next to a cigar factory. The cigar factory may have employed Chinese labor, since the Chinese dominated the cigar manufacturing industry in San Francisco at the time. Yee Wah (b. 1858, immigrated 1881), who spoke English, and his partner, Yee Jung (b. 1855, immigrated 1881), probably owned the laundry.[53] The laundry may have been started by a relative, who in the 1880 census manuscript was listed as Wan See (b. 1857), one of two Chinese laundrymen in Carlin who lived with three other Chinese men, including a servant. In some rural communities the Chinese laundryman spoke English, served as the intermediary between the Chinese and Euro-American communities, and was also a leader of the Chinese community. In Carlin two mercantile families might have been more prosperous and would therefore have held the leadership position in the Chinese community there.

Merchants formed the most important group in most Chinese communities in the American West. Because they usually were literate to varying degrees, spoke English and Chinese, and provided goods to the general community, they were well suited to serve as the intermediaries between the Chinese and Euro-American populations. After the 1882 Chinese Exclusion Act, merchants were among the few classes of Chinese able to travel to China and back. They also had the privilege of bringing their wives and children to the United States if they so desired and could afford to do so.

Typically, in the late nineteenth century through the early twentieth century, the principals and shareholders in a Chinese business were relatives or were from the same district. They created a chain migration pattern as original settlers sent for relatives and neighbors to assist them in the continuation of businesses in specific areas. They often used a rotating credit system in order to finance their businesses.[54] They catered to local residents and often were links in a chain of merchandising firms located in towns throughout the West owned by relations or friends. Their stores served as social and recreational centers, especially if the community did not have a formal one, such as a "joss house" or association building. Because of Chinese merchants' privileged ability to travel to and from the United States, the Immigration and Naturalization Service, with the help of the Treasury Department, kept records, usually partnership lists, on them. These records gave the most revealing information about the Chinese in Carlin.

THE CEMETERY AND DECEASED

There is no record of Chinese ownership or a Chinese lease of the federal land on which the cemetery was located. Archaeological evidence suggests that the cemetery was in use from before 1900 through 1924, and from the little evidence available, it may have been under the Ning Yuen *huiguan*'s affiliate organization concerned with burials. According to records located at the Bureau of Land Management and the Elko County Courthouse, John W. Puett, a farmer, homesteaded the Carlin cemetery site, an eighty-acre parcel of land, on October 25, 1920, and recorded it on July 21, 1923, in accordance with the Homestead Act.[55] He apparently allowed its continued use as a Chinese cemetery in 1923, because the last burial was in 1924.

The graves formed a single line that was oriented roughly northwest-southeast on a low sloping ridge that overlooked Maggie Creek near the edge of the Humboldt River (see fig. 4.1). Chinese *fengshui* favored a location facing a body of water with great natural beauty, in this case the creek, in the front and distant mountains in the back. Based on evidence from the grave goods, the earliest graves were at the southeast end of the alignment and the most recent at the northwest end. American coins in Burials 1, 2, 4, and 5 date these to no earlier than the late 1890s.[56] The Burials were excavated from southeast to northwest and were numbered consecutively beginning with 2. The original location of Burial 1 is unknown, as the ground surface was bladed after the Elko County Sheriff's Department removed the burial.

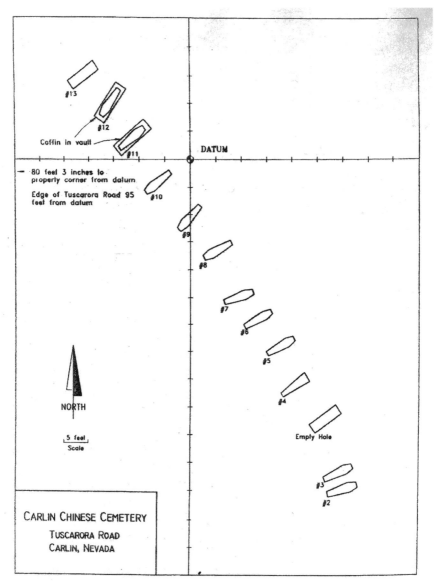

Figure 4.1. Map of Carlin's Chinese Cemetery. By Donna Murphy. The exact location of coffin 1 was unknown. The cemetery was located near the town of Carlin, which was founded in 1869 as an important station for the Central Pacific Railroad.

Each grave contained the remains of a single Chinese male interred in a wooden coffin. While the burials shared some attributes, there were also differences. The graves were excavated into partially cemented terrace deposits. In most cases the original depth of burial could not be determined because of the land leveling. Many appeared to have been quite shallow, consistent with Chinese burial practices. The deepest ones, located at the northwest end of the cemetery, were up to four feet deep.

With one exception, the coffins were of good quality. Ten were almost identical mass-produced, pinch-toe-type coffins made of redwood. The primary differences among them were the length of the coffin and the type of hardware used. These coffins were narrow at the head and feet and wide at the shoulders. The fit was snug, even for these individuals, who were relatively small. Each side of the coffins was made of a single piece of curved lumber. The bases and lids were made of two or three pieces of lumber that were probably glued together. Exposed edges were rounded. The bases, ends, and sides were attached to one another with nails. Several coffins had the size stamped on them, either 5.9 feet or 6.0 feet.

Three coffins differed from the generalized description above. Two (Burials 11 and 12) were of fine quality, probably having been professionally constructed. One was rectangular and made from redwood. Both the sides and ends sloped outward. The other, also made of redwood, was a quadrilateral coffin that was narrow at the feet and wide at the head. The third coffin (Burial 3) was a crude box made of rough, probably reused, lumber; it was the only coffin without any hardware. The poor quality of this coffin suggests that the deceased was a person lacking financial means.

Twelve coffins bore hardware such as handles, brass decorations, and lid locks. Each coffin had a different style or type of hardware, suggesting that the hardware was customized for each individual purchaser or was reflective of market availability. Coffin handles associated with Burials 1 and 2, 5 through 10, and 13 were nickel or chrome plated. All were decorated, with patterns that included oak leaves and acorns, interlocking feathers, and scrolls. Makers' marks and pattern numbers, found on most of the handles, indicate the use of Euro-American coffin makers and possibly undertakers.

The most elegant coffins were in graves 11 and 12. Carved, black lacquered, wooden handles were found on the coffins. Both coffins were placed within wooden vaults. The vaults were rectangular redwood boxes that were larger than the coffins. The coffin lid of Burial 11 had a nickel-plated plaque with the inscription, "AT REST." This lid also had red pigment on the surface, possibly the remains of a piece of red cloth that covered the coffin. Both Burials 11 and 12 had identification bricks, described later.

SKELETAL ANALYSIS

In 1997 a team of physical anthropologists headed by Douglas Owsley from the Smithsonian Institution in Washington, DC, performed an osteological analysis of the skeletons, the first such data ever collected on Chinese Americans of the turn of the twentieth century.[57] The deceased ranged in age from the early twenties to the mid-sixties. Burials 2 and 9 were between twenty and thirty years of age at the time of death. Burials 3, 5, 7, 8, and 10 were of men between thirty and forty-nine years of age. Burial 1 was between forty-five and fifty-nine years old. Burials 4, 6, 11, 12, and 13 were between fifty and sixty-five years old.

Burial 2 was a mummified man between the ages of twenty and thirty,[58] with brown hair that probably had been bleached by the sun or by postmortem changes in the coffin. Good preservation of the coffin as well as ground conditions naturally mummified the body. The corpse had a high mercury content, suggesting that he was a placer miner (with sun-bleached hair) or an individual trying to cure himself of a venereal disease (mercury was a common remedy for the problem at this time). He had a shoulder fracture. Several other skeletons had partially mummified parts, such as fingers and toes, but only Burial 2 was completely mummified.

The bodies in all intact burials were found in a supine position. All had their legs fully extended, with the exception of Burial 3, who had one leg and one arm flexed. Most had arms extended along the side of the torso, with the exception of Burial 9, who had one arm across the chest and the other arm flexed upward, and Burials 6, 8, and 11, who had their hands crossed on the pelvis.

Burial 8 had some desiccated tissue, and his facial features indicated that he may have been of mixed ancestry. He was between thirty and thirty-nine years old, and had trauma to his body and pelvis, indicating a violent death. Burial 10 also had suffered a violent death. There was no evidence of burial goods provided for these two men.

Burial 12 had been badly vandalized, and its arrangement could not be determined. Seven of the deceased had their heads oriented to the northeast, and four or possibly five (Burial 12) were oriented to the southwest. Burials 2 through 7 and 11 were oriented to the northeast, seemingly in accordance with *fengshui*, while Burials 8 through 10 and 13 had their heads oriented to the southwest. Burial 12 appeared to be oriented to the southwest, but the degree of vandalism prohibited positive identification of orientation. The variations of head-feet orientation probably were due to whether a Chinese who knew *fengshui* directed the burial or the American mortician laid the deceased to rest. The later burials were located in the northwestern end of the cemetery.

While all of the individuals had suffered from some disease and/or trauma during their lives, the skeletal evidence of all but burials 8 and 10 suggests that these problems were not out of the ordinary. Healed antemortem trauma and disease were identified in nine burials. All thirteen had suffered fractured bones,[59] one had a lesion on a rib, and two had periostitis, or inflammation of the connective tissues of the bones. One of the latter also apparently had torn a ligament during his lifetime. Nine individuals had varying degrees of arthritis, from minor to severe.

An analysis of the degree of development in muscle attachment sites and the location and degree of arthritic development provided insight into the work history of the individuals. Burials 2, 3, 10, and 13 showed evidence of strenuous labor. Burial 9 also was involved in strenuous labor, but it affected only his upper body. Evidence for moderately strenuous activity was found in Burials 1, 4, and 5. Burial 6 had slight to moderate muscle attachment development. Burial 8 had moderate muscle development only in his arms. Burials 7, 11, and 12 showed no evidence of habitual strenuous labor. None of the skeletons showed characteristics of frequent horseback riding, despite the fact that some Chinese in the region were cowboys by occupation.

Trauma was identified in Burials 2, 4, 5, 6, 8, 9, 13 (all had healed). Two, Burials 8 and 10, suffered violent deaths. Burial 8's clavicle, sternum, and several ribs were broken, perhaps from a severe beating (these injuries are consistent with blows from hitting, kicking, and stomping) or a work-related accident (involving moving machinery or a moving train). His head, arms, and legs showed no trauma. Burial 10 had facial and rib fractures and appeared to have died from blows to the head and chest region, consistent with a beating. Violence in frontier America around the turn of the century, especially against Chinese, was not uncommon. Violence also occurred among the Chinese.

Dental analysis could be performed on eleven of the skeletons. Although most suffered from poor dental hygiene and dental care, their dental health appeared to be partially attributable to age. The youngest individual, Burial 2, had no dental problems. All those over forty-five had experienced some tooth loss. Those in early middle age were most variable. Two between the ages of thirty and forty-five had healthy teeth with the exception of calculus deposits and, in the case of Burial 8, the loss of a single molar. Others of similar age had suffered serious dental disease. Many individuals had decayed or missing teeth. Of the eleven burials, seven showed extensive tooth loss and/or active caries, abscesses, and periodontal disease. Burial 10 had a cavity in the second molar packed with a hard substance that may have been a filling, indicating some dental care. Burial 12 had complete antemortem tooth loss, and a full set of dentures was found in the coffin. Hypoplastic lines on the teeth of three individuals indicate that they had suffered a period of nutritional or health problems early in life. Eight were heavy smokers, as evidenced by the black stains on their teeth, and some of these may have smoked opium. To date the analysis on tooth residue from tobacco and opium smoking has not been completed.

HAIRSTYLES AND CLOTHING

Hairstyles provided an avenue for estimating burial dates. The hair of the individual in Burial 2 was braided into a queue that was thirty centimeters long. Black woven cordage was braided into his queue to extend it by another sixty-five centimeters. The hair of the individuals in Burials 1, 5, 6, and 7 was short, but a false queue of braided woven cordage was placed beneath, or perhaps attached to, the head of each.

The presence of the queues suggests that the southeastern seven graves dated prior to the 1911 revolution in China. The foreign Manchu rulers of China had imposed the queue as the required hairstyle for Chinese men in 1644. In China, those who did not have a queue were subject to immediate death. With the start of China's anti-Manchu uprising, the revolutionaries and their supporters cut their hair as an act of defiance. In America, those who supported the revolution or who had no intention of returning to China adopted American hairstyles. After the 1911 overthrow of the Manchu government, almost all of the young Chinese American men, and most of the older generation, made the transition to a Western hairstyle.

The clothing also suggests a transition to American styles. Based on a study of photographs of Chinese men in Nevada in the late nineteenth to early twentieth century, some of the Chinese men wore American-made baggy canvas overalls and black quilted Chinese jackets. Others wore Chinese- or Western-style pants, and Western-style shirts with metal buttons or Chinese-style cotton tops or jackets with small, brass-like, round Chinese buttons. Some wore Western hats, while others wore bamboo hats. Many preferred American boots for the rugged terrain, while some purchased thick-soled, cotton, Chinese boots. Some of the men probably knew how to sew their simple Chinese-style clothing, while others purchased imported wear in Chinese stores. In the more isolated Nevada communities, like Carlin, with few Chinese stores, it was more practical and convenient to buy ready-made American clothing for everyday wear.

Although textile analysis and artifact accessioning has not been fully completed for the thirteen burials,[60] it appears that Burials 1 through 7 contained a higher percentage of Chinese-style attire than Burials 8 through 13. These earlier seven graves all contained Chinese round metal buttons on upper-torso apparel, as well as a dominance of Chinese traditional shoes, of which only the soles and trim remained. Accustomed to soft Chinese shoes, most of these men probably preferred to be buried in them rather than in American boots, if indeed they specified a choice to their close friends or family members.

Burial 1 contained several round metal buttons as well as eighteen non-Chinese metal buttons, three of which appear similar to those on Levi's pants. There was no indication of what kind of shirt he wore. Burial 2 (mummy) wore Levi's, Western woolen socks, a light American-made shirt, and a brown wool cloak or cape that was fastened with Chinese round metal buttons. His shoes were Chinese style. Burial 3 wore traditional Chinese shoes, and two Chinese brass-like buttons were found in the coffin, indicating traditional dress. Burials 4 and 5 also probably wore traditional clothing. Only Chinese metal buttons were found, and Burial 5 had Chinese shoes. Burial 6, in addition to several Chinese ball buttons, contained ten non-Chinese metal buttons, one rivet (from Levi's pants?), and a leather belt with a metal buckle. Burial 7 wore the traditional black Chinese jacket. Burial 8 had the remnants of a metal buckle and ferrous metal buttons. Burial 9 wore a brown coat with a black lining, brown American pants, suspenders, Euro-American cuff links, and an American-made watch. This was also the only individual who wore American heavy leather boots, possibly indicating that he had adopted American-style clothing as his favorite dress. Burial 10 had a single Chinese round metal button associated with it. Burial 11 contained shell buttons as well as the remnants of Chinese cloth shoes. Burial 12 had brass snaps, metal buttons, and a leather strap (a belt?), suggesting American clothing. Table 4.2 summarizes the data from the Carlin burials.

GRAVE GOODS

Grave goods were more abundant in the first seven graves. The Chinese believed in burying items with the dead for use in the afterworld. These ranged from necessities like eyeglasses and dentures to favorite, often inexpensive, objects. Burial 1 contained various seeds and pods, including gingko and lichee seeds, indicating the favorite foods of the deceased; one dime and three nickels (corrosion prevented determination of dates); and a dragon-carved, wooden pipe with a long bamboo stem for smoking tobacco. A bundle of twenty-eight matches was included, probably to be used in the afterworld for lighting his pipe and/or cooking. Burial 2 held a corroded brass Chinese coin as well as peanut shells, a knife, a spoon, matches, burned incense sticks, and a leather thong. A 30-caliber bullet cartridge casing, wooden matches, and a

Table 4.2. Summary of Burial Data

No.	Age	Cause of death	Notes	Hair/racial type	Clothing/other grave contents	Dental	Burial direction
#1	45–59		Excavated by Elko County Sheriff	Short hair; false queue	Possible Western wear		Unknown
#2	20–30		Naturally mummified	Brown hair; queue with false extension	Western clothing; Levi's, wool socks, brown sweater		NE
#3	35–45		Muscular; suggests strenuous work. Leg and arm flexed. Maggot pupa cases near head	No hair	Chinese shoes not only on feet, but placed near feet; crude coffin	Dark black stains, suggesting smoker	NE
#4	50–59		Probably no heavy labor; arthritis; leg fractured; skull smashed postmortem			Dark black stains, suggesting smoker	NE
#5	35–44		Left handed; arthritis; healed fractures	Short hair; false queue	Chinese black silk	Poor teeth	NE
#6	32–36		Skeletal development anomalies	Black hair; short, false queue	Chinese vest or shirt that might be silk	Poor teeth	NE
#7	40–49		Probably no heavy labor	Short hair; false queue	Western garments	Habitual smoker	NE

(continued)

Table 4.2. (continued)

No.	Age	Cause of death	Notes	Hair/racial type	Clothing/other grave contents	Dental	Burial direction
#8	30–39	Trauma to body and pelvis	Short in stature; healed fractures	Possible mixed ancestry		Probable smoker	SW
#9	22–25		Short in stature; physical labor; healed fractures	Short hair	Western; leather shoes and pants (dress clothes?) and cuff links	Probable smoker	SW
#10	40–49	Trauma to head and chest	Possibly Yee Hong Shing; strenuous physical labor; arthritis			Probable smoker; poor teeth	SW
#11	45–54		Yee Wei Yuen (Yu Weiyuan) on identification brick; short in stature; no heavy labor; arthritis	Black hair with some gray	Elegant coffin	Smoker; five teeth abscessed	NE
#12	50–65		Ung Bak Chong (Wu Baizong) on identification brick #3, aka Sing Lee; vandalism, disturbed; no heavy labor; arthritis		Elegant coffin	Full set of dentures	SW?
#13	50–59		Heavy physical labor	Brown hair; beard			SW

highly oxidized blob of metal were found below the calf of his left leg. Burial 3 had a bowl fragment and bone fragment. Burial 4 contained a Barber dime and two Liberty nickels, all dating to 1896 and 1897. Burial 5 had three dimes from the 1880s and 1890s, a sawn rib, and tiny metal half spheres. Burial 6 contained nutshells. Burial 7 contained two Barber dimes (1897? and 1909?) and a clay marble. No grave goods were found in Burials 8, 9, and 10.

Burials 11 and 12 were the two most important individuals because of their position in the community, as evidenced by their elaborate coffins. Burial 11 had an unidentified Chinese ceramic fragment and bundle of six stick matches, as well as a cut food bone, in the excavation fill, but nothing was found in the coffin. An identification brick was found between the lower legs with the long axis of the brick parallel to the legs. The vandalized Burial 12 had its own identification brick, described later, that was situated perpendicular to the long axis of the coffin at the northwest end. A small board had been placed over the brick. A wrapper from Double Yum Gum, introduced by the Life Saver Company in 1975, and a small shovel were partial evidence of the vandalism that had occurred after 1975. Burial 13 had 22-caliber shell casings and other unidentified metals.

CHINESE DEATHS IN CARLIN

Information about deaths of the Carlin Chinese has been difficult to ascertain. The 1870 census records noted the deaths of three Chinese: Wy Coup, age thirty-one, in October 1869 from an accident; Hin Yea, age twenty-three, in December 1869 as a result of smallpox; and Hong Lee, age thirty-one, in March 1870, also from smallpox.[61] While the deaths of Euro-Americans were published regularly in the newspapers, the passing of Chinese residents was seldom acknowledged unless there were unusual, sensational circumstances like murder or a tragic accident. The deaths of longtime merchants Sing Lee of Carlin and Hong Lee of nearby Island Mountain received no notice in the newspapers, possibly because they died during World War I, when the newspapers covered wartime news.

Death certificates and reports from the coroners' inquests detailed the deaths of eight Carlin individuals. (1) Ah Quang or Quoy was shot to death on November 16, 1869. He worked for the railroad and was a Sanyi District Association member. He had quarreled with Ah Yang over money that Ah Yang's woman owed him.[62] (2) Lee Quong Fay (or Foy) died in Carlin around June 4, 1903, from dementia of the brain and exposure to cold weather.[63] (3) Yee Hong Shing, a sixty-two-year-old worker for the Southern Pacific, died in January 1916 from blows to his body and head.[64] (4) Sing Lee died in November

1918.[65] (5) Jim Now (or Sow or Som), a sixty-one-year-old laborer and married man, died from natural causes on September 16, 1924. The Carlin coroner conducted an inquest, and friends in Carlin buried Jim, presumably in Carlin, a day later.[66] (6) Lao Jim, a widower and Chinese cook for the Overland Cafe, died at the age of fifty-eight in Carlin on April 22, 1929, after a long illness.[67] (7) Leo Chang (Lee Sheung) died in early August 1930.[68] (8) Yee Lee Wah, a single man about forty-three years old, died on August 19, 1930, of natural causes in the Elko County Poorhouse and was buried in Elko's public cemetery.[69] Of these eight, only Lee Quong Fay, Yee Hong Shing, Sing Lee, and Jim Now *may* have been buried in the Carlin Chinese Cemetery.

IDENTIFYING THE CARLIN CHINESE CEMETERY BURIALS

Given the sketchiness of existing obituaries, coroners' reports, newspaper stories, and death records, the identification of the thirteen Carlin Chinese Cemetery individuals is very difficult. However, the discovery of three identification bricks, usually used for exhumation and reburial, made the identification of Burials 11 and 12 definite, as Yee Wai Yuen (Cantonese; Yu Weiyuan in pinyin) and Ung Bak Chong (Wu Baizong), respectively. Another identification brick (Brick 1), for Yee Bak Gee (Yu Baizhi in pinyin), was found near Burials 6 and 7. It was not in either of the coffins, and the ground had been disturbed. However, Brick 1 indicates the owner had been a merchant, and both Burials 6 and 7 were men who had not engaged in heavy work. Finally, comparison of the physical evidence with the data from newspaper reports, death certificates, and coroners' reports suggests that Lee Quong Fay, Yee Hong Shing, and Jim Now might be the individuals found in Burial 3, Burial 10, and Burial 13, respectively, if one assumes that there were no other Chinese men in the area who died under similar circumstances and conditions.

THE IDENTIFICATION BRICKS

The bricks have been the most interesting clues to identification. The earliest brick was found on the ground surface. This identification brick, measuring four inches wide, eight and one-quarter inches long, and two and one-quarter inches high, was discovered in the vicinity of Burials 6 and 7. It is unknown whether this brick was related to any particular coffin, as the plow or the tractor blade unearthed it when leveling the lot. Either piece of equipment could have transported the brick some distance from its original location. While the brick could have been placed over or next to one of the graves, it could not have come from inside any of them; the contents of the coffins were undisturbed, despite the fact that the equipment had impacted some.

The presence of the burial brick indicates that the deceased was someone who could afford reburial through death insurance paid to the Zhigongtang, burial association, or district association. With the exception of Burials 11 and 12, already identified, only Burials 6 and 7 indicate someone in an upperclass situation, perhaps a merchant. Because the physical evidence suggests that Burial 7 was an individual who probably did little or no heavy labor, had short hair but also a false queue, and wore a Western garment, he was probably someone of wealth, most likely a merchant.

Brick 1

The inscription on Brick 1 reads: "[From] Ning Yuen [part of Toishan (Taishan) in the Four Districts, or Siyi, of Guangdong], [name of village unclear]"; in large characters in the center: "the grave of Yee Bak Gee [Cantonese; Yu Baizhi in pinyin]"; on the left: "died Xuanzong first year [1909], first month, twenty-first day [February 11], in the afternoon, at the age of [unclear; possibly sixty]."

Chinese men, in general, had at least two names—a formal family name (*ci*) and a familiar name (*hao*)—and could have seven first or familiar names during their lifetimes. However, they usually were buried with their formal name on the headstone. Two Chinese families, the Ung/Ng (Cantonese; Wu in pinyin) and the Yee (Yu), dominated the merchandising stores in Carlin. The merchants provided essential goods to Chinese in town and in neighboring mining communities. The reoccurrence of family names along the major towns on the transcontinental railroad route indicates that chain migration took place. Euro-Americans were often confused by Asian names because the family name was given before the familiar name. They also called Chinese men by their store or business names, adding to the multitude of different names. American government officials often picked random transliterations for Chinese names and reversed first and family names. The Chinese also had a birth name, generation name, formal name, and informal names. Based on a survey of papers from the Immigration and Naturalization Service in the National Archives and Records Administration in Washington, DC, the Chinese would sign their romanized name either right to left or left to right.

The phenomenon of "paper sons,"[70] men who claimed to be the son of a particular Chinese American but who actually might have been from another clan, added to the confusion. The passage of Chinese exclusion acts between 1882 and 1902 and the Immigration Act of 1924 forced many Chinese to use a paper family name in order to immigrate. In such cases, all American records had the man's paper name, but all Chinese records, including that of his burial, had his real family name. Chinese business partnership records might have any of the aforementioned combinations of names.

Yee Bak Gee (Yu Baizhi in pinyin) was probably one of the Chinese merchants in Carlin, or he was related to the Yee (Yu in pinyin) family that operated a store there. The Cantonese pronunciation of his name, Yee Bak Gee, was not found in the census, business partnership records, or any other documents.

Yee probably was known by his familiar name, and the only name close to this was Yee Tung Back (Yee is Yu, Back is Bai), a Carlin Chinese merchant. The largest, and probably oldest, Chinese merchandising store in Carlin's Chinatown was Quong Wing and Company, which was owned by Yee Dung in the 1890s. His partners Yee Chung and Yee Hing lived in Carlin, while Yee Qung, Yee Wong, Yee Young Park, and Ton One Hoy were in China.[71] Each partner invested $1,000, totaling $7,000, so this was the larger of the two Chinese stores in Carlin. By 1902 each partner had various amounts invested. The four partners then living in Carlin were Yee Quong ($1,000), Yee Bon Huey ($700), Yee He Jung ($700), and Yee Soon Jung ($500). Yee Soon Jung was working at the Chinese railroad camp selling goods when the Treasury Department agent, who had charge of immigration, surveyed the business.[72] None of these men were listed in the 1900 or later census manuscripts with these names.

In addition to Sing Lee and Gee Toy, mentioned earlier, the 1910 census manuscript listed three other merchants, who lived together: Yee Hah (b. 1862, immigrated 1881, married 1880), Yee N. Wah (b. 1861, immigrated 1886, married 1880), and Yee H. Wah (b. 1850, immigrated 1874, married 1870). In all probability, these were the same three men who appeared in the Quong Wing and Company business records as Yee Quong, Yee Bon Huey, and Yee He Jung. No women were reported to be living with them. This was not surprising, since the phenomenon of separated Chinese American families was common in the late nineteenth century due to the 1875 Page Law and Chinese exclusion acts.

Other investors in Quong Wing and Company included Yee Wah, a laundryman in the Sin Wah Laundry in Elko ($500) and Yee Man Jung ($600), who was on a steamer en route either to or from China. Yee Tung Back had been a partner in this firm but sold out in 1896. The stock on hand was valued at $3,000. According to the Treasury Department agent working for the Immigration and Naturalization Service, the company also rented rooms for $6 per month and had opium bunks but no visible signs of gambling other than the presence of fan tan tables.

Yee (Yu) Tung Back (Bai)'s name in Chinese has two of the same characters as Yee Bak Gee (Yu Baizhi) and would be a possible candidate as the owner of the brick. There is a strong possibility that it belonged to a member of the Yee clan of Quong Wing and Company. Since the identification bricks were sent to China with the exhumed remains, it is highly unlikely that the brick would have been left behind. The brick probably was placed near the headstone, which disappeared with the passage of time. The calligraphy on the brick shows a skilled hand, and in all probability, the deceased was a person of some wealth. Matching the brick to the physical descriptions indicates that it probably came from Burial 6 or 7. The writing was well preserved because of the dry landscape at the upper end of the cemetery.

Bricks 2 and 3

The remaining two bricks were found in the coffins and provide a more positive identification. Brick 2 was found in Burial 11 and reads: first line, "Taishan [Toishan] district"; second line, "person from Dayuan village"; then reading vertically from right to left: "died Republic of China thirteenth year [1924], fourth month [May]"; the characters for the day are illegible but might be 12. The next vertical line in larger characters gives the man's name, probably Yee Wai Yuen (Cantonese; Yu Weiyuan in pinyin). The last line gives his age as fifty-nine years old. Thus he was born in 1866. This makes him a little older than the physical evidence, but this was not unusual among Asian Americans. Burial 11 performed no heavy labor. His elaborate burial indicates that he was probably related to the Yee family merchants of Carlin, but there are no historical documents or records that link him to Quong Wing and Company (see fig. 4.2).

Unfortunately, the 1910 and 1920 Elko County census manuscripts list no one with a name even remotely close to Yee Wai Yuen. However, Yee Wai Yuen was his formal name, and he most likely was known by his informal name. Three men in the 1910 and 1920 state census manuscripts might be him: Yee Nam, a merchant; Yee Fong, another merchant; and Yee Chee, a man with his own income. Nor does the body fit the profile of Jim Now, age sixty-one, a laborer who died of cerebral apoplexy in Carlin on September 16, 1924, because of the month (four) noted on the brick.

Brick 3 was discovered in the northern end of Burial 12, which was vandalized, so it was difficult to determine the orientation of the individual. It appeared that a long leg bone lay beside the brick, which suggests that the man's head had been oriented to the southeast. Brick 3 had writing on both sides, but the ink had faded and was difficult to read since it was closer to the river (moist soil). This brick reads: "Originally from [faint—probably Ning Yuen, a part of Taishan district in the Four Districts (Siyi) of Guangdong], the grave of Ung Bak Chong [Cantonese; Wu Baizong in pinyin], an official [or person

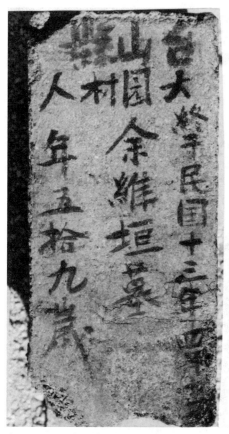

2 top horizontal lines

Taishan district

Dayuan Villager

right vertical line

Died Minguo 13 (1924)

4th month 12th day (?) (May 15?)

(day of death unclear)

center vertical line

Yee Wai Yuen (Yu Weiyuan)

left vertical line

59 years old

[b. 1866]

Figure 4.2.   Identification brick of Yee Wai Yuen (Yu Weiyuan). Photograph by Sue Fawn Chung. Yee Wai Yuen (1866–1924) of Taishan, Guangdong Province, was in coffin 11.

of high status; *guan*]." On the reverse side the Chinese writing is unclear, but the number 9 stands out, and this corresponds to Chinese merchant Sing Lee's death date, as given in the Elko County Recorder's Office, of November 9, 1918; the Chinese give the year (Minguo, 7), then month (*yue*, 11), and finally day (9) of death. Thus the date in Chinese was the American calendar's date. Based on the death certificate from the Elko County Recorder's Office,[73] Sing Lee died from influenza, which had reached epidemic proportions in the American West during that winter, and was buried by a Euro-American undertaker in Carlin.

Sing Lee and Company was the second-largest Chinese merchandising store in Carlin. In 1894 Sing Lee and Company was owned by Wu, or Ng (Ung) Bak (Buck) Dong, Ng (Ung) Hing, Ng (Ung) Shue — all living in Carlin but not appearing in the census manuscript for Carlin—and Ng (Ung) Fun On, Lee Yung, and Lee Sam You—all living in China. Each had an investment of one thousand dollars, totaling six thousand dollars.[74] In a sworn statement of 1894, Ung Buck Dung, variously spelled Ng Bak Dong or Ung Bak Dung (signed in Cantonese; Wu Baizong in pinyin), affirmed the members of the firm and stated that he had resided in Carlin and managed the business for the past fifteen years—since 1879. Based on the Chinese signature of the 1894 partnership document, the body in Burial 11 was that of Ung Bak Dong, or Sing Lee, as he was commonly known. He may have been related to Sing Car, a merchant listed in the 1870 census manuscript for Carlin. Chain migration of relatives was especially important in places with a small Chinese population in the American West.

The 1880 census manuscript for Carlin did not list any Chinese merchants. However, Ung Fang On (Ng Fun On), Lee Yung, and Lee Sam You undoubtedly lived there earlier and had amassed enough funds to return to China either for a visit or permanently, and probably were the ones who had previously sent for the others who were living in Carlin in 1894. By 1902 the company had changed partnerships. The 1900 census manuscript shows Ung Bak Dong (listed as Sing Lee, born 1862, immigrated 1878) living in a house with Charley Sing (born 1855, immigrated 1875), both of whom spoke English. Partnership papers indicate that Lee Sam You and Ung Fang On moved to Spokane Falls, Washington; Lee Fong to Denver, Colorado; and Ung Hing to China.[75] Census takers often listed a Chinese man's business name or firm name as his personal name, since the Euro-American community referred to him as such and never bothered to learn his real name, perhaps because it was too difficult to pronounce in English. Sing Lee also appeared on the 1909 Elko County tax list.[76] Because of the economic decline in the town in the early 1900s, the Chinese business partnership papers in the National Archives and Records Administration in San Bruno, California, show that Sing Lee and Company's assets dropped to forty-two thousand dollars.[77] Their stock of Chinese merchandise on hand was worth fifteen thousand dollars, and they supplemented their income by renting rooms to Chinese prostitutes, whose names never appear in the census manuscripts, for four to five dollars per month.

The Ung/Ng/Woo (Wu in pinyin) clan also had relations in Lovelock to the west and in Elko to the east around the turn of the twentieth century,[78] which may have strengthened their business relationships. The clan also might have been connected to the prominent merchandising store of Hi Loy and Company in Elko, reputed to be one of the oldest Chinese merchandising firms. One of the important managers was a man named Ung Fun Chung, who, in 1909, was applying to reenter the United States after spending ten years in

China.[79] Among the Ung family members who lived in Elko in 1910 were Ung Kee Fong, Ung Chang, and Ung Yee.[80] Clan businesses dominated South China in the late nineteenth and early twentieth centuries, but the practice in the United States had to be modified in many cases to include extended maternal relatives and countrymen from the same village or district (*tongxiang*). Clan business connections, if strong enough, often allowed these small merchandising stores to survive during economic downturns.

Therefore, two, and possibly three, of the bodies buried in the eastern Chinese cemetery in Carlin were those of Chinese merchants. One can be positively identified as the man known as Sing Lee in the Euro-American community. The others were Yee Bak Gee (Yu Baizhi) and Yee Wai Yuen (Yu Weiyuan). Since all three bricks indicate that the individuals were from Toishan (Taishan) district, the cemetery probably belonged to the Ning Yuen or Ning Yung District Association. The only extant marble headstone of a Chinese male in the western Carlin public cemetery was that of a Mr. Yen (Cantonese; Yan in pinyin) from Toishan (Taishan), so one might presume that he did not belong to the Ning Yuen District Association or died at a later date, when the Chinese cemetery no longer was visible. Taking into account the brick dated 1924, presumably John W. Puett allowed the land to be used as a Chinese cemetery even after he had secured a land patent, but no later than 1924.

Since the other coffins did not have bricks for identification, little is known about them, but some suppositions can be made by coordinating burial dates and descriptions. Burial 3 might be Lee Quong Fay (or Foy), who died on June 4, 1903. He was found naked three hundred yards from the railroad tracks on the south side, east of Carlin and west of Golden Gate. According to the inquest testimony of T. A. Buckles, a fifteen-year-old who had gone fishing, Lee was found stretched out, with his face and neck half eaten off by maggots.[81] This is consistent with the physical findings of hundreds of maggot pupa cases at the head end of the coffin and might account for the roughly made box used for his coffin. Earlier the Chinese community leaders had offered a reward for finding Lee because they knew he might wander aimlessly.[82] The coroner concluded that Lee had died of exposure and dementia. Burial 3 was placed with the arms and legs partially flexed and extended. The remains of Chinese shoes were found in the coffin, but not on his feet, only in the vicinity of his feet. While fragments of clothing were found, only two round metal buttons, typical of Chinese jackets, were in the coffin. All of this suggests a hasty burial.

Burial 10 may be that of Yee Hong Shing, a sixty-two-year-old worker for the Southern Pacific Railroad. The coroner's inquest of January 1916 indicates that Yee had died of blows to the body and head. Doctor T. H. Harper reported that his chest and ribs were caved in by some blunt instrument. Internal organs appear to be pretty well smashed. . . . Scalp wound on back of head and on top of head, and one extending from left cheek over left eyebrow to middle of forehead. Small surface wound on lower jaw two inches to left of chin. Fracture of lower jaw bone. Surface wound two inches long over the pubes.[83]

This description compares favorably with the findings of the osteological report for Burial 10, which shows at least two distinct blows, one to the chest region and another to the head. The impact to the chest was apparently on the left side and fractured eight ribs, four on each side of the body. This blow would have been fatal, causing severe trauma to the heart and lungs. The other blow was to the left cheek, fracturing the zygomatic, the upper portion of the left eye orbit, the maxilla, and the mandible.[84] However, there are some inconsistencies. The inquest report gave his age as sixty-two, while the osteological analysis put his age at between forty and forty-nine. A roughly ten-year difference might not be significant given the possibility of error in age estimation or that the witness in the coroner's report gave the man's age as being older than he was. Also, Burial 10 contained many insect pupa cases, suggesting death and burial occurred during warmer weather; however, Yee died in January, when there was no insect activity. On the other hand, the insects may have been capable of burrowing to reach the body at a later time.

Figure 4.3.   Mummy. Photograph by Donna Murphy.

The last possible identification, though very weak in nature, is that of the laborer named Jim Now or Sow. This conclusion is based on the age range, fifty to fifty-nine, and the fact that the deceased did heavy physical labor. Jim Now, a laborer, died in September 1924 of cerebral apoplexy at the age of sixty-one and was buried in Carlin by his friends.[85] The other two deaths officially recorded occurred in 1929 and 1930, long after Puett had taken possession of the property, and therefore the men were unlikely to be buried there.

CONCLUSIONS

The Chinese came to Nevada beginning in the mid-nineteenth century, and many remained there for the rest of their lives. Although they tried to adhere to traditional Chinese funeral and burial practices, they made accommodations to their new environment and circumstances from the outset. Relatives and close friends, often working with family or district associations, were in charge of the funerary rituals instead of the wife and nuclear or extended family. Important aspects of a traditional Chinese funeral and burial, such as the placement of the tablet in the ancestral hall and the duties of the immediate family, seldom took place in the male-dominated Chinese American communities. Euro-American undertakers took the place of Chinese ones.

For the Carlin Chinese burials, J. A. Bieler handled most of the interments. At the turn of the twentieth century, the traditional Chinese funeral processions, as described by the local newspapers, had a distinctive Chinese identity, but gradually, between 1916 and 1921, the Chinese Americans incorporated more American aspects, including American ministers, morticians, and musicians. In general, Euro-Americans viewed the entire Chinese mortuary process as something very alien, so probably denied that the Chinese were accommodating themselves to the new culture. The Chinese themselves probably also felt that they were adhering to tradition. However, important deviations had been made. For example, for the funeral of Henry Leong, an American minister performed the services accompanied by an American vocalist,[86] and old customs were satisfied with the probable exhumation and shipment of his bones to China, where his wife and one son resided and where his tablet was placed.[87] As exemplified by the recently discovered graves in Carlin, many Chinese in Nevada were buried in their adopted homeland—becoming immigrants, not sojourners.

Based on the archaeological evidence, by the early twentieth century many Chinese had made some adjustments to American society by adopting American hairstyles, wearing American-made clothing, and having American objects buried with them. It is interesting that the first seven burials had false queues and that six of these men had short Western-style haircuts. This probably meant that they were more comfortable with their Western hairstyles but needed the queues for formal Chinese social events or in case they returned to China. They were uncertain as to whether they might need the queue in the afterworld.

The archaeological evidence corresponds to local newspaper reports and historical photographs that indicate the adoption of things American—dress, hairstyles, names, housing, and, in some cases, religion—by the 1890s to early 1900s in Nevada. Billy Ford (Chinese name: Min Chung) and his Sacramento-born wife, Loy Lee Ford, of Tonopah, Nevada, not only wore American-style clothing by 1900 but also, between 1899 and 1916, were among the first Chinese Americans in Nevada to give all of their children American names at birth.[88] The adoption of a Western name also was seen in Carlin in 1944. Felipe Ma, a waiter for the Western Pacific Railroad, had the Chinese name of Mar Wah Leung. He died at the age of fifty-two on December 21, 1944, and his two names were noted as such in the court records.[89] In rural frontier America these changes took place sooner than in urban America, which had large Chinatowns that preserved Chinese culture more effectively.

There was no question that life was arduous for most of the men. Physical trauma, including two violent deaths, fractured bones, and limited health care were part of their lives. Their dental health was poor, because after 1892 Chinese dentists fell into the excluded category and could not immigrate to the United States; few Chinese already here could afford to go to Euro-American dentists. Eight of the men buried in Carlin smoked, and some of these might have been opium smokers. One was buried in a crude box, indicative of his poor financial status. However, three showed that they had an easier lifestyle, and extra money was spent on their coffins. This suggests a modicum of wealth and class stratification in Carlin's Chinese community.

The archaeological evidence from the Carlin cemetery indicates that the Chinese in the American West took aspects of the East and West with them into the afterworld. Some burials—those lacking the false queues and containing Euro-American apparel rather than Chinese clothing and footwear—were more acculturated than others. As more acculturation occurred, the traditional preoccupation with ancestors and spirits became less important. With each succeeding generation of Chinese Americans, fewer and fewer of the traditional rituals and more of the American practices were observed. The burials in Carlin demonstrated this gradual trend toward accommodation and acculturation in the early twentieth century. Although it is unfortunate that we cannot presently identify all of the individuals at this site, their remains have provided us with a small window into the Chinese American past. Perhaps future study will shed new light on the many questions that still persist.

NOTES

1. Fred Frampton and Timothy Murphy provided much of the information in this section.

2. Food offerings included apples, oranges, a bunch of bananas, and a container of cookies. A bottle of brandy or whiskey, placed as an offering, was later poured out on the site.

3. *Virginia City (NV) Territorial Enterprise*, April 12, 1871. We are indebted to University of Nevada, Las Vegas, graduate students LuAnn Caressi, Sondra Cosgrove, and Gerhard Grytz for their assistance in this project. Nevada newspapers often are only four to six pages in length; stories about the Chinese appear on pages 1 or 4 as a general rule.

4. Five of the best accounts of the Chinese involvement in the construction of the railroads are: David H. Bain, *Empire Express: Building the First Transcontinental Railroad* (New York: Penguin Putnam, 1999); Stephen E. Ambrose, *Nothing Like It in the World* (New York: Simon and Schuster, 2000); George Kraus, *High Road to Promontory: Building the Central Pacific (Now the Southern Pacific) across the High Sierra* (Palo Alto: American West, 1969); David F. Myrick, *Railroads of Nevada and Eastern California*, 2 vols. (Berkeley: Howell-North Books, 1962–1963); and Tzy Kuei Yen, *Chinese Workers and the First Transcontinental Railroad of the United States of America* (Ann Arbor: Xerox University Microfilms, PhD diss., 1977).

5. *Winnemucca (NV) Silver State*, April 3, 1882.

6. John Fong, interview by Sue Fawn Chung, tape recording, Carlin, NV, July 2000, University of Nevada, Las Vegas, Lied Library, Special Collections. Mr. Fong operated one such restaurant for many decades.

7. For an occupational breakdown, see Gregg Lee Carter, "Social Demography of the Chinese in Nevada: 1870–1880," *Nevada Historical Society Quarterly* 18, no. 3 (Summer 1976): 85–86.

8. Him Mark Lai, "Chinese Regional Solidarity: Case Study of the Hua Xian (Fah Yuen) Community in California," in *Chinese America: History and Perspectives, 1994*, ed. Marlon Hom and others (San Francisco: Chinese Historical Society of America, 1994), 19–60, which reports on this group's domination of the butchery industry.

9. This is discussed in detail in Marlon K. Hom, "Fallen Leaves' Homecoming: Notes on the 1893 Gold Mountain Charity Cemetery in Xinhui," in *Chinese America: History and Perspectives, 2002*, ed. Colleen Fong and others (San Francisco: Chinese Historical Society of America, 2002), 36–50.

10. State of Nevada, *General Statutes of Nevada* (Carson City, NV: State Printing Office, 1879), chapter 38.

11. Sucheng Chan, *Asian Americans: An Interpretive History* (Boston: Twayne, 1991), and Shih-shan Henry Tsai, *The Chinese Experience in America* (Bloomington: Indiana University Press, 1986), both argue this as part of their main thesis.

12. *Tuscarora (NV) Times-Review*, July 7, 1882, describes the exhumation of the Chinese in Tuscarora. William Skewes from Salt Lake City, Utah, undertook the task.

13. *Elko (NV) Independent*, July 7, 1925. See also James William Hefferon, "Bad Eye[,] Last of the CP Chinese Workers Left in Elko, Nevada," interview by John Eldredge, February 1, 1986, Golden Spike National Historic Site, National Park Service, at www.nps.gov/gosp/research/hefferon.htm.

14. Elko County Recorder's Office, *Deaths*, book 1. We are indebted to the staffs at the Nevada State Archives and the Office of Vital Statistics in Carson City for their assistance in this. Death certificates after 1920 were transferred to Vital Statistics in Carson City.

15. Mary Rusco's photographs of the Chinese cemetery in Lovelock are on file at the University of Nevada, Las Vegas, Special Collections, Asian American photographs file.

16. Sue Fawn Chung, personal observation. A grant from the Nevada Humanities and the National Endowment for the Humanities allowed Chung to travel around the state to do research on the Chinese in Nevada.

17. Emily M. Ahern, *Chinese Ritual and Politics* (Cambridge: Cambridge University Press, 1981), 21–22.

18. Lu Cai, "The Errors of Geomancy," trans. Chunyu Wang, in *Chinese Civilization: A Sourcebook*, 2nd ed., rev., ed. Patricia Buckley Ebrey (New York: Free Press, 1993), 120–124.

19. Elko County Recorder's Office, *Deaths*, book 1.

20. The term "joss house" probably originated in the Portuguese word *deus* or in the fact that incense sticks (also known as joss sticks) were burned at the altar. Americans called the Chinese buildings with altars "joss houses," even though some of the organizations housed in the buildings did not serve any religious function.

21. Christian Jochim, *Chinese Religions: A Cultural Perspective* (Englewood Cliffs, NJ: Prentice-Hall, 1986), 166–169, summarizes the funeral rites. For a comparison, see Ann Maxwell Hill, "Chinese Funerals and Chinese Ethnicity in Chiang Mai, Thailand," *Ethnology* 31, no. 4 (October 1992): 315–330.

22. Sue Fawn Chung, personal observations. See also Susan Naquin, "Funerals in North China: Uniformity and Variation," in *Death Ritual in Late Imperial and Modern China*, ed. James L. Watson and Evelyn S. Rawski (Berkeley: University of California Press, 1988), 43.

23. Sylvia Sun Minnick, *Samfow: The San Joaquin Chinese Legacy* (Fresno: Panorama West, 1988), 287–298, discusses funerals, burials, exhumation, death records, and the Qingming festival. See also Zhiyuan Zhang and Zunguan Huang, "A Brief Account of Traditional Chinese Festival Customs," *Journal of Popular Culture* 27, no. 2 (Fall 1993): 13–25; Shuang Li and Yong Fang Li, "The Funeral and Chinese Culture," *Journal of Popular Culture* 27, no. 2 (Fall 1993): 113–121; and Roberta S. Greenwood, *Down by the Station: Los Angeles Chinatown, 1880–1933* (Los Angeles: Institute of Archaeology, University of California, Los Angeles, 1996) for additional information.

24. Fred P. Frampton and Sue Fawn Chung, personal observations in the late 1990s.

25. Cindy L. Baker and Mary L. Maniery, *Historical Summary of Chinese Cemeteries in Folsom, Sacramento County, California: Final Report* (Sacramento, CA: PAR Environmental Services, 1995), 17.

26. Liping Zhu, "A Chinaman's Chance on the Rocky Mountain Frontier," *Montana: The Magazine of Western History* 45, no. 4 (Autumn/Winter 1995): 48; see also his book *A Chinaman's Chance: The Chinese on the Rocky Mountain Mining Frontier* (Niwot: University Press of Colorado, 1997), which describes this situation.

27. Tin-Yuke Char, comp. and ed., *The Sandalwood Mountains: Readings and Stories of the Early Chinese in Hawaii* (Honolulu: University of Hawai'i Press, 1975), 134–138. See also Carol Stepanchuk and Charles Wong, *Mooncakes and Hungry Ghosts: Festivals of China* (San Francisco: China Books and Periodicals, 1991), 61–80.

28. *Reno (NV) Evening Gazette*, December 16, 1916.

29. How Cat, How Suy Get (b. 1856), also known as Sing Lee, not to be confused with the prominent merchant also known as Sing Lee, discussed later.

30. Elko County Clerk's Office, *Coroner's Inquests*, Sing Lee, July 20, 1921.

31. *Elko (NV) Independent*, July 20 and 22, 1921; and *Humboldt (NV) Star*, February 27, 1924.

32. The advertisement, published in the *Carlin (NV) Commonwealth* on November 9, 1910, announced that the Ong Company was opening the Overland Cafe, with meals costing thirty cents. Both news articles, published on January 25 and February 1, 1911, related the editor's opinion of the wastefulness of the Nevada State policeman who had traveled three hundred miles to entice Carlin Paiutes to induce "a Chinaman and an ignorant Greek to go out and get them some whiskey. Then the modern sleuth . . . arrested the hop-headed chink and the ignorant little Greek, fastened the poor fools together with handcuffs and triumphantly took them to jail in Elko," since it was against the law to sell whiskey to Native Americans.

33. *Elko (NV) Daily Independent*, February 25, 1907.

34. *Daily Elko (NV) Independent*, March 26, 1870.

35. *Winnemucca (NV) Daily Silver State*, June 8, 1878.

36. *Weekly Elko (NV) Independent*. June 16, 1878.

37. *Winnemucca (NV) Silver State*, May 14, 1877.

38. *Weekly Elko (NV) Independent*, May 8, 1905; *Elko (NV) Daily Independent*, May 8, 1905.

39. *Winnemucca (NV) Humboldt Star*, August 1, 1930; *(Reno) Nevada State Journal*, August 1, 1930.

40. Department of Vital Statistics, Carson City, NV: death certificate for Lee Sheung, August 5, 1930.

41. Department of Vital Statistics, Carson City, NV: death certificate for Sing Lee, November 9, 1918.

42. Chen Lanbin, *Shih Mei jilue* [Brief Record of a Mission to America], originally published in *Xiaofanghu zhai yudi congchao* (Shanghai: Zhuyitang, 1877–1894), *ce* 63, 2a–b.

43. *Elko (NV) Free Press*, April 30, 1909.

44. State of Nevada, *General Statutes of Nevada* (Carson City, NV: State Printing Office, 1885), 322–323, sections 1128–1133. We are indebted to Jeffrey Kintop of the Nevada State Archives for his assistance in locating this citation. As an example of the avoidance behavior discussed, one enthusiastic official in a nearby county re-

ported that he had visited the mining community of American Canyon to collect the poll taxes levied on foreigners and found only one Chinese present; typed manuscript in the Lovelock Public Library; David Valentine provided the senior author with a copy of this memoir. Additionally, the Zhigongtang caretaker said he was the only person there, but the official noted numerous picks and equipment scattered about. Therefore, the official returned later in order to collect the equipment; when he attempted to do so, many Chinese miners appeared to stop him, and thereafter he collected a tidy sum from the site.

45. United States Census Manuscript, 1870, Nevada, Elko County, Carlin. Details also can be found at http://dmla.clan.lib.nv.us/docs/shpo/NVCensus/FindPeople/year .asp.

46. United States Census Manuscript, 1870, Nevada, Elko County, Carlin.

47. United States Census Manuscript, 1870 and 1880, Nevada, Elko County, Carlin.

48. National Archives and Records Administration, United States Immigration and Naturalization Service (hereafter abbreviated INS) Record Group 85, Chinese Partnership records of Quong Wing and Company, Carlin, Nevada, dated 1902, file #13562/305; and Sing Lee and Company, Carlin, Nevada, dated 1894 and 1902, file #13562/304 (National Archives, San Bruno, California). A third company, Hong Lee, although listed in Carlin, was actually in Island Mountain, about seventy miles to the northeast. See file #13562/284.

49. United States Census Manuscript, 1880, 1900, 1910, 1920, Nevada, Elko County, Carlin. The 1890 census manuscript was destroyed in a fire in Washington, DC. An examination of the business records (see notes 69 and 72, below) shows that many important Chinatown figures were not included in the census.

50. *Reno (NV) Evening Gazette*, March 5, 1941, devoted a long article to his accomplishments and death.

51. Ruth Hamel and Tim Schreiner, "Land along the Track," *American Demographics* 10, no. 6 (June 1988): 50–52; and William G. Roy and Philip Bonacich, "Interlocking Directorates and Communities of Interest among American Railroad Companies, 1905," *American Sociological Review* 53, no. 3 (June 1988): 368–380.

52. United States Census Manuscript, 1910, Nevada, Elko County, Carlin.

53. United States Census Manuscript, 1900 and 1910, Nevada, Elko County, Carlin, lists both these laundrymen, who had been married since 1875 but had no wives listed as living with them.

54. In this system, contributors, usually relatives or close friends or association members, pooled their funds and had an annual contest in which the winner could use the mutual funds to establish a business. See Maurice Freedman, "The Handling of Money: A Note on the Background to the Economic Sophistication of Overseas Chinese," *Man* 59 (1959): 64–65; and David Y. H. Wu, "To Kill Three Birds with One Stone: The Rotating Credit Associations of the Papua New Guinea Chinese," *American Ethnologist* 1, no. 3 (August 1974): 565–575.

55. We are indebted to Donna L. Murphy for this information. The site T. 33 N., R. 52 E., Sec. 26, W1/2 NW1/4, was recorded on July 21, 1923, in P7/574, Bureau of Land Management and Elko County Recorder's Office, *Book of Deeds*, 1923.

56. The single Chinese coin from Burial 2 was very corroded and has not yet been dated.

57. Douglas Owsley and others, "Osteology and Paleopathology of the Carlin Chinese Cemetery," report dated November 1997, on file at the University of Nevada, Las Vegas, Special Collections Library, Asian American file #93. We are indebted to Amy Dansie of the Nevada State Museum for the report from the seven Smithsonian Institute physical anthropologists.

58. Two experts from Connecticut studied the mummy as part of the *National Geographic* special "Mummy on the Road," an Engel Brothers Media production, which aired in 2001. Their age estimate differs from that in Owsley's report, below.

59. This differs from the findings in the report by Owsley and others, "Osteology."

60. The grave goods and clothing will be the subject of a future article by Timothy Murphy.

61. United States Census Manuscript, 1870, Nevada, Elko County, Carlin.

62. Elko County Recorder's Office, *Coroner's Inquests*, Ah Quang, December 2, 1869.

63. Elko County Recorder's Office, *Coroner's Inquests*, Lee Quong Fay, June 4, 1903.

64. Elko County Recorder's Office, *Coroner's Inquests*, Yee Hong Shing, January 1916.

65. Elko County Recorder's Office, *Deaths*, Book 2, filed in the Nevada State Vital Statistics Office, Carson City.

66. Department of Vital Statistics, Carson City, NV: Death certificate for Jim Now, September 17, 1924.

67. Ibid.; Death certificate for Lao Jim, April 22, 1929.

68. Ibid., Death certificate for Lee Sheung, 5 August 1930.

69. Department of Vital Statistics for Elko County, Carson City, NV, Elko County death certificate, Yee Lee Wah, August 19, 1930.

70. Madeline Hsu, "Gold Mountain Dreams and Paper Son Schemes: Chinese Immigration Under Exclusion," in *Chinese America: History and Perspectives*, ed. Marion K. Hom et al. (San Francisco: Chinese Historical Society of America, 1997), 46–60. See also her book, *Dreaming of Gold, Dreaming of Home: Transnationalism and Migration between the United States and South China, 1882–1943* (Stanford: Stanford University Press, 2000) and Erika Lee, *At America's Gates: Chinese Immigration during the Exclusion Era, 1882–1943* (Chapel Hill: University of North Carolina Press, 2003).

71. National Archives and Records Administration, INS Record Group 85, Chinese partnership records of Quong Wing and Company, Carlin, Nevada, 1902, file #13562/305 (San Bruno, CA: National Archives, Pacific Sierra Region). We are indebted to Neil Thomsen, now retired, of the National Archives and Records Administration, for his assistance, and to Vincent Chin, a volunteer at NARA, and Mary and Elmer Rusco for introducing us to these documents.

72. National Archives and Records Administration, INS Record Group 85, Chinese partnership records of Quong Wing and Company, Carlin, Nevada, 1902, file #13562/305.

73. Recorder's Office, *Deaths*, book 2, filed in the Nevada State Vital Statistics Office, Carson City.

74. National Archives and Records Administration, INS Record Group 85, Chinese partnership records of Sing Lee and Company, Carlin, Nevada, 1894 and 1902, file #13562/304 (San Bruno, CA: National Archives, Pacific Sierra Region).

75. United States Census Manuscript, 1900 and 1910, Nevada, Elko County, Carlin.

76. *Elko (NV) Free Press*, October 9, 1909, listed Sing Lee's tax as $50.

77. National Archives and Records Administration, INS Record Group 85, Chinese partnership records of Sing Lee and Company, Carlin, Nevada, 1894 and 1902, file #13562/304 (San Bruno, CA: National Archives, Pacific Sierra Region).

78. *Elko (NV) Free Press*, December 17, 1920; Ng Hung Let brought his wife and son to Elko. It is possible that he moved the business from Carlin to Elko, but there is no concrete evidence to indicate this.

79. *Elko (NV) Free Press*, May 28, 1909, mentioned that Ung Fun Chung, formerly of Hi Loy and Company of Elko, one of the oldest Chinese merchandising firms in the West, had returned from China and was in San Francisco. L. J. DeHart, inspector for the district of Utah, was investigating his reentry case. See also Erika Lee, *At America's Gates*.

80. Bryan Lee Dilts, comp., *1910 Census Index* (Salt Lake City: Index, 1984), gives an alphabetical listing by last name. However, the index is not completely accurate when compared with the census manuscript.

81. Elko County Recorder's Office, *Coroner's Inquests*, Lee Quong Fay, June 4, 1903.

82. Elko County Recorder's Office, *Coroner's Inquests*, Lee Quong Fay, June 4, 1903.

83. Elko County Recorder's Office, *Coroner's Inquests*, Yee Hong Shing, January 1916.

84. Owsley and others, "Osteology."

85. Department of Vital Statistics, Carson City, NV: death certificate for Jim Now, September 17, 1924.

86. *Elko (NV) Free Press*, November 9, 10, 1938.

87. Since Leong's name did not appear on extant Elko cemetery markers, verified by a search of the Elko Cemetery, and confirmed by Jean and Roger Ferrel, *Nevada State Cemeteries*, vol. 1, (n.p., n.d.), 96–133, Nevada State Archives and Library, Carson City, Nevada, one might assume that his body was exhumed for shipment to China, where his wife and son could care for his spirit.

88. See Sue Fawn Chung, "Ah Cum Kee (1878–1927) and Loy Lee Ford (1882–1920): Between Two Worlds," in *Ordinary Women, Extraordinary Lives*, ed. Kriste Lindenmeyer (Wilmington, DE: Scholarly Resources, 2000), 179–195.

89. Justice Court of Carlin, County of Elko, Verdict of Coroner's Jury, filed December 23, 1944, no. 435.

5

Respecting the Dead:
Chinese Cemeteries and Burial Practices
in the Interior Pacific Northwest

Terry Abraham and Priscilla Wegars

In the latter half of the nineteenth century, following a variety of job opportunities, Chinese workers drifted east toward the newly opened interior parts of the intermountain West. Anti-Chinese racism encoded in harshly punitive laws restrained the Chinese from following the more usual Euro-American patterns of immigration and assimilation. In spite of the efforts by the dominant culture to enforce and maintain these immigrants' "otherness," the Chinese over time accommodated themselves to that culture by, for example, learning English, adopting Western clothing, raising families, and converting to Christianity. As the Chinese acculturated, Euro-Americans gradually altered many of their stereotyped perceptions of the Chinese, enabling the latter to become included in an increasingly pluralistic American society.

Such acculturation is clearly evident when the material remains of funerary customs are examined. Changes in burial practices and cemetery markers demonstrate how Chinese Americans progressively relinquished Chinese cultural traditions and adopted Euro-American ones instead. Today we recognize that Chinese cemeteries and grave markers from earlier times, long abandoned or ignored, are silent monuments memorializing Chinese contributions to the growth and development of the West.

In mining communities, as in other resource-dependent economies, once the resource is depleted the laborers move on to other areas. This was particularly true of the placer mining communities in the West. Placer mining, in contrast to lode or deep mining, is a low-capital effort with a relatively quick loss/reward indicator. Although canvas boomtowns sprang up to provide services to miners, they quickly disappeared or shriveled to near invisibility once the economic base withered. For example, eastern Oregon's Auburn was bigger than Portland in 1862; within two years it was about a quarter that size; and today there is no vestige of the town site.[1]

In most gold mining regions of the West, the Euro-American miners initially excluded the Chinese from claim ownership. Later, before the placers were completely exploited, the Euro-American miners permitted the Chinese to purchase or lease their claims. Such transfers often kept some boomtowns afloat for enough additional years for other economic forces to develop, enabling the community to remain intact into the present century. One such example is Pierce, Idaho, in the remote Clearwater River country, near where Idaho's first gold discovery occurred in 1860.[2] Today, the local place name Shanghai Road recalls Pierce's once-prominent Chinese occupation.

Sources for the study of the Chinese presence in the West include census documents, funeral and cemetery records, gravestones, fire insurance maps, signs, newspapers, photographs, city and county records, oral histories, and reminiscences. In addition, U.S. topographic maps often identify specific places related to the Chinese.[3]

There are apparently few records in Chinese of burials in the West. Even if there were many, problems of translation and transliteration between Mandarin, Cantonese, Toishan dialect, and English limit the analysis of such documentary records. A grave marker from Grangeville, Idaho, provides an illustrative example. One person, a Mandarin speaker, transcribed the marker as "The grave of Mr. Jinming Li, Tianyuan village, Taishan [Toishan], in 1942."[4] However, a Toishanese speaker (Toishanese is a dialect of Cantonese), asserted that Mr. "Le'a's" home village was Yuan-Tain.[5] In Grangeville, Mr. Li or Le'a was known as Lee Mann,[6] a close approximation of his Toishanese name, Le'a Ma-An.[7] Emma Woo Louie has examined similar confusing problems with regard to Chinese names.[8]

Another common problem, documented in regard to the Chinese cemetery in Ballarat, Australia, demonstrates that the dominant culture's accounts of early Chinese burials seldom reflected the Chinese name of the deceased. Where the marker is still legible and can be transcribed by one familiar with various dialects, it is possible to make the necessary biographical link. Inscription chronicler Linda Brumley states:

> The only really personal information was on the fast disintegrating gravestone, and only by linking gravestone with European record could a track be made of an individual from China. The gravestone contained the real Chinese name of the deceased, and the place where he was born. It had to be recorded—and linked.[9]

CHINESE CEMETERIES

In many western communities, the Chinese population established duplicate civic services. One of the main reasons was that the community had reached a sufficient size. Intriguingly, one researcher notes that in Nevada City, California, in 1861, a local newspaper demanded that the Chinese discontinue using the local city cemetery because of their "pagan [burial] rituals" and exhumation practices. Nevertheless, the separate Chinese cemetery there is documented only from 1891, although burials appear to have taken place in it as much as a decade earlier.[10]

Duplication of such functions followed the pattern established by Euro-American enclaves in Guangzhou (Canton) and other Chinese ports. In Baker City, Oregon, and Lewiston, Idaho, for example, the Chinese community had both a temple and a cemetery. In Baker City, the land housing the Chinese cemetery was owned by, and presumably purchased by, the Chinese community under the auspices of the Chinese Consolidated Benevolent Association (CCBA), transliterated as Zhonghua, Jung Wah, or Chung Wah Association. Within the last decade, after the Baker County commissioners exchanged some of the cemetery property for a local developer's road, the CCBA of Portland stepped forward to reassert its ownership of the land.[11] Although Baker County Historical Society volunteer Alvin Ward installed a fence around the cemetery in 1997,[12] it is not known if the cemetery had a fence while it was in use.

In Lewiston, Idaho, the Chinese cemetery was originally sited atop the bluff overlooking the Snake River, but in 1888 the city made it illegal to bury anyone within the city limits.[13] Subsequently, in 1891, "Jung Wah" entered into a ninety-nine-year lease agreement with the Ancient Free and Accepted Masons, the Knights of Pythias, the Independent Order of Odd Fellows, and the Mayor of Lewiston for a 79-by-115-foot portion of Lewiston's Normal Hill cemetery. The lease required the lessee to pay two hundred dollars in advance for this parcel and "to fence said ground in the same manner as the city cemetery."[14] Toward the end of the ninety-nine-year period, Lewiston's Chinese community expressed concern about the lease's ending, so the then-mayor announced that the Chinese buried in the Lewiston cemetery could remain there.[15] In 1891, at the time the lease was drawn up, the signers probably expected that then-current exhumation practices would empty the cemetery of Chinese remains by the time the lease expired in 1990.

Chinese cemeteries, unlike landscaped Euro-American plots, were generally left in their "natural" state, a point made by local informants about the Chung Wah (CCBA) cemetery in Folsom, California.[16] Marjorie Fong, a

Baker City, Oregon, Chinese American pioneer, recalled that the Chinese cemetery in her town was "full of sagebrush."[17]

This "untended" appearance often gave the impression of abandonment to Euro-Americans who had other development plans for the area. Chinese custom, however, decreed that graveyard visits primarily occurred during spring's Qingming festival.[18] American custom is somewhat similar; people visit the cemeteries and make floral offerings primarily on Memorial Day in late May. Chinese in Victoria, British Columbia, also performed similar rites during the autumn Chongyang festival.[19] In China, ceremonial visits to the cemetery occur during both of these festivals.

According to one account, burials were not the only activity to take place in Chinese cemeteries. In 1872, in Idaho City, Idaho, the Euro-American sheriff was called on as an independent witness to a "purging" ceremony. The accused and accusers, along with the sheriff, visited the cemetery, where participants placed a paper "oath of innocence" on a grave and sacrificed a white rooster. The paper oath, the rooster, and the cleaver were then buried.[20] This ceremony ensured that wandering spirits were laid to rest and no longer bothered the innocent.

PHYSICAL ORIENTATION

Although graves in the inland Northwest's Chinese cemeteries are often placed parallel to one another, these are usually not in the neat rows found in Euro-American cemeteries. In Warren, Idaho, geographer Samuel Couch mapped the Chinese cemetery to show that all of the graves (i.e., exhumation pits) were placed parallel to the slope of the land toward the southwest.[21] In Stanley, British Columbia, all of the graves except two are aligned north-south.[22] Interestingly, in Jacksonville, Oregon, about 1873, Father François Xavier Blanchet observed that burials were placed "so that the head is lowest."[23]

In order for a burial to be "correct," a person skilled in geomancy was necessary, and such a person could not always be found in mining communities in the American West. For many Chinese, however, general principles were known and applied.

Even so, Stewart Culin observes that, in Philadelphia and other eastern sites in 1890, "little if any attention is paid to the character of the site selected for the grave or to the direction in which the body shall rest."[24] Chinese cemeteries in the Northwest, not yet examined archaeologically, may also prove to have no specific orientation of the individual graves, similar to that found for the Chung Wah (CCBA) Cemetery in Folsom, California.[25]

FENGSHUI AS SEEN IN THE PACIFIC
NORTHWEST'S CHINESE CEMETERIES

Most of the West's Chinese immigrants were from southern China and brought with them many rituals and beliefs. These led to a singular transformation of the western landscape, since Chinese cemeteries in the West follow a pattern common to cemeteries in southern China; they are often located on a sloping, encompassing hillside. This is a distinctive feature of the Chinese concept of geomancy, or *fengshui* (see chapter 1). Over time, this centuries-old geomantic system[26] became common at all levels of Chinese society, from emperor to peasant.[27] Yet, not all graves were placed according to *fengshui*, and not all the dead were accorded the benefits of the full three-stage burial process.[28] In one case, in Moscow, Idaho, the Chinese cemetery was located on a steep, north-facing slope. It was eventually abandoned, and the remaining graves were moved to the nearby city cemetery.

In the context of burials of Chinese miners in remote western communities, it is only the first stage of this process that is visible, the interment of the body immediately following death. The second and third stages involved placing the bones in an urn, often exposed, and, much later, erecting a permanent tomb.

In many parts of China, this first burial after death is performed almost without ritual, although there are elaborate funeral ceremonies that take place before the body is removed to the burial place. Anthropologist Rubie Watson notes, "At this stage little attention is given to the choice of burial site because it is assumed that this is not the permanent resting place."[29] While different assumptions are apparently the rule in some Taiwanese villages, reflecting practices prescribed in ancient Chinese texts, this reflects locally divergent traditions.[30]

Since the initial impetus for the practice of *fengshui* was in siting graves,[31] it is logical for Western scholars to seek *fengshui* principles in Chinese cemeteries in the West. For example, David Chuenyan Lai has ascribed *fengshui* principles to the placement of two sites in Victoria, British Columbia:

The [first] site was near two creeks and a lake and flanked on both sides by ridges. . . . According to the *Feng Shui* concept, water was an emblem of wealth, and mountain ranges were life-giving breaths of Nature. The site had good *Feng Shui*—i.e., was in harmony with Nature. It was an auspicious spot where, in geomantic terminology, the "Azure Dragon," the higher ridge on its left, and the "White Tiger," the lower ridge on its right, converged.[32]

The [second] site, backed by Gonzales Hill, is flanked on both sides by rock platforms of higher elevation and commands an open view of the Strait of Juan de Fuca. In geomantic terms, the site was guarded by the "Azure Dragon" on its left and by the "White Tiger" on its right and was embraced by a wide stretch of water—a symbol of wealth and affluence. Furthermore, it was believed that the souls of the deceased hovering over their tombs would enjoy viewing passing vessels bound for China.[33]

Similarly, another scholar has recently analyzed a remote Chinese cemetery for its adherence to the practice:

> From a *feng shui* perspective, the cemetery [at Warren, Idaho,] is sited perfectly. It lies in the center of a south-facing hill above a meandering creek on the valley floor. Ridges to the left and right would form the "Azure Dragon" and "White Tiger," respectively. . . . Guarded by the "horseshoe" shape of surrounding ridges, the site channels the clouds and mist (*feng* and *shui*), thus harmonizing the site for the revered dead.[34]

Whether actual *fengshui* applications can be demonstrated or not, very specific traditional concepts appear to be at work. In central Idaho, on the remote Salmon River, the "River of No Return," the burial site of Charles A. (Charlie) Bemis is one such example. Although he was Euro-American, his Chinese wife, Polly Bemis, undoubtedly selected his grave site. She chose a slight rise in front of an enveloping hillside facing a creek flowing into a river, all significant *fengshui* characteristics. This suggests that even common people were familiar with the basic principles of *fengshui*.

Polly Bemis died some years later and was buried in Grangeville's Prairie View Cemetery. In 1987, her remains were exhumed and reinterred just outside her cabin, across the river from where Charlie is buried; he was interred where he died, on the opposite side of the river from their home. Her present location, chosen by Euro-Americans, lacks adherence to *fengshui* principles, in contrast to the "Chineseness" of her husband's grave site.[35]

Another physical indication of the practice of *fengshui* in the rural West would be the existence of geomantic compasses among the material remains of Chinese immigrants. The widespread availability of such geomantic compasses in China[36] suggests that individuals other than the "priesthood" commonly attempted to determine the harmonious qualities of particular sites. Although geomantic compasses have not yet been found, or have not been recognized, in an archaeological context in the intermountain West, such a compass, marked with hexagrams, has been identified among the holdings of the Chinese Museum in Barkerville, British Columbia.[37] This artifact suggests that at least some Chinese in the West practiced *fengshui*.

It is worth noting that the apparent lack of contemporary documentary evidence means that all discussion of *fengshui* practices in nineteenth-century rural western sites is based on later interpretations. Such readings must be cautiously applied, since an important component of the belief is that unsuitable sitings can be made harmonious through "retrofitting, [that is,] realignment [through] ritual or talismans."[38]

Because the burials in rural western sites were considered temporary, with a more permanent and carefully sited interment to take place close to family at a later date, Chinese cemeteries in the inland Northwest lack the omega-shaped tombs (Ω) set into the hillside, a common type of mortuary monument in China.[39] Although evident in Chinese cemeteries on the Hawaiian island of Oahu (see chapter 6), similar features have not yet been observed in rural western cemeteries.[40] In China, this form of monument is characteristic of secondary burials, part of the ritual that transforms the deceased into an ancestor spirit.[41] The Chinese seldom performed this stage of the process in the nineteenth-century interior West.

REMOVAL OF REMAINS FROM
PACIFIC NORTHWEST CEMETERIES

Where a distinctly separate Chinese cemetery exists, it may be possible to isolate certain common features; chief among these are empty graves. According to Chinese custom, Chinese immigrants, nearly all of whom planned to return to China after making their fortune in the West, made provision for the possibility of their death in a foreign land by arranging in advance for their remains to be returned to China (see chapter 1). Accordingly, they paid a death "insurance" fee to cover the costs of exhumation and reburial in south China.

While this practice is often attributed to a desire to be buried in one's native soil,[42] it is more correct to state that Chinese belief in the continuity between this life and the afterlife required one's material remains to be cared for by one's family after death. This veneration ensured that the ancestors would watch out for and protect the living descendants. It is this family responsibility that prompted the practice of exhumation and removal.

Disinterment was not uncommon in southern China, where the relocation of remains to ensure favorable *fengshui* placement was carried out in a similar fashion. There, after seven to ten years, specialists would excavate the wooden coffins, scrape the bones clean, and place them in large urns for reburial.[43] This practice, adapted to new conditions in North America, resolved one difficulty a Chinese laborer faced when traveling abroad for what was often dangerous work. He could be assured that after death his remains would receive proper care by his family in China and that traditional rituals would ensure a good afterlife in the spirit world. Although the exact time for exhumation varied in the

United States, it was usually at least three years after death and burial. At the appropriate time, an agent of the CCBA, as successor to the family associations that had earlier managed this task, would appear in the community and direct the exhumations.

Newspapers often reported on this practice.[44] For example, one account described the exhumation of forty Chinese from the Walla Walla, Washington, cemetery in 1905.[45] Of particular concern was the obligation to count all the small bones to make sure none were missing. The bones were grouped together in bags: arms, legs, body, head. Valued belongings, such as eyeglasses, also were included. In the context of Western medical doctors performing foot amputations, Beverley Jackson observes that traditional beliefs required that all the bones remain together, so they would be together in the afterlife.[46]

In Baker City, Oregon, in the mid-1930s, ironworker Herman C. Webb made sheet metal boxes for the exhumed bones. He constructed about thirty boxes, measuring ten by twelve by thirty inches, of .28-gauge metal. After they were filled, he soldered them shut and delivered them to the agent for shipment to China through San Francisco.[47]

In the war-torn turmoil of the 1930s, during the worldwide economic depression, it became increasingly difficult to manage such shipments to China; this, combined with the smaller numbers of Chinese who wished to be returned, brought the enterprise to a halt. In a 1994 conversation with then–federal archivist Waverly Lowell, in San Bruno, California, Samuel Couch learned that records of the CCBA's removal activities, which would have provided much documentary evidence on the early Chinese laborers in the West, were reportedly destroyed in the 1950s.[48] Many had already been lost in the fire following the 1906 San Francisco earthquake.

The effect of this removal activity is still apparent in many locations throughout the West, since, once exhumed, the graves were not backfilled. These exhumation pits are clearly visible in Warren, Pierce, and Florence, Idaho, as well as in Baker City, Oregon. The empty graves could thus more easily be reused as necessary,[49] a practice that meant that Chinese cemeteries could be smaller than Euro-American ones serving similarly sized populations.[50] Except where local health concerns dictated otherwise, burials in Chinese cemeteries were shallow, eighteen inches deep rather than the more traditional six feet, permitting easy exhumation.[51]

In Moscow, Idaho, the cemetery deed book lists Chinese burials and notes subsequent removals (fig. 5.1). The book of handwritten entries also indicates that empty grave sites were resold for reuse by Euro-Americans.[52]

Not all Chinese participated in the removal activity. The reasons were undoubtedly individual, but could be categorized as a greater degree of assimilation, a lack of connection with family back in China, or insufficient funds

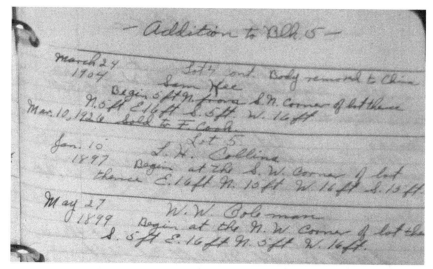

Figure 5.1.   Deed book, Moscow Cemetery, Moscow, ID. Photograph by Priscilla We-gars. Note upper right, Sam Kee, "Body removed to China" and lot resold.

to purchase the death insurance. There is, for instance, at least one burial re-maining in what was an extensive Chinese cemetery on the slope above Sil-ver City, Idaho.[53] Those who were able to bring families to North America, particularly merchants, would have satisfied the need to have descendants to care for their remains.

Some women appear to have been excluded from the practice of removal. The emphasis on patrilineal descent and the lack of respect accorded women were contributing factors. In addition, the bringing of Chinese women to the United States removed them from the familial system in which they would become the curators of their husband's filial obligations. This may mean that some Chinese cemeteries, considered empty through removal, are actually still holding female burials.

In recent years, with the reopening of China's borders, removal practices have been revived. Today, however, the traffic is in the opposite direction. Immigrants are bringing the remains of their direct ancestors to North America for reburial here (see chapter 8), thus maintaining the pattern of familial responsibility.

GRAVE AND BURIAL MARKERS

Graves of men and women interred permanently in western cemeteries were marked in a variety of ways. Wooden markers were common in forested regions and elsewhere, but very few now remain. One from the inland Northwest has been illustrated elsewhere,[54] as has one from Nevada.[55] Markers for those who were exhumed and returned were often simple wooden plaques giving name and date of death for cross-checking with the CCBA's records. Chinese ink (often called "India ink") would usually endure through the years prior to exhumation.[56] A flat wooden fragment among the exhumed pits at Warren, Idaho, may possibly be from such an identifier. Once the body was removed, a marker was no longer needed. Because wooden markers tended to rot, they lost the capability to memorialize the deceased, so other, more substantive, materials, such as stones, concrete, and bricks, were preferred as grave markers.

Another attempt at preserving identification for later exhumation was a wooden slat placed in a bottle; one was found at a northeastern Oregon cemetery.[57] It reportedly stated, "Lee Gooey buried at cemetery. Died at midnight, Dec. 4, 1924. Good heart."[58] Bottles were also used to protect linen strips[59] and paper slips[60] containing written information about the deceased.

Marked bricks seem to have been primarily used as identification for later exhumations.[61] The bricks were marked with the person's name and home village, and sometimes other details such as age or date of death. This information was then transferred to the shipping container.

The use of bricks as markers has recently received some attention (see chapters 3 and 4), but there has been little else published by way of description or analysis. In 1995 an abandoned cemetery was discovered during seismic retrofitting in San Francisco. Chinese burials uncovered there included some with character-marked bricks.[62] An exhibit viewed in April 1998 at the Jake Jackson Museum in Weaverville, California, contained an inscribed brick described as a grave marker, and the museum in Forbestown, California, exhibited a similar brick from a 1918 burial.[63] The aptly named family history *Bury My Bones in America* uses a photograph of this identical inscribed brick on the back of the book jacket,[64] but does not identify it.

Anthropologist Linda Sun Crowder has offered an alternative explanation for the bricks, however. She noted that "poor people may place bricks in their coffins in imitation of the manner of the emperors who placed real gold bricks in their coffins. These bricks are uninscripted."[65]

Historian Nancy Wey reports a different use for bricks in a Chinese cemetery in Quincy, California, where eleven graves are set off with bricks. Although Wey does not state whether the bricks were marked with characters,[66] it is unlikely. The Cloncurry Chinese Cemetery in Cloncurry, Queensland, Australia, contains one grave with a "simple extruded brick surround" outlining the grave plot.[67] Brick outlines are also seen in many non-Chinese cemeteries.

Although bricks have not been identified as components of Chinese burials in the inland Northwest, grave markers viewed at cemeteries in Walla Walla, Washington; Grangeville, Idaho; Moscow, Idaho; the Mount Hope Cemetery in Baker City, Oregon; and the Morris Hill Cemetery in Boise, Idaho, show similar characteristics and patterns. The text on the markers ranges from all Chinese through a combination of English and Chinese to all English. Physically, the markers range from rectangular blocks set flat in the ground, to upright slabs, to slabs on pedestals. These shape variations are little different from those in Euro-American burials.

The form and the language of the marker frequently resulted from the circumstances of the death and burial. Local taxing districts often place very simple generic markers. Funeral homes may provide a simple metal tag with removable letters to mark graves for which no stone has been provided. Where gravestones are in Chinese, family members or others supervising the burial provided the characters for the local stonemason to copy.[68]

Although markers with both Chinese and English characters indicate a measure of acculturation, it is important to recognize that it is usually the survivors, not the deceased, who undertake the memorial activities. Accordingly, the acculturation measured is not necessarily that of the deceased. However, when close friends or relatives supervised the creation of the markers, an effort was made to fulfill the perceived desires of the deceased.

Sometimes markers have been placed by Euro-Americans. Herman Koppes, a resident of Centerville, Idaho, reported that in the late 1920s he placed a memorial stone on the grave of a local Chinese friend.[69] Mr. Koppes was unable to locate that stone in the early 1990s,[70] perhaps because the stone had been stolen or vandalized, or he had forgotten the location.

In the Baker City Chinese Cemetery, amidst all of the exhumation pits, lies a substantial, but modest, granite stone for Lee Chue, who died in 1938 (fig. 5.2). Lee Pak Chue was born in Victoria, British Columbia, in 1882.[71] He eventually arrived in Baker City, where he became an herbalist, retiring in the 1930s.[72] He died on May 5, 1938, of "cardio ren[a]l disease"; his funeral was charged to his estate.[73] At the time of his death, he had a widow and son, Lee Bing Yuen, in China.[74] The son's name indicates that Lee Chue's surname was Lee, not Chue, even though Lee Chue's funeral record is alphabetized under *C*.

Baker City native Marjorie Fong stated that his bones were not sent back because "he didn't want them to be"; she recalled that he had a son who might have lived in northeastern Oregon somewhere.[75] Even if that were not the case, most bone shipments to China had already ceased by that date.

Another form of marker, not yet identified in the Pacific Northwest, was flattened sheet iron. An example, with nail-punched characters, has been

Figure 5.2.   Lee Chue marker surrounded by exhumation pits, Chinese Cemetery, Baker City, OR. Photograph by Priscilla Wegars.

found at a remote mining site in Australia.[76] Other nearby cemetery markers, lacking the punched characters, were made by flattening corrugated galvanized iron, fuel cans, or food tins. It is possible that they originally had inked inscriptions, now weathered away.

FUNERARY STRUCTURES

One feature often seen in Euro-American cemeteries is the mausoleum or massive funerary structure. Many Chinese cemeteries have shrines or altars for ritual observances such as the offering of food after the funeral and during the Qingming or Chongyang festivals.[77] Others have a "bone house," a repository for the urns and boxes of the exhumed awaiting shipment and reburial. Geographer David Chuenyan Lai has described those once found in Victoria, British Columbia,[78] and historian Sue Fawn Chung has noted one in Elko, Nevada.[79] The authors have visited the bone houses at two Chinese cemeteries on the Hawaiian island of Oahu. There are no comparable equivalents to these three types of structures—mausoleums, shrines, and bone houses—among the western cemeteries examined.

The more common singular feature of Chinese cemeteries and of the Chinese sections of Euro-American cemeteries is the "burner." This brick or masonry structure, usually over seven feet tall, serves as a safe place for the ritualized burning of spiritual tributes.[80] Often paper and cardboard facsimiles of money, clothing, possessions, and even houses, these objects are to serve the deceased in the afterlife. Burning them passes them to the spirit realm for use by the deceased.

In addition to replica artifacts, burning the deceased's personal effects was common. Father François X. Blanchet in southern Oregon noted this practice about 1873: "They offer all the provisions to the dead and dispose of them by burning it on the graves, as the whites or the savages would otherwise steal it."[81] At the Folsom, California, Chung Wah (CCBA) Cemetery, a large depression near the entrance, rather than a burner, facilitated this practice. Cindy Baker and Mary Maniery report that in Folsom a "brick oven with steel doors" near the temple was used to burn actual belongings of the deceased.[82] Historian Nancy Wey observes that the Nevada City Chinese Cemetery "is one of the few [in California] which still has a burner for paper money and offerings."[83] Wey also lists a vandalized burner at Auburn in Placer County, California, and another in the San Jose cemetery, "which although only 6 feet by 6 feet is monumental in its simplicity."[84]

Vacaville, California, native Yee Ah Chong noted the transition from burning in an open pit to using an incinerator:

> The Chinese in this country when anybody dies their few possessions are burned. They take them out to the cemetery and burn them. . . . Along with this money, paper money, an offering and a little ceremony goes with it. It invariably set the countryside on fire. All that dry grass and weeds would just go up in fire. So they run them [the Chinese] out of Vacaville. They wouldn't let them have them [the burnings] anymore so they went to Fairfield . . . with the provision that they would burn in an incinerator. It's there yet. You can drive around and see the old incinerator sitting there yet. . . . You can tell it's a brick incinerator. You know, there's nothing anywhere else like it. They made them do that to burn their stuff in it and also to burn the paper offering.[85]

Similar problems were reported in Nevada City, California.[86] In parts of China, particularly Hong Kong, "accidental" wild fires from graveside rituals are a continuing problem.[87]

The burner in the Chinese section of the Walla Walla cemetery is a large, square, red-brick-faced structure with a sloping concrete cap. A course of protruding bricks gives it the appearance of an undersized two-story building. The south face has a large circular opening, while two smaller arched openings appear in each of the other three faces. Inside one can see the concrete block core of the structure and a metal grate, on which, in 1997, were several burned or rusted tin cans.

The burner at the elegant Morris Hill Cemetery in Boise, Idaho, is also brick but painted white (fig. 5.3). The faces are smooth and rise to a sloping, white concrete cap. Only the south face is blank. The north face contains a tall, narrow opening nine courses high with a triangular "shoulder" and rounded top. The east and west faces are identical; bricks have been omitted, leaving a cross-shaped opening. This structure contained debris that may or may not have resulted from funerary rituals.

Since vandals destroyed the original some time ago, the burner at the Baker City Chinese Cemetery is a reconstruction. It is based in part on the reminiscences of an elderly Chinese American native of Baker City, now deceased. The new burner, some eight feet tall, is of thick masonry construction, measuring seven feet square by six feet, three inches high. The gabled masonry is topped by a corrugated iron roof on a framework of cast-iron pipe, based on remains of the original found at the site.

Another vandalized burner is at Olney Cemetery at Pendleton, also in eastern Oregon; documentation exists of Chinese rituals there.[88] Here the upper brick courses have been removed and a flat concrete cap placed on top. This burner presently measures six feet square by five feet high.

In other locales, burners range from modest to elaborate. Historian Ian Jack, comparing burners in California, Macao, and Australia, notes: "The

Figure 5.3. Burner, Morris Hill Cemetery, Boise, ID. Its brick base measures 4 feet 4 inches square by 4 feet 10 inches tall; its concrete cap is 4 feet 8 inches square by 2 feet tall. Photograph by Priscilla Wegars.

most striking feature of Chinese Australian practice is the lavishness of the best burners. . . . [One] is astonishing by world standards."[89] Those found in Pacific Northwest cemeteries tend toward the more unpretentious end of the scale as compared to ones at Australian cemeteries.

FUNERARY RITUALS

In addition to the burning of paper symbols of goods, funerary rituals involved leaving material offerings, such as food and liquor, for the spirits. Numerous contemporary accounts describe such funerary practices.[90] When a young man from Hong Kong, working as a servant in turn-of-the-century Victoria, British Columbia, was asked about this practice, his explanation of the shadowy nature of the spirit world was quite explicit:

> "You see," replied he quickly, taking up a cup, and holding it in front of a lamp so that a sharp shadow was thrown on to the white tablecloth. "You see that," pointing to the shadow, "dead men all the same that, he eat all the same that [shadow] of food and wine, I this," flicking the cup with his finger; "if I no get all the same this, food and wine, me pretty soon die quick."[91]

Glass and ceramic containers from such offerings, usually broken, may be found today at the sites of Chinese burials.[92] We visited one museum exhibiting a small group of such fragments collected at the local Chinese cemetery and asked if they were planning a similar exhibit of artifacts from the Euro-American cemetery. When we next visited, the display had been removed.

Paper reproductions of contemporary material culture, for use in funerary or memorial ceremonies, are available for purchase today. One store in Vancouver, British Columbia, visited in 1995, had paper videocassette recorders, televisions, and cell phones.[93] Before burning the paper objects at the cemetery, relatives or other purchasers write the deceased's name and hometown on them[94] or speak the name aloud.[95] Euro-American novelty stores, unaware of the cultural significance of them as paper funerary tokens, often sell "hell banknotes" and other such items to equally unsuspecting purchasers. "Hell banknotes" are one form of "mock money" that is burned during ceremonies honoring the deceased. Burning it sends it to the realm of the dead, where it becomes real money that the spirit can use to purchase needed items.[96]

CHINESE IN EURO-AMERICAN CEMETERIES

Civic leader Oscar Fong often organized the burials of Chinese in the Baker City, Oregon, Chinese Cemetery.[97] However, the Christian and much-acculturated

Fong family interred their own deceased at the other end of town, in Baker City's Mount Hope Cemetery, which had separate sections for Chinese and Japanese burials, as well as for Catholics, Masons, and Odd Fellows.

Where the Chinese were, or later became, a much smaller population, there was less need for a completely distinct burial ground. Today, many communities have a separate Chinese section in the Euro-American cemetery, such as the Morris Hill Cemetery in Boise, Idaho; the Normal Hill Cemetery in Lewiston, Idaho; and the Walla Walla, Washington, cemetery. Although secondary historical sources sometimes discuss the Chinese in these communities, many do not mention funerary practices.[98]

The disposition of remains is also subject to changes in belief patterns. Those Chinese who had become more acculturated, even to the point of adopting Christianity, were more likely to want to follow Christian patterns in interment. Funeral records for Baker City, Oregon, list five Chinese Catholics who were buried in the Euro-American Mount Hope Cemetery, possibly in the Catholic section.[99] Father O'Rourke officiated at the funeral of another Chinese man, who died in 1930, but who was buried in the Chinese Cemetery.[100]

Having a Chinese section in a cemetery already partitioned off for Catholics, Masons, and Odd Fellows is not that unusual. One example, in Idaho City, Idaho, is the Boise County Pioneer Cemetery. A local guidebook notes: "Sections of the cemetery have been consecrated by the Masonic and Odd Fellows Societies, the Roman Catholics, and the Chinese."[101]

This segregation, in some cases, may be a function of the CCBA's role as community caretaker and family stand-in. Individuals would not purchase a grave site in advance, for it would be bad luck to do so; this role was left to the surviving family or community association. Rather than buy individual grave sites, the CCBA would acquire a block of cemetery land, and individual sites would be allocated within the section.[102]

Self-segregation must also be considered. Consultant Frederick Chin advised the funeral industry that "Chinese people prefer graves near those of other Chinese."[103] Funeral director Charles Belanger stated that his Chinese clientele believe that the deceased "talk to each other in the ground."[104]

Not all Chinese were buried in separate sections. Ah Sam, a long-term resident of Warren, Idaho, was interred in that community's Euro-American cemetery, not the Chinese cemetery, after his death in 1933. He had been named "honorary mayor" only a few years before[105] and was a well-known character in the Warren district. His deeds of kindness and charity won him a warm spot in the hearts of his friends and acquaintances.[106] Another writer agreed, noting that Sam was greatly respected and loved by all Warren residents. Hours before dawn, on cold winter nights, Sam would go from one end of the sleepy Warren town to the other, kindling dying embers in each stove so that the residents would have warm homes when they awakened. In return, the residents put out pastries, cold cuts, and other tasty foods [for him].[107]

During the 1880s Chinese workers helped construct the Northern Pacific Railroad across the northern Idaho mountains into Montana. Chinese section gangs and Chinese support services were later based in the remote community of Hope, Idaho. An early Hope cemetery once existed in the narrow area outside of town between the hills and Lake Pend Oreille, and Chinese were reportedly buried there.[108] Much of this graveyard was destroyed by later highway construction. Although a few gravestones remain, they are only for Euro-Americans; there are no markers or depressions to indicate that Chinese people were once interred there also. Funeral home records, however, indicate that at least three Chinese were buried at that cemetery.[109]

A Chinese woman named May Den died in Hope in 1925 and is buried in the town's main cemetery. As is often the case, Chinese characters on May Den's tombstone give her Chinese name and that of her birthplace in China. The tombstone reads, "Grave [of a woman whose maiden name was] Ou [Cantonese, Ow] [who married into the] Liu [Cantonese, Lau; Toishanese, Lew] clan of Wong Poon Ling village, Wong Sui [heung (a group of villages)], Toishan [district]"[110] (fig. 5.4). A woman's gravestone, such as this one, often recorded more information about the deceased's husband than about the dead woman herself.[111]

EFFORTS TO MAINTAIN CEMETERIES

"Abandoned" Euro-American cemeteries in remote western places are often subject to vandalism and/or illicit excavation. Chinese graves and Chinese cemeteries are exposed to the same evils.[112] However, many such sites are on federal land, and agencies such as the Forest Service and the Bureau of Land Management are increasing their efforts to locate and preserve them. This has resulted in interpretive signs, brochures, and other efforts to recognize the Chinese contributions to western history. In Oroville, California, in 1972, the Butte County Board of Supervisors designated Oroville's Chinese cemetery as a Pioneer Memorial Park,[113] and in Wheatland, California, local Euro-American residents reportedly rebuilt the vandalized burner in the Chinese American cemetery.[114]

Figure 5.4. **Tombstone of May L. Den, Hope Cemetery, Hope, ID. Photograph by Priscilla Wegars.**

In several cases, local citizens and agencies have stepped in to document and preserve these historic locations, thus ensuring that the sites are afforded a measure of respect as cemeteries. For example, in Baker City, Oregon, adult and teenage representatives from Portland's Chinese Consolidated Benevolent Association have twice cleaned up the grounds. The CCBA and the Baker County Historical Society have recently published an illustrated brochure on the Baker City Chinese Cemetery.[115] The local group has placed interpretive signs, cleared brush, erected a fence, created paths, rebuilt the masonry burner, and, in 2002, installed a three-sided pavilion imported from China.

Similarly Pierce, Idaho, has placed this sign at the site of its Chinese cemetery, now a city park:

Chinese Cemetery
This is the site of the graves of the Chinese who died in Pierce. All bodies have been returned to their homeland. Chinese artifacts[,] broken tools[,] and rotting cabins are still found in the nearby hills.

Occasionally, concerned individuals, with the best of intentions, have tried to ensure that such cemeteries remain memorials to those who helped create and develop the American West. In 1980, a former resident of a remote Idaho community commemorated the local Chinese by erecting a welded sheet-metal dragon at the town's Chinese cemetery.[116] This object is proving to be an interpretive problem for the Forest Service, which now owns the site.

At the other extreme is abandonment and disregard. Elk City, Idaho, in remote Idaho County, had a Chinese cemetery in the latter half of the nineteenth century. By the mid-1970s the site had, to many, lost its character as a burying ground, and a personal residence was built there.[117] This tragedy has been repeated elsewhere in the West (see chapter 4).

CONCLUSIONS

In the interior Pacific Northwest during the late nineteenth and early twentieth centuries, Chinese laborers lived, worked, and died far from home. Chinese belief systems required that the dead be properly cared for, and an established body of Asian funerary customs and traditions manifested itself on the western slopes of the Rocky Mountains.

Many communities had Chinese cemeteries that provided temporary resting places for the deceased. Careful siting of the burial grounds often ensured good fortune, both for the deceased and for the living; contented denizens of the spirit world would not harass the living and spread bad fortune.

Most Chinese expected, and made arrangements for, their bones to be disinterred and shipped back to the home village. Early Chinese cemeteries in the mountain West thus still contain exhumation pits that were once graves.

The emphasis on removal of the bodies dictated a variety of efforts to properly mark the graves; wooden markers were ephemeral, while stones, concrete, and bricks provided more permanent memorials. Some bricks, incised or marked with ink, were buried with the deceased. Paper or wooden slats sealed in bottles were another means to keep track of the deceased and his—and sometimes her—home village.

Several Chinese cemeteries in the interior Pacific Northwest feature a masonry structure that served as an incinerator for paper offerings to benefit the deceased. Often called a burner, it is a prominent landmark in cemeteries in Boise, Walla Walla, Baker City, and elsewhere.

Increasing acculturation coupled with international events halted the shipment of bodies back to China, and thus many Chinese are now permanently located in Euro-American cemeteries across the West. Their markers are often indistinguishable from those of their Euro-American neighbors, except for the name and, often, Chinese characters.

As we have seen, the funerary remains of the West's Chinese residents persist, both in the documentation and in the landscape. Once overgrown and overlooked, these monuments are now visible reminders of the history of the Chinese in the interior Northwest.

NOTES

1. Priscilla Wegars, *The Ah Hee Diggings: Final Report of Archaeological Investigations at OR-GR-16, the Granite, Oregon "Chinese Walls" Site, 1992 through 1994,* University of Idaho Anthropological Reports 97 (Moscow: Alfred W. Bowers Laboratory of Anthropology, University of Idaho, 1995), 32.

2. Leonard J. Arrington, *History of Idaho,* vol. 1 (Moscow: University of Idaho Press, 1994), 186.

3. Thomas A. McDannold, "Chinese Placenames and Their Significance," in *Origins and Destinations: 41 Essays on Chinese America* (Los Angeles: Chinese Historical Society of Southern California and UCLA Asian American Studies Center, 1994), 181.

4. Yixian Xu, trans., "Translation Notes: Gravestone of Lee Mann," Asian American Comparative Collection, University of Idaho, Moscow, 1993.

5. Gorden Lee, letter to Priscilla Wegars, October 29, 1997. Gorden Lee is not known to be related to Lee Mann.

6. M. Alfreda Elsensohn, *Pioneer Days in Idaho County,* vol. 1 (Cottonwood: Idaho Corporation of Benedictine Sisters, 1965), 167–168.

7. Gorden Lee, letter to Priscilla Wegars, October 29, 1997.

8. See, for example, Emma Woo Louie, "A New Perspective on Surnames among Chinese Americans," *Amerasia Journal* 12 (1985–1986); "Surnames as Clues to Family History," in *Chinese America: History and Perspectives 1991,* ed. Marlon K. Hom and others (San Francisco: Chinese Historical Society of America, 1991); "Chinese American Name Styles and Their Significance," in *Origins and Destinations: 41 Essays on Chinese America* (Los Angeles: Chinese Historical Society of Southern California and UCLA Asian American Studies Center, 1994); and *Chinese American Names: Tradition and Transition* (Jefferson, NC: McFarland, 1998).

9. Linda Brumley, "Turning History into People: The People on the Chinese Gravestones in 19th Century Ballarat Cemeteries," in *Histories of the Chinese in Australasia and the South Pacific,* ed. Paul Macgregor (Melbourne: Museum of Chinese Australian History, 1995), 323–324.

10. Wallace R. Hagaman, *A Short History of the Chinese Cemetery at Nevada City, California and Chinese Burial Customs during the Gold Rush* (Nevada City, CA: Cowboy Press, 2001), [2].

11. Wegars, *Ah Hee Diggings*, 20.

12. *Baker City (OR) Herald*, September 8, 1997.

13. City of Lewiston, *Charter and General Ordinances of the City of Lewiston* (Lewiston, ID: Teller, 1896), 104.

14. Nez Perce County Leases, Book N (Lewiston, ID: Nez Perce County Courthouse, 1891), 226. The original Chinese cemetery site is now Prospect Park.

15. Priscilla Wegars, "Chinese at the Confluence and Beyond: A Case Study of Asian Entrepreneurs and Other Pioneers in Early Pierce and Lewiston" (working paper, 1996), 123–125.

16. Mary L. Maniery and Cindy L. Baker, "National Register of Historic Places Registration Form, Chung Wah Cemetery, Folsom, California" (Sacramento, CA: PAR Environmental Services, 1995), [6] (hereafter "Chung Wah Cemetery"); see also Ronald G. Knapp, "The Changing Landscape of the Chinese Cemetery," *China Geographer* 8 (Fall 1977): 7.

17. Priscilla Wegars, "Marjorie Fong, a Chinese American Pioneer of Baker City, Oregon" (working paper, 1996), 15.

18. L. Eve Armentrout Ma, "Chinese Traditional Religion in North America and Hawaii," in *Chinese America: History and Perspectives 1988*, ed. Him Mark Lai, Ruthanne Lum McCunn, and Judy Yung (San Francisco: Chinese Historical Society of America, 1988), 139, 144. During these ceremonies, the graves, although not necessarily the grounds, were swept and offerings were made.

19. David Chuenyan Lai, "The Chinese Cemetery in Victoria," *BC Studies* 75 (1987): 27–28. The Chongyang festival is celebrated on the ninth day of the ninth month. Then, in northern China, chrysanthemums are in full bloom.

20. Betty Derig, "Celestials in the Diggings," *Idaho Yesterdays* 16 (Fall 1972): 13.

21. Samuel L. Couch, "Topophilia and Chinese Miners: Place Attachment in North Central Idaho" (PhD diss., University of Idaho, 1996), 195–196.

22. Larry Peters, "Green Dragons and White Tigers on Gold Mountain: *Feng-Shui* in Barkerville," *B.C. Historical News*, Fall 1998, 19.

23. François Xavier Blanchet, "Ten Years on the Pacific Coast," trans. Don Wilkins (Seattle: University of Washington [WPA Projects nos. 4185 and 5606], 1937), 70. Typescript carbon in the University of Idaho Library. These graves were on the side of a hill, so "head . . . lowest" meant down the slope.

24. Stewart Culin, "Customs of the Chinese in America," *Journal of American Folk-Lore* 3 (1890): 195.

25. Maniery and Baker, "Chung Wah Cemetery," [5].

26. William Winterbotham, *An Historical, Geographical, and Philosophical View of the Chinese Empire* (London: Ridgway, 1795), 357. Although Winterbotham does not use the term *fengshui*, he refers to certain "superstitious practices," one of which is "the choice of ground and situation proper for a burying-place."

27. Evelyn S. Rawski, "A Historian's Approach to Chinese Death Ritual," in *Death Ritual in Late Imperial and Modern China*, ed. James L. Watson and Evelyn S. Rawski (Berkeley: University of California Press, 1988), 25.

28. Rubie S. Watson, "Remembering the Dead: Graves and Politics in Southeastern China," in *Death Ritual in Late Imperial and Modern China*, ed. James L. Watson and Evelyn S. Rawski (Berkeley: University of California Press, 1988), 207–209.

29. Watson, "Remembering," 208.

30. Emily M. Ahern, *The Cult of the Dead in a Chinese Village* (Stanford, CA: Stanford University Press, 1973), 181; Knapp, "Changing Landscape," 8; Stuart E. Thompson, "Death, Food, and Fertility," in *Death Ritual in Late Imperial and Modern China*, ed. James L. Watson and Evelyn S. Rawski (Berkeley: University of California Press, 1988), 104.

31. Couch, "Topophilia," 63.

32. Lai, "Chinese Cemetery," 29–30.

33. Lai, "Chinese Cemetery," 30. See also Chuen-Yan David Lai, "A Feng Shui Model as a Location Index," *Annals of the Association of American Geographers* 64, no. 4 (December 1974): 507.

34. Couch, "Topophilia," 192–193, poetically translating *fengshui*.

35. Priscilla Wegars, "Polly Bemis: Lurid Life or Literary Legend?" in *Wild Women of the Old West*, ed. Glenda Riley and Richard W. Etulain (Golden, CO: Fulcrum, 2003), 66.

36. J. Dyer Ball, *Things Chinese, or Notes Connected with China* (Hong Kong: Kelly and Walsh, 1903), 314.

37. Peters, "Green Dragons," 20.

38. Roberta S. Greenwood, *Down by the Station, Los Angeles Chinatown, 1880–1933* (Los Angeles: UCLA Institute of Archaeology, 1996), 13.

39. C. Fred Blake, "Gravestones in the Chinese Diaspora" (paper presented at the regional meeting of the Association for Asian American Studies, Honolulu, March 1996).

40. One similarly shaped structure, from Nevada City, California, is pictured on the inside front cover of Hagaman, *Short History*, but it apparently is a memorial site, not a tomb. Omega-shaped tombs are found in Chinese cemeteries in Colma, California, where urban San Francisco's burials were relocated, starting in the 1890s; see chapter 7.

41. Watson, "Remembering," 209–210.

42. Ma, "Chinese," 144.

43. Ahern, *Cult*, 130–131; Watson, "Remembering," 208. Forensic archaeologists have noted that it generally takes about six to seven years for a body to become fully skeletonized; see A. M. Pollard, "Dating the Time of Death," in *Studies in Crime: An Introduction to Forensic Archaeology*, ed. John Hunter, Charlotte Roberts, and Anthony Martin (London: Batsford, 1996), 141. However, contemporary accounts suggest that scraping the bones was an accepted part of the job; see Linda Sun Crowder, "Mortuary Practices in San Francisco Chinatown," *Chinese America: History and Perspectives, 1999*, ed. Marlon Hom and others (San Francisco: Chinese Historical Society of America, 1999), 34.

44. See, for example, *Spokane (WA) Spokesman-Review*, May 25, 1902.

45. *Spokane (WA) Spokesman-Review*, September 24, 1905.

46. Beverley Jackson, *Splendid Slippers: A Thousand Years of an Erotic Tradition* (Berkeley: Ten Speed, 1997), 134, 137.

47. Wegars, *Ah Hee Diggings*, 19.

48. Couch, "Topophilia," 216.

49. Maniery and Baker, "Chung Wah Cemetery," [6].

50. Cindy L. Baker and Mary L. Maniery, *Historical Summary of Chinese Cemeteries in Folsom, Sacramento County, California: Final Report* (Sacramento, CA: PAR Environmental Services, 1995), 16.

51. Sylvia Sun Minnick, *Samfow: The San Joaquin Chinese Legacy* (Fresno, CA: Panorama West, 1988), 293.

52. Moscow Cemetery Deed Book, "Addition to Blk. 5," (unpaginated manuscript, Moscow City Cemetery, Moscow, ID, 1897–1930).

53. Betty Derig, "The Chinese of Silver City," *Idaho Yesterdays* 2 (Winter 1959): 4.

54. See, for example, Jane Trombley Frink, Helen Woodroofe, and Julie Reese, eds., "Chinese Performed Memorial Rites at Olney Cemetery," *Pioneer Trails* 16 (Summer 1992): 4, Umatilla County Historical Society. The authors imply that the illustrated grave marker is from Pendleton, Oregon, but we did not see it in the cemetery there.

55. Joseph M. Moore, *The Test Excavation of 26MN540, Acme Playa, Mineral County, Nevada*, NDOT Archaeological Technical Report Series, No. 2 (Carson City, NV: Nevada Department of Transportation, 1986), 107–111. The once-painted characters are now visible in relief due to differential weathering, but the extent of their deterioration is such that translators do not agree on their meaning.

56. Minnick, *Samfow*, 288; Yee Ah Chong, "Chinese Burial Customs," an unnumbered chapter in "The Chinese in Vacaville," interview by Ron Limbaugh, February 4 and 12, 1977, transcript, 52, Vacaville Museum, Vacaville, California.

57. John Meek, telephone conversation with Priscilla Wegars, 1997.

58. Baker County Historical Society, "Chinese Cemetery Pavillion [*sic*] Dedication," *Baker County Historical Society* (newsletter), Fall 2000, [2]. This person is probably Lee Kee, aged seventy-eight or eighty-five, who was a placer miner in Auburn and Clark Creek and who was buried in the "China cemetery"; Baker Funeral Records, *Funeral Records of Baker, Oregon*, microfilm (Salt Lake City, UT: Genealogical Society of Utah, [1950?]), reel 2, H-R, from West and Company records, vol. 13. Because each typed card has the notation "West and Co." and a volume number, the entries were presumably taken from sequential books of funeral records compiled by West and Company, a former Baker City funeral home, now Gray's West and Company.

59. Hagaman, *Short History*, [6]; Minnick, *Samfow*, 292.

60. Bruce Edward Hall, *Tea That Burns: A Family Memoir of Chinatown* (New York: Free Press, 1998), 205.

61. Baker and Maniery, "Chinese Cemeteries," 16; Yee, "Chinese Burial Customs," 52; Hagaman, *Short History*, [5]; Minnick, *Samfow*, 292.

62. Candy Kit Har Chan, "31 Historic Chinese Corpses Discovered in Abandoned Cemetery," *Asian Week*, April 14, 1995, 4.

63. *Marysville (CA) Appeal-Democrat*, July 27, 1998; Xiaoyun Yao, trans., "Translation Notes: Burial Brick of Ru Chui Zhen" (pinyin), Asian American Comparative Collection, University of Idaho, Moscow, 1999.

64. Lani Ah Tye Farkas, *Bury My Bones in America* (Nevada City, CA: Carl Mautz, 1998), back cover; Yao, "Translation Notes."

65. Linda Sun Crowder, e-mail message to Chinese Cemetery Study Group, authors' collection, March 23, 1997.

66. Nancy Wey, comp., "Chinese Sites in California" (photocopy, unpaginated, arranged by county, Asian American Comparative Collection, University of Idaho, Moscow, n.d.), Plumas County: Quincy.

67. Godden Mackay Heritage Consultants, *Queensland Historical Burial Places Study*, vol. 1 (Queensland, Australia: Queensland Department of Environment, 1997), appendix F, Cloncurry, Cloncurry Chinese Cemetery.

68. This still happens today. In 2001, for example, Priscilla Wegars purchased a replacement for the shattered gravestone belonging to "Jim Yee-Ott" and had it installed in the Lewiston, Idaho, Normal Hill Cemetery. Former Lewiston resident Gorden Lee commissioned the inscription from a Chinese calligrapher in San Francisco, and a non-Chinese monument company copied the characters onto the new stone. Interestingly, the Chinese characters revealed that the deceased's surname was actually Ng and his given names were Yee-Ott.

69. Herman Koppes, interview by authors, Centerville, ID, July 30, 1993; telephone conversation with Priscilla Wegars, October 7, 1993; letter to Priscilla Wegars, December 4, 1996.

70. Herman Koppes, interview by Linda Morton-Keithley, August 4, 1994, transcript, 16, Idaho State Historical Society, Boise.

71. Baker Funeral Records, *Funeral Records*, reel 1, A–G, West and Company, vol. 20.

72. Wegars, "Marjorie Fong," 13.

73. Baker Funeral Records, *Funeral Records*, reel 1, vol. 20.

74. Baker Funeral Records, *Funeral Records*, reel 1, vol. 20.

75. Wegars, "Marjorie Fong," 15.

76. Justin McCarthy, "Tales from the Empire City: Chinese Miners in the Pine Creek Region, Northern Territory, 1872–1915," in *Histories of the Chinese in Australasia and the South Pacific*, ed. Paul Macgregor (Melbourne: Museum of Chinese Australian History, 1995), 198–199.

77. Baker and Maniery, "Chinese Cemeteries," 26.

78. Lai, "Chinese Cemetery," 32, 35–39.

79. Sue Fawn Chung, e-mail messages to authors citing *Elko (NV) Independent*, July 7, 1925, 1; August 24, 1999; and August 25, 2000.

80. For a preliminary list of such structures, see Terry Abraham, "Chinese Funerary Burners: A Census," at www.uidaho.edu/special-collections/papers/burners.htm (accessed November 25, 2003).

81. Blanchet, "Ten Years," 71.

82. Baker and Maniery, "Chinese Cemeteries," 17.

83. Wey, "Chinese Sites," Nevada County: Nevada City; see also Hagaman, *Short History*, [8] and illustration on inside front cover.

84. Wey, "Chinese Sites," Santa Clara County: San Jose. The authors visited this cemetery in 2002; the burner is intact.

85. Yee, "Chinese Burial Customs," 52; quotation courtesy Vacaville Museum, Vacaville, California. The authors visited the incinerator in 2002.

86. Hagaman, *Short History*, [2].

87. Elizabeth Kenworthy Teather, "Themes from Complex Landscapes: Chinese Cemeteries and Columbaria in Urban Hong Kong," *Australian Geographical Studies* 36 (1998): 30.

88. Andy Bellomo, "Olney Cemetery: Pioneer Park Served First as Burial Place," *Pioneer Trails* 5 (November 1980): 23–24, Umatilla County Historical Society; Frink, Woodroofe, and Reese, "Chinese," 3–5.

89. R. Ian Jack, "Chinese Cemeteries outside China," in *Histories of the Chinese in Australasia and the South Pacific*, ed. Paul Macgregor (Melbourne: Museum of Chinese Australian History, 1995), 303–304.

90. See, for example, Leslie Dowell, "Funeral Rites 50 Centuries Old Bury Boy," *Los Angeles (CA) Examiner*, October 1, 1922.

91. Florence Baillie-Grohman, "The Yellow and White Agony: A Chapter on Western Servants," in *Fifteen Years' Sport and Life in the Hunting Grounds of Western America and British Columbia*, by William A. Baillie-Grohman (London: Horace Cox, 1900), 338.

92. See, for example, Paul J. F. Schumacher, "Current Research: Pacific West, Shasta-Trinity National Forest," *Society for Historical Archaeology Newsletter* 12 (June 1979): 21.

93. "Funeral Ephemera," *Asian American Comparative Collection Newsletter* 12, no. 4 (December 1995): 3.

94. Bill Guthrie, conversation with Priscilla Wegars, Moscow, Idaho, July 10, 1998.

95. Valery M. Garrett, *Chinese Clothing: An Illustrated Guide* (Hong Kong: Oxford University Press, 1994), 146.

96. Rita Aero, *Things Chinese* (New York: Dolphin/Doubleday, 1980), 117.

97. Oscar Fong was born in Dutch Flat, California, in 1852. He later worked as a laborer there and lived with a Presbyterian minister's family, where he learned English and became a Presbyterian. He then worked as a salesman for the Monarch Coffee Company. Before the turn of the century, he went to Baker City, Oregon, selling coffee. At Baker City he met Cuie Emow, who was born there. They married in 1898 and had four children—two boys, Arthur and Edwin [Eddie], and two girls, Marjorie [Margie] and Christine. The family spoke only English at home. The Fongs first had a store, Suey Kee, which sold Chinese candy, Chinese merchandise, and canned food, and in 1918 Mr. Fong opened the American Restaurant, serving only American food. Mrs. Fong continued to run the store and was the hostess for the restaurant. Following Mrs. Fong's death in 1920, Mr. Fong raised the children by himself. He died in 1940; Wegars, "Marjorie Fong," 4–8.

98. See, for example, Drew Ackerlund, "Walla Walla's Chinese Population: The History of Walla Walla's Chinatown, 1862–1962," in *Annals of the Chinese Historical Society of the Pacific Northwest*, ed. Paul D. Buell, Douglas W. Lee, and Edward Kaplan (Bellingham, WA: Chinese Historical Society of the Pacific Northwest, 1984), 59–69.

99. Baker Cemetery Records, *Cemetery Records of Baker, Oregon*, microfilm (Salt Lake City: Genealogical Society of Utah, 1959); Baker Funeral Records, *Funeral Records*.

100. Baker Funeral Records, *Funeral Records*, reel 1, vol. 17.

101. Mary Ellen McMurtrie, *Bricks and Boardwalks: A Walking-Tour Guide to Historic Idaho City* (Idaho City, ID: Idaho City Historic Foundation, 1995), 14.

102. Charles L. Belanger (director, Lee Funeral Home, Washington, DC), telephone conversation with Priscilla Wegars, April 1999.

103. Frederick K. Chin, "Chinese Funeral Traditions," *American Funeral Director*, October 1995, 52.

104. Belanger, telephone conversation.

105. Couch, "Topophilia," 203.

106. M. Alfreda Elsensohn, *Idaho Chinese Lore* (Cottonwood: Idaho Corporation of Benedictine Sisters, 1970), 80.

107. Jeffrey M. Fee, "Idaho's Chinese Mountain Gardens," in *Hidden Heritage: Historical Archaeology of the Overseas Chinese*, ed. Priscilla Wegars (Amityville, NY: Baywood, 1993), 74.

108. Judy Nelson, "The Final Journey Home: Chinese Burial Practices in Spokane," in "The Chinese in the Frontier Northwest" (special issue), *Pacific Northwest Forum*, 2nd ser., 6, no. 1 (Winter–Spring 1993): 74.

109. Judy Nelson, "The Chinese in Spokane, 1860–1915" (master's thesis, Eastern Washington State University, 1994), 235–236.

110. Emma Woo Louie, letter to Priscilla Wegars, September 19, 2002, citing *Index of Clan Names by Villages for Toishan District* (Hong Kong: American Consulate General, Consular Section, 1963; reprint, Oakton, VA: Center for Chinese Research Materials, 1973), I–IV, IX, 81. May Den was originally "Miss Moy Shee" from Hope, Idaho. In October 1909 she married Soo Kee, a Bonners Ferry, Idaho, laundryman, in an English ceremony performed by a Euro-American clergyman. May Soo Kee, as she then became known, had several children in the next few years, and was pregnant again when her much-older husband died in 1916. By late 1919 she was married again, to Lewis [also known as Louie] Den of Hope. Since there is no record of her children by Soo Kee moving to Hope with her, they probably went to live with family members on their father's side, in accordance with Chinese custom. While married to Louie Den, May Den had at least three more children, the oldest of whom was just five years old when May Den committed suicide, by hanging, aged thirty-five; Priscilla Wegars, "The History and Archaeology of the Chinese in Northern Idaho, 1880 through 1910" (PhD diss., University of Idaho, 1991), 366–373.

111. Louie, *Chinese American Names*, 170–171, 173.

112. See, for example, Schumacher, "Current Research," 21; Wey, "Chinese Sites," Placer County: Auburn.

113. Susan Book, "Ashes to Ashes . . . Chinese Cemeteries in Butte County—1880," *Diggins* 18 (1974): 4.

114. Wey, "Chinese Sites," Yuba County: Wheatland.

115. [Eloise Dielman, comp.], *The Chinese Cemetery at Baker City, Oregon* (Baker City, OR: Baker County Historical Society and the Chinese Consolidated Benevolent Association, 1997).

116. Greg Burton, "A Sojourn among Chinese Miners," *Lewiston (ID) Morning Tribune*, July 24, 1994.

117. Wanda Jo Gallaher, *Report of a Preliminary Archaeological Reconnaissance of the Elk City Planning Unit, Idaho County, Idaho,* University of Idaho Anthropological Research Manuscript Series 27 (Moscow: Laboratory of Anthropology, University of Idaho, 1976), 69.

6

Remembering Ancestors in Hawai'i

Sue Fawn Chung and Reiko Neizman

The Chinese, more than many other groups, have a strong affiliation with the deceased. Shortly after they settled in Hawai'i, the Chinese recognized the need to be concerned with funerals and burials, so if their employers or relatives did not perform the tasks, associations assumed these functions. At first fraternal organizations that were concerned with the welfare of their members performed these duties, but later the Chinese established specific cemetery associations to purchase the land; pay the taxes; keep up the facilities; and sponsor the traditional festivals, one in the spring and one in the autumn, connected with remembering the dead. Most of the associations hired a residential caretaker whose duties were to guard and maintain the grounds and assist in the festivals. Some Chinese cemeteries, especially those owned by individual families or defunct companies, have fallen into disrepair.

This is a study contrasting the oldest and most important Chinese cemetery on Oahu with the smaller ones on Maui, with some reference to those on the big island of Hawai'i, in order to show the preservation of some Chinese traditions and the transformation of practices in a predominantly Asian American environment.[1] Because many of the Chinese who settled in Hawai'i came from one district in Guangdong (Kwangtung) Province, Zhongshan (also known as Heungshan and Chungshan), many of their practices were the same and came to be regarded by the local population as "the standard." This differed from the experience of mainland Chinese Americans, who had to alter and modify customs because they originated from different parts of south China and because of their circumstances and the environment, as described in other chapters of this book.

Nobody knows when the first Chinese arrived in Hawai'i, but there is evidence that they visited the islands as early as 1788 or 1789 as part of trading expeditions. These early Chinese visitors called Hawaiʻi, in Cantonese, Tan Heong Shan, "the Sandalwood Mountains." A few of the early settlers became sugar, coffee, or rice masters because of their agricultural knowledge; they also helped develop the plantation system. Between 1820 and 1840 they sent for others to assist them in their potentially prosperous businesses; by 1852 they, along with non-Chinese owners, had begun hiring contract laborers to work on the plantations.

The first Western-style sugar plantation began in 1835, and because of the labor-intensive work required, the plantation owners turned to China as a source of inexpensive, diligent workers. In 1852, some 200 Chinese arrived under the 1850 Masters and Servants Act and became part of the first large group of Chinese settlers. Only about 20 were hired to be servants, and the rest became plantation workers. By 1884, the 18,254 Chinese in Hawaiʻi made up 22.6 percent of the total population, and by 1886, among the agricultural workers, only 803 Chinese were contract laborers, while 4,736 were "free" laborers.[2] Prior to annexation in 1898, an estimated 46,000 Chinese had immigrated to the islands.[3] Only about half of the contract laborers remained longer than their five-year contract. The main motivation for immigrating was a desire for wealth and a better life either in their native land or in Hawaiʻi. This was the dream of many immigrants regardless of race or ethnicity.

As on the mainland, the large influx of Chinese led to restrictions on Chinese immigration. In 1883 the government limited the entry of Chinese to six hundred for every three-month period. When the United States annexed Hawaiʻi in 1898, the national 1882 Chinese Exclusion Act and additional, more stringent, immigration acts took effect. Chinese laborers could no longer freely immigrate and were replaced by growing numbers of Japanese and Filipino immigrants.

In common with the mainland, most of the early Chinese immigrants were men. Some had married and left their families behind, while others were single men, who tended to be more adventurous. Because of the shortage of Chinese women, many Chinese bachelors ended up marrying native Hawaiians or women from other ethnic groups. As a result some of the Chinese cemeteries include people of interethnic marriages. However, the majority of Chinese immigrants remained single and had to rely on kinsmen or people from their home district or fraternal organizations to finalize burial arrangements when they died.

The majority of Chinese came from two distinct groups: the Punti, who made up 75 percent of the immigrants, and the Hakka, who made up the remainder. Among the Punti, many came from Zhongshan District (formerly called Heungshan in Cantonese and now includes Zhuhai and Doumen) in

Guangdong Province and therefore shared a common dialect and cultural practices, including burial and funerary rites. Their large numbers gave them the financial and numerical strength to establish the largest and oldest Chinese cemetery, at Manoa on the island of Oahu. The Hakka-speaking people, also from the Pearl River Delta region, had a long tradition of feuding with the Punti.[4] Cultural and religious values differed. Clan wars between the Hakka and Punti were fierce and unforgiving. The Hakka established their own cemetery and followed different burial practices from those of the Punti.[5] In other aspects of life in this new environment, however, the two groups coexisted in relative harmony.

Since the growing Chinese population needed services, some immigrants went into merchandising and other businesses, thus developing a middle class. The leaders of the communities recognized the need for burial grounds and for the continuation of traditional rituals, especially funerary rites, so they established organizations, often called "companies," "societies," or "associations," to achieve these goals.[6] Many immigrants wanted to be permanently buried in their home village in China so that descendants would remember their spirits during the Qingming and Yulanpen festivals commemorating the dead. As part of their mutual aid functions, these organizations took care of temporary burials in Hawai'i as well as subsequent exhumations for reburial in Guangdong Province.[7] In some cases the land was needed for other uses, so exhumation and reburial took place. For those who wanted to remain in Hawai'i, their final resting place often was a Chinese cemetery.

THE MANOA CHINESE CEMETERY, OAHU

Early Chinese immigrants to Oahu recognized the need to organize themselves for their own protection and interests. They modeled their associations after village organizations in their place of birth. In 1854 a group from Zhongshan established the Manoa Lin Yee Wai, the oldest of these associations; it was concerned with burials of kinsmen.[8] In 1889 the name was changed to the Lin Yee Chung Association, and three years later the association acquired title to the Manoa Chinese Cemetery.[9] With the help of noted geomancer Lum Ching, who used the traditional Chinese compass, called a *low poon*, and a light-reflecting mirror, the leaders selected an ideal place for their cemetery: a hillside overlooking a body of water—in this case, the ocean—that was surrounded by mountains on two sides.[10] The natural landscape of mountains and water played an important role in the siting. The founding members, including merchants and physicians/herbalists, donated six months or more of their earnings to purchase the C-shaped cemetery, which has picturesque mountains to the north (rear) and faces the sea to the south (see chapter 1). Here members could be buried with their head to the north and their feet facing south, as dictated by Lum Ching and *fengshui* principles (fig. 6.1).

The association coordinated traditional Chinese funeral rites. Most Chinese performed Daoist or Buddhist death rituals, or a combination of the two, since overseas Chinese tended to reinterpret the canonical practices. The Daoist rituals focused on gaining merit for the deceased's next life, while the Buddhist rituals reminded the living of the impermanence of life and the wheel of life.[11] Whatever religious rituals were performed, the important aspect was social conformity and the fulfillment of family or clan beliefs and social obligations.

Some associations arranged for remains to be exhumed and returned to China for permanent burial whenever the deceased or relations had so requested. Following exhumation, the Chinese used brown, green, or white glazed stoneware urns to store the bones that had been cleaned and often sandpapered, wrapped in paper or cloth in an organized manner, and marked according to the part of the body with the skull at the top. The urns were clearly marked on the outside with information about the deceased, including name, birth and/or death date, and often birth and death place.[12] The size of these jars varied according to the length of the deceased's longest bone (fig.

Figure 6.1.   Overview of Manoa Chinese Cemetery, Oahu. Photograph by Sue Fawn Chung.

6.2). The containers were kept in a "bone house" until they could be taken back to the home village in China to be reburied. When the Department of Health stopped the practice of sending bones back to the native village in China for reburial and began allowing only cremated remains to be sent,[13] the association built a more permanent "bone house" for those members who wanted their ancestors' remains to be kept in urns. Some Chinese believed that the disinterment of remains, washed and properly placed in permanent crockery containers or even suitcases, would bring forth both prosperity and more descendants to future generations, even though the remains could not be reburied in China. Although some chose cremation, many southern Chinese regarded it as a Buddhist practice and would not select this option for themselves or their ancestors. Accordingly, few cremated remains were sent to China. Thus bone houses can be found in other Chinese cemeteries in Hawai'i and elsewhere in the United States.[14]

Following Lum Ching's death,[15] his tomb, called the Grand Ancestor's Tomb, was erected as the main feature of the cemetery (fig. 6.3). In 1914,

Figure 6.2. Example of ceramic bone container for Huang Menxie (d. 1917). Photograph by Priscilla Wegars.

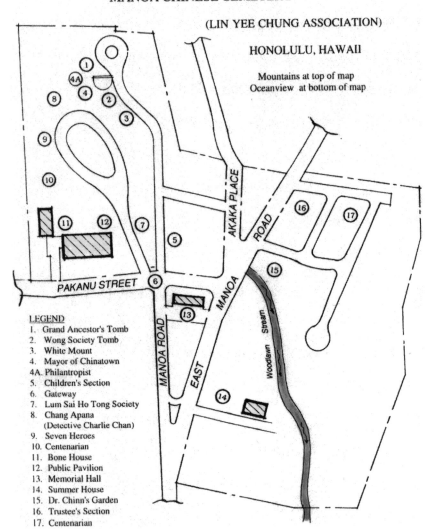

MANOA CHINESE CEMETERY

(LIN YEE CHUNG ASSOCIATION)

HONOLULU, HAWAII

Mountains at top of map
Oceanview at bottom of map

LEGEND
1. Grand Ancestor's Tomb
2. Wong Society Tomb
3. White Mount
4. Mayor of Chinatown
4A. Philantropist
5. Children's Section
6. Gateway
7. Lum Sai Ho Tong Society
8. Chang Apana
   (Detective Charlie Chan)
9. Seven Heroes
10. Centenarian
11. Bone House
12. Public Pavilion
13. Memorial Hall
14. Summer House
15. Dr. Chinn's Garden
16. Trustee's Section
17. Centenarian

Figure 6.3. Map of the Manoa Chinese Cemetery showing points of interest. Drawing adapted by Sue Fawn Chung.

Lum Ching's distant cousin, Lum Sum, planted a banyan tree for shade by the Grand Ancestor's Tomb. Lum Sum later became president of the Republic of China (Taiwan), thus adding to the prestige of the Grand Ancestor's Tomb. In the late twentieth century a new spirit gateway, designed by architect James C. M. Young, further highlighted the site. The purpose of the spirit gate was to keep the living from coming into the Grand Ancestor's Tomb and keep the spirits of the dead from wandering out of it.[16] The gate has been made the focal point of the Qingming festivals at this cemetery.

Besides being the oldest Chinese cemetery in Honolulu, the Manoa Chinese Cemetery has several notable graves and features. For example, Chang Apana and Henry Awa Wong are both buried in the main part of the cemetery. Chang Apana (1874–1933) was the bullwhip-toting Honolulu police detective who served the force from 1898 until 1932 and on whom the famous fictional character Charlie Chan was based (fig. 6.4). Henry Awa Wong, the "mayor of Chinatown," built the world-famous Wo Fat Restaurant in Chinatown in 1882 and founded the Hawaiian Oak Liquors Company. By the late twentieth century only the prestigious members of the Zhongshan-Hawaiian community could be laid to rest in the main part of the cemetery.

Another noteworthy feature in the Manoa Chinese Cemetery is the special tomb that the Wong Kong Har Tong Society constructed for their Wong family ancestors. Sections were designated for the burial of infants and for centenarians.[17] Husbands and wives were buried side by side so that their descendants could honor them easily during the April Qingming festival. In this way the clan members could be considered close in life and close in death.

Near the Grand Ancestor's Tomb is the "White Mound," a common grave of three hundred unknown Chinese Americans. The mass grave served as a final resting place for many whose original cemetery site on Oahu was destroyed by natural forces. The scattered headstones made identification of the deceased impossible. This same kind of concern for "homeless" Chinese Americans was seen in the Huang Kang Charity Cemetery in Xinhui District, Guangdong, which was established for "Gold Mountain" returnees without relatives or identification.[18] Members of the returnees' *huiguan* (District association) or *tongxiang* (fellow regionals) paid for their burial or reburial in their birthplace. Another section, the "Tomb of the Unknown Chinese Soldiers," holds the remains of the "Seven Heroes," six Chinese pilots and soldiers, and one woman, who died during the Burma campaign in World War II. Concern for the deceased often went beyond the family and clan.

The markers on the Manoa Chinese Cemetery graves vary in size and shape. Some have photographs, sepia or tinted, of the face of the deceased, while others have images of favorite items, like roses or even a Corvette, engraved on the headstone. An omega- or armchair-shaped masonry wall with a cement platform fronts some.[19] During Qingming, the descendants place food and drink and burn incense on the platform. A few tombs have an image of the Dragon Spirit, a benevolent spirit symbolizing the fertilizing rain so important to agricultural Chinese.[20] Many tombstones note the deceased's date of birth, birthplace, and date of death. Some have a combination of English and

Figure 6.4. Elaborate cemetery marker for Chang Apana, the model for fictional detective Charlie Chan. Photograph by Sue Fawn Chung.

Chinese, while others have only one language. For example, Hu Tom Shee's marker bears her photograph and the English inscriptions "Beloved Mother," "Dec. 20, 1871," and "Dec. 18, 1959," as well as her surname, birthplace, birth date, and death date in Chinese.

Much of the preservation and beauty of the cemetery is due to the Young family. During his last illness Kee Nam Young, a Chinese doctor and herbalist, told his two sons, George and James, to take care of the cemetery, and the sons did.[21] George C. K. Young (1925–2001)[22] served as the president of the Lin Yee Chung Association for thirteen years and directed many of the improvements. The brothers refurbished the grounds by planting new trees and replacing the termite-eaten wooden gateway arches with new ones. Two Taiwanese, Danny H. C. Young and Harry H. W. Young, who were not relatives of George C. K. Young, contributed to the expenses of renovating the grounds.

The Young family of Honolulu also played a major role in the adherence to Qingming, a Chinese tradition that involves remembering the dead and taking care of graves. In ancient times the holiday was celebrated with dancing, singing, picnicking, and courting as part of the welcoming of spring, but over time the holiday gave way to a focus on death, as a time of quiet solitude and the remembrance of ancestors.[23] George Young also broke a long-standing tradition and allowed non-Chinese to be buried in the cemetery with the society's approval.

Details of the celebration of Qingming at the Manoa Chinese Cemetery resemble traditional practices, but there are some innovative features. The opening Qingming ceremonies are held every April 5th, except for leap years, when they are held April 4th. The observances take place in front of the Grand Ancestor's Tomb. Incense and candles are lit and flowers and paper banners are placed on each of the headstones, anchored down with a stone or a clod of earth. Special chopsticks, brown with resin tips, are thrust into the ground to the right of the incense and candles as memorial markers to denote that descendants have visited the grave. Long "longevity" incense sticks are lit and placed on the grave in order to awaken the ancestors' souls so that they know they are being honored. Smaller incense sticks can convey the same message. Red candles are lit, and the smoke curls skyward to establish the communication between those on earth and those in the other world.

A banquet of five courses is arranged for the deceased. It includes offerings of fish, chicken, and pork, together with stewed oysters, tofu (bean curd), shrimp, mushrooms, duck eggs, roast pork, and roast duck. Each component has symbolic meaning. For example, the pork is the sacrifice to the Pig Demon of the underworld. This demon controls the release of the souls of the deceased who are paying their debts to the different realms of the nether world. The oysters mean good news or blessings, while the tofu signifies abundant wealth. The shrimp are offerings to the watery realm; because they multiply quickly, they bring the good fortune of many offspring. Chicken with mushrooms is a sacrifice to the heavens, and mushrooms are the food of the immortals. Duck eggs symbolize the *yin* and *yang* (principles of universal life), and their oval shapes represent a feeling of well-being and tranquility. Other items, such as beer, wine, liquor, and cigars, might be included, too, if they were favorites of the deceased during life.

On the right side of the grave a small altar contains incense, candles, and a plate of boiled pork, for the land god's simple tastes, and two unsalted duck eggs, pronounced *ya*, meaning "to suppress," implying the suppression of evil. These practices also are found in Guangdong, showing a continuation of ancient traditions.

The oldest living male descendant bows three times before the grave, symbolizing happiness, prosperity, and longevity; then the oldest son, other sons, grandsons, and other male descendants follow suit. Finally, the females do the same. Upon the completion of this ritual, symbolic paper money printed in gold and silver is offered three times and then burned. The rituals conclude with firecrackers, set off to chase away the evil spirits that might be present in the graveyard.

The main part of the formal rites takes about one hour and has three major sections: preparation and decoration (steps 1–13); offering of tea, wine or Chinese liquor, and food (steps 15–23); and reading of the eulogy and presentation, by burning, of the ceremonial paper money and paper images of clothing, household items, and, more recently, computers and cameras (steps 25–28).[24] The rites are followed by a closing ceremony (steps 29–34). This thirty-four-step religious service, presided over by a Buddhist or Daoist priest, or both, is as follows: (1) brief ritual of thanks for blessings of Mother Earth; (2) call to gather and stand at attention; (3) lighting of three rounds of firecrackers; (4) beating of drums and gongs; (5) loud musical fanfare by a Chinese band; (6) soft musical presentation by a Chinese band; (7) head of ritual (president) in position, advancing one step; (8) ceremonial assistants advancing one step; (9) all other participants preparing to perform; (10) presentation of red banner and ornaments; (11) presentation of bamboo torches and guide strips; (12) presentation of large lighted incense three times; (13) presentation of fresh flowers three times; (14) bowing three times as sign of respect by relatives; (15) offering of tea, lifting of center cup, performed five times; (16) offering of wine, lifting of center cup, performed five times; (17) offering of rice, lifting center bowl; (18) offering of entrée (fish or meat or pork); (19) offering of vegetable dish; (20) cutting up of roast pork; (21) offering of roast pork; (22) offering of sugar buns; (23) offering of fresh fruits; (24) bowing three times; (25) presentation of reader of eulogy; (26) presentation of eulogy; (27) presentation of assortment of paper images; (28) burning of paper images; (29) bowing three times for final time; (30) retreat of head of ritual one step; (31) retreat of ceremonial assistants one step; (32) retreat of reader of eulogy one step; (33) completion of ceremony; (34) lighting of firecrackers.[25] For centuries this ritual has been followed by the Chinese, but it has been recently forgotten by the younger generation of Chinese Americans.

Following the conclusion of the ceremonies, the family of the deceased and their guests and association members eat the food offerings at a nearby banquet hall located at the entrance of the cemetery. Since the gods have now blessed this food, its benefits will be conferred on those who partake.

The process of acculturation has contributed American additions to the traditional services. These include American musicians and music, the use of

U.S. and Hickam Air Force Base color guards, the playing of the U.S. national anthem, a twenty-one-gun salute, a helicopter flower drop and pigeon release, and speeches by Hawaiian government officials. When incorporated, all of these activities precede the traditional Chinese rites.

The Chinese on Oahu, especially those connected with the Manoa Chinese Cemetery, preserved traditional rituals but incorporated American aspects. The Lin Yee Chung Association set the precedent for following certain practices for the other non-Christian Chinese and Hakka cemeteries on Oahu. Similar rites probably could be seen in other death rituals of Zhongshan Chinese Americans throughout the Chinese diasporas. At the same time, because of the wealth and large number of the Zhongshan immigrants and their descendants, the Manoa Chinese Cemetery conducted elaborate commemorations of their dead. Other Chinese American cemetery groups aspired to conduct similar practices.

As of 1999 there were approximately seventy cemeteries in Honolulu County, and at least seven were predominantly for Chinese.[26] However, many, like the Manoa Chinese Cemetery, include people of other races who often were connected to the Chinese through marriage, adoption, and other situations. In other locations, such as on the island of Maui, adaptations and modifications had to take place because of the nature of the economy and the greater mix of ethnic groups.

CHINESE CEMETERIES ON MAUI

Like those on Oahu, the Chinese on Maui maintained their ties with China. The growing of sugarcane was well under way by the 1830s on Maui, but the need for Chinese workers to augment the native workers was recognized as early as 1850. Chinese labor contractors recruited many of the nineteenth-century Chinese settlers on the island. Some of these early workers spoke Cantonese, but a few spoke Fujianese,[27] thus creating a linguistic distinction between the immigrants. One unifying aspect was that many pre-1911 Chinese immigrants on Maui belonged to one of the six Hongmen (often designated "Triad" in the United States) secret brotherhoods dedicated to the overthrow of Manchu rule in China and the restoration of Chinese political leadership.[28] Their ties to China were expressed in their support of Sun Yat-sen's revolutionary movement, which led to the establishment of the Republic of China in 1911.[29] This was not surprising, since Sun came from Zhongshan, had been educated in Hawai'i, and espoused a government structure similar to that of the United States.

On Maui there are over thirty cemeteries, but only seven are designated as "Chinese."[30] The ratio reflects the small percentage of Chinese on the island. The cemeteries are differentiated by district of origin in China, dialect, and religion. Unlike the cemeteries on Oahu, some of the Maui Chinese cemeteries were connected to workplaces. An examination of each by location sheds light on the evolution of the cemeteries and the variety of practices on one small island.

In the early days the Chinese were buried within the plantation where they worked, and today these graves can be found in the middle of sugar or pineapple fields, and even in the middle of a golf course. One of the most notable, relatively isolated, burials is the Tam Sing grave, which is located in the middle of the present-day Pukalani Square Shopping Center on the slopes of Haleakala, Maui's famous volcano. Richard Tam Sing, a historian and grandson of Mr. (first name unknown) Tam Sing, knows little about his ancestor other than that he was born in 1853, died at the age of fifty-nine in 1912, and worked for the Pu'unene Sugar Mill until his death.[31] The site, in the Makawao district, is regularly maintained and in excellent condition. An iron fence, similar to those found around grave sites elsewhere in America, surrounds and protects the grave.[32]

The Pu'unene Chinese Cemetery, located in central Maui on Aholo Road, is another plantation cemetery. According to Alice Tihada, who grew up in Pu'unene, it is one of the oldest on the island.[33] Hawaiian Commercial and Sugar Company, the owner of all of the sugar plantations on Maui, owns this poorly kept, difficult-to-access, .25-acre cemetery east of Pulehu Road behind the quarry. Bobby Motooka, safety administrator for the company, stated that there is only one recorded English-language tombstone at this site, but others in Chinese exist.[34] A photograph of the cemetery shows an upright concrete grave marker with Chinese characters. Unfortunately, since the grave recorders could not read Chinese, all but one of these markers have been relegated to the "unknown" burial category. A major barrier to the recording in English of Chinese headstones is the transliteration of the person's name; the surname of Zhang (pinyin) can be variously spelled Chung, Cheung, Jeung, Jung, and Chang, for example.[35] Recorders are hesitant to transliterate the name incorrectly.

Another plantation-connected cemetery, in the town of Lahaina, is the Man Fook Tong Chinese Cemetery on Honoapi'ilani Highway, which connects west Maui to the rest of the island (fig. 6.5). It is a small cemetery of .26 acres with twenty-six recorded tombstones and over seven unmarked graves.[36] The Man Fook Tong is the cemetery organization associated with the Wo Hing Society, whose temple has been restored and is a historical site. The Wo Hing Society was a branch of the political anti-Manchu Zhigongtang (Chee Kung

Tong), which prior to 1911 vowed the restoration of Chinese rule. It has been linked with the Tiandihui (Heaven and Earth Society) and the Triads, both anti-Manchu secret societies in southeastern China. As a mutual aid society, the organization also cared for its members upon death. Usually new members had to be sixty or under[37] so that each member contributed funds for funerary services for several years. The leaders of the Wo Hing Society were community leaders, and because of this position they sponsored elaborate funerals with traditional music. In the late nineteenth and early twentieth centuries the society conducted Qingming festivals as well as recreational activities like opium smoking and gambling. The majority of those buried in this cemetery worked for the Pioneer Mill, the only sugar plantation on Oahu's west side, or for Maui Land and Pineapple Company, which owned pineapple fields on the west side. Entire families are buried at the Man Fook Tong Chinese Cemetery. The large number of babies known to be buried in unmarked graves demonstrates the high death rate for infants. This infant-burial section is similar to the one at the Manoa Chinese Cemetery. Several of the men buried here were born in the early 1860s. Despite their arduous lives, a few, like Tong Lai and Chang Wong, lived into their nineties.[38]

On the slopes of Haleakala on the Hana Highway is the Pa'ia Chinese Cemetery, on 7.5 acres of land. The land was deeded in 1883.[39] There are at least eighty graves, sixty-six of which have English on the headstones; four

Figure 6.5.   Grave marker at Man Fook Tong Cemetery, Maui. Photograph by Reiko Neizman.

have Chinese only, and ten graves are unmarked.[40] Like the Manoa Chinese Cemetery on Oahu, the Heong Sam Chong Cemetery Association, presently headed by Ah Hong Chee, is primarily for Chinese who originated in Zhongshan, Guangdong Province, but Chinese from other districts have also been buried at this cemetery. For example, an undated tombstone for Long Shum indicates that he was from Leong Sheoy Hang in the Siyi (Four Districts). The headstones vary in material, shape, and size. Some are of marble or granite, and others are of concrete. Some are raised and others are upright; some are flat and others are obelisks. The first burial recorded here occurred in 1915, when Agnes G. Tong Nap, age twenty-nine, died; hers is the only rock headstone. The oldest person buried was Mrs. Chut Moi Tam Wong, who was 104. The last burial at this site, in 1985, was of Ngun Moi Shinn Hew. The average age of those buried here is fifty-nine, perhaps an indication of the hard life these immigrants led. The earliest recorded birth dates are 1864 and 1865, indicating that some of the pioneers of Maui were buried at the Pa'ia Chinese Cemetery. Their longtime residency indicates that they were immigrants, not sojourners, as many have called the Chinese.

Another cemetery located along Haleakala is the Fook On Tong Chinese Cemetery, situated on 4.5 acres.[41] There are over 150 graves,[42] but only 37 have been recorded in English; these burials average fifty-four years of age. The Kwock Hing Society, which is affiliated with a church group,[43] originally established this cemetery. Undoubtedly Christian services took precedence over traditional Chinese rituals. Gertrude Ceballos, a society member, stated that most of those buried in this cemetery worked for sugar or pineapple plantations.[44]

The first burial here took place in 1912. Chong Chung, born in 1851, was sixty-one at the time of his death. Another early burial was that of Mrs. Shee Chong Ching, whose marker is made of wood. Many of the grave sites are elaborately constructed with concrete borders or half enclosures that resemble couches, often called omega-shaped. The one for See Dang, who died in 1924 at the age of sixty-six, was not erected until 1966. Undoubtedly he was placed in a temporary site until the family or society had sufficient funds to construct the more monumental marker. The last burial was in 1985, when Mrs. Len Kyau Fong Ching, age eighty-eight, passed away. Once again, Chinese traditions in the grave markers were combined with American beliefs in the religious services.

On the remote easterly side of Maui is the Hana Chinese Cemetery, where five graves can be found: Mrs. Ah Lee Sam, also known as Ah Loikeau; C. Pak Chong, died 1918; Loo Yau Jang; Kim Chun Pai, died 1916; and Hu Young.[45] Kee Chin Chang, a merchant in Hana, owned the land, not far from the Hana Harbor. Despite the fact that he was not a rich man, he offered the use of one acre of his land as a burial site for those Chinese immigrants who had no family or money. Located on Uakea Road behind the old Hana School and present Hana Community Center, the graves are in fair condition. All of those buried at the site worked on the sugar or pineapple plantations in Hana. According to Kee Chin Chang's son, Roland Chang, the last burial took place in 1961, some time after his father's burial in the early 1950s.[46] As in other locations in frontier America, the Japanese cemetery in Hana is located nearby. In death, as in life, the minorities had to be physically separated until recent times.

The last of the small cemeteries surveyed was the Chang Family Cemetery, on .25 acres on Old Makena Road, north of Keawalai Church, near Makena Bay in south Maui. Difficult to find because it is located in thick brush, the cemetery holds eight members of the Chang family.[47] David Chang, the family historian, stated that Haehae Kukahiko was his grandfather's sister; she was married to a Hawaiian who had died many years before Haehae and was buried in a plantation cemetery.[48] Ying Chang, David's grandfather, worked at Pu'unene Sugar Mill as a laborer when he first arrived on Maui. When his contract expired, Ying Chang established a very successful fish-market business, where John Ying Chang and Robert T. Y. Chang, David's uncles, worked. Ying Chang bought the land for the cemetery when it was still considered dry and uninhabitable. The five recorded graves are for John Ying Chang (1899–1928), Ying Chang (1865–1932), Robert T. Y. Chang (1912–1937), Hattie K. Chang (1883–1946), and Haehae Kukahiko (1860–1961). The graves are relatively flat and bounded in marble or granite. Today, Makena is still somewhat undeveloped, but luxury hotels are slowly spreading toward the town. Continuation of recreational development could potentially threaten the Chang Family Cemetery's continued existence at this location.

These small cemeteries are dwarfed by the Kwong Fook Tong Chinese Cemetery, located on Highway 140 in Waiehu in central Maui. The property was deeded in 1888.[49] Unlike some of the other cemeteries, this was an inclusive, rather than exclusive, cemetery. There are approximately three hundred burials in this 2.4-acre cemetery owned by the Waiehu Chinese Cemetery Association, but only seventy-six are recorded in English.[50] There are more than twenty unmarked graves. The site has a "spirit gate" at the entrance, a "bone house" at the top of the hill, and an omega-shaped "central altar" at the front of the site. As at the Manoa Chinese Cemetery, Qingming rituals are performed at the central altar. The first burial at the Kwong Fook Tong Chinese Cemetery occurred in 1904, with only the name John Lani noted. Several of the other men buried here were born in the 1850s. Three of the burials have upright wooden markers: Mrs. Shee Chong Ching, Mrs. Ho Shee Wong, and Mr. Tai Lee, probably indicating very early burials. There are two concrete vaults. One is for See Kong, who died in 1947, and the other is for Yin Moy Zane Ching, who died in 1956. Two men were in the military: Robert Fong and See Fook Hew, who both died in 1928. Several graves have crosses, indicating the Christian beliefs of the deceased. Most of the headstones, however, are uniformly upright and made of concrete, marble, or granite, thus resembling gravestones at mainland cemeteries. They are not like the concrete omega-shaped markers or obelisks found in other Chinese cemeteries in Hawai'i. The most recent burial was Annie Kukahiko Foo Sum, who died in 1971. She was from the well-known Hawaiian Kukahiko family but was married to a Chinese man. A number of other gravestones are carved with Hawaiian surnames rather than Chinese ones, indicating the widespread intermarriages that had occurred. This cemetery is connected with the smaller Kwock Hing Society Cemetery.[51] More work must be done to uncover the burial sites of pioneering families and interethnic families.

One of the reasons for the existence of "bone houses" and burial urns is land usage. As urbanization encroaches on cemetery sites, graves are moved. In 1947 in Wailua, thirty-eight graves were exhumed from the Wailua Valley Cemetery and moved to the Wauhu (Wailaku) Cemetery because the land was needed for other purposes. It was rumored that these were early Hana sugar plantation workers.[52] The bone houses hold the burial urns until they are reburied, or they are held there for the descendants.

CONCLUSIONS

The cemeteries in Hawai'i reinforce the connection between the living and the dead in accordance with Chinese beliefs. Modifications in the performance of rituals and burial practices have been made. Because of its wealth and importance, the Manoa Chinese Cemetery on Oahu became a model for other Chinese American cemeteries in Hawai'i. In general the early Zhongshan immigrants were wealthier and held positions of power and influence in the community, so they could afford the ideal cemetery location. The prime real estate location has been refurbished and is regularly maintained. This large membership of the Lin Yee Chung Association permitted the preservation of traditional ceremonies on festival days, especially Qingming. As the decades passed, the association began conducting American funerary practices before Chinese traditional rites, demonstrating the unification of cultural customs.

Although people of various religious beliefs are buried at Manoa, on Maui there are cemeteries segregated by religious beliefs as well as by occupational and family affiliations. The ones on Maui demonstrate the need to adapt to the economic and ethnic concerns. As with the Chinese cemeteries on the mainland, maintenance has been a major issue for the smaller and more isolated sites, such as the Man Fook Tong Chinese Cemetery. Fortunately the latter, located near the Kaanapali Beach Hotel, is maintained by the hotel. The cemeteries on Maui have adapted to a more leisurely, Hawaiian approach in their observation of Chinese customs.

Unlike in cemeteries in China, families are not always buried together in these Chinese Hawaiian cemeteries. For example, in the case of the Lim Kyau family (fifteen children) of the island of Hawai'i, ancestors were buried in ten different cemeteries on two different islands.[53] Remembrance of ancestors usually is done through tablets and at the grave sites of the parents.

What is remarkable about these Chinese Hawaiian cemeteries is the individuality of their character. No two are alike in the types of rituals performed or types or sizes of markers used. Burial practices and grave sites show a combination of Chinese and American customs. This is seen in the shapes of the markers and the writing on the markers, first in Chinese only, then in a combination of Chinese and English, and finally in English only. But the mixture of Chinese and American practices is deeper, especially when one observes the American activities that precede the traditional Chinese rituals at the Manoa Chinese Cemetery. As many of the markers demonstrate, these people in Hawai'i were immigrants, not sojourners.

NOTES

1. We are indebted to the late George C. K. Young for providing information on Oahu's Manoa Chinese Cemetery.

2. Tin-Yuke Char, "The Chinese Experience in Hawaii—1800–1980," in *The Chinese American Experience*, ed. Genny Lim (San Francisco: Chinese Historical Society of America and Chinese Cultural Foundation of San Francisco, 1981), 196. See also Tin-Yuke Char and Wai Jane Char, "The First Chinese Contract Laborers in Hawaii, 1852," *Hawaiian Journal of History* 9 (1975): 128–134; and Eleanor C. Nordyke and Richard K. C. Lee, "The Chinese in Hawai'i: A Historical and Demographic Perspective," *Hawaiian Journal of History* 23 (1989): 196–216.

3. Clarence E. Glick, *Sojourners and Settlers: Chinese Migrants in Hawaii* (Honolulu: University of Hawai'i Press, 1980), 23–29. For a general background on Chinese immigration, see Kil Young Zo, *Chinese Emigration into the United States, 1850–1880* (1971; reprint, New York: Arno, 1978).

4. For more information, see Kristofer Allerfeldt, "Race and Restriction: Anti-Asian Immigration Pressures in the Pacific North-West of America during the Progressive Era, 1885–1924," *History* (Great Britain) 88, no. 289 (2003): 53–73.

5. On Hakka burial traditions see V[alentine] R[odolphe] Burkhardt, *Chinese Creeds and Customs*, vol. 3 (Taipei: Book World, 1958), 79–81. One major difference

in funerary practices is the food for the deceased. The Hakkas leave rice, water, salt fish, and dried octopus in an earthenware cooking pot in the funeral home and at the cemetery, while the Punti leave cooked foods such as chicken and pork.

6. These rituals have been delineated in Chu Hsi [Zhu Xi] (1130–1300), *Chu Hsi's Family Rituals: A Twelfth Century Chinese Manual for the Performance of Cappings, Weddings, Funerals, and Ancestral Rites*, trans., annotated, and introduced by Patricia Buckley Ebrey (Princeton: Princeton University Press, 1991), chapter 4. The Chinese societies are discussed in detail in Tin-Yuke Char, comp. and ed., *The Sandalwood Mountains: Readings and Stories of Early Chinese in Hawaii* (Honolulu: University of Hawai'i Press, 1975), chapter 5; and Glick, *Sojourners*, chapter 10.

7. For more on reburials, see Elizabeth Sinn, "Moving Bones: Hong Kong's Role as an 'In-between Place' in the Chinese Diaspora" (paper presented at the Association for Asian Studies Conference, Washington, DC, 2002).

8. Glick, *Sojourners*, 87.

9. See Lin Yee Chung Association, "General Information Sheets," n.d. [ca. 1998], University of Nevada, Las Vegas, Lied Library Special Collections, Asian American Folder 93, no. 13.

10. Nanette Napoleon Purnell, "Oriental and Polynesian Cemetery Traditions in the Hawaiian Islands," in *Ethnicity and the American Cemetery*, ed. Richard E. Meyer (Bowling Green, OH: Bowling Green State University Popular Press, 1993), 193–239. We are indebted to Terry Abraham for this information.

11. For more details, see Vivian Lim Tsui Shan, "Specializing in Death: The Case of the Chinese in Singapore," *Southeast Asian Journal of Social Sciences* 23, no. 2 (October 1995): 63–88; and David K. Yoo, *New Spiritual Homes: Religion and Asian Americans* (Honolulu: University of Hawai'i Press, 1999).

12. Burkhardt, *Chinese Creeds*, 2:135–137.

13. Burl Burlingame and Kathryn Bender, "Grounds for Respect," *Honolulu Star-Bulletin*, March 30, 1998.

14. See, for example, chapter 5, p. 158, on the bone house in Elko, Nevada.

15. Glick, *Sojourners*, 187. Another variation of the spelling of the Grand Ancestor's name is Lau Jack.

16. Purnell, "Oriental," 194.

17. The two best-known centenarians interred here, as cremations, are Mrs. Young Sim Tong (1886–1987) and Ella M. Q. Wong, who died at 103.

18. Marlon K. Hom, "Fallen Leaves' Homecoming: Notes on the 1893 Gold Mountain Charity Cemetery in Xinhui," in *Chinese America: History and Perspectives, 2002*, ed. Colleen Fong and others (San Francisco: Chinese Historical Society of America, 2002), 36–50.

19. Such grave sites are called omega-shaped because of their resemblance to the last letter of the Greek alphabet, omega, written Ω.

20. Tin-Yuke Char and Wai Jane Char, comps. and eds., *Chinese Historic Sites and Pioneer Families of the Island of Hawaii* (Honolulu: Hawaii Chinese History Center and University of Hawai'i Press, 1983), 16, discuss the symbolism of the Dragon Spirit.

21. Esme Nii, "Sons Fulfill Monumental Obligations," *Honolulu Advertiser*, April 3, 2000.

22. See Pat Gee, "George C. K. Young, Community Leader: Visionary Guided Rebirth of Isle Chinese Cemetery" (obituary), *Honolulu Star-Bulletin*, November 6, 2001.

23. Carol Stepanchuk and Charles Wong, *Mooncakes and Hungry Ghosts: Festivals of China* (San Francisco: China Books and Periodicals, 1991), 62–63.

24. Lin Yee Chung Association, *The Story of the Manoa Chinese Cemetery: With a Discussion of Ancestor Worship* (Honolulu: Lin Yee Chung Association, 1988), 5. George Young took Fred Blake, Priscilla Wegars, Wendy Rouse, Melissa Farncomb, Terry Abraham, Sue Fawn Chung, and several others on a tour of the cemetery in 1996.

25. See Purnell, "Oriental," 198–199, for a similar list.

26. Cemeteries in Hawai'i are gradually being listed in Maggie Stewart, "Hawaii Cemetery Records Now Online," USGenWeb Archives: Hawaii Cemetery Project, at www.rootsweb.com/~usgenweb/hi/hicem.htm (accessed November 20, 2003). See also Char, *Sandalwood Mountains*, 172–173.

27. Glick, *Sojourners*, 9.

28. Glick, *Sojourners*, 190.

29. Glick, *Sojourners*, 285.

30. Reiko Neizman, "Chinese Cemeteries in Maui," manuscript, University of Nevada, Las Vegas, Lied Library Special Collections, Asian American Folder 93, no. 13. See also Gail Bartholomew, *Maui Remembers: A Local History* (Honolulu: Mutual, 1994); and Char, *Sandalwood Mountains*, 174–175.

31. Richard Tam Sing, interview by Reiko Neizman, 1999.

32. *Island of Maui: Cemetery (Map and History) Directory* and *Site Data Form* (Maui: Government Printing Office, 1990), 213 (hereafter cited as *Site Data*).

33. Alice Tihada, interview by Reiko Neizman, 1999.

34. Bobby Motooka, interview by Reiko Neizman, 1999.

35. Emma Woo Louie, *Chinese American Names: Tradition and Transition* (Jefferson, NC: McFarland, 1998).

36. *Site Data*, 167 and 155–156.

37. Char and Char, *Chinese Historic Sites*, 8.

38. Anthony Vierra, interview by Reiko Neizman, 1999. Mr. Vierra, the caretaker for the Man Fook Tong Chinese Cemetery, has family members buried there.

39. Char, *Sandalwood Mountains*, 175.

40. *Site Data*, 181, 198–201.

41. *Site Data*, 124 and 6–8.

42. Char, *Sandalwood Mountains*, 174.

43. For more information about Christianity and the Chinese in Hawai'i, see Char and Char, *Chinese Historic Sites*, chapter 5.

44. Gertrude Ceballos, interview by Reiko Neizman, 1999.

45. *Site Data*, 130 and 14.

46. Roland Chang, interview by Reiko Neizman, 1999.

47. *Site Data*, 123 and 5.

48. David Chang, interview by Reiko Neizman, 1999.
49. Char, *Sandalwood Mountains*, 175.
50. *Site Data*, 160 and 101–104.
51. Gertrude Ceballos is in charge of both cemeteries.
52. Char, *Sandalwood Mountains*, 174–175.
53. Char and Char, *Chinese Historic Sites*, 130–131.

7

The Chinese Mortuary Tradition in San Francisco Chinatown

Linda Sun Crowder

The clear, melodic notes of a brass band marching along Chinatown's Stockton Street catch the attention of an Asian woman picking over produce at a sidewalk vegetable stand. As the band turns the corner at Clay Street to continue its march north up Grant Avenue, she and the storekeeper pause to look at a large, floral-framed portrait propped up in the back of the vintage black Cadillac convertible that follows the band. Not recognizing the photograph, they cursorily note the length of the procession, then return to their business. Tourists on the street corners quickly pull out their pocket and video cameras to capture moments of a real "Chinese" ritual being performed.

This scene is a typical one in San Francisco Chinatown—the only Chinatown in North America whose streets, on a regular and frequent basis, continue to have extensive funeral processions with a marching brass band and picture car.[1] This custom of honoring the dead with pageantry is a residual of a long, progressive commingling of Chinese and European traditions particular to San Francisco Chinatown. Such hybrid funeral rituals illustrate the identity of Chinatown as an American Chinese community forged by the constraints of the American polity, the endurance of Chinese culture, and unique demographics and political-social mechanisms. As a symbol of what is Chinese in the American context, Chinatown is a cultural performance arena for funerals in which individuals express degrees of "Chineseness," American style.

From a sequestered, nineteenth-century bachelor town organized along the lines of the traditional village social structure prevalent in rural south China, Chinatown burgeoned into a modern, Americanized, Chinese community. In 1850, rapid growth, caused by the gold rush and the progressive development of the West, demanded laborers in large numbers. Thousands of Chinese

195

males from Guangdong (Kwangtung) Province answered this need and entered the United States through San Francisco, the main port of entry from the Pacific. Escaping the poverty and chaos of war-torn China, these early sojourners came to California, or "gum san" (*jinshan*, "Gold Mountain"), to find work, build a fortune, and then return to China. The early settlement was called the "Chinese Quarter" by outsiders and "Tong Yan Gai," or "the street of the people of Tang," by insiders. District and family associations formed to assist newcomers with employment, housing, protection, and communication links to China.

In the early twentieth century, the quarter's architectural and cultural profile was dramatically altered, first by the 1906 earthquake and subsequently by its reconstruction into a modern, pseudo-Oriental tourist attraction.[2] The demise of imperial China and the emergence of the Chinese Republic in 1911 stirred both nostalgia for a bygone era and optimism for a new modern China. These events and sentiments captured the pride and imagination of overseas Chinese and influenced the style and tone of Chinatown's development. By then the community had become known as "Chinatown." Its demographic profile now included second- and third-generation Chinese who increasingly voiced their rights and claims as American citizens. The status of Chinese as Americans continued to gain rightful recognition when China became an ally of the United States in World War II, and when the discriminatory Chinese exclusion laws were repealed in 1943.

By 1965 new immigration laws had liberalized the entry of Asian immigrants, and Chinese from many different countries and economic and social backgrounds entered the United States. Chinatowns became havens for some of these various Chinese immigrants, who were no longer predominantly males from rural Guangdong Province. In San Francisco's Chinatown, this demographic change became evident in the diversity of funeral rituals performed. Such individual public displays express the different self-perceptions, beliefs, and identities of Chinatown folk.

THE CULTURAL SIGNIFICANCE OF CHINESE FUNERALS

Chinese cultural tradition regards funerals as major life-passage rituals that surpass weddings in priority, expense, and significance. Reverence for ancestors, formalized in Confucianism, is the cornerstone of Chinese cultural belief, social structure, and religious practice. With death, a family member can become a beneficent ancestor, and funerals are the ritual means of accomplishing this transition. A ritually well-disposed corpse will have a safe, contented spirit that will reward its family with good fortune for many generations to come. Such concern with spirit welfare and familial duty is expressed and judged by the funeral procured, particularly if the funeral is for one's parents: a respectable presentation to show filial duty, respect, and honor is necessary to "save face" (fig. 7.1).[3]

Many of the early Chinese sojourners never intended to remain in America and be permanently buried there. Once the immigrant landed in America, he "immediately arranged for his body to be shipped to China for burial in case he should meet with an accident in America; he believed that if his body was buried in a strange land, untended by his family, his soul would never stop wandering in the darkness of the other world."[4]

This arrangement was usually made with the person's district association, or *huiguan*. With the rapidly enlarging Chinese population in the 1850s, the increased duty of disinterring bones and shipping them back to China for reburial became delegated to separate organizations known as *shantang*, or "benevolent halls."[5] In addition to the *shantang*, "very many remains were sent home by personal friends in America, the expenses being paid by relatives in Guangdong."[6]

Some labor contracts covered such arrangements: "In all contracts the Chinese signed with relation to their passage money or their labors were clauses

Figure 7.1.   A proper funeral and ritual offerings to the deceased demonstrate a family's respect, honor, and devotion. Photograph by Linda Sun Crowder.

touching the matter of eventualities in case of death. The great passion of
every Chinaman, from the wealthiest merchant to the humblest coolie, was to
have his bones returned to the tomb of his ancestors."[7]

Not just bones were returned, but embalmed corpses as well. Cargo inventory in 1858 for the French ship *Asia* records carrying 321 embalmed Chinese
bodies to China, and that of the *Flying Cloud* included 200 corpses.[8] At the
close of the 1850s, approximately 10,000 bodies had been shipped from the
United States back to China.[9] These numbers dwindled in the twentieth century and the practice all but discontinued with the Communist takeover in
1949.

Since the 1970s, mortuary directors in the Bay Area have noticed an increase in instances of remains received from China and other areas for permanent repose in the United States. As more Chinese immigrants make their
home in America, the remains of loved ones overseas are reunited with the
present generation, reversing the previous custom (see chapter 8). Such immigrants include many from Hong Kong, who feel that the Communist repos-
session of their island will bring uncertainties regarding cemetery land use.[10]

BURIALS AND BONES

District associations have owned their own cemeteries ever since the Chinese were not allowed burial in the other cemeteries of nineteenth-century
San Francisco. The first Chinese cemetery (1851) was at Lone Mountain at
the edge of the city. It was moved to a site in the present area of Lincoln Park
in 1872[11] and then to Colma, a suburb south of San Francisco, in the 1890s.
Eventually, in 1912, all burials within the city limits of San Francisco were
prohibited,[12] and Colma became the new repository site for all the city's
dead. The Chinese cemeteries there include Look San (land purchased in
1889), the largest cemetery established by the Chinese Consolidated Benevolent Association (CCBA), or Six Companies; Tung Sen (1936), also part of
the CCBA; Ning Yung (1898); Hoy Sun (1987), recently added to Ning
Yung; and Golden Hill (1994), a private corporation that caters to the Chinese.[13] Committees within the district associations continue to look after
cemetery business. Non-Chinese cemeteries in Colma, such as Woodlawn
and Cypress Lawn, also serve a large number of Chinese, and Skylawn
Memorial Park in San Mateo has developed *fengshui*-designed sections
named Bai Ling, or "one hundred years of longevity," that appeal to many
Chinese. These last three cemeteries hold special Buddhist ceremonies during Qingming, the spring grave-cleaning memorial festival, to market to
Chinese clients.[14]

In the past, association plots were almost free, since burial was not permanent. The body was interred for as brief a period as five months[15] to a maximum of ten years,[16] until decomposition left only the bones. Because of religious beliefs and strong ties to China, it was important that bones be exhumed and sent to the deceased's native place as soon as possible. In the mid-1800s, representatives of each *shantang* under each association would travel to burial sites

> checking up deaths, making calculations for decomposition, gathering up the relics of their late members. . . . The procedure in such instances was very meticulous. The first thing to be removed from the coffin was the longest bone. This was measured and a box was made of proper length, two feet wide. Each bone was then dipped in a bucket of brandy and water and polished with a stiff brush until it shone. The polishers were careful never to touch the bones but handled them with great dexterity with two sticks. Great care was taken to see that no bones were missing.[17]

In an interview, longtime Chinatown resident Bobby Gee (1920–1997) recollected his experience as a teenager in the 1930s exhuming bones for shipment back to China. Each exhumation took him about five hours. Bones were collected by sifting them on a screen to remove the dirt and assure that the smallest bones were salvaged. It was imperative to get every piece of bone so that there was a complete body. A bone chart was used with a list of bones to be checked off. The bones for the left hand were placed in one small bag, those for the right hand in another; the bones for the left foot were placed in a third bag, and those for the right foot placed in a fourth. These four bags together with the other bones were placed in a galvanized tin box on which the association wrote the person's name and native village. Gee received $2.50 for each exhumation.[18]

CHINATOWN MORTUARIES

In the villages in China each family handled the care and disposition of the corpse. The body lay in state at home in the courtyard or in the street in front of the house, sometimes under a canopy constructed for the purpose. Mourners came to pay their respects, and the proper rituals were performed to help the soul make its transition to the next world.[19] In nineteenth-century Chinatown the large numbers of sojourners living apart from their immediate families depended on relatives, friends, or benevolent societies to perform these rituals and handle the final disposition of the corpse. The need for undertakers developed.

By the late nineteenth century, Chinatown undertakers had been established to prepare the corpse to lie in state in their small, single-parlor mortuaries. According to historian Him Mark Lai, sources such as the directories of Chinese businesses, association histories, and interviews with former mortuary owners indicate that San Francisco had seven Chinese mortuaries in business at one time or another from the late 1870s to the early twentieth century. The earliest listing, in 1878, was for Main Fook undertakers at 732 Pacific Avenue.[20] By 1913 Quon Fook Sang and Wing Sun were the only ones listed.[21] They remained in business into the 1960s.

Wing Sun, at 21 Brenham Place (now Walter U. Lum Place) on Portsmouth Square, was started perhaps as early as 1878 by Wong Tin Gut, his brother Wong Tin Pang, and a cousin. From 1927 to 1967, Wing Sun received most of the contracts to exhume bones for shipment to China; the contracts were renewed after each shipment of bones, which occurred every ten years. The mortuary was sold in 1968 to Nicholas Daphne, who later consolidated it with his other Chinatown mortuary, Cathay Wah Sang on Powell Street, from 1975 to 1981.[22]

Cathay was started by Nicholas Daphne in 1946 and closed in 1993. For almost forty-seven years, the centrally located Cathay Wah Sang was considered the principal mortuary serving Chinatown. With Cathay gone, the only other mortuary in the Chinatown vicinity was the Green Street Mortuary in the Italian sector of North Beach.

Today Green Street Mortuary serves the largest number of Chinese in the United States. In San Francisco, it is the only full-service mortuary serving the Chinatown–North Beach area. It caters particularly to ethnic Chinese, who make up 95 percent of its clientele. Each of the chapels is outfitted with a burning facility and vent system for the burning of paper items to accompany the dead to the spirit world. The mortuary supplies items such as casket blankets, colored yarn bows, spirit money, and food offerings for the typical Chinese customs practiced in San Francisco Chinatown. Most staff members are bilingual, each speaking at least one dialect of the Chinese language. Green Street Mortuary is also the single producer of all the funeral processions that presently march through Chinatown. Of the roughly seven hundred Chinese funerals conducted each year, approximately 30 percent include a band with picture car and procession through Chinatown. Green Street contracts its own marching band to meet this high demand.[23]

Other mortuaries known to serve the Chinese population in San Francisco today include Halsted's, owned by Halsted N. Gray-Carew and English, on Sutter Street, and Ashley and McMullen Mortuary, owned by the Daphne family, in the Richmond district. Both also hire bilingual Chinese counselors and cater to Chinese traditional customs. Their Chinese funerals occasionally include a marching brass band, but this occurrence is not as frequent as in Chinatown; nor is the procession route, outside of Chinatown, as extensive.[24]

PAST CHINATOWN FUNERAL PROCESSIONS AND MORTUARY PRACTICES

Public displays of funeral processions create opportunities to show honor, respect, status, and prestige. For the Chinese, funerals are more significant than birthdays or weddings, and the funeral procession is the most celebrated aspect of the funeral. According to the prominent historian and intellectual Gu Jiegang (Ku Chieh-kang), "A marriage celebration may be embellished to impress people, but its lavishness can never compare with a funeral. . . . The most elaborate part of a funeral is the procession because it passes through city streets and avenues where spectators gather."[25]

L. Eve Armentrout Ma has written that "the rites and practices associated with death and burial are of special importance in China," noting, "Perhaps the most important of these public rites is the funeral procession. . . . If finances permit, the funeral procession will be quite elaborate."[26] At the 1964 funeral of Dai Wah Low in San Francisco, Joseph Quan, a Four Family (Lung Kong Tin Yee Association) leader, is quoted in the *San Francisco Chronicle* as saying, "Everyone is here [at the funeral] because we Chinese consider that a departure is more important than a birth or birthday. . . . It is an occasion when we tell the young about the accomplishments of the elders."[27] It is this emphasis on the achievements of a lifetime, of living a full life and then becoming an ancestor, that renders funerals more significant than weddings or birthdays, echoed Steven J. Lee, national grand president of the Lee Family Association of the U.S.A.[28]

In village China, processions were necessary simply to convey the corpse from the home to the burial grounds. The minimum procession would include the coffin followed by mourners who traveled on foot. If affordable, the way was paved with spirit money, firecrackers, chanting Daoist and/or Buddhist priests, and Chinese music bands to appease evil spirits and comfort the soul of the deceased.[29] In the cities of imperial China, these processions became opportunities for opulent displays of status, honor, and prestige. High-ranking or prosperous personages had lengthy processions that included lanterns, banners, and military brass bands, as well as traditional Chinese music bands, floats, umbrellas, name and rank placards, sedan chairs carrying both the soul tablet and female mourners, paper effigies of spirit deities, and so on.[30]

Like the funerals in village China, those of the early Chinese poor in San Francisco were simple affairs,

> confined to the beating of gongs, the firing of a few strings of crackers, and the scattering of fluttering bits of red paper as the hearse and carriages dragged their way over the sand dunes to the dead man's temporary resting place. But, presently, there came a time when one of the wealthy merchants of the quarter died and the residents of the town were treated to a Chinese funeral in the grand manner.[31]

Though not as extensive as those witnessed by Gu in the cities of late imperial China, the grand and elaborate "big shot" funerals of San Francisco Chinatown were pageants that caught the attention of writers such as Charles Keeler, in 1902:

> A Chinese funeral is an event that forces itself upon the attention of every wayfarer. The beating of tom-toms, scattering of imitation paper money to the devil, the express-wagon full of baked hogs and other food, are all matters of note. And then there are the antiquated hacks drawn by raw-boned horses that eminently suit them, the professional mourners, the sallow-visaged friends of the deceased. The train proceeds to the cemetery keeping up its infernal din the while. When the body is interred, a portion of the baked meats and confections are placed over it together with some lighted punks. The remaining viands are then taken back to Chinatown where the whole party unite in a feast in honor of the dead. At a later period the body is exhumed, the bones are scraped, and all that remains of the departed is shipped to his beloved resting place—the Flowery Kingdom.[32]

The deceased was almost always a businessman and a community, association, or *tong* (*tang*) leader. One of the best recorded and memorable funerals of the nineteenth century was for the notorious gangster Fong Ching, better known as Little Pete (see chapter 1).[33] Henceforth, all other grand funerals were compared to Little Pete's.[34]

The nineteenth-century funerals held in San Francisco Chinatown typically included—to varying degrees of elaboration or inclusion—funeral elements characteristic of Qing dynasty China: walking mourners, professional wailers, family members dressed in sackcloth mourning garb with bare feet, Daoist and Buddhist priests, a picture of the deceased or a name tablet, the scattering of red paper spirit money, paper goods for burning, firecrackers, banners, Chinese funeral bands, Western bands, whole cooked animals, meat and other food offerings, liquor and tea, incense and candles, and *li shi* (lucky money wrapped in red paper).[35] Canopied platforms were often constructed to lay the body in state and display the rich funeral offerings.[36]

In the first half of the twentieth century, influential and respectable Chinatown notables continued to have spectacular funeral processions. Journalists and historians, along with the mainstream press, recorded the funerals of prominent citizens as public events. Mrs. Yick Jung Shee Ghee's funeral was the subject of a 1937 *Chronicle* article containing a half-page photo in which the picture truck carrying her portrait looked like a float covered with greenery.[37] In 1938 a news report detailed Chin Lain's funeral, during which "the walking procession, at two abreast, stretched for more than four blocks . . . followed by 222 automobiles, interspersed with several bands and a Chinese orchestra followed by a troupe of actors in symbolic roles."[38]

Goon Dick Wong's 1941 front-page funeral account sported the banner title "Blast of Firecrackers, Blare of Brass Horns—Chinatown's Largest Funeral: Wong Goon Dick Goes to Sit with His Ancestors at the Councils of Confucius."[39] The *Chronicle* said the following about Bing Shun Fong's funeral in 1947: "Chinatown in years past has seen many colorful funeral processions but old-timers said yesterday's memorial for the 52-year-old 'unofficial' mayor of Chinatown was one of the most impressive."[40] Dai Wah Low's funeral ceremony in 1964 proved that

> East and West do meet in San Francisco. The two services for Dai Wah Low were Chinese and American, Buddhist and Christian, with some of the traditions of the centuries as well as the glint of gleaming Cadillacs almost fresh off the assembly line. . . . A 43-car cortege was led by a 12-man Musicians Union band and then by a Cadillac convertible bearing his large, flower-wreathed portrait. ("So those who do not know his name will know who he was," a friend said.)[41]

In all these funeral accounts, the funeral procession is mentioned. Being public, such processions are observable and salient, offering up something special for the eye to behold. Always notable are the colorful and "exotic" traditional Chinese elements and their striking contrast with Western customs of mourning. These funeral accounts reveal the admixture of East and West in Chinatown funeral rituals and show the gradual inclusion and adaptation of Western elements into the San Francisco Chinatown funeral. Pardee Lowe's 1937 observation of Chinatown life notes:

> Funerals in Chinatown are distinctly eclectic by nature. It is by no means unusual to witness corteges with Chinese orchestras and American brass bands, Christian ministers and Taoist devotees scattering ghost money to purchase the right of way for the dead, several hundred motor cars, and the immediate family of the deceased clad in white sackcloth and straw sandals followed by the leaders of the Chinese community flawlessly groomed in frock coat, striped trousers and silk top hat.[42]

Less seen now than in the nineteenth century are the off-white sackcloth mourning garb, walking barefoot, and platforms to display offerings. Western brass bands are more common and Chinese music less so. Vehicles, Christian elements, and black mourning clothes have become typical.[43] Mourners continue to walk, and the picture of the deceased has its own vehicle. Offerings, candles, and incense are displayed less publicly; the coarse spirit money is now off-white instead of red; and firecrackers appear less regularly.

By World War II, funeral processions had become less frequent and less ostentatious. Chinatown historians and observers speculate that wartime frugality and changing tastes minimized the importance of public displays. The resurgence in traditional customs and the increased frequency of funeral processions did not occur until the influx of new Chinese immigrants in the 1960s and 1970s revitalized San Francisco Chinatown.

THE CHINATOWN FUNERAL TODAY

With the 1965 Immigration Act came an incursion of Chinese immigrants into the United States from Southeast Asia, Hong Kong, Taiwan, and the People's Republic of China. No longer mainly male Cantonese peasants, these new Chinese immigrants include urbanites, hail from dissimilar regions, have different levels of education,[44] and bring a wider variety of funeral rituals to Chinatown. That such a broad range of practices exists reflects the tolerance of Chinatown, and the inclusive nature of Chinese religious and cultural practice, in accommodating the diverse ethnic Chinese who have settled in Chinatown. Many practices brought to the United States have been modified to conform to the tastes and legalities of American society. The resulting variations—still distinctly different from the practices of second- or third-generation Chinese Americans—have made a typical modern Chinese funeral recognizably different from those of the past.

Within the broad range of rituals practiced in San Francisco's Chinatown there is such a thing as a typical or usual Chinese funeral with slight modifications for Christian or Buddhist services. The sequence consists of (1) the visit, (2) the funeral service proper, (3) the procession, (4) the burial, and (5) the traditional supper or longevity meal. The visit and traditional meal tend to be more informal and intimate in tone and structure than the funeral proper, which has a presentational, formal style. The procession through the crowded public areas of Chinatown is highly presentational, with a sense of pomp. The burial in outlying cemeteries, by contrast, is sequestered from the curious eyes of a general spectatorship and takes on an intimacy and solemnity occasioned by the limited attendance of family and close friends.

The Visit

The visit is comparable to a one-hour wake. It typically occurs the day before the funeral and is the occasion when the family accepts visitors informally.

Guests approach the casket to pay their respects by bowing three times to the deceased (some Christians and non-Chinese will stand at the casket and observe a moment of silence) and then turn to the family seated on the side to either bow once to them or shake their hands to offer condolences. The guests then sit in the chapel for the remainder of the time to keep company with the family and the deceased. There is generally no speaker or program addressing an audience.

The chapel or parlor holds a portrait wreath plus all the bouquets and wreaths already sent to the mortuary. The portrait wreath is usually rectangular, with flowers framing a large photograph of the deceased, and is set on a stand. For viewing, the body often lies in state with an incense burner and a narrow table placed before it. On this table are a pig's head; a whole, boiled chicken; a plate of vegetarian stew or *cai*; three cups each of tea and whiskey; three pairs of chopsticks; and a bowl of rice (fig. 7.2). Sometimes paper money is burned by the staff or by family members.

Halfway through the visit, members of the family perform the blanket ceremony, considered the last act of caring for the deceased. The first blanket is white for death and the second is red for life. These are laid by the eldest son and his wife. The subsequent blankets given by the other children of the deceased can be of any color, print, or number.[45]

Before leaving, guests again go forward to pay their respects. They are given *li shi* and candy by family assistants who station themselves at the chapel door. Often two envelopes are handed out together—a white one containing a piece of candy and a coin, plus a red one with just a coin.[46] The red color of the envelope serves to ward off death's bad luck and make a restatement of life, and the candy is to remove the bitter taste of death signified by the white envelope. The coins are "good luck" money to be spent right away, preferably on something sweet.

Open caskets are the usual custom at both the wake and the funeral services. Printed mock money, called "devil money" or "hell banknotes," is usually placed in the coffin for the deceased to spend. A silver coin, such as a pre-1964 dime, is sometimes placed on the lips of the deceased as the toll to pay the guardian of the underworld. Personal effects such as clothes, jewelry, money, and cherished items are often placed in the coffin by the family during the visit. Paper models of goods and effigies (houses, cars, servants, gold and silver mountains, treasure chests containing paper clothes) are set up for display; these will be burned at the grave during the burial (fig. 7.3).

Bereaved families typically wear black suits, dresses, or pant suits with black armbands. In addition, sons wear a black waistband, and female relatives wear a square, black net veil on their heads along with colored yarn bows in their hair. The color indicates a woman's or girl's relationship to the

Figure 7.2. A food offering table is presented to the deceased at the mortuary during the visit and at the formal service. Photograph by Linda Sun Crowder.

deceased: white bows are worn by wives, daughters, and daughters-in-law during the funeral. The white bow is tossed into the grave at the burial and immediately replaced with a blue one that is worn for three days, discarded, and replaced with a red one that is worn for at least a month. Granddaughters wear green bows at the funeral; these are later tossed into the grave and re-placed by red ones that are discarded after the longevity dinner. The symbolic color scheme designates white for death, blue for mourning, red for life and good luck, and green for fertility and perpetuity. Variations are numerous, with individuals having their own particular interpretations and customs.[47] The mortuary provides the bows, arm- and waistbands, and veils.

Figure 7.3. Paper model offerings of a furnished home with two spirit servants and other necessities for the deceased's spirit life will be burned at the grave. Photograph by Linda Sun Crowder.

The Funeral Service

The formal funeral service is usually scheduled for the next day in the same chapel, set up as it was at the end of the visit. Guests arrive, sign the register, and seat themselves. Church organ music is piped in. The last to be seated are the six to eight pallbearers, who wear white gloves, boutonnieres, and black bow ties. The body remains on view in the open casket at the front of the chapel, which is like an alcove to stage and frame the casket. The family sits perpendicular to the coffin out of view of the congregation.

The minister or speaker opens the service by welcoming the guests and eulogizing the deceased. A brief, often nonsectarian sermon is delivered to comfort the mourners, after which everyone is invited to pay last respects. The funeral director instructs those assigned to hand out the *li shi* to pay their respects first, then the pallbearers. The director then signals the last row of the congregation to pay their last respects, working forward until all have done so. Finally the two designated picture wreath bearers pay their respects and carry the wreath into position for the march out of the chapel.

On leaving the chapel, the guests, staff, helpers, and family are handed *li shi* and candy.

In the meantime the pallbearers are stationed at the entry to receive the casket, which is rolled out on a wheeled bier. They carry the casket to the hearse, following the portrait wreath, which is placed nearby. The family, led by the eldest son carrying a giant incense stick, follows the casket (fig. 7.4). The purpose of the incense is to generate fragrance for mourners to follow to the cemetery. The hierarchy in traditional Chinese families is established by the males: father, then sons in order of age with their wives, then the wife, and then daughters in order of age with their spouses. The family watches the coffin being placed onto the hearse before they enter their limousines. Sometimes, the family will kneel down before the hearse to show respect. The other mourners then go to their cars.

Occasionally the funeral service is held at a location other than the mortuary. Members of Buddha's Universal Church in Chinatown traditionally hold their funerals at the church. For esteemed and high-ranking members of associations, the funeral is held at Victory Hall, a large auditorium belonging to the CCBA (fig. 7.5). Such a funeral is most likely if the member had served prominently for the Guomintang (Kuomintang) government of Taiwan and held national and international office in the associations. The flag of the Republic of China is often placed atop the casket. Funeral services for such persons are long, elaborate, and logistically complex affairs. Representatives from the numerous related associations come to pay their respects formally by presenting flowers and bowing three times in unison before the corpse. Many eulogies are spoken; numerous couplet banners are hung on the walls to eulogize the deeds of the deceased and wish his or her spirit well; floral wreaths abound; and the attending crowd is enormous. Police are usually on hand to control traffic for the long cortege, which often includes multiple bands. There is no doubt that a dignitary is being honored.

The Procession

If a band has been hired to lead the procession through Chinatown, its members will have been waiting outdoors at one side of the entrance for the casket to exit. Guests leaving the building wait on the other side of the entrance. The appearance of the picture wreath at the top of the mortuary stairs signals the beginning of a drumroll and gong that continue while the picture is brought down and until the casket appears. When the casket begins its descent down the stairs, the drumroll is joined by the solemn beatings of a bass drum, and the band begins to play its signature opening tune, "Amazing Grace." The pallbearers carry the casket down to the street, place

Figure 7.4. The eldest son as the chief mourner carries a giant incense stick to lead the procession to the cemetery. Here, he also carries a spirit flag or soul name banner to guide the soul while it is in transit to its final resting place. Photograph by Linda Sun Crowder.

Figure 7.5. The funerals for prominent members of Chinatown typically take place at a special association hall where floral wreaths and condolence banners are displayed during an elaborate service. Photograph by Linda Sun Crowder.

it in the hearse, and remain in position at the back of the hearse until the tune is finished.

At the conclusion of "Amazing Grace," which is signified by a gong, the family members are led to their limousines and the guests to their cars. The band positions itself in the street in front of the mortuary, parallel to the family limousine. There they play either a Chinese folk song or a Christian hymn while the mourners and staff members organize themselves for the procession. The band then moves to the end of the block to lead off the procession. The picture wreath is placed in the back seat of the picture car—a vintage 1960s Cadillac convertible—which is then positioned in the center of the street behind the band (fig. 7.6). The hearse follows, then the family limousines, and then the guest cars.

At eight out of ten Chinese funerals produced by the Green Street Mortuary, the hearse makes a stop at the deceased's home, business, or association for the deceased's spirit to make a final visit. This is done regardless of whether a band has been contracted or the stop is outside of Chinatown. In a typical stop at a home in Chinatown, the hearse stops and the funeral director

Figure 7.6.　The most visually striking feature of the procession is the picture car—a convertible with a giant picture of the deceased wreathed in flowers. Photograph by Linda Sun Crowder.

opens its back door. He goes to the front of the house to take down a hanging black wreath (Western style, provided by the mortuary) and places it on the casket in the hearse. The picture wreath is brought out of the picture car and set up adjacent to the back of the hearse facing the house. The funeral director and limousine drivers then stand at respectful attention in a line next to the picture. In unison they bow three times in the direction of the home and toss spirit money into the air (fig. 7.7). If the band is present, they play a tune at this stop, and at its conclusion the staff performs the bowing ritual. Sometimes the family will get out of the limousines and kneel down in the street before the casket while the staff does the bowing ritual. Ritual performed, the hearse is then closed, the picture is replaced in the car, and the procession regroups to proceed through Chinatown with the band playing. In some cases, family and friends of the deceased are waiting at the home or association to greet the spirit with offerings of incense, candles, food, and paper money for burning (fig. 7.8).

Intermittently throughout the procession within the boundaries of Chinatown, the hearse driver throws out spirit money (fig. 7.9).[48] This is plain, unbleached, coarse, off-white paper in the shape of bills with curved slits cut in it to divert malevolent spirits. When this money is tossed into the air, it is commonly believed that mischievous spirits lingering about will chase after it and pass through the curved holes. Since spirits are believed to travel only in straight lines, these spirits will be confused and thus kept from causing havoc with the corpse. Another prevalent interpretation views this cheap money as a payoff to poor, lowly ghosts in the same way that tossing out a few copper coins to pestering beggars would clear the roadway of distraction in imperial China.

During the procession the band plays between ten and twelve tunes, depending on the route, the number of stops, and the number of cars in the procession (fig. 7.10). The usual route is about fourteen blocks through the heart of Chinatown and concludes on a street corner as the cortege continues on to one of the cemeteries outside the city proper. As the hearse and family limousine pass, the bandleader bows reverently to the deceased and to the family. The band plays on this corner until all the cars in the cortege have passed.

Figure 7.7.   A stop is often made at the deceased's home, association, or workplace for the soul to bid farewell to his earthly life. The funeral staff performs the bowing ceremony and tosses spirit money. Photograph by Linda Sun Crowder.

Figure 7.8.   Offerings of food and incense and the burning of mock ritual money are occasionally presented at stops to honor the visiting spirit. Here, the stop is at the Wong Family Association, where the deceased was an officer. Photograph by Linda Sun Crowder.

Sometimes a prominent person's funeral includes two or even three bands. On very rare occasions there is a Chinese band in the procession playing Chinese funeral music with traditional instruments, either alone or at the same time the Western band plays. Instead of marching, the five Chinese musicians ride in the back of a pickup truck (fig. 7.11).

Figure 7.9.   During the procession, the hearse driver tosses out spirit money to "buy the road" by paying off and distracting away malicious spirits who might wreak havoc on the corpse and spirit. Photograph by Linda Sun Crowder.

In a variation of the procession the mourners walk through Chinatown. This is usually done by ethnic Chinese who have recently emigrated from mainland Southeast Asia. Instead of riding in limousines, the mourners are led on foot by the eldest son or chief mourner, who may carry an ancestral tablet on a tray with offerings of incense, candles, and three cups of tea (fig. 7.12). An evergreen branch, symbolizing longevity and family continuity, and a thin bamboo staff, symbolizing the walking cane used to support one weak with grief, are often carried as well. Each family member wears a version of the traditional Chinese mourning clothes of neutral-colored sackcloth. Walking and wearing rough, colorless cloth are signs of respect, grief, and distraction (fig. 7.13). Often accompanying the family and mourners are Daoist and/or Buddhist priests in traditional garb playing cymbals and gongs. Most of the longtime residents of Chinatown regard this form of ritual as an "old style" village custom and view it as something that a modern, Americanized Chinese would not do. Such sentiments often form a kind of community consensus that discourages, if not constrains, particular cultural expressions.

In one walking funeral procession for a Chinese family from Southeast Asia, there was the usual Western brass band and picture car followed by the hearse. Behind the hearse marched the family, dressed in traditional Chinese mourning outfits, walking barefoot, and accompanied by Daoist/Buddhist priests wearing ceremonial robes and playing gongs and cymbals. An assistant followed—dragging a live chicken on a string.[49]

The funeral director had not been informed about the chicken. Soon after, he received a call from animal rights activists, who complained about the chicken's mistreatment. Members of the Chinatown community also called the mortuary, expressing their displeasure that the mourners were walking bare-footed; this made Chinatown look "shabby." The implication was that they were embarrassed by behavior they considered backward and bad for the image of Chinatown.[50] Though the use of animals in religious rituals is permitted in San Francisco, and being barefooted is not unheard of, the complaints received by the mortuary are expressive of community sensibilities and tastes rather than insistence on enforcing legalities. In the interest of community relations, the funeral home might discourage mourners from such practices in

Figure 7.10.   The marching brass band leads the funeral procession down Grant Avenue, the main thoroughfare of San Francisco Chinatown. Photograph by Linda Sun Crowder.

Figure 7.11.   Sometimes a Chinese band is hired to play traditional Chinese funeral music. Instead of marching, the five musicians play seated in the bed of a pickup truck. When a Western band is also hired, both bands play simultaneously, creating a mix of sounds. Photograph by Linda Sun Crowder.

the future, but its influence is limited. A more persuasive source would be the mourners' district or family association, which might be prevailed on to curtail its members' ritual practice in the interest of social harmony.

Bounded by community consensus and American regulatory laws, ritual variations seldom depart radically from the typical funeral described. The typical range of practice comprises those modern and traditional elements that more often than not reinforce American urban middle-class values rather than Chinese village or rural ones.

The Burial

At the cemetery the portrait wreath and all the other bouquets and wreaths brought from the mortuary are arranged upright and placed at the head of the grave. The pallbearers carry the casket to the grave and remain lined up on each side. The minister says a few words and a prayer, after which the pallbearers lower the casket into the grave. The pallbearers bow three times to the grave, then remove their bow ties, boutonnieres, and gloves and toss them into the grave, sometimes with a clump of dirt. The funeral assistants pick flowers from the wreaths and hand each person a flower to toss into the grave as he or she pays last respects. If there are paper goods for burning, they are burned at this time. The eldest son plants the giant incense stick in the ground at the head of the grave. He and his wife bow three times and toss in their flowers and armbands. Occasionally tossed in are rice, coins, and a clump of dirt.[51] The other family members follow suit in the order of males by seniority first, then females by seniority, and then the mourners.

When everyone is done, the funeral director removes the portrait from the picture wreath and gives it to the eldest son, with the portrait facing out, to be taken home. Occasionally banners with memorial sayings that have been hung in the chapel for the visit and the funeral will be brought to the grave, laid atop the casket, and buried; sometimes, instead, they are burned or taken home.

The Traditional Supper

Following the burial at the cemetery, the family and friends typically return to Chinatown to have a meal at a restaurant. This practice is prevalent

Figure 7.12.   Some Chinese ethnic groups prefer to have the more traditional walking procession and don off-white mourning clothes. Walking signifies humble respect and distracted grief for the deceased. Photograph by Linda Sun Crowder.

Figure 7.13. Traditional Chinese mourning clothes were typically made of sackcloth with burlap or hemp accents. Neutral or off-white is the color of death for close family members of the deceased. The lack of pigmentation represents the corporeal decay and the absence of life. Photograph by Linda Sun Crowder.

enough that many restaurants have special set menus appropriate for this occasion. A communal meal at the end of the funeral day is both practical and symbolic. Since the funeral and burial may involve a few hours and a missed meal, mourners are ready to eat. Going to a restaurant after the burial also provides a detour and a place to go to leave behind the airs of death before returning home.[52] The traditional supper is also a way for the family to thank friends for their attendance. The shared meal provides closure, sustenance, support, and reintegration into social life. The Chinese name for the traditional supper, *gaai wai jau* (Cantonese) or *jie huai jiu*, means "to wash away sorrow."[53]

The seven-course menus usually consist of the mandatory roast pork; boiled chicken; a vegetarian stew; soup; and other seafood, meat, and vegetable dishes. Strict Buddhists have a vegetarian menu. Though most people would find the food appetizing and impressive,[54] the traditional supper is considered simple fare compared to what is expected at most Chinese banquets. The idea is that a funeral is not a joyous occasion to be celebrated with elaborate dishes. Eating is done out of necessity, since feelings of sadness curb the appetite.

The traditional supper is occasionally referred to as a "longevity banquet," or *sauh tsaan*, by some people from China. "Longevity" in this context refers to the wish for a long next life after death due an elderly person (usually over seventy) who has lived a full, prosperous life and left descendants to continue the lineage (another form of longevity). Longevity symbols are commonly seen at funerals in the form of stylized calligraphic emblems on the caskets and as embroidered designs on the burial clothes, which are also referred to as "longevity clothes." Most of the local (second- and third-generation) people in San Francisco Chinatown know the meal as "plain meal," or *sou tsaan*. This concept has an association with the Buddhist tradition of serving vegetarian dishes at ritual meals to memorialize the dead. "Plain" in this context refers to the meatless dishes served on such occasions. Now it just refers to the simple, modest food served after the funeral.[55]

There are always seven courses served and odd numbers of tables ordered. For the Cantonese, seven is the number associated with death, and some odd numbers are associated with incompleteness, death, and spirits. A token single cup of white rice liquor is placed in the center of each table in honor of the deceased. If more people attend than there are seats, guests crowd themselves to make places at the available tables—no further tables are added. Some food items associated with longevity in the celebratory sense are deliberately avoided, such as noodles for long life or a fish served whole. The head and tail of a whole fish represent the beginning and end of a hoped-for completed life that is long and fortunate. At a funeral banquet the deceased being commemorated has had that completed life. It cannot be relived. This sense of completeness would also symbolize that everyone is together, which, since the deceased is absent, is obviously not the case. Thus, a whole fish would be inappropriate. Some Chinatown folk believe that beef should also be excluded from funeral banquets, not so much for any symbolic meanings or associations but in keeping with the local practice of their natal region; it is just not a commonly eaten item in south China.[56]

Funerals tend to bring into play those unquestioned, conservative traditions that are comfortingly familiar and that reconnect people to their origins and past. As social events for saying a final farewell to the deceased, they bring together family and friends for comfort and support. The funeral banquet concludes the proper sending off of the deceased and launches the life-renewal process for the mourning family around a communal meal.

MAJOR FUNERAL VARIATIONS

The following major funeral variations have structural differences premised either on the religious concepts of the soul and spirit world or on the secular ideals of social service. In the most general terms, Christians believe that the soul leaves the body at death and continues its existence in either heaven or hell. The soul has no further interaction or relationship with the living. Christian funerals celebrate the life of the person and entreat for the mercy of the deceased's soul through prayer. For Buddhist-Daoists, the soul has aspects that reside in different contexts, and it relies on an interactive, cause-and-effect relationship with humans to sustain itself. Thus Buddhist-Daoist funerals are ritually oriented, with rites that have consequences for the future existence of the soul.

Secular Chinatown funerals of distinctive note honor a life that has been distinguished by public service, business success, and political office. These "big shot" funerals make the community aware of the extensive influence and regard the deceased has cultivated during his lifetime.

Christian Funerals

For Protestants, the deceased himself is responsible for his soul, so sermon themes tend to comfort the bereaved and remind them of the importance of following God's will in making life choices. Since no ritual acts by the living have spiritual consequences for the dead, religious rituals at the visit, funeral, and burial are limited to prayers of thanks, blessings and forgiveness for the living, and mercy for all.

Catholics appeal to Christ, the Virgin Mary, or the saints to intervene on behalf of the deceased to send the soul to purgatory, if not to heaven. Saying the rosary and holding masses for the dead help in this respect, but the soul remains divorced from the living as a social member, and movement of the body in transition is not spiritually dangerous. The Catholic mortuary sequence typically includes an additional segment: a mass for the dead held at the church with the corpse present. The body is transported back to the mortuary if a visit or funeral service is to be held.

While variations exist, the Christian funeral is functionally structured in two major parts: the formal services to pay respects, eulogize the deceased, and comfort the living, and the burial to permanently place the body. The visit, devoid of religious ritual function, has the purpose of keeping informal company with the family. There are some Christians who view the blanket ceremony as an act of caring and include it in the visit. Others, viewing it as a ritual tradition associated with ancestor reverence or Buddhism-Daoism, will not. There is usually no burning of mock ritual money or goods by Christians, since a Christian soul does not journey through a series of ten hells, nor does it have a spirit existence that would require money and goods. *Li shi*, however, considered a Chinese social custom, is almost always handed out at the visit and the formal service.[57] Both Catholic and Protestant Chinese funerals may have a Chinatown procession with band and picture car (no spirit money is thrown) and a traditional dinner after the burial, since these events are considered customs with no religious overtones.

BUDDHIST, DAOIST, AND BUDDHIST-DAOIST FUNERALS

In San Francisco, Buddhist, Daoist, and combined Buddhist-Daoist funerals have three critical phases involving the body and the soul: the preparing of the body for its final placement and of the soul for the spirit world; the transition to the cemetery; and the burial. The preburial rituals, most of which are performed during the visit, aim at localizing, placating, and feeding the soul. For devout Buddhists or Daoists the formal service is often an extension of the visit with further rituals and chanting performed. Eulogies and formal presentations by a master of ceremonies are often absent. The movement of the corpse to the burial plot is considered spiritually dangerous, and most Buddhist and Daoists contract a procession or at least include the stop ceremony en route to the cemetery. Music is an important element in this transitory stage. The final disposition plants the body and soul in their new and permanent home. Rituals are conducted that purify the grave, enrich the spirit before its departure, cast off death pollution clinging to the mourners, and ease the separation for the living and the deceased.

A typical Chinese Buddhist funeral is very similar to the Chinatown standard described earlier, but with the following modifications. If the deceased had been a vegetarian, the table offering would include fruit and vegetable dishes instead of the pig's head and the whole, boiled chicken. During the visit or the formal funeral, nuns or monks, often with shaved heads and dressed in simple, long, solid-colored robes, perform as a group, chanting appeals to Bodhisattvas for mercy on behalf of the deceased's soul. Leading the family and mourners, they circle the casket or aisle in multiples of three rounds. At the grave, instead of or in addition to flowers, small lit incense sticks (either one or three) are distributed to the mourners to be placed at the foot of the grave in a mound of soil. Food offerings are often left at the grave for the spirit of the deceased to savor their essence. Additional prayers and chants are said by the officiant, and paper goods, money, and incense are burned. Burning tends to be associated with Buddhist ceremonies, but it is done in combination with Christian elements and contexts as well. This kind of synthesis is characteristic of most Chinese religious ritual practice.

A Buddhist funeral that deviates from the above structure is the type practiced by members of Buddha's Universal Church. Contemporary in appearance with its absence of statues, incense, priests, or nuns, the church focuses on the spiritual principles of Buddhism rather than on the ritual performances. At its funerals the deceased is brought to the church, where the visit and formal funeral are held. Services are simple and may include the blanket ceremony.

Daoist death rituals tend to be flamboyant, actor-centered presentations by male priests. Dressed in bright, colorful raiment embroidered with symbols and wearing miters, they contrast sharply with the austerely dressed Buddhist nuns and monks. Their funeral chants are accompanied by more ritual activity and employ more paraphernalia than those of the Buddhists, who predominantly just chant. Daoist chants and rites are directed to many gods, as well as Bodhisattvas and the harnessing of nature's cosmic forces. Some Daoist priests have charismatic personas and perform dramatic, mystifying rituals such as spraying wine from their mouths onto the casket and grave and brandishing a sword over them for purification by scaring away evil spirits. On occasion they strike the casket hard with the sword to cause a crack that will facilitate decomposition. These rituals of protection work to safeguard the soul of the deceased from negative spirits and energies and to solicit the assistance of positive ones to produce a powerful ancestor.

Unlike Buddhists, who are opposed to killing and do not use blood in their rituals, Daoists incorporate animals in their ceremonies. At the cemetery the priest will sometimes toss a chicken lengthwise across the open grave to be caught by the chief mourner. The priest cuts the crest of the chicken's comb and lets its blood drip around the grave to protect it. If the chicken is to be killed, the throat is cut and the blood is squirted out around the grave.[58]

Each Daoist sect has specialists with their own particular litany, set of practices, and key deities, creating a range of variation and differences. Almost all Daoists incorporate some Buddhist elements, figures, and practices; Buddhists may also incorporate some Daoist ones to a certain extent. Some Buddhist sects have high-level mortuary rituals with fanciful setups, use symbolic objects, and have a chief priest or nun wearing elaborate vestments that rival those of the Daoists. The Chinese folk beliefs that dominate most San Francisco Chinatown funerals typically intermingle the concepts, deities, and customs of both religions, leading people to generally characterize those beliefs as Buddhist-Daoist.

In the Buddhist-Daoist worldview, the actions of the living during the mortuary process make a difference in the disposition of the spirit. The spirit world, mirroring the earthly one—with the same social structure and material need for sustenance—requires that ancestral spirits be fed, clothed, and supplied with money to live well. The soul's journey through the ten Buddhist hells is assisted with talismans, prayerful chants, and rituals of purification, absolution, and protection. The deceased is provisioned with money, food, personal items, and charms to facilitate his passage to the next life. The focus is on the transformation of the soul from its state in a living person to that of its spirit existence as an ancestor. The transport of the body to the grave is literally and ritually a transitional movement of the soul from the earthly world to the unseen one.[59]

The visit is the family's opportunity to perform the last acts of preparation for the body and soul of the deceased and is often the busiest ritual phase in the Buddhist-Daoist funeral process. It may incorporate any of the following rites and elements. Corpse preparation may include the ritual washing of the body by family members. Buddhist and/or Daoist chanting and death rituals are performed to guide, purify, and calm the spirit in accepting its new condition and prepare it for its journey. A spirit flag or banner made of white paper with the deceased's name written on it may be made and staked in the casket spray to keep the hovering spirit close to the body. The family may wail to share their grief with the spirit, wear traditional white funeral clothes, and actively participate in the rituals under the direction of the ritual specialists. Food, liquor, and tea, along with incense, mock ritual money, and paper provisions to be burnt, are offered in front of the casket.

In the casket the deceased is laid out with items such as "hell banknotes," lotus-shaped prayer papers, spirit money, Buddhist prayer beads, a passport for the spirit world, a silver dime in the mouth, and jewelry. Blankets are given, sometimes a gold colored one with Buddhist prayers and mantras printed on it in red ink. Burial clothes occasionally have holes burnt into them as a ritual of reversal and of separation, to indicate that the deceased is no longer of this material world. Buttons and zippers are sometimes removed and the burial clothes are secured with cloth ties so the deceased will be comfortable during his long rest. A rice bowl with or without the deceased's name or the longevity emblem on it is sometimes placed in the casket so the deceased will have something to use. Crocks of real food (chicken, egg, and rice) are occasionally placed with the corpse. Some families place a layer of tea and herbs in the casket as a desiccant. On very rare occasions, a brick is placed in the casket with the deceased's name, natal place, and birth and death dates written on it. The brick, a remnant from the past practice of secondary burials, used to be buried with the body to identify the bones when they were exhumed in case the grave marker had been lost or destroyed. Some widows also break a comb, placing one half into the casket and throwing the other half on the floor. This symbolizes the breaking of the matrimonial bond and indicates the widow's freedom to remarry.

At the formal service there may be further chanting, the burning of paper offerings, and a formal eulogy. When final respects have been paid and the casket is to be closed, the family and guests often turn away or avert their eyes to avoid bad luck. *Li shi* and candy are handed out at the end of both the visit and the funeral services to dispel the airs of death and reaffirm life.

The procession to convey the body from the mortuary to the cemetery embodies multiple ritual elements to honor the deceased and protect and tether the soul. In the simplest procession, spirit money is thrown to distract negative ghost-spirits (*gui*). In others, the presence of incense, spirit flags, ancestral tablet, and music serve to keep the soul close to the corpse and to alert the living to the presence of death. Mourners may decide to walk in the procession as a traditional act of respect. The stop ceremony during the procession for the spirit to pay a final visit at its former home or association is a sign of the spirit's reluctance to leave this worldly life of social attachments and its need to continue such attachments as a spirit. The stop functions as part of a ritual sequence to separate the soul and gradually ease its transition out of this world by allowing it to say goodbye before burial.

Until proper burial, the corpse pollutes and corrupts its surroundings with the airs of death and is in danger of being possessed by other malicious spirits. As discussed above, some officiating Daoist priests or shamans cleanse and protect the grave by waving a sword, spraying liquor, and sprinkling chicken's blood over the grave. The grave, one of the repositories for securing the soul, is chosen, if possible, for its *fengshui* properties of optimal access to the earth's cosmic energies. The timing of the burial, the geomantic positioning of the grave, and grave rituals for the final disposition of the body all determine the eternal welfare of the deceased and the future luck of the family. The spirit flag, placed at the grave, stations the soul there, where it can be propitiated with burnt offerings and the essences of food, incense, and flowers.

Once the casket is placed in the grave and offerings are made, mourners begin to wean themselves from the death sphere with rituals of transition. White yarn bows, black armbands, and other funeral paraphernalia are tossed in the grave, the traditional white mourning clothes are burned, the spirit flag is planted, and liquor is spilled on the grave to get rid of death's pollution. Once something has been used for the dead or dedicated to them, it becomes part of the death sphere and is typically left behind. If it enters the life sphere, it is believed to bring bad luck. Mourners shift from colors symbolizing death and decomposition (neutral off-white)[60] to colors of mourning (black), somber sadness (blue), and life (red) by changing their hair bows and clothing items, and receiving a final item with a life color such as the red *li shi*. The transition to the social life sphere is signified by the mourners' engaging in a life-affirming, group-shared activity, the traditional meal.

Like the preburial funeral rites, the rituals and elements involved at the grave site are as varied as the beliefs and needs of each family involved. Not all Buddhist-Daoist funerals include the burial features mentioned, but when they are present in whatever combination, they serve the ceremonial purposes described. Again, the ritual motives are to cleanse and safeguard the grave, feed the spirit, and protect the living.

"Big Shot" Association Funerals

Another major type of funeral with a different structure is the association funeral. The primary focus here is to honor the deceased in relation to his association affiliation and show public respect. Often referred to as "big shots," those who receive exalted association funerals are influential public figures in Chinatown. Their identity and the mortuary rituals are commensurate with their social position and extend beyond the concerns of the family. While personal and religious beliefs may be addressed at the visit, the spiritual state or disposition of the soul is not as prominently ritualized as are the civic contributions of the person's life. The formal service is the single dominant phase of the mortuary structure. A major public event, it celebrates the status of the "big shot" whose life, larger than his private self, in a sense belongs to Chinatown.

For esteemed and high-ranking officers of associations, the funeral is held at Victory Hall, a large auditorium belonging to the CCBA. Such a funeral is most likely if the member had served prominently for the Guomintang government of Taiwan and held national and/or international office in major associations. Funeral services for such persons are long, logistically complex, elaborate affairs. If the deceased was a president of the national Lee Family Association, for example, delegates from each Lee chapter in the United States attend to pay their respects. As each chapter is announced, its representatives are directed to approach the deceased, present the deceased with hand bouquets of flowers, and bow three times to show respect. The proceedings, designed to recognize an ideal life of prominent service, are very dignified, formal, and choreographed. Several speeches eulogizing the deceased are delivered. Numerous couplet banners are hung on the walls praising the life and significance of the deceased and wishing his spirit well. Floral tributes abound and the attending crowd is enormous. When the casket is closed, the Taiwanese flag is draped on it. Everyone receives *li shi* before leaving to join the procession through Chinatown. Police are usually on hand to control traffic for the long cortege, which extends several blocks and will make at least one stop at the association building. At least two, if not three, bands are contracted. The public show is a significant factor in leaving no doubt that a dignitary is being honored.

THE CATHAY BAND TRADITION IN CHINATOWN FUNERALS

Of all the major Chinatowns in North America, San Francisco's is the only one in which the tradition of a funeral procession with a marching band flourishes. The perpetuation of this tradition is strongly linked to the historic formation of a Chinatown Western-style marching band. Its story illustrates how a fusion of multicultural elements creates a unique entity with new characteristics that give it an identity of its own. Because of this particular history and because the band is the most salient element of today's funeral procession, it is appropriate to include an in-depth description of the tradition's development.

Along with Chinese funeral bands, Western marching bands have been a part of the Chinatown ritual scene since as early as 1897, when a popular orchestra played the funeral march from the opera *Saul* for the fanciful funeral procession of infamous Chinatown gang leader Little Pete.[61] However, Western funeral bands became a Chinatown cultural fixture when a group of Chinese boys, endorsed by the Six Companies, formed the first Chinese Western-style marching band in America.

This tradition began in 1911 with "the first organized social interaction between American and Chinese youths":

> On a Saturday afternoon the American boys arrived [in Chinatown] in a large bus. . . . When they got out of the bus . . . the Columbia Park boys lined up and started serenading their peers with "America" and other tunes. After a few numbers, Evans [the headmaster of the Columbia Park School] asked the Chinese boys to join them in a march, and so, with the band playing, [the Chinese boys] fell into line . . . to the applause of a large crowd that gathered to watch them marching to and fro along Stockton Street. . . . Never before had young Chinese and American groups even mingled to talk, let alone develop friendships and exchange ideas with each other.[62]

This encounter was the inspiration for the Chinese Boys Band. The thirteen Chinese boys who participated in this meeting approached the Chinese Six Companies Association for sponsorship. The Six Companies, then holding the leadership role in Chinatown, felt that such a band playing Western music would be a positive activity for the youths and a benefit to their community, which was acquainted mainly with the music of Chinese opera. The director solicited funds from the community and in a few days raised two thousand dollars for the purchase of instruments and the hiring of a band teacher, and provided a practice room in the association building. Thomas Kennedy, a retired U.S. Navy concertmaster, was the band's first musical director. When he retired a couple of years later, one of the original band members, Thomas Lym, succeeded him and led the band for the next fifty years, until it stopped playing in 1962.[63]

As the band grew, it changed its name several times. In 1914 it merged with the Chinese Boys Band of Oakland and was renamed the New Cathay Boys Band, later modified to just the Cathay Boys Band. When its growth led to the addition of junior bands, the band changed its charter; in 1916 it created a club called the Cathay Musical Society. By 1928 the society's development included sports, community service, and social activities. A rewriting of the society's charter created a parent organization, the Cathay Club Limited, in 1930. Its main band became the Cathay Club Band or, as it was commonly called, the Cathay Band.[64]

The Cathay Club Band became a prize-winning band. Its bookings ranged from the 1915 Panama Pacific International Exposition, to the Orpheum Theater circuit, to free concerts for the Chinatown community. At its peak it had over a hundred members, with as many as sixty musicians playing at once. It was in demand at Chinese New Year dances, parades, parties, charitable events, and funeral processions:[65]

> In our Chinatown, participation of bands in funeral processions [is] a tradition and form[s] an important adjunct in prominent ceremonies. Heretofore, the band had usually been composed of American musicians but with the advent of the Chinese band the latter was favored. They became firmly established as part of nearly every funeral with the exception of week-day burials. Income from this source formed a valuable asset to the finances of the band. Others soon became aware of this fact, and during 1913, two other rival bands were organized. But either due to poor management or discouragement, these rival bands were soon forced to withdraw from the field of competition.[66]

Band member Wilson Wong remembers the funeral processions taking about an hour (double the present length) and going through all the streets of Chinatown, even alleyways. For funerals the band wore maroon, military-style uniforms with black belts. Their signature song when the casket came out of the funeral home was "Nearer My God to Thee." The funeral repertoire of twelve pieces comprised elegies and Christian hymns. "It didn't matter to the Chinese as long as it sounded good!" Wong claims. The Cathay Band was always first in the procession. In the 1930s and 1940s each band had twenty-five to thirty members. When a "big shot" died and needed three bands, the

Cathay Band would assemble three groups of fifteen or twenty, depending on the availability of players. At that time, there were sixty musicians capable of playing.[67]

It is unclear when the band began playing for funerals, but it eventually played in nearly every funeral procession until the mid-1950s. Author Herbert Haim implies that the Chinese Boys Band played for funerals as early as 1913, and Wilson Wong remembers seeing the Cathay Musical Society band marching in funeral processions in the late 1920s. The band was a hobby for the amateur players, and they played for funerals usually only on Sundays, when most of the funerals took place. In the 1950s, the demand for this mortuary practice was large enough to attract the attention of the Musicians' Union, which required that only unionized bands play for funerals. The Cathay Band could perform as an auxiliary band if a union band was hired; otherwise the Cathay Band had to join the union, or it would be picketed. Since union dues far exceeded the good luck *li shi* or the token fee given to the club, the band ceased playing for funerals, and by 1964 it stopped its public performances altogether.[68]

The Cathay Club was a Chinatown institution that maintained a visible presence at every social and seasonal occasion for over fifty years. It was a modern, American Chinese development that emerged from within Chinatown as an assimilative result of contact with the larger society. The club carried on the funeral band tradition in its own fashion, establishing a Chinatown custom that was transferred to the union bands. The legacy of the Cathay Club Band remains evident in the unionized funeral band today. Some of the pieces played are taken directly from the funeral music folio used by the Cathay Club Band, and one of the band's former members serves as an occasional adviser to the mortuary band. The Cathay Club Band is one of the distinguishing features in San Francisco that is absent in the histories of other American Chinatowns. Its success as an active Chinatown institution for two generations may partially explain the continued popularity of the funeral band and procession in San Francisco.

THE GREEN STREET BRASS BAND

The current Chinatown funeral band is the Green Street Brass Band, managed and led by a female jazz saxophonist, Lisa Pollard. Under exclusive contract with Green Street Mortuary, they are the sole band that plays for Chinatown funerals. Composed of ten first-rate unionized musicians, none of whom are of Chinese descent, the band plays a combination of military funeral marches, European elegies, Christian hymns, and an occasional Chinese folk song. Pollard works with Clifford Yee, the Green Street Mortuary manager, to develop dramatic yet decorous presentations to show respect and honor. Continually seeking out and arranging appropriate music, she is conscious of her role in the Chinatown funeral tradition. She has consulted with Wilson Wong on the music used by the Cathay Band and has adapted some of the Cathay Band's selections for her band. Pollard is a world-class musician who has toured with Duke Ellington and played at presidential inaugurations; her band has also played for many of the celebrity non-Chinese funerals in the San Francisco area, such as those for Jessica Mitford and Herb Caen.[69]

The band's success is evident in the continued demand for its services and the attention paid it by the media. In mid-October of 1996, a big, splashy article on the band and Chinatown tradition appeared in the Sunday edition of the *San Francisco Examiner and Chronicle*.[70] This article generated interest from the television media, and in late October, for their Halloween and death theme stories, local channels 2 and 5 and the national Cable News Network featured the funeral band and this unique Chinatown way of celebrating the dead.

As a tourist attraction, the funeral procession with band stands out in any visitor's tour of Chinatown, and travel magazines are quick to point this out. A U.S. Airways in-flight magazine mentioned watching for a funeral procession when visiting San Francisco Chinatown, and in the January 1997 issue of *Travel and Leisure*, an article on San Francisco's Asian neighborhoods and Chinatown quotes novelist Amy Tan's recommendation "for an offbeat, quintessential tour of Chinatown . . . to follow the brass marching band that plays for Chinese funerals."[71]

SUMMARY

The conventions and traditions brought to America by the early southern Chinese were Chinese in general and regional in particular, reflecting the different rural villages from which they came. Generally speaking, Chinese American funeral and burial practices are characterized by the southern Chinese custom of secondary burials, an emphasis on patrilineage, the fear and placation of evil spirits, the solicitation of good luck, and the view that the afterlife parallels the earthly one, meaning that the deceased will have similar material needs in the spirit world.

Until the twentieth century, the funeral customs in San Francisco were similar to what would have been practiced in the native village. District and clan associations may have contributed to a standardization of practices distinctive to their group.

With the birth of the Republic of China in 1911, the Chinese in America became conscious of being modern Chinese while harboring nostalgia for the fading traditions of imperial China. This mixture of sentiments became evident in funeral rituals, especially as San Francisco rebuilt itself into a modern city after the 1906 earthquake. Prior to World War II, immigration restrictions, urban growth, limited assimilation of second- and third-generation American Chinese, and racial biases that continued to restrict many Chinese and their culture to Chinatown all contributed to a Chinatown-style, Americanized version of Chinese cultural expression and funerary rites.

This cultural expression continues to change with the different traditions introduced by the numerous and diverse ethnic Chinese who have immigrated to America since 1965. Within the American cultural framework, their customs and practices are modified by community consensus and governmental regulations. In San Francisco Chinatown, the tolerance for cultural tradition allows for traditions most reminiscent of those of the nineteenth century: sackcloth mourning clothes, walking processions sometimes in bare feet, the presence of Daoist or Buddhist priests, picture car and band, incense, spirit money, and the occasional presence of sacrificial animals. At the other extreme are Western-style Christian funerals, with only scant traits relating to Chinatown custom: the picture car and band.

CONCLUSIONS: ENDURANCE AND PERPETUATION

Several factors may explain why funeral processions with marching bands persist in San Francisco's Chinatown when they have diminished in other major North American Chinatowns, such as those in New York and Vancouver. In many ways San Francisco Chinatown remains the cultural symbol for the Chinese in America. As the oldest American port of entry and settlement for the Chinese, it became the official seat of the Chinese government in America and the regional and national headquarters for many of the district and clan associations. Rebuilt in the image of a stereotypical Chinese town after the 1906 earthquake, it is visually the most "Chinese" and colorful of all the Chinatowns[72] and a major tourist attraction.[73] Having been rebuilt, it also became one of the newer and more modern Chinatowns, fitting in with the progressive spirit of the early twentieth century. This spirit is evident in the formation of the Cathay Club Band, a unique San Francisco Chinatown tradition that became an integral part of the local funeral scene. The Cathay Club Band made the inclusion of a marching band a common and typical part of Chinatown mortuary rites.

The influence of the associations is not to be dismissed. As the backbone of Chinatown's social structure, they were a conservative element that valued the Chinese tradition of honoring an esteemed member with pomp and ceremony. Their funeral rituals for prominent members set the standard of what was due a revered person whose life fulfilled Confucian ideals.

The continued increase in Chinese immigrants to the United States is a major factor in revitalizing and perpetuating cultural traditions in Chinatown. First-generation immigrants commonly cling to the familiar traditions of their homeland for emotional comfort and because they are unfamiliar with the customs of their host culture. Many of the recent immigrants are more economically solvent than were their nineteenth-century predecessors and can afford to realize fully the ceremonial ideals of their traditions. In addition, their demographic diversity is accompanied by a diversity in mortuary ritual practices, many of which are best tolerated in Chinatown.

The liberality of Chinatown has manifold causes. Historically it has always been left somewhat alone to contend with its lifeways as an ethnic enclave. In this regard, Chinatown has always expressed itself publicly in ways not permitted in other neighborhoods. Sidewalk vending, firecracker use, the throwing of spirit money, the blocking of traffic to accommodate custom, and the sale of live animals for food are practices not easily accepted elsewhere.

As a cultural symbol, Chinatown, through its district associations and chamber of commerce, exercises a political clout that has as its foundation the expanding Chinese and Asian voting population in the Bay Area. How Chinatown is treated politically by the city of San Francisco is indicative of the city's attitude toward Asians. Chinese electoral clout empowers the leaders of Chinatown, who exercise influence, if not control, over the permissiveness and restraint of public cultural practices such as funeral processions.

Chinese cultural practices thrive as sanctioned lifeways in public Chinatown. The community remains physically and culturally sequestered within the city, offering Chinatown residents the opportunities, cultural conveniences, and familiarity of an ethnic enclave. In varying stages of acculturation, residents continue proudly to exercise Chinese traditions, which also attract tourists as something "exotic" and novel.[74] Tourism is a major source of income to Chinatown and the city of San Francisco. To this end the Chinese chamber of commerce self-consciously cultivates an image of Chinatown as a safe, colorfully traditional "Oriental" place. This image serves not only to draw tourists but also to lure corporate sponsors for community projects; the market interests and surveys of these sponsors perceive a cultural link between Chinatown and the Asian consumer population in the Bay Area.[75]

Last but not least, the endurance and perpetuation of Chinese mortuary customs is credited to the mortuary that handles the Chinatown funeral processions. The manager's personal concern and respect for his community and its cultural practices encourages a variety of ritual expression. In many respects this attitude is attributable to the policies of Service Corporation International (SCI), Green Street Mortuary's parent corporation, which allow the local management to do business in a manner sensitive to Chinatown needs.

As an ethnic enclave carved out of racism, economic opportunity, and a deeply ingrained Chinese cultural tradition, Chinatown has become a defining patch in the increasingly multicultural American quilt. In the process of its development it has synthesized American as well as various types of Chinese cultural characteristics to form a modified version of Chinese culture in America. City politics, global marketing and capital, immigration, tourism, and special interest groups inside and outside of Chinatown are additional factors that influence decisions regarding how people in Chinatown express themselves as being Chinese in America.

NOTES

This article is a revised version of Linda Sun Crowder's "Mortuary Practices in San Francisco Chinatown," in *Chinese America: History and Perspectives 1999*, ed. Marlon Hom and others (San Francisco: Chinese Historical Society of America, 1999), 33–46. For additional information see Linda Sun Crowder, "Mortuary Practices and the Construction of Chinatown Identity" (PhD diss., University of Hawai'i at Manoa, 2002).

1. The major Chinatowns in North America included in my research were New York, Los Angeles, and Vancouver, BC. In New York Chinatown a ten-piece Italian band plays at the mortuary, then waits to play on a corner of Mott Street (the main street of Chinatown) while the motor procession passes by. The musicianship is very simple. Walking processions by mourners or the band are discouraged because the slower pace holds up traffic; Martha Yick (owner) and staff, Wah Wing Sang Mortuary, interviews by author, June and September 1997. In Los Angeles the custom was revived by new Chinese immigrants from Southeast Asia, but the route is shorter and processions occur much less frequently. Band members wear blue plastic pith helmets instead of the military-style caps worn in San Francisco; Kevin Porter (musician), interview by author, April 1998. Marching funeral processions in Vancouver, BC, stopped in the late 1980s owing to the unavailability of musicians on weekdays, when most funerals take place, since the cemeteries do not permit burials during the weekend; James Kelly (manager) and staff, Armstrong Mortuary, interview by author, July 1997.

The "new Chinatown" in the Richmond-Sunset district of San Francisco has the processions also, but infrequently (one out of every twenty funerals as opposed to the four out of ten in Chinatown) and with a route of only a few blocks. People from Vietnam tend to hire the bands; Daphne Daphne (owner, Ashley and McMullen Mortuary), interview by author, January 1998. In the "suburban Chinatown" of Monterey Park, near Los Angeles, the majority of the Chinese are from Taiwan, and they do not tend to hire bands. When the community became predominantly Chinese in the late 1970s, the custom was observed occasionally, but pressures from the city discouraged its practice; Henry Kwong (owner, Universal Chung Wah Funeral Homes), interview by author, April 1998.

2. Philip P. Choy, "The Architecture of San Francisco Chinatown," in *Chinese America: History and Perspectives, 1990*, ed. Marlon K. Hom and others (San Francisco: Chinese Historical Society of America, 1990), 37–66.

3. C. K. Yang, *Religion in Chinese Society* (Prospect Heights, IL: Waveland, 1961), 38, 44–53.

4. Shih-shan Henry Tsai, *The Chinese Experience in America* (Bloomington: Indiana University Press, 1986), 10.

5. Him Mark Lai, "Historical Development of the Chinese Consolidated Benevolent Association/*Huiguan* System," in *Chinese America: History and Perspectives* 1987, [ed. Him Mark Lai, Ruthanne Lum McCunn, and Judy Yung] (San Francisco: Chinese Historical Society of America, 1987), 33.

6. A. W. Loomis, "The Six Chinese Companies," *Overland Monthly* 1 (September 18, 1868): 224, cited in Tsai, *Chinese Experience*, 49.

7. Charles Caldwell Dobie, *San Francisco's Chinatown* (New York: D. Appleton-Century, 1936), 67.

8. Richard H. Dillon, *The Hatchet Men* (New York: Coward-McCann, 1962), 16.

9. Dobie, *Chinatown*, 68.

10. However, the San Francisco Nam Hoy District Association sent a delegation to China in late 1997 on a mission to reclaim their cemetery and ensure that remains sent to China in the future would have a burial place. The reason for sending the delegation was that the association cemeteries in Colma are reaching their capacity, and the cost of acquiring the additional needed land is prohibitive. As it turned out, the cemeteries in the Nam Hoy district had already been filled almost to capacity, eliminating the prospect of returning bodies to China for burial. Since then the Look San Cemetery committee has voted to construct a brick wall around its cemetery in Colma that would be based on a design resembling the Great Wall of China. It would house only cremated remains and thus provide space to accommodate its members for many years into the twenty-first century; Larry Chan (member of Look San Cemetery committee), interviews by author, October 1997 and April 1998.

While there are no bone houses at Look San, bodies in the old, lower section, where burials were supposed to be temporary, are periodically exhumed (perhaps after twenty-five years) and reburied closer together on the upper part of the slope. The Kong Chow Association part of Look San is said to have a small plot set aside for burying ashes. There also used to be a plot in Look San set aside for prostitutes, paupers, and others whose ancestral county may have been unknown; Horatio Jung (Look San Cemetery Committee member, CCBA), interview by author, March 1998.

11. When buildings in the Lincoln Park area were being retrofitted for earthquake safety in the early 1990s, thirty-two Chinese graves with remains were uncovered and

relocated to Golden Hill Cemetery; George Lee (Golden Hill Cemetery staff member), interview by author, June 1998.

12. Lone Mountain was such a popular cemetery that when the board of supervisors ordered all the city's cemeteries to close in 1912, there was such a public outcry to save Lone Mountain (renamed Laurel Hill in 1867) that its closing was deferred until 1937; Oscar Lewis, *San Francisco: Mission to Metropolis* (San Diego: Howell-North, 1980), 76.

13. The establishment dates of the Chinese cemeteries in Colma are from San Francisco Chinese American historian Him Mark Lai's research of district association documents.

14. Although Qingming was not originally a Buddhist festival, Buddhists now observe it, at least in California.

15. Dobie, *Chinatown*, 68.

16. Bobby Gee, interview by author, January 1997.

17. Dobie, *Chinatown*, 68.

18. Gee, interview.

19. Wu Ting-Fang, the Chinese minister to the United States, wrote an article titled "China and the Chinese People" for *Collier's Weekly* that was reprinted in the *Los Angeles Times* of July 15, 1900. In it he compares the social customs of the Chinese to those of Americans and describes funeral practices in some detail. In a 1997 interview by the author, Bobby Gee recalled his parents' description and his own observations of handling the dead in village China. Gee's recollection is similar to what is described by Wu.

20. Wells Fargo and Company, *Wells Fargo and Co.'s Express Directory of Chinese Business Houses, San Francisco, Sacramento, Marysville, Portland, Stockton, San Jose [and] Virginia City, Nev.* (San Francisco, Wells Fargo, 1878), 20. It is the only Chinese undertaker listed in the 1878 directory. Main Fook is also mentioned as a Nanhai Sanyi business in Sam Yup Association, *A History of the Sam Yup Benevolent Association in the United States, 1850–1974* (San Francisco: Sam Yup Association, 1975).

21. [Wong Kin, ed.], *International Chinese Business Directory of the World for the Year 1913* (San Francisco: International Chinese Business Directory, 1913), 1452, 1459.

22. Frank Dunn, interview by Him Mark Lai, 1975; Daphne, interview; Pacific Telephone and Telegraph Company, *Pacific Telephone Directory for San Francisco, Including Brisbane, Colma, and Daly City* ([San Francisco]: Pacific Telephone and Telegraph Company, 1968); Pacific Telephone and Telegraph Company, *San Francisco, Including Daly City, Brisbane, and Colma Yellow Pages Directory* ([San Francisco]: Pacific Telephone and Telegraph Company, 1975; 1981).

23. Bill Steiner, interviews by author, April 1996, May 1997, August 1998; Clifford Yee, interviews by author, April 1996, May 1997, August 1998; Lisa Pollard, interviews by author, April 1996, May 1997, August 1998.

24. Daphne, interview; Pollard, interview, 1998; Green Street Mortuary staff, interview by author, August 1998.

25. Ku Chieh-Kang (Gu Jiejang), "Funeral Processions," in *Chinese Civilization and Society: A Source Book*, ed. Patricia Buckley Ebrey (New York: Free Press, 1981).

26. L. Eve Armentrout Ma, "Chinese Traditional Religion in North America and Hawaii," in *Chinese America: History and Perspectives, 1988*, ed. Him Mark Lai, Ruthanne Lum McCunn, and Judy Yung (San Francisco: Chinese Historical Society of America, 1988), 131.

27. Joseph Quan, quoted in Ralph Craib, "Two Worlds at a Funeral," *San Francisco Chronicle*, April 24, 1964, 3.

28. Steven J. Lee, interview by author, February 1996.

29. Yang, *Religion*, 31–32.

30. Ku, "Funeral Processions," 289.

31. Dobie, *Chinatown*, 63–64.

32. Charles Keeler, *San Francisco and Thereabout* (San Francisco: California Promotion Committee of San Francisco, 1902), 67.

33. City and County of San Francisco, *San Francisco, the Bay and Its Cities*, American Guide Series (New York: Hastings House, 1940), 225–226. An extensive description of Little Pete's funeral is also given in Dillon, *Hatchet Men,* 335–339. Dillon quotes a lengthy excerpt from Frank Norris's firsthand account of the event published in the literary magazine the *Wave*.

34. See, for example, Dillon, *Hatchet Men*, 175–177:

> In true gangster tradition, Little Pete's cohorts attempted to give him a magnificent funeral. After two hours of intricate last rites, performed by four priests from his favorite joss house, his casket was placed in a resplendent hearse drawn by six black-draped white horses. Hired mourners preceded the hearse, burning joss sticks and wildly beating the air with uplifted arms. From a carriage, four Chinese busily tossed out bits of paper punched with square holes—to confuse the devils seeking to make off with the spirit of the departed. The fantastic cortege, led by a popular orchestra playing the funeral march from *Saul*, proceeded through streets lined with spectators to the Chinese Cemetery down the Peninsula. Here a mob of onlookers—not hoodlums, but respectable San Franciscans indignant over losing bets on race horses doped by Pete's henchmen—greeted priests and mourners with hoots and clods of earth. The Chinese were compelled to haul the coffin back to the city where, at the old Chinese cemetery, Little Pete's remains were interred pending arrangements for shipment to China. The wagonloads of roast pig, duck, cakes, tea, and gin left beside the grave were guzzled by the crowd of white onlookers.

Dillon describes the funeral of Low Yet, founder of the Chee Kung Tong, and compares it to that of Little Pete. See also Neil Hitt, "Blast of Firecrackers, Blare of Brass Horns—Chinatown's Largest Funeral: Wong Goon Dick Goes to Sit with His Ancestors at the Councils of Confucius," *San Francisco Chronicle*, February 17, 1941, 1. In this extensive news article, Hitt writes:

> Some of the old-timers thought perhaps the funeral of Little Pete might have been as large in the horse and carriage days before the fire, but later admitted themselves mistaken when they saw the procession of 1600 in the Wong cortege, with 400 automobiles, five bands and three huge truck loads of flowers. Too, Little Pete's funeral was an old-fashioned affair,

with women paid to mourn and scream, priests hired to exorcise and pay heavy tribute to the evil spirits, and a special guard to stand and keep the sun out of Pete's eyes. Little Pete, leader of the Sam Yups at a time when pistols were supplanting lathing hatchets, had been killed in a Washington St. barber shop when he committed the indiscretion of sending his body guard out for results of the old Bay District horse track. With a few minor exceptions, the funeral of Wong Goon Dick yesterday was a modern affair, and in keeping with this, the 30th year of the great Republic of China.

35. *Li shi*, in Cantonese romanization, is *lai see* or *leih sih*, sometimes written *lei-sz* or *li-sz*. *Li shi* are also known as "red envelopes" (*hongbao, hung-pao*).

36. Dobie, *Chinatown*, 63–69; Dillon, *Hatchet Men*, 175–177, 336–339; Ku, "Funeral Processions," 289–293; Wu, "China," 6.

37. Stanton Delaplane, "A Journey to Her Ancestors!" *San Francisco Chronicle*, January 18, 1934, 4.

38. Thomas W. Chinn, *Bridging the Pacific: San Francisco Chinatown and Its People* (San Francisco: Chinese Historical Society of America, 1989), 178.

39. Hitt, "Blast."

40. *San Francisco Chronicle*, October 26, 1947.

41. Craib, "Two Worlds."

42. Pardee Lowe, "Good Life in Chinatown," *Journal of the American Asiatic Association*, February 1937, 127–131.

43. See Hitt, "Blast."

44. The 1965 Immigration Act ended the discriminatory national origins quota system and instituted the eight-category preference system to reunite families with close relatives and admit aliens with specially needed skills and talents on a "first come, first served" basis in each category. The act also provided an annual limitation of 170,000 immigrants from the Eastern Hemisphere, with a limitation of 20,000 from each country. The Western Hemisphere had a limit of 120,000, with no limit as to country and no preference system. Spouses and children of U.S. citizens and parents of children over twenty-one were exempt from numerical ceilings. To control the admission of skilled or unskilled foreign workers, the act instituted requirements for labor certification. It authorized the annual admission of 10,000 refugees. This legislation resulted in an increase in a new type of Chinese immigrant: men and women with high skills and intellectual attainments, of middle-class and usually affluent families from Shanghai, Tianjin, and other parts of China coming via Hong Kong or Taiwan, speaking Mandarin rather than the Cantonese dialects, and usually fluent in English. Such immigrants often felt more at home in entirely American surroundings than in the Cantonese-dominated Chinatowns; Jack Chen, *The Chinese of America* (San Francisco: Harper and Row, 1980), 216–217.

45. As practiced in San Francisco Chinatown, the white and red blankets are given by the chief mourner. Additional blankets may be given by the deceased's children or other relatives as an option; the author has seen up to ten given. If the family decides on the blanket ritual, the minimum requirement is usually the white and red. Variations exist in different areas. In Vancouver Chinatown, blankets with prints are given by the daughters only. At one Chinese mortuary in New York's Chinatown, the cas-

kets come with the first blanket: white or creamy beige for men and pink for women. The second blanket is always red, and the subsequent blankets can be of any color. At another Chinese mortuary on the same street in New York, the first blanket is always red if the deceased is over sixteen years of age. The subsequent blankets can be of any color. If the deceased is younger than sixteen years old, red is not used, but other colors or prints are acceptable. The director at this mortuary commented that the San Francisco Chinese, by using white, are more traditional in their practices. Some Buddhists use a special gold-colored blanket printed with red charms and symbols in lieu of the white and red blankets.

46. *Li shi* given at the mortuary always contain one coin or bill because things associated with funerals are always in odd numbers. *Li shi* given at the Lunar New Year and other life-affirming celebrations are generally in pairs and even numbers.

47. The variations in practice remain consistent within the larger logic system of lineage continuity. For instance, some families insist the in-laws wear green, while others insist that it should be the grandchildren. In the Chinese patrilineage system, the male line is perpetuated through the fertility of the son's wife, the daughter-in-law, and her issue, the grandchildren who will continue their father's line. Whether it is the daughter-in-law or the descendant grandchildren who wear green, the general concept applies. For additional information and academic analysis of color symbolism, fertility, and death in funeral rituals, see James L. Watson, "Of Flesh and Bones: The Management of Death Pollution in Cantonese Society," in *Death and the Regeneration of Life*, ed. Maurice Bloch and Jonathan Parry (Cambridge: Cambridge University Press, 1982), 155–186; Stuart E. Thompson, "Death, Food, and Fertility," in *Death Ritual in Late Imperial and Modern China*, ed. James L. Watson and Evelyn S. Rawski (Berkeley: University of California Press, 1988), 71–108.

48. Spirit money is thrown within the borders of Chinatown, specifically between Powell and Kearny, and Broadway and Bush. Beyond these streets, the mortuary runs the risk of littering; Yee, interview, 1997. Hence a ritual boundary is established based on the tolerance and consensus of Chinatown, and the intolerance of Chinese ritual tradition by the non-Chinese community. This consensus may change in the future if there are increasing complaints by community leaders about the mess made by the tossed spirit money. One suggestion has been to charge the mortuary for cleanup services; Wei Teng, "Keeping the Public Clean Is Beneficial to You and Others," *Chinese Express*, May 1, 1996, 3.

49. The chicken is a symbol of fertility, and its blood is a protection from evil. The rooster or cockerel in particular is associated with new beginnings and continuity because it welcomes the new day by crowing at the rising of the sun, and because of its sexual, propagating character.

50. Steiner, interview, 1996.

51. Rice is thrown into the grave for good luck and fertility for the lineage. Coins are also thrown for good luck and as passage money for the soul. Handfuls of dirt are thrown in by family and friends as a gesture of closure and saying goodbye, and as a way of participating in the burial; Green Street Mortuary staff, interview by author, July 1996.

52. Many Chinatown folk believe that one should never go directly home after a funeral because the bad luck of death from the funeral would follow you there. A stop should be made to "drop off" the bad luck or confuse malevolent spirits that might follow you home.

53. Bernard Wong, PhD, interview by author, June 1997.

54. The traditional meal always includes roast pork, boiled chicken, a vegetarian stew, soup, and rice. The other dishes may be shrimp and greens, Peking ribs, bean cakes, chicken with cashews, barbecued duck, stir-fried scallops, or honey walnut prawns. One restaurant said that beef traditionally is not served, while another restaurant included it in the suggested menu.

55. Reverend Tam, a Methodist minister from Guangzhou (Canton) who served the Chinatown community for over thirty years and who has presided over numerous funerals, formerly used the term "longevity meal" but changed to using the more ambiguous "traditional meal" to avoid confusion. The people who used the term "longevity meal" did not find it inconsistent with the term "plain meal"; they recognized it as being the same thing. Those who used the term "plain meal" found the term "longevity meal" to be inappropriate and did not associate the two. That *sauh* and *sou* are of similar sound and are used to refer to the same thing is consistent with the Chinese love of homophones to make puns and confer double meanings.

56. Camellia Lau, interview by author, June 1997; B. Wong, interview; S. Lee, interview; Lychee Garden Restaurant staff, interview by author, June 1997; Great Eastern Restaurant staff, interview by author, June 1997.

57. *Li shi* is accepted as a Chinese custom, as something that is done out of good manners and courtesy independent of specific ideologies. In Chinatown, a family would be highly criticized if no *li shi* were given at a funeral. And if it is offered, one must accept it as a goodwill gesture of social exchange or risk offending the giver.

58. Given American sensibilities about animal abuse, the cut comb is the more frequent practice. The priests are very circumspect and bring in the chicken discreetly hidden in a paper bag. Once the chicken's purpose is fulfilled, the bird is quickly squirreled away out of sight. Some families request that the funeral director escort away from the grave non-Chinese guests and other mourners who may be squeamish or offended by the blood rituals. Other families will not bring out the animal if they see any non-Chinese strangers in the vicinity of the grave site. Occasionally the solemnity of the burial is comically disrupted by an uncooperative chicken that escapes and is chased about the cemetery by the priest and mourners. According to some Chinatown folk, the chicken is supposed to be killed, taken home to be cooked, and brought back the following day as an offering to the new ancestor (ancestors partake of cooked food offerings; gods accept raw or natural foods).

59. In the Buddhist-Daoist worldview, the soul, upon death, is believed to hover over the body for three days in a volatile state of disorientation. Bewildered in its new state outside the body, it is at risk of wandering away from it. The family's wailing before the body not only sets the mood and lets the deceased know that people care about him, but also serves as an appeal to the soul not to leave the body; Yang, *Religion*, 35. During the funeral process, the soul, comprised of two classic major aspects, is prepared for two contexts. One, the heavenly aspect (*yang*) of the soul (*hun*) is as-

sisted in its spirit journey context through a series of hells to account for its lifetime of sins before it resides in paradise. The second, the earthly aspect (*yin*) of the soul (*po*) resides in the grave context. In Chinese folk belief, another part of the *hun* resides in the ancestral tablet that is placed at home or at a temple; Stevan Harrell, "The Concept of Soul in Chinese Folk Religion," *Journal of Asian Studies* 38 (1979): 518–528; Tu Wei-Ming, ed., "Soul: Chinese Concept," in *Encyclopedia of Religion*, ed. Mircea Eliade, vol. 13 (New York: Macmillan, 1986), 447–450. Once the souls are situated in these contexts, they will continue to depend on the living for ritual sustenance. This reciprocal exchange of offerings for blessings engages the prospective ancestor and descendants in an interactive relationship. Hence the spirit continues to have a social role and position in the family from the spirit plane as a beneficent ancestor.

60. Some Chinese distinguish death and decomposition as a separate category from grief and mourning and signify it with the color symbols of noncolor: white, natural, or off-white. Death and decomposition are associated with pollution from death airs (bad luck) and the dangerous volatility of the spirit before proper burial. This pollution and danger warrant their own rituals and symbols and are concerns separate from the personal grief and mourning felt from losing a loved one.

61. Dillon, *Hatchet Men*, 336–339; Doris Muscatine, *Old San Francisco: The Biography of a City from Early Days to the Earthquake* (New York: G. P. Putnam's Sons, 1975), 406.

62. Chinn, *Bridging*, 202.

63. Sally Swope, "Cathay Club: Chinatown's First Marching Band Celebrates 75th Year," *East-West*, September 11, 1986, 10–11; Chinn, *Bridging*, 55–59, 201–202; Wilson Wong, interview by author, April 1996.

64. In 1914 the Chinese Boys Band of Oakland (formed in 1912) merged with the San Francisco Chinese Boys Band to become fifty-eight pieces strong. It changed its name to the New Cathay Boys Band. The bands were indirectly affiliated with each other, since they were both supported by the Six Companies; Herbert J. Haim, "Cathay Club of San Francisco," Cathay Club Band Scrapbook (San Francisco: Cathay Club, 1934), 2–3. Between 1919 and 1943 thirteen auxiliary bands were formed, such as a jazz band, a dance orchestra, and girls' bands; Swope, "Cathay Club," 10–11.

65. Swope, "Cathay Club"; Chinn, *Bridging*, 55–59; W. Wong, interview.

66. Haim, "Cathay Club," 2.

67. W. Wong, interview; Wilson Wong, interview by author, January 1997.

68. Swope, "Cathay Club," 10–11; Chinn, *Bridging*, 55–59; W. Wong, interviews.

69. Pollard, interviews, 1996 and 1997.

70. Carl Nolte, "How Sweet the Sound," *San Francisco Examiner and Chronicle*, October 13, 1996, zone 6, 1.

71. Alan Brown, "Asia Minor: Wayne Wang, Amy Tan, and Others Lead an Insider's Tour through the Far East—in San Francisco," *Travel and Leisure*, January 1997, 88–97, 118–120.

72. Christopher L. Salter, *San Francisco's Chinatown: How Chinese a Town?* (San Francisco: R and E Research Associates, 1978), 15–42; Choy, "Architecture," 37–66.

73. Calvin Lee, *Chinatown, U.S.A.* (New York: Doubleday, 1965), 88–101.

74. Teng, "Keeping."

75. Chinese New Year Parade Office, San Francisco, literature for public relations distribution, 1996; Chinese New Year Parade Office staff, San Francisco, interviews by author, March 1997, August 1998.

8

Old Rituals in New Lands:
Bringing the Ancestors to America

Roberta S. Greenwood

With a mixture of awe and amazement, nineteenth-century newspapers from New York to Los Angeles reported observations—filtered through their own biases and perceptions—of the elaborate traditions of Chinese funerals, processions to the cemetery, and ritual honors subsequently paid to the deceased. Prompted mostly by tradition and also by overcrowding in local cemeteries and pressures for land development, selective exhumations for shipment of the remains back to the homeland followed interment. Around the turn of the twentieth century, there were increasing accounts of burials that were disinterred and forwarded from the New World to China. The tide, so to speak, is turning now, with many ancestors being removed from family graves in China and brought to this country, where families settled permanently in the United States can observe traditional customs of honor and respect.

In years past, primary interments in rural China were consigned to graves scattered in the hillsides, although more recently, they are concentrated in graveyards. The principles of *fengshui*, thought to have arisen originally with respect to burial customs, favored a location on a hillside. Families were free to make a grave on any unoccupied land, but when the government or a commune opted to use the land, the families were obliged to move the remains. Archaeological evidence shows that burials took place as deep as thirty-three feet in 167 B.C., in tightly sealed coffins containing solutions of mercuric sulfide and other chemicals for preservation.[1] Other preservatives used were mercury and charcoal, and the body was placed deep in the earth so that the dead could find peace free from disturbance.[2]

As is the case here, observances take place on the traditional holidays, particularly Qingming (Pure Brightness), in the spring, and Yulanpen (Hungry Ghosts), a lesser ancestral commemoration in the fall. The family may provide offerings at seven, fourteen, twenty-one, and on up to forty-nine days after the funeral, in the traditional seven-day mourning cycle, and on the birth date or anniversary of death of the deceased.[3] From three to seven years later, members of the family or, less often, part-time specialists, dig open the grave, clean the bones, and place them in an established order in a pottery urn called a "golden pagoda," *jinta* (*chin-t'a*), or "golden womb."[4] The urn is then partially buried in the hillside. Whether it is reburied in the same place or not depends on the recent fortunes of the family. The ideal last stage, rarely observed now, is to build a tomb to contain the urns of all the ancestors.[5] Confucianism prohibited the altars from containing tablets of juvenile males, unmarried women, or married couples without sons.[6]

Historically, it was the fervent wish of Chinese in this country, whether the isolated workingman or the prosperous merchant, to be buried in the homeland. To this end, perhaps as far back as the gold rush[7] and well into the 1930s, exhuming those interred along the West Coast became ever more regularized as an annual spring event.[8] The benevolent associations hired men to search for temporary graves along the route of the Central Pacific Railroad, so that the bones could be recovered, bundled, and rafted to Victoria for shipment.[9] In southern California, the bodies of railroad workers were sent to Sacramento for transshipment.[10] Newspapers in Bakersfield reported the disinterment and boxing of remains for shipment as early as 1880.[11] In St. Louis, where the Chinese population was too small to support a united chinese benevolent association, the On Leong Tong was responsible for exhumations and shipment to San Francisco from at least 1873 until the 1960s; one hundred individuals were sent home in 1927.[12] So it was distinctly newsworthy when gold rush pioneer Yee Ah Tye instructed his family to bury his remains in this country permanently; in fact, he obtained a piece of land near Point Lobos in San Francisco, which he gave to his association (Kong Chow) in 1864 for the express purpose of creating a cemetery. This was one of the cemeteries that would be physically relocated in 1900 when the city needed more room, and Ah Tye's own remains were later moved once again to Oakland, where other family members were buried.[13] The relocation of whole cemeteries, as well as of individuals, was to become a recurring phenomenon and also occurred in Tucson and other locations.[14]

The cemeteries where Chinese were buried typically had shrines in which representations of goods, money, and even servants were burned to accompany and serve the dead. Remains of such a shrine in Ah Tye's cemetery survive on the first hole of the Lincoln Park Golf Course in San Francisco. One was erected in Santa Cruz in the 1890s,[15] and there was another in Yreka.[16] They often occur in pairs, both historically and in the present. In Los Angeles, the earliest duo was built in Evergreen Cemetery in 1888, and after Chinese burials were no longer accepted there, a later pair was built in the new Chinese Cemetery in 1924. "Two sacrificial paper burners" once existed in Bakersfield[17] and another two were built in Colma.[18] Other historic pairs are known from Australia to British Columbia,[19] while a set of iron burners on wheels made in 1991 now stands in front of the Kuan Yin Teng (Goddess of Mercy Temple) on Pitt Street in Penang, Malaysia.

In Los Angeles, there are references to early burials in the "city" cemetery on Fort Moore Hill in 1871 and 1872. Evergreen Cemetery was created in 1877, and the city operated about five acres of it as a potter's field. Perhaps as early as 1877, the city allowed the Chinese community to use part of this parcel.[20] The shrine was erected in 1888 with two brick and mortar furnaces, each twelve feet high, flanking a central altar and a stone stele (fig. 8.1). The whole covered approximately one thousand square feet. Historical photos show the altar with pots of plants, and the stele's inscription can be literally translated as "Respect as still exists," implying that people should respect those who have gone before as if they are still with us. The shape of the burners re-creates old traditions. Particularly in north China, earth was piled up over the grave in a cone-shaped mound,[21] and the mounds were re-formed at each of the postfunerary rites.[22] Tomb covers of the ancient dynasties had the same shape as the shrines: square at the base and tapered on top. The lower portion of the tomb covers would be decorated with scenes from the lives of people, while the tapering upper portions would have images of the heavenly elements. The shape is thus a metamorphic expression of the structure of the universe as a whole.[23]

After the primary burial, ritual visits to the cemetery were made twice a year, and the observances were much the same throughout the West. One such seasonal ceremony in Ventura was described as follows in 1884:

About 25 Chinamen went out to the graveyard last Saturday to perform a religious ceremony. The ceremony consisted of placing goat pork [*sic*] and chicken, oranges, rice, cereal, candles etc. about the graves of two Chinamen. . . . A celestial explained to us that after a Chinaman died he went to China and then came back to the place of his burial. He further informed us that the deceased Chinamen had returned and for several nights had caused considerable trouble in Chinatown, but that their wrath and hunger had been appeased by going through the above "ceremony."[24]

A similar ritual, which a newspaper compared to Memorial Day observances, was called a "picnicky" in Santa Barbara:

Yesterday morning several carriages were drawn up in line in front of the Chinese temple. . . . They proceeded to the graveyard east of the city to decorate the

Figure 8.1.   Burners and altar, Evergreen Cemetery, Los Angeles, 1900. Courtesy University of Southern California, on behalf of the USC Specialized Libraries and Archival Collections, no. 7166.

> graves of their countrymen with roast pig, Chinese ginger and tea. . . . They burned paper and made gestures with their hands. . . . They gathered together and indulged in a feast. A circle was formed and apples, oranges, and candies were passed around.[25]

Both residence and interment in early California were typically regarded as temporary. Individuals who prospered wished to return to their home villages to live out their lives in comfortable retirement. Those who died in America often relied on the *huiguan* (district associations) to render assistance and serve the deceased. As reported by Huang Tsun-hsien (Huang Gongdu; pinyin, Huang Zunxian), Chinese consul general in San Francisco, the *huiguan*, later consolidated and chartered as the Chinese Consolidated Benevolent Association (CCBA), imposed an exit fee on members to pay for burial services and boat fare. A typical assessment in 1894 was nine dollars per person, of which three dollars was allocated to the CCBA and three dollars to the local *huiguan*; the balance paid for temporary burial in the United States and later shipment back to China. Documents show that the sequence was more expensive, and voluntary contributions were sought in the homeland as early as 1858 to carry out the recovery of bones from places such as British Columbia, Idaho, and Tennessee. The Guangzhou *huiguan* issued the last exit fee receipt only in 1951.[26] Local cemeteries or authorities imposed other fees. The Santa Barbara Board of Health charged ten dollars for each of the forty to fifty graves removed in 1895.[27] In Ventura as well, the benevolent associations cared for the dead, putting a burial brick identifying the deceased and his village of origin into each coffin, and exhuming the body for shipment within a decade of death.[28]

Before the urbanization of Chinatowns, thousands died in isolated work camps, on farms, or while building the railroads, and the associations sent special teams to gather remains from remote sites and prepare them for shipping.[29] One historian reports that "all cemeteries in the Monterey region underwent these periodic exhumations," and it has been estimated that ten thousand boxes of bones left the United States for China in 1913 alone.[30] A Sacramento newspaper reported that "the accumulated bones of perhaps 1,200" Chinese workers on the Central Pacific passed through in 1870.[31] At least one Chinese individual was removed from a grave on San Nicolas Island for reburial by 1897,[32] and Chinese cemetery plots in Oregon are marked "vacated."[33] A total of 188 bodies were returned from Watsonville from 1902 to 1913, and in just two weeks during 1913 the CCBA exhumed from the Watsonville Chinese Cemetery sixty-eight additional individuals who had died in the past eleven years. In a previous episode, 120 bodies were shipped.[34] In the northern California mining town of La Porte, only the numerous depressions in the ground mark the locations where burials have been exhumed.[35] The practice was observed in the East as well, where the recovery and shipment of remains in Baltimore could be arranged through the CCBA, district associations, or family associations.[36] The total may never be known; for example, records in China document a charity cemetery in the small village of Xinhui containing the unclaimed remains of 387 natives that were returned from California between 1888 and 1892.[37]

In Los Angeles, three Chinese benevolent associations disinterred remains of 850 Chinese in 1937 for return to the homeland. The skeletons were assembled with great care so that they would be complete. Each was placed into a white cotton bag, and the bags set into a metal urn; the urns were packed eight to a wooden crate (fig. 8.2). Once the remains arrived in China, the skeletons would be wired in a fixed position, sealed in earthenware jars, and placed in family tombs.[38]

The disinterred bones were shipped in metal containers or, later, wooden boxes. Prior to reburial in the ancestral village, the remains of each individual were placed in an unglazed jar about three feet high with an opening one and one-half feet in diameter, wide enough to accept the skull and rib bones.

Figure 8.2.   Crates being packed for shipment to China, 1937. Photograph, *Los Angeles Times*, "Remains to Rest Peacefully in Orient," July 31, 1937, courtesy Young Research Library, Department of Special Collections, University of California Los Angeles, collection no. 1429.

Smaller jars were used to rebury cremations.[39] The choice of the final resting place was often conditioned by the principles of *fengshui*, which recommended certain environmental settings said to be auspicious. In 1900 the Chinese minister to the United States recognized the importance of those he called "geomancers" in selecting whether a place is lucky for a burial ground, especially for the rich.[40]

Although incomplete, available cemetery records indicate that women, infants, and victims of violence were less apt to be removed, either for return to China or for relocation to a different local cemetery.[41] This seems to parallel the historic tradition whereby family altars in China never contained "soul tablets" of juvenile males or unmarried women.[42] Confucianism and village culture invoked lesser obligations to those who had not completed the circle of life through reproduction; thus their deaths, and especially those of female infants, did not occasion public expression of grief.[43]

> The funerary treatment of the deceased who are not destined to remain part of the lineage and become ancestors illustrates all the more clearly the principle of preservation underlying the funeral observances which are reserved for the

dead who are accepted as ancestors. The whole range of ritual practices . . . are aimed at preservation, both of their remains—a function served by funerary observances—and of the symbolic component, the soul.[44]

The marking of female graves in the United States in later years may be attributed to a change in values, the possible influence of Christianity, the need for women in a largely male society, and the increasing affluence of a resident Chinese community.

Remains from Santa Barbara were shipped by Wells Fargo and Company, one individual each to a redwood box three feet long and one foot square.[45] In Los Angeles, such mass exhumations (fig. 8.3) were regarded as indecent,[46] and in 1878, the state passed a law called "An Act to Protect Public Health from Infection Caused by Exhumation and Removal of the Remains of Deceased Persons." Thereafter, permits to exhume bodies were required from county health officials, and the Federal Trade Commission and the State of California became the regulatory agencies.[47] The associations were held responsible for seeing that all bones were present, and the shipments were insured in transit by the Fireman's Fund Insurance Company.[48] The belief in the eternal bond between the living and the dead was illustrated in one example when the deceased expressed discomfort to a living descendant that not all of his bones were present in the reburial. The vacated grave was reopened, a finger joint was recovered, and a later communication to the living expressed that all was now well.[49]

Except for the sea voyage and the distance traveled, the concept of removing remains from the original grave is not too different from traditions prevailing even now in southern China. Burial has been nearly universal in rural areas of Guangdong (Kwangtung) Province; while cremation is encouraged by the government because of increasing economic pressure on land use, it has made little headway until recently. Beginning in the 1950s, attempts were made to mandate cremation, placement of the remains in a legal columbarium or official cemetery, and abandonment of "feudal superstitions." Among these undesirable traditions were "good *fengshui*," auspicious geomantic aspects of the burial site, the ritual observances, and even the very practice of interment.[50]

The shipment of human remains back to China was discouraged in 1937 during and after the Japanese invasion, and again in and around 1949 when the People's Republic was established.[51] The numbers of individuals transported depend on both the political situation and immigration statistics. Nixon's visit in 1972 opened the door to emigration. Margaret Thatcher's agreement in 1984 to end the British lease on Hong Kong prompted increased emigration, as did Carter's opening of diplomatic relations with China and

Figure 8.3.   Exhumations from Chinese cemetery at east end of Evergreen Cemetery, Los Angeles, about 1897. Photograph by Olive Percival. This item is reproduced by permission of the Huntington Library, San Marino, California, album 217:129.

ending of diplomatic relations with Taiwan. Vietnamese Chinese boat people came to the United States in the 1970s and 1980s, and Chinese students arrived in high numbers in the 1990s. As many achieved citizenship and established families and livelihoods here, the direction of the dead was reversed, and the number of burial remains shipped out of China has grown steadily since the 1970s. The need for more cemetery space in the Bay Area has been caused in part by this movement. The spacious new Golden Hill Memorial Park in the San Francisco Bay area helps families with the arrangements and plans to open offices in Hong Kong and on the mainland to bring ancestors' ashes to America.[52] Another big new mausoleum is being built in Vancouver, British Columbia, in part to accommodate Chinese immigrants wishing to bring their ancestors to join them.[53]

In New York, the search for a pleasant resting place and the pull of tradition has turned many Chinese away from the cramped inner-city cemeteries, and they are buying spacious plots in suburban areas, including in Westchester, Long Island, and New Jersey. They charter buses for the semiannual rituals, and the new cemeteries allow them to observe traditional ceremonies, make the burned offerings, and erect elaborate headstones. They take great care in selecting grave sites with good *fengshui*, preferring high ground, open views, an eastern or southern exposure, proximity to water, and spacious plots.[54] It is not only descendants of mainland Chinese who are bringing their ancestors for reburial in the United States. Cremations are coming from Taiwan,[55] Hong Kong, Korea, Vietnam, Indonesia, and Myanmar.[56] In Orange County, California, the community of Little Saigon created the Vietnamese Veteran Cemetery in a corner of Westminster Memorial Park to receive remains of Vietnam War soldiers who were first buried abroad.[57]

A Chinese funeral director related that reburial in this country results more directly from the location of residence than from religion or culture. People fear that the Communists might prevent them from returning to observe the annual customs, and the trip is costly and difficult, yet they want to reunite families so that they can maintain the favor and goodwill achieved through ceremonial respect for the ancestors. Both males and females have been reburied in Los Angeles, but no children.[58]

The following personal account is cited with the permission of the family.[59] Yook Chew Tong, age seventy-two when interviewed in 1999, was born in a village on the Pearl River Delta, three hours by bus from Guangzhou, or an overnight trip by barge. He came to the United States in 1952 to join a brother and sister already here. He had another brother, sister, and mother-in-law in Hong Kong, and a nephew at university in China. Although Tong's father (fig. 8.4) was born in San Francisco in 1873, he frequently went back and forth to China and, because of his poor health, remained there permanently after 1925 with his second wife. His father and one brother starved to death under the Communist regime; his stepmother died of gangrene; and his sister-in-law, a doctor, drowned herself in fear of being shot. The family members were buried on a piece of their own land, a private plot about a mile from their village, with the expectation that their remains would be dug up three to five years later and put securely into an urn. Each family in Tong's village had its own area.

It was Tong's nephew, now a prosperous electrical engineer in Hong Kong, who recommended that Tong reunite and rebury the family in the United States, including *his* own father, Tong's brother, a cook who had been buried in Kansas. Tong accepted the idea willingly, since he had been unable to attend his father's funeral, give him a proper ceremony, or provide for the regular observances. Tong's father, sister-in-law, and younger brother were originally buried without caskets; before she left China, Tong's wife arranged to have their remains dug up and reburied in big urns so that they could be exhumed at a later time. The U.S. State Department sent documents to Hong Kong for a visa, and the Chinese government required that the remains be cremated prior to shipment.

The cousin still in China helped arrange for the six cremations and the shipments. The remains of Tong's father, mother, stepmother, two brothers,

Figure 8.4.   Yook Chew Tong and his father, Tong Gin Gee, Hong Kong, 1940. Courtesy Yook Chew Tong family.

and one sister-in-law were delivered by air cargo and truck directly to Tong's home in southern California, and the remains of the third brother were brought from Kansas. Tong inserted a 1998 silver dollar into each round marble urn, symbolizing payment for entrance at the gate of heaven; in a primary burial, the coin would have been placed in the mouth of the deceased. At the Rose Hills Cemetery in Whittier, California, on August 22, 1998, the urns were first placed on a table covered with a white cloth (fig. 8.5) while Tong read a poem he had composed.[60] Twenty-two members of the family gathered and burned symbolic spirit money, imitation gold bars, and representations of gold coins. Tong stated, "It was a way to pay respect [because] I couldn't give them a proper burial or visit the grave site."

The family placed flowers at each grave, burned incense, and kowtowed three times to each of the deceased. Each urn was then buried in a square

Figure 8.5. Urns prepared for reburial, 1998. Courtesy Yook Chew Tong family.

vault of cement painted to look metallic (fig. 8.6). Later, when the nephew came from Hong Kong, the family had a second, smaller service with a roast pig and other food offerings. The expenses, including shipping the remains of the relative from Kansas, came to approximately five thousand dollars, and ten local burial plots were purchased for about twenty-five thousand dollars. When Tong's own wife had died in 1993, he had visited her grave every week for several years; in later years, he paid visits on Mother's Day, Father's Day, Christmas, Qingming (Pure Brightness) in early spring, and Yulapen (Hungry Ghosts) in late autumn.[61]

The service for a reburial is simpler than that for a primary funeral, and the customs differ depending partly on where the family comes from. Mainland Chinese tend to have more secular funerals, stemming from the Communist rejection of religion, while overseas Chinese have religious ceremonies. Those from the Philippines tend to be Catholic, whereas Malaysians and Taiwanese are mostly Buddhist, but they pay the same respects.[62] There might be a portrait on display, but a reburial usually lacks the procession, band, ritual mourners, traditional garb, and other elements described in historical accounts of a primary funeral.

One practice that crosses over the religions is the burning of incense sticks, spirit money, gold (foil) ingots, "hell banknotes," and representations of items used in daily life. The Win Sense Trading Company in Los Angeles

Figure 8.6.   Urns in vaults, ready for reburial, 1998. Courtesy Yook Chew Tong family.

offers paper replicas of contemporary checkbooks, credit cards, cell phones, televisions with remote and VCR, Rolex watches, both traditional houses and modern ranch houses, passports and bank statements, human servant figures, and words of a chant on a yellow disk (fig. 8.7), and sells them as far away as Texas. Funeral bundles being sold for the same purpose at the old Man Mo Temple in Kowloon, Hong Kong, in 1999 included candles, fireworks, and incense as well as paper money (fig. 8.8). When these objects burn, they ascend for the use of the deceased. Cemeteries like Rose Hills that do not have permanent shrines or furnaces purchase bright red portable burners wholesale in Chinatown and sell them to the customers. The mortuary also offers a choice of twenty-five burial urns variously made of wood, cloisonné, marble, acrylic, and bronze, in different sizes.[63]

In this country, it is the oldest descendants who make the decision to exhume relatives buried in China and rebury them here. If the deceased have been cremated, the removal is easier and more likely to occur; if they have been interred originally, it is a more complex and costly procedure. Usually, the living descendants bring back family members only to the grandparents' generation. At Rose Hills, the balance between men and women has been fairly even, but no children have been returned for reburial.[64] Reminiscent of the same selectivity observed early in the twentieth century, when remains were exhumed from Los Angeles for shipment to China,[65] the very young,

Figure 8.7. Spirit goods for burning, including paper servant, cell phone, and house model, for sale in Los Angeles Chinatown, 1999. Photograph by J. A. Rasson.

women, criminals, or those associated with violence are less likely to be exhumed in the homeland and brought to this country.

The remains are usually contained in an urn of marble or ceramic, which is then placed in a vault. Most families prefer to bury the vaults in the ground, rather than install them in a columbarium or niche in a wall. The urn is oriented so that the name of the deceased faces forward, if it is to be placed aboveground, or outward if it is buried on a slope. The vaults used for either reburial or cremation range in cost from $395 for the minimum concrete box, to $1,995 for one lined with stainless steel over Strentex (a nonwoven plastic bonded to the concrete for hermetically sealed protection), to $2,395 for one that is copper and so lined. In contrast, friends and relations would strenuously oppose the scattering of ashes at sea.

The U.S. Customs Service does not require a declaration for either bones or cremations, and local funeral homes and cemeteries assist with burial permits.

Figure 8.8.   Traditional offerings to ancestors, Man Mo Temple, Kowloon, Hong Kong, 1999. Photograph by R. S. Greenwood.

There is some irony in the fact that immigration is restricted, but the dead may come. Shippers like Federal Express and United Parcel Service do not accept burial parcels because of the liability, but the U.S. Post Office must transport them. However, it is considered more respectful to carry the ancestors personally, and lacking a family member to accompany the remains, funeral directors or couriers sometimes carry cremations in both directions. There is greater regulation for a body in a casket: before shipment, customs must stamp a release on the airway bill; the body must enter the country at a facility with public health officers on site; and they must inspect the corpse and seal and quarantine the casket. Most ignore this option since it is costly and time-consuming.[66] Through his own small company, the Universal Chung Wah funeral home, director Henry Kwong sends about ten to twenty individuals a year back to China, while receiving almost one a week from China.[67] The Wah Wing Sang Mortuary in Los Angeles has been receiving fifteen to twenty reburials a year, and expects the number to increase.[68] Cypress Lawn Memorial Park in Colma, California, receives ten requests a month to receive cremated remains.[69] At Rose Hills, fewer than one hundred deceased were sent to China in 1998. But in a trend that started with the first two sets of remains brought here from Asia in 1991, about five hundred are now returned to California each year, and the number of reburials is expected to increase.[70]

Contrary to what one might first assume, all those interviewed agreed that the people who are the most acculturated are the most apt to bring their ancestors to the New World. In years past, part of the yearning to return to the homeland resulted from the prejudice, isolation, and exclusion experienced in America.[71] But as subsequent generations made permanent homes in the United States, their ties to the homeland became attenuated, and the obligations of the annual observances increasingly burdensome. The primary concern was not the actual place of burial, but rather the wish to ensure the safety of the remains and facilitate access to them. The exchanges between the living and the dead represent a reciprocal relationship. Through the presentations of food and the other observances, the descendants hope to ensure a good life for themselves: wealth, health, good harvest, and offspring.[72]

The relocating of human remains—in either direction—is neither unusual nor a new custom, nor even limited to the well-documented historical return to China of individuals who died in this country. Exhumation of graves in China has long been practiced for the ritual cleaning of bones and placement of bones in urns, and the urns might be reburied in a different location and ultimately moved again if the family relocated or constructed a tomb. Mass relocations occurred when the government wished to develop an auspicious property. In the village of Xinhui, descendants were ordered to remove thousands of graves; if they did not comply, the local government would "dispense with them."[73] The custom of relocation was particularly strong in Cantonese society, much less so in north China.[74] In this country, burials were very apt to be relocated because cemeteries were full or closed, or to bring family members together, or when a family moved to a different location.[75] Henry Kwong related moving burials from one cemetery to another, even within Los Angeles County.[76] The incentives for facilitating access to the ancestors to fulfill ceremonial obligations are cultural and of long standing.

Death rituals have been prominent in Chinese culture for more than two thousand years, as demonstrated by contemporary archaeological research. In imperial China, officials promoted the elaborate Confucian rituals. During his lifetime—between 500 and 400 B.C., when feudalism and vice were pervasive—Confucius urged the Zhou dynasty rulers to bring moral order to the land. While this is not the only influence on Chinese burial customs, one of the most important Confucian precepts is to honor one's father and mother. This responsibility extends beyond death, because good fortune for the living depends on the blessings of the dead who are treated well.[77] It was during the Han dynasty (206 B.C.–A.D. 221) that people became concerned about a favorable spot for the burial ground; the principles of *fengshui*, governing the direction of surrounding objects and the physical configuration of the landscape, were applied primarily to grave sites of those of high rank.[78]

It has been said that food and burial practices are among the strongest indicators of ethnic identity. Traditions concerning the selection, preparation, and consumption of food are amply confirmed in the archaeology of Chinese sites in the New World. It appears that the relatively new practice of bringing the remains of ancestors buried in the homeland to cemeteries in the United States may represent one of the last holdouts against assimilation. Ethnicity has not receded to a position of being incidental in a multicultural society. Rather, it is being reinforced by the reinvigoration of everything from lion dances to the extension of *fengshui*, which arose from concern over the placement of noble graves, to mundane applications like furniture arrangement in the home.

The underlying motive, that proper care and honor expressed to the dead benefit the living, reveals a distinct contrast to Euro-American attitudes toward human remains and the place where they are interred. The difference seems to be in the levels of regard expressed for the actual physical remains, as opposed to the grave or cemetery where they are buried. Early American faiths discouraged concern for bodily remains, as this implied a lesser confidence in eternal life.[79] In the prevailing social attitudes of Victorianism, Americans expected and assumed that graves would be permanent.[80] Since cremation began to be promoted in the United States in the 1870s, it has been declared acceptable to all the major religions, as well as desirable for reasons of sanitation.[81] The burial plot was regarded as not much more than a place to store the dead, although some later became imbued with historical importance (e.g., the Granary Burying Ground and several others carefully preserved in the middle of downtown Boston), and others were embellished with elaborate statuary or memorials as a public display of wealth or status. The plots themselves were protected more as a link to the past, as open green space or historic landscape, than for the individuals resting there—except, of course, for celebrities. This concern for the place rather than the individual is reflected in various ways. In a Kentucky county, the court denied a landowner permission to move a small cemetery even though some of the graves had already been disturbed. The Indiana legislature is considering a bill to make it a felony to remove any gravestone, and illegal to move a cemetery for any reason.[82] The idea of the cemetery as a final resting place seems more important than the individual remains; the importance of the plot would thus vary inversely with the level of concern for the remains buried therein.

In China, the place of burial was not closely linked to a community, as here, because traditional graves were usually on family land rather than in institutional cemeteries. As land use intensified, burial locations were simply moved, rather than being preserved. Moreover, as families attained citizenship in the United States, ties to the homeland often weakened; and for reasons of time, cost, age, and/or politics, fewer were able to make regular visitations to honor the ancestors. Cemetery locations in the United States have become places of historical, even secular, value. An example is the shrine in Evergreen Cemetery in Los Angeles. The Chinese Historical Society of Southern California acquired the physical remains of the old features as well as the land immediately surrounding the shrine. The burners and altar have been restored (fig. 8.9), rededicated, and declared a City Historic-Cultural Monument. Although there is no continuing association with any of those once buried there and long since removed, the annual Qingming observance that was discontinued in the 1960s was reinaugurated in 2001 as a historical commemoration. The physical remains and the traditions of honor are important, not the place of interment.

Immigrant communities are shaped by forces originating in the larger societies that surround them. Structuralists argue that immigrants are attracted to more advanced capitalist countries either as low-wage employees or

Figure 8.9.   Restored shrine at Evergreen Cemetery, rededicated in 1997. Photograph by R. S. Greenwood.

small-business entrepreneurs and are affected by forces of discrimination, politics, and the prevailing economy of the host community. Thus in a comparison of Los Angeles and New York, which have almost identical Chinese populations in percentage and absolute numbers, the Los Angeles Chinese economy is based more on high-value-added and high-skill occupations, while New York offers more work in low-wage, low-skill occupations.[83] Chinese business activity in Los Angeles has shifted from the old ethnic consumer service center in Chinatown to global outposts and producer services; as Chinatown has become congested, and individuals have prospered, activities have tended to move to suburbs such as Monterey Park and the San Gabriel Valley.[84]

In addition to the more diverse socioeconomic profiles among the recent immigrants, there is another consideration prompting the relatively new trend toward bringing ancestors to the New World. Prior to the Chinese Revolution in 1949, most of the Chinese in Los Angeles were first-wave immigrants from a peasant background in Guangdong Province or their descendants. Since that time, the Chinese in Los Angeles have become overwhelmingly second-wave immigrants, many professionals or elites fleeing the homeland. In the 1990 census, 77 percent of the Chinese in Los Angeles were foreign born.[85] They brought their families, capital, and skills or professions, with every expectation of permanence. Migration reinforces the need to preserve a sense of "rootedness" defined in relation to past generations, and by bringing the ancestors to new homes, the local group finds one means of expressing its identity.[86]

The Chinese burial customs relate directly to a continuing association between the living and the ancestors, for the ultimate benefit—it must be said—of the living. The actual place of burial is secondary to being able to visit and honor those who have gone before. Its function, whether in China or this country, is to sustain the sense of roots and identity by honoring the continuity of patrilineal lineage. Through the dead, the living define their identity, and migration only reinforces the need for territorial and cultural affiliation with the past.[87] Therefore, whether a family moves across an ocean or within the same county, relocating the remains is efficacious in lowering the level of guilt, thus easing the burden of the traditional seasonal observations. Just as the earliest Chinese in the New World expressed their hopes of dying in China, or of having their remains shipped back there for their spirits to be cared for by the family, fed, and made to feel a part of the living world,[88] so it is this bond between the living, the dead, and the ancestral village[89] that is paramount and that makes the actual first place of interment increasingly irrelevant.

Yook Chew Tong expressed this movingly in the poem he composed to read at the reburial of his family members:

Neither the tallest mountain, nor the longest river can match a parent's never-ending love of their child;
Neither the oldest cedar, nor the senior pine can match a child's eternal devotion to their parent.[90]

NOTES

1. John Grabowski, rough translation of *Xi han gushi jianjie* [Introduction to the Western Han Preserved Corpse], (manuscript, 1982, photocopy on file, Greenwood and Associates, Pacific Palisades, CA).

2. Jung Chang, *Wild Swans: Three Daughters of China* (New York: Doubleday Anchor, 1992), 172.

3. William L. Parish and Martin King Whyte, *Village and Family in Contemporary China* (Chicago: University of Chicago Press, 1978), 262–263. Qingming, the Pure Brightness festival, is a time for cleaning the graves, sometimes called "sweeping the tombs" or the "Chinese Memorial Day." Yulanpen (Hungry Ghosts) is celebrated in the seventh moon to satisfy the ghosts that might seek revenge (see chapter 2).

4. Stuart E. Thompson, "Death, Food, and Fertility," in *Death Ritual in Late Imperial and Modern China*, ed. James L. Watson and Evelyn S. Rawski (Berkeley: University of California Press, 1988), 104.

5. Parish and Whyte, *Village*, 265.

6. Tsuyoshi Katayama, "Ritual Spaces for Soul Tablets" (Noon Lecture Series, UCLA Center for Chinese Studies, December 6, 2001).

7. Darryl Fears, "America, the Sweet Hereafter: Tradition-Minded Asians Bring Ancestors' Ashes to U.S.," *Washington (DC) Post*, July 15, 2002, sec. A, 1.

8. *Humboldt (CA) Standard*, April 16, 1908.

9. Sky Lee, *Disappearing Moon Cafe* (Seattle: Seal, 1990), 11–18.

10. Harris Newmark, *Sixty Years in Southern California* (Boston: Houghton Mifflin, 1930), 388.

11. Gilbert Gia, "Our Fair City: What Became of the Old Chinese Cemetery?" in *The Bakersfield Blackboard*, photocopy on file, Greenwood and Associates, Pacific Palisades, CA; Gilbert Gia, "Bakersfield's Old Chinese Cemetery," Historic Bakersfield and Kern County, at www3.igalaxy.net/~ggia/ (accessed October 15, 2003).

12. C. Fred Blake, "The Chinese of Valhalla: Adaptation and Identity in a Midwestern American Cemetery," in *Markers X*, ed. Richard E. Meyer (Worcester, MA: Association for Gravestone Studies, 1993), 54, 80.

13. Lani Ah Tye Farkas, *Bury My Bones in America* (Nevada City, CA: Carl Mautz, 1998), 80–81.

14. Homer Thiel, letter to author, October 8, 1998.

15. Sandy Lydon, *Chinese Gold: The Chinese in the Monterey Bay Area* (Capitola, CA: Capitola Book Co., 1985), 264–265.

16. Bessie Jeong, MD, interview by Suellen Cheng and Munson Kwok, tape recording and transcript, December 17, 1981, and October 17, 1982. Southern California Chinese-American Oral History Project, vol. 7, interview 157, 3–4, Young Research Library, Department of Special Collections, University of California, Los Angeles.

17. Gia, "Our Fair City."

18. Farkas, *Bury*, 139, 149.

19. Terry Abraham, "Chinese Funerary Burners: A Census," at www.uidaho.edu/ special-collections/papers/burners.htm (accessed November 25, 2003).

20. Edwin H. Carpenter, letter to Jack Lazenby, Evergreen Cemetery, July 17, 1990, photocopy on file, Greenwood and Associates, Pacific Palisades, CA.

21. Susan Naquin, "Funerals in North China: Uniformity and Variation," in *Death Ritual in Late Imperial and Modern China*, ed. James L. Watson and Evelyn S. Rawski (Berkeley: University of California Press, 1988), 44.

22. William R. Jankowiak, *Sex, Death, and Hierarchy in a Chinese City* (New York: Columbia University Press, 1993), 288.

23. Eugene Cooper, PhD (professor of anthropology), interview by author, University of Southern California, Los Angeles, May 17, 1999.

24. *Ventura (CA) Free Press*, April 5, 1884.

25. *Santa Barbara (CA) Daily Independent*, November 15, 1895.

26. Marlon K. Hom, "Fallen Leaves' Homecoming: Notes on the 1893 Gold Mountain Charity Cemetery in Xinhui," in *Chinese America: History and Perspectives, 2002*, ed. Colleen Fong and others (San Francisco: Chinese Historical Society of America, 2002), 39–40.

27. *Santa Barbara (CA) Daily Independent*, November 15, 1895.

28. Olen Adams, interview, tape recording, 1982, Oral History Collection, Ventura County Museum of History and Art, Ventura, CA.

29. Hom, "Fallen," 39.

30. Lydon, *Chinese Gold*, 132.

31. *Sacramento (CA) Reporter*, June 30, 1870.

32. Steven J. Schwartz and Kelly A. Rossbach, "A Preliminary Survey of Historic Sites on San Nicolas Island," in *Proceedings of the Society for California Archaeology* 6 (1993): 194.

33. Laurel Gerkman, "Chinese Burial Practices," in *Curry County Echoes* 30, no. 1 (December 2001–March 2002): 13, Curry Historical Society, Gold Beach, OR.

34. Lydon, *Chinese Gold*, 132.

35. Farkas, *Bury*, 135.

36. Murray Lee (curator of Chinese American history, San Diego Chinese Historical Museum), "Grandfather's Bones: A Chinese American Family History" (working paper, n.d.).

37. Hom, "Fallen," 43.

38. *Los Angeles Times*, July 31, 1937.

39. Hom, "Fallen," 43.

40. Wu Ting-Fang, "China and the Chinese People," *Los Angeles Times*, July 15, 1900.

41. Roberta S. Greenwood, *Down by the Station: Los Angeles Chinatown, 1880–1933* (Los Angeles: Institute of Archaeology, University of California, 1996), 34.

42. Katayama, "Ritual Spaces."

43. Blake, "Chinese," 86.

44. Beatrice David, "The Evacuation of Village Funerary Sites," *China Perspectives* 5 (May–June 1996): 23, Centre d'Etudes Français sur la Chine Contemporaire, Hong Kong.

45. *Santa Barbara (CA) Daily Independent,* November 15, 1895.

46. *Los Angeles Times*, December 11, 1902.

47. Lydon, *Chinese Gold*, 133.

48. William Bronson, *Still Flying and Nailed to the Mast: The Extraordinary Study of America's Boldest Insurance Company* (New York: Doubleday, 1963), 52.

49. Lee, "Grandfather's Bones."

50. David, "Evacuation," 23.

51. Hom, "Fallen," 40.

52. Gerrye Wong, "Golden Hill Memorial Park Helps Families Plan for the Future," *AsianWeek*, October 29, 1993, 8.

53. Hunter T. George, "The View Is to Die For, but There's a Catch Involved," *Moscow-Pullman (ID-WA) Daily News*, May 16–17, 1998, sec. A, 1, 10.

54. Winnie Hu, "For Chinese, Bliss Is Eternity in the Suburbs," *New York Times*, May 6, 2001, 1, 48.

55. Robert Jablon, "Asians Reburying Ancestors in the U.S.," *Torrance (CA) Daily Breeze*, August 19, 2002, sec. A, 5.

56. Larry Gordon, "Laid to Rest Again—in a New Land," *Los Angeles Times*, December 2, 2002, sec. A, 1, 25.

57. Chelsea J. Carter, "A Final Resting Place," *AsianWeek*, June 22–28, 2000, 14.

58. Henry Kwong, interviews by Judith Rasson, PhD, Alhambra, CA, February 23 and June 11, 1999.

59. Yook Chew Tong, interview by Judith Rasson, PhD, Pasadena, CA, May 14, 1999.

60. *Los Angeles Times*, December 2, 1998.

61. Tong, interview; see note 3 for an explanation of these festivals.

62. Trace Simmons, interview by Judith Rasson, PhD, Rose Hills Cemetery, Whittier, CA, 1999; Kwong, interview, June 11, 1999.

63. *Los Angeles Times*, August 29, 1994.

64. Simmons, interview.

65. Greenwood, *Down by the Station*, 34.

66. Fears, "America."

67. Kwong, interview, June 11, 1999.

68. Jablon, "Asians."

69. Fears, "America."

70. Simmons, interview.

71. Hom, "Fallen," 38.

72. Thompson, "Death," 73.

73. Hom, "Fallen," 37.

74. Naquin, "Funerals," 58.

75. Farkas, *Bury*, 139.

76. Kwong, interview, February 23, 1999.

77. Fears, "America."

78. Martin C. Yang, *A Chinese Village: Taitou, Shantung Province* (New York: Columbia University Press, 1945), 88.

79. Everett J. Bassett, e-mail to HISTARCH mailing list, March 31, 1999, at http://lists.asu.edu/archives/histarch.html.

80. Jose Cardenas, "Diversity, Time Alter Rituals of Death," *Los Angeles Times*, April 5, 2000, sec. E, 1, 3.

81. Stephen Prothero, *Purified by Fire: A History of Cremation in America* (Berkeley: University of California Press, 2001), 1–30.

82. Jeannine Kreinbrink, e-mail to HISTARCH mailing list, March 31, 1999, at http://lists.asu.edu/archives/histarch.html.

83. Yu Zhou, "How Do Places Matter? A Comparative Study of Chinese Ethnic Communities in Los Angeles and New York City," *Urban Geography* 19, no. 6 (1998): 532–535.

84. Wei Li, "Los Angeles's Chinese Ethnoburb: From Ethnic Service Center to Global Economy Outpost," *Urban Geography* 19, no. 6 (1998): 505.

85. Zhou, "How Do Places Matter?" 535, 538.

86. David, "Evacuation," 36.

87. David, "Evacuation," 26.

88. Lydon, *Chinese Gold*, 13.

89. David, "Evacuation," 25–26.

90. Yook Chew Tong, "Tong Family Remembrance," composition read at graveside, August 22, 1998. Used with permission.

Bibliography

Abraham, Terry. "Chinese Funerary Burners: A Census." At www.uidaho.edu/special-collections/papers/burners.htm.

Ackerlund, Drew. "Walla Walla's Chinese Population: The History of Walla Walla's Chinatown, 1862–1962." In *Annals of the Chinese Historical Society of the Pacific Northwest*, ed. Paul D. Buell, Douglas W. Lee, and Edward Kaplan, 59–69. Bellingham, WA: Chinese Historical Society of the Pacific Northwest, 1984.

Adams, Olen. Interview. Tape recording. Oral History Collection, Ventura County Museum of History and Art, Ventura, CA, 1982.

Aero, Rita. *Things Chinese*. New York: Dolphin/Doubleday, 1980.

Ahern, Emily M. *Chinese Ritual and Politics*. Cambridge: Cambridge University Press, 1981.

———. *The Cult of the Dead in a Chinese Village*. Stanford, CA: Stanford University Press, 1973.

Aijmer, Goran. *Burial, Ancestors, and Geomancy among the Ma On Shan Hakka, New Territories of Hong Kong*. [Göteborg], Sweden: IASSA, Göteborgs Universitet, 1993.

Allerfeldt, Kristofer. "Race and Restriction: Anti-Asian Immigration Pressures in the Pacific North-West of America during the Progressive Era, 1885–1924." *History* (Great Britain) 88, no. 289 (2003): 53–73.

Ambrose, Stephen E. *Nothing Like It in the World*. New York: Simon and Schuster, 2000.

Arkush, R. David, and Leo O. Lee, trans. and eds. *Land without Ghosts: Chinese Impressions of America from the Mid-Nineteenth Century to the Present*. Berkeley: University of California Press, 1989.

Arrington, Leonard J. *History of Idaho*. Vol. 1. Moscow: University of Idaho Press, 1994.

Baillie-Grohman, Florence. "The Yellow and White Agony: A Chapter on Western Servants." In *Fifteen Years' Sport and Life in the Hunting Grounds of Western*

America and British Columbia, by William A. Baillie-Grohman, 331–361. London: Horace Cox, 1900.

Bain, David H. *Empire Express: Building the First Transcontinental Railroad.* New York: Penguin Putnam, 1999.

Baker Cemetery Records. *Cemetery Records of Baker, Oregon.* Microfilm. Salt Lake City: Genealogical Society of Utah, 1959.

Baker, Cindy L., and Mary L. Maniery. *Historical Summary of Chinese Cemeteries in Folsom, Sacramento County, California: Final Report.* Sacramento, CA: PAR Environmental Services, 1995.

Baker City (OR) Herald. September 8, 1997.

Baker County Historical Society. "Chinese Cemetery Pavillion [*sic*] Dedication." *Baker County (OR) Historical Society* (newsletter) [1–2] (Fall 2000).

Baker Funeral Records. *Funeral Records of Baker, Oregon.* No. 1, A–G; no. 2, H–R; no. 3, S–Z. Microfilm, 3 reels. Salt Lake City: Genealogical Society of Utah, [1950?].

Ball, J. Dyer. *Things Chinese, or Notes Connected with China.* Hong Kong: Kelly and Walsh, 1903.

Bartholomew, Gail. *Maui Remembers: A Local History.* Honolulu: Mutual, 1994.

Bassett, Everett J. E-mail to HISTARCH mailing list. March 31, 1999. At http://lists.asu.edu/archives/histarch.html.

Belanger, Charles L. (director, Lee Funeral Home, Washington, DC). Telephone interview by Priscilla Wegars, April 19, 1999.

Bell, Edward L. "The Historical Archaeology of Mortuary Behavior: Coffin Hardware from Uxbridge, Massachusetts." *Historical Archaeology* 24, no. 3 (1990): 54–78.

Bellomo, Andy. "Olney Cemetery: Pioneer Park Served First as Burial Place." *Pioneer Trails* 5 (November 1980): 23–24, Umatilla County Historical Society.

Berling, Judith A. "Death and Afterlife in Chinese Religions." In *Death and Afterlife: Perspectives of World Religions*, ed. Hiroshi Obayashi, 181–192. New York: Greenwood, 1992.

Blake, C. Fred. "The Chinese of Valhalla: Adaptation and Identity in a Midwestern American Cemetery." In *Markers X: Journal of the Association for Gravestone Studies*, ed. Richard E. Meyer, 53–89. Worcester, MA: Association for Gravestone Studies, 1993.

———. "Gravestones in the Chinese Diaspora." Paper presented at the Hawai'i Pacific and Pacific Northwest Asian American Studies Joint Regional Conference, Honolulu, March 1996.

Blanchet, François Xavier. "Ten Years on the Pacific Coast." Trans. Don Wilkins. Seattle: University of Washington (WPA Projects nos. 4185 and 5606), 1937. Typescript carbon in the University of Idaho Library.

"Bok Kai Supplement." *Marysville (CA) Appeal-Democrat*, 1985, 10–11, 27.

Book, Susan. "Ashes to Ashes . . . Chinese Cemeteries in Butte County—1880." *Diggins* 18 (1974): 3–10.

Bronson, William. *Still Flying and Nailed to the Mast: The Extraordinary Study of America's Boldest Insurance Company.* New York: Doubleday, 1963.

Brook, Timothy. "Funerary Ritual and the Building of Lineages in Late Imperial China." *Harvard Journal of Asiatic Studies* 49, no. 2 (December 1989): 465–499.

Brown, Alan. "Asia Minor: Wayne Wang, Amy Tan, and Others Lead an Insider's Tour through the Far East—in San Francisco." *Travel and Leisure* (January 1997): 88–97, 119–120.

Brumley, Linda. "Turning History into People: The People on the Chinese Gravestones in 19th Century Ballarat Cemeteries." In *Histories of the Chinese in Australasia and the South Pacific*, ed. Paul Macgregor, 320–326. Melbourne: Museum of Chinese Australian History, 1995.

Burkhardt, V[alentine] R[odolphe]. *Chinese Creeds and Customs*. 3 vols. Taipei: Book World, 1958.

Burlingame, Burl, and Kathryn Bender. "Grounds for Respect." *Honolulu Star-Bulletin*, March 30, 1998.

Burton, Greg. "A Sojourn among Chinese Miners." *Lewiston (ID) Morning Tribune*, July 24, 1994.

Buschmann, Clark A., ed. *Third City*. [Marysville, CA]: Yuba Sutter Arts Council, 1991.

Campany, Robert F. "Return-from-Death Narratives in Early Medieval China." *Journal of Chinese Religions* 18 (Fall 1990): 91–125.

Cardenas, Jose. "Diversity, Time Alter Rituals of Death." *Los Angeles Times*, April 5, 2000, sec. E, 1, 3.

Carlin (NV) Commonwealth. November 9, 1910–February 1, 1911.

Carpenter, Edwin H. Letter to Jack Lazenby, Evergreen Cemetery, 17 July 1990. Photocopy on file, Greenwood and Associates, Pacific Palisades, CA.

Carter, Chelsea J. "A Final Resting Place." *AsianWeek*, June 22–28, 2000, 14.

Carter, Gregg. "Social Demography of the Chinese in Nevada: 1870–1880." *Nevada Historical Society Quarterly* 18, no. 3 (Summer 1976): 85–86.

Cathay Mortuary, Inc. v. San Francisco Planning Commission. 207 Cal.App.3d 275, no. AO39937. January 20, 1989.

Ceballos, Gertrude. Interview by Reiko Neizman, 1999.

Chace, Paul G. *The Bok Kai Festival of 1931 in Historic Marysville, Creating a California Community*. Yuba City, CA: River City Printing, 1994.

———. "Dancing with the Dragon: A Study of Ritual and Inter-Ethnic Community Relations." In *Origins and Destinations: 41 Essays on Chinese America*, 189–205. Los Angeles: Chinese Historical Society of Southern California and UCLA Asian American Studies Center, 1994.

———. *A History of Marysville's Bok Kai Temple*. [N.p.: Privately printed for a temple benefit by the Marysville-Peikang Sister City Association], 1999.

———. "Interpretive Restraint and Ritual Tradition: Marysville's Festival of Bok Kai." *Journal of Contemporary Ethnography* 21, no. 2 (1992): 226–254.

———. "Jiao Rites in Chinese California." Working paper, n.d.

———. "The Oldest Chinese Temples in California: A Landmarks Tour." *Gum Saan Journal* 14, no. 1 (1991): 1–19.

———. "On Becoming American: Chinese Rites for Death and Ghost-Spirits in an Urban American City." Escondido, CA: Paul G. Chace and Associates, 1998.

———. "Returning Thanks: Chinese Rites in an American Community." PhD diss., University of California, Riverside, 1992.

———. "The Turtle Dove Messenger: A Trait of the Early Los Angeles Chiao Ceremony." *Gum Saan Journal* 12, no. 2 (1989): 1–9.

Chan, Candy Kit Har. "31 Historic Chinese Corpses Discovered in Abandoned Cemetery." *AsianWeek*, April 14, 1995, 4.

Chan, Larry (officer of Ning Yung Association and member of the Look San Cemetery committee). Interviews by Linda Sun Crowder, August 1997, October 1998.

Chan, N. C. *Handbook of Chinese in America*. New York: People's Foreign Relations Association of China, 1946.

Chan, Sucheng. *Asian Americans: An Interpretive History*. Boston: Twayne, 1991.

———. "Chinese Livelihood in Rural California: The Impact of Economic Change, 1860–1880." *Pacific Historical Review* 53, no. 3 (1984): 273–307.

———. *This Bittersweet Soil: The Chinese in California Agriculture, 1860–1910*. Berkeley: University of California Press, 1986.

Chang, David. Interview by Reiko Neizman, 1999.

Chang, Jung. *Wild Swans: Three Daughters of China*. New York: Doubleday Anchor, 1992.

Chang, Roland. Interview by Reiko Neizman, 1999.

Char, Tin-Yuke. "The Chinese Experience in Hawaii—1800–1980." In *The Chinese American Experience*, ed. Genny Lim, 196–197. San Francisco: Chinese Historical Society of America and Chinese Cultural Foundation of San Francisco, 1981.

———, comp. and ed. *The Sandalwood Mountains: Readings and Stories of the Early Chinese in Hawaii*. Honolulu: University of Hawai'i Press, 1975.

Char, Tin-Yuke, and Wai Jane Char. *Chinese Historic Sites and Pioneer Families of the Island of Hawaii*. Honolulu: University of Hawai'i Press, 1983.

———. "The First Chinese Contract Laborers in Hawaii, 1852." *Hawaiian Journal of History* 9 (1975): 128–134.

Chen, Gang. "Death Rituals in a Chinese Village: An Old Tradition in Contemporary Social Context." PhD diss., Ohio State University, 2000.

Chen, Jack. *The Chinese of America*. San Francisco: Harper and Row, 1980.

Chen Lanbin. *Shih Mei jilue* [Brief Record of a Mission to America]. In *Xiaofanghu zhai yudi congchao*. Shanghai: Zhuyitang, 1877–1894, ce 63, 2a–b.

Chen, Yong. *Chinese San Francisco, 1850–1943: A Trans-Pacific Community*. Stanford, CA: Stanford University Press, 2000.

Cheng, Te-Kun. *Archaeology in China*. Vol. 2, *Shang China*. Toronto: University of Toronto Press, 1960.

Chin, Frederick K. "Chinese Funeral Traditions." *American Funeral Director* (October 1995): 52, 54, 112, 114, 116, 118.

Chinese Directory Service. *Chinese Business Directory, Sacramento–Marysville and Vicinity*. San Francisco: Chinese Directory Service, 1952.

"Chinese 'Funeral Baked Meats.'" *Overland Monthly* 3 (July 1869): 21–29.

Chinese Historical Society of Southern California. "19th Century Chinese Memorial Shrine Preservation Project." At http://www.chssc.org/shrinefull.html.

Chinese New Year Parade Office, San Francisco. Literature for public relations distribution. 1996.

Chinese New Year Parade Office staff, San Francisco. Interviews by Linda Sun Crowder, March 1997, August 1998.

Chinn, Thomas W. *Bridging the Pacific: San Francisco Chinatown and Its People*. San Francisco: Chinese Historical Society of America, 1989.

Chinn, Thomas W., H. Mark Lai, and Philip P. Choy, eds. *A History of the Chinese in California: A Syllabus*. San Francisco: Chinese Historical Society of America, 1969.

Choy, Philip P. "The Architecture of San Francisco Chinatown." *Chinese America: History and Perspectives, 1990*, ed. Marlon K. Hom and others, 37–66. San Francisco: Chinese Historical Society of America, 1990.

Chu Hsi (Zhu Hsi). *Chu Hsi's Family Rituals: A Twelfth Century Chinese Manual for the Performance of Cappings, Weddings, Funerals, and Ancestral Rites*. Trans. and annotated by Patricia Buckley Ebrey. Princeton, NJ: Princeton University Press, 1991.

Chung, Sue Fawn. "Ah Cum Kee and Loy Lee Ford: Between Two Worlds." In *Ordinary Women, Extraordinary Lives: Women in American History*, ed. Kriste Lindenmeyer, 179–195. Wilmington, DE: Scholarly Resources, 2000.

———. E-mail messages to Terry Abraham and Priscilla Wegars citing *Elko (NV) Independent*, July 7, 1925, 1. August 24, 1999, August 25, 2000.

City and County of San Francisco. *San Francisco, the Bay and Its Cities*. New York: Hastings House, 1940.

City of Lewiston, ID. *Charter and General Ordinances of the City of Lewiston. In the State of Idaho*. Published by authority of the City Council. Lewiston, ID: Teller, 1896.

City of Marysville, CA. "Assessor's Plat Book." History Room, Yuba County Library, Marysville, CA.

Cohen, Myron L. "Souls and Salvation: Conflicting Themes in Chinese Popular Religion." In *Death Ritual in Late Imperial and Modern China*, ed. James L. Watson and Evelyn S. Rawski, 180–202. Berkeley: University of California Press, 1988.

Comber, Leon. *Chinese Ancestor Worship in Malaya*. Singapore: Donald Moore, 1957. Reprint, Singapore: Eastern Universities Press, 1963.

Cooper, Eugene, PhD (professor of anthropology, University of Southern California, Los Angeles). Interview by Roberta S. Greenwood, May 17, 1999.

Couch, Samuel L. "Topophilia and Chinese Miners: Place Attachment in North Central Idaho." PhD diss., University of Idaho, 1996.

Craib, Ralph. "Two Worlds at a Funeral." *San Francisco Chronicle*, April 24, 1964, 3.

Crowder, Linda Sun. E-mail message to Chinese Cemetery Study Group, March 23, 1997. Collection of Terry Abraham and Priscilla Wegars.

———. Interview by Wendy L. Rouse, October 23, 1998.

———. "Mortuary Practices and the Construction of Chinatown Identity." PhD diss., University of Hawai'i, Manoa, 2002.

———. "Mortuary Practices in San Francisco Chinatown." *Chinese America: History and Perspectives 1999*, ed. Marlon Hom and others, 33–46. San Francisco: Chinese Historical Society of America, 1999.

———. "Mortuary Rituals and the Public Identity of San Francisco Chinatown." Paper presented at the Hawaii/Pacific and Pacific Northwest Asian American Studies Joint Regional Conference, Honolulu, March 1996.

The Cuba Commission Report: A Hidden History of the Chinese in Cuba. Introduction by Denise Helly. 1876. Reprint, Baltimore: Johns Hopkins University Press, 1993.

Culin, Stewart. "Customs of the Chinese in America." *Journal of American Folk-Lore* 3 (1890): 191–200.

———. *The Religious Ceremonies of the Chinese in the Eastern Cities of the United States*. Philadelphia: privately printed, 1887.

Daily Elko (NV) Independent. March 26, 1870.

Daphne, Daphne (owner-operator of the Daphne group of mortuaries in San Francisco). Interview by Linda Sun Crowder, January 1998.

David, Beatrice. "The Evacuation of Village Funerary Sites." *China Perspectives* 5 (May–June 1996): 20–26. Hong Kong: Centre d'Etudes Français sur la Chine Contemporaire.

de Groot, J. J. M. *The Religious System of China*. Vol. 1. Leiden, Netherlands: E. J. Brill, 1892.

———. *The Religious System of China*. Vol. 3. Leiden, Netherlands: E. J. Brill, 1897. Reprint, Taiwan: Ch'eng Wen, 1969. Page references are to the Ch'eng Wen edition.

Delaplane, Stanton. "A Journey to Her Ancestors!" *San Francisco Chronicle,* January 18, 1934, 4.

Department of Vital Statistics, Carson City, NV. Death certificates for Old Jake Chinaman, August 3, 1917; Sing Lee, November 9, 1918; Louis Sing Tong, August 3, 1922; Jim Now, September 17, 1924; Yap Choi, July 25, 1925; Lao Jim, April 22, 1929; Lee Sheung, August 5, 1930; Yee Lee Wah, August 19, 1930.

Derig, Betty. "Celestials in the Diggings." *Idaho Yesterdays* 16, no. 3 (Fall 1972): 2–23.

———. "The Chinese of Silver City." *Idaho Yesterdays* 2, no. 4 (Winter 1959): 2–5.

Desmond, M. Belinda. "The History of the City of Marysville, California, 1852–1859." Master's thesis, Catholic University of America, 1962.

Dicker, Laverne Mau. *The Chinese in San Francisco: A Pictorial History*. New York: Dover, 1979.

[Dielman, Eloise, comp.]. *The Chinese Cemetery at Baker City, Oregon*. [Baker City, OR: Baker County Historical Society and the Chinese Consolidated Benevolent Association, 1997].

Dien, Albert E. "Chinese Beliefs in the Afterworld." In *The Quest for Eternity: Chinese Ceramic Sculptures from the People's Republic of China*, ed. Susan Caroselli, 1–15. San Francisco: Chronicle Books for the Los Angeles County Museum of Art, 1987.

Dillon, Richard H. *The Hatchet Men*. New York: Coward-McCann, 1962.

Dilts, Bryan Lee, comp. *1910 Census Index*. Salt Lake City, UT: Index, 1984.

Dobie, Charles Caldwell. *San Francisco's Chinatown*. New York: D. Appleton-Century, 1936.

Doten, Alfred. *The Journals of Alfred Doten, 1849–1903*. Vol. 2. Ed. Walter Van Tilburg Clark. Reno: University of Nevada Press, 1973.

Dowell, Leslie. "Funeral Rites 50 Centuries Old Bury Boy." *Los Angeles Examiner,* October 1, 1922, sec. 2, p. 5.

Dunbar, A. R. *A. R. Dunbar's Chinese Directory of the United States, British Columbia, Canada and Honolulu, H. I.* Portland, OR: A. R. Dunbar, 1892.

———. *A. R. Dunbar's United States Chinese Directory, 1900, including Hong Kong, Canada, and Hawaiian Islands.* San Francisco: A. R. Dunbar, 1900.

Dunn, Frank (owner-operator of the former Wing Sun Mortuary in San Francisco Chinatown). Interview by Him Mark Lai, 1975.

Dunn, Mary E. Phelps. "The Chinese in California." *Plumas Memories* 25 (June 4, 1967): 9–10. Plumas County Historical Society.

Eatwell, W. "On Chinese Burials." *Journal of the Anthropological Institute of Great Britain and Ireland* 1 (1872): 207–208.

Eberhard, Wolfram. "Economic Activities of a Chinese Temple in California." In *Settlement and Social Change in Asia by Wolfram Eberhard, Collected Papers.* Vol. 1, 264–278. Hong Kong: Hong Kong University Press, 1967.

Ebrey, Patricia Buckley, ed. *Chinese Civilization and Society.* New York: Free Press, 1981.

———. *Confucianism and Family Rituals in Imperial China: A Social History of Writing about Rites.* Princeton, NJ: Princeton University Press, 1991.

Elko County (NV) Recorder's Office. *Book of Deeds*, 1923. Site T. 33 N., R. 52 E., sec. 26, W1/2NW1/4, recorded on July 21, 1923; P7/574, Bureau of Land Management.

———. *Coroner's Inquests.* Ah Quang, December 2, 1869; Lee Quong Fay, June 4, 1903; Ng Quong, February 13, 1908; Yee Hong Shing, January 1916; Ong Wing, February 13, 1919; Chong Ong, July 13, 1921; Sing Lee, July 20, 1921.

———. *Deaths*, books 1, 2. Nevada State Vital Statistics Office, Carson City.

Elko (NV) Daily Independent. May 8, 1905–January 20, 1909.

Elko (NV) Free Press. April 30, 1909–November 10, 1938.

Elko (NV) Independent. July 20, 1921–July 7, 1925.

Elsensohn, M. Alfreda. *Idaho Chinese Lore.* Cottonwood: Idaho Corporation of Benedictine Sisters, 1970.

———. *Pioneer Days in Idaho County.* 2 vols. Cottonwood: Idaho Corporation of Benedictine Sisters, 1965.

Eu, March Fong (secretary of state for California). Letter to Paul G. Chace, March 27, 1992.

Farkas, Lani Ah Tye. *Bury My Bones in America.* Nevada City, CA: Carl Mautz, 1998.

Farncomb, Melissa. "Historical and Archaeological Investigations at Virginiatown: Features 2 and 4." Master's thesis, California State University, Sacramento, 1994.

Fears, Darryl. "America, the Sweet Hereafter: Tradition-Minded Asians Bring Ancestors' Ashes to U.S." *Washington (DC) Post*, July 15, 2002, sec. A, 1.

Fee, Jeffrey M. "Idaho's Chinese Mountain Gardens." In *Hidden Heritage: Historical Archaeology of the Overseas Chinese*, ed. Priscilla Wegars, 65–96. Amityville, NY: Baywood, 1993.

Ferrel, Jean, and Roger Ferrel. *Nevada State Cemeteries.* Vol. 1. N.p.: n.d.

Feuchtwang, Stephen. "Domestic and Communal Worship in Taiwan." In *Religion and Ritual in Chinese Society*, ed. Arthur Wolf, 105–129. Stanford, CA: Stanford University Press, 1974.

Fong, John (longtime restaurant operator, Carlin, NV). Interview by Sue Fawn Chung, July 2000. Tape recording. University of Nevada, Las Vegas, Lied Library, Special Collections.

Freedman, Maurice. "Geomancy." *Proceedings of the Royal Anthropological Institute of Great Britain and Ireland*, 1968, 5–15.

———. "The Handling of Money: A Note on the Background to the Economic Sophistication of Overseas Chinese." *Man* 59 (1959): 64–65.

———. *The Study of Chinese Society: Essays by Maurice Freedman*, ed. G. William Skinner. Stanford, CA: Stanford University Press, 1979.

French, Stanley. "The Cemetery as Cultural Institution: The Establishment of Mount Auburn and the 'Rural Cemetery' Movement." *American Quarterly* 26, no. 1 (March 1974): 40.

Frink, Jane Trombley, Helen Woodroofe, and Julie Reese, eds. "Chinese Performed Memorial Rites at Olney Cemetery." *Pioneer Trails* 16, no. 2 (Summer 1992): 3–5. Umatilla County Historical Society.

"Funeral Ephemera." *Asian American Comparative Collection Newsletter* 12, no. 4 (December 1995): 3.

Gallaher, Wanda Jo. *Report of a Preliminary Archaeological Reconnaissance of the Elk City Planning Unit, Idaho County, Idaho*. University of Idaho Anthropological Research Manuscript Series 27. Moscow: Laboratory of Anthropology, University of Idaho, 1976.

Garrett, Valery M. *Chinese Clothing: An Illustrated Guide*. Hong Kong: Oxford University Press, 1994.

Gates, Hill. "Money for the Gods." *Modern China* 13, no. 3 (July 1987): 259–277.

Gee, Bobby (active Chinatown community member). Interview by Linda Sun Crowder, January 1997.

Gee, Pat. "George C. K. Young/Community Leader: Visionary Guided Rebirth of Isle Chinese Cemetery" (obituary). *Honolulu Star-Bulletin*, November 6, 2001.

George, Hunter T. "The View Is to Die For, but There's a Catch Involved." *Moscow-Pullman (ID–WA) Daily News*, May 16–17, 1998, sec. A, 1, 10.

Gerkman, Laurel. "Chinese Burial Practices." *Curry County Echoes* 30, no. 1 (December 2001–March 2002): 13–14. Gold Beach, OR: Curry Historical Society.

Gia, Gilbert. "Bakersfield's Old Chinese Cemetery." Historic Bakersfield and Kern County. At www3.igalaxy.net/~ggia/.

———. "Our Fair City: What Became of the Old Chinese Cemetery?" In *Bakersfield Blackboard*. Photocopy on file, Greenwood and Associates, Pacific Palisades, CA.

Glick, Clarence E. *Sojourners and Settlers: Chinese Migrants in Hawaii*. Honolulu: University of Hawai'i Press, 1980.

Godden Mackay Heritage Consultants. *Queensland Historical Burial Places Study*. Vol. 1. Queensland, Australia: Queensland Department of Environment, 1997.

Gong, Eng Ying, and Bruce Grant. *Tong War!* New York: Nicholas L. Brown, 1930.

Gordon, Larry. "Laid to Rest Again—in a New Land." *Los Angeles Times*, December 2, 1998, sec. A, 1, 25.

Grabowski, John. Rough translation of *Xi Han Gushi Jianjie* [Introduction to the Western Han Preserved Corpse]. Manuscript, 1982, photocopy on file, Greenwood and Associates, Pacific Palisades, CA.

Great Eastern Restaurant staff, San Francisco. Interview by Linda Sun Crowder, June 1997.

Green Street Mortuary staff, San Francisco. Interviews by Linda Sun Crowder, July 1996, August 1998.

Greenwood, Roberta S. *Down by the Station: Los Angeles Chinatown, 1880–1933*. Los Angeles: Institute of Archaeology, University of California, Los Angeles, 1996.

Griggs, Veta. *Chinaman's Chance: The Life Story of Elmer Wok Wai*. New York: Exposition, 1969.

Gust, Sherri M. "Animal Bones from Historic Urban Chinese Sites: A Comparison of Sacramento, Woodland, Tucson, Ventura, and Lovelock." In *Hidden Heritage: Historical Archaeology of the Overseas Chinese*, ed. Priscilla Wegars, 177–212. Amityville, NY: Baywood, 1993.

Guthrie, Bill. Conversation with Priscilla Wegars, Moscow, ID, July 10, 1998.

Hacker-Norton, Debi, and Michael Trinkley. *Remember Man Thou Art Dust*. Research Series 2. Columbia, SC: Chicora Foundation, 1984.

Hagaman, Wallace A. *A Short History of the Chinese Cemetery at Nevada City, California and Chinese Burial Customs during the Gold Rush*. Nevada City, CA: Cowboy Press, 2001.

Haim, Herbert J. "Cathay Club of San Francisco." Cathay Club Band Scrapbook. San Francisco: Cathay Club, 1934.

Hall, Bruce Edward. *Tea That Burns: A Family Memoir of Chinatown*. New York: Free Press, 1998.

Hamel, Ruth, and Tim Schreiner. "Land along the Track." *American Demographics* 10, no. 6 (June 1988): 50–52.

Harrell, Stevan. "The Concept of Soul in Chinese Folk Religion." *Journal of Asian Studies* 38 (1979): 519–528.

———. "When a Ghost Becomes a God." In *Religion and Ritual in Chinese Society*, ed. Arthur Wolf, 193–206. Stanford, CA: Stanford University Press, 1974.

Hefferon, James William. "Bad Eye[,] Last of the CP Chinese Workers Left in Elko, Nevada." Interview by John Eldredge, February 1, 1986, Golden Spike National Historic Site, National Park Service, at www.nps.gov/gosp/research/hefferon.htm.

Herr, Sally. "Bok Kai Temple Prayer Director Combines Religion and Philosophy in His Preaching." *Yuba-Sutter Business* 3, no. 3 (1984): 6–7.

Hill, Ann Maxwell. "Chinese Funerals and Chinese Ethnicity in Chiang Mai, Thailand." *Ethnology* 31, no. 4 (October 1992): 315–330.

Hitt, Neil. "Blast of Firecrackers, Blare of Brass Horns—Chinatown's Largest Funeral: Wong Goon Dick Goes to Sit with His Ancestors at the Councils of Confucius." *San Francisco Chronicle*, February 17, 1941, p. 1.

Hom, Marlon K. "Fallen Leaves' Homecoming: Notes on the 1893 Gold Mountain Charity Cemetery in Xinhui." In *Chinese America: History and Perspectives, 2002*, ed. Colleen Fong and others, 36–50. San Francisco: Chinese Historical Society of America, 2002.

Hoy, William. "Native Festivals of the California Chinese." *Western Folklore* 7, no. 3 (1948): 240–250.

Hsu, Madeline. *Dreaming of Gold, Dreaming of Home: Transnationalism and Migration between the United States and South China, 1882–1943*. Stanford, CA: Stanford University Press, 2000.

———. "Gold Mountain Dreams and Paper Son Schemes: Chinese Immigration under Exclusion." In *Chinese America: History and Perspectives, 1997*, ed. Marlon K. Hom and others, 46–60. San Francisco: Chinese Historical Society of America, 1997.

Hu, Winnie. "For Chinese, Bliss Is Eternity in the Suburbs." *New York Times*, May 6, 2001, 1, 48.

Hughey, Michael W. *Civil Religion and Moral Order: Theoretical and Historical Dimensions*. Westport, CT: Greenwood, 1983.

Humboldt (CA) Standard. April 16, 1908.

Humboldt (NV) Star. February 27, 1924.

Ibanez, Reuben, ed. *Historical Bok Kai Temple in Old Marysville, California*. Marysville, CA: Marysville Chinese Community [Inc.], 1967.

Index of Clan Names by Villages for Toishan District. Hong Kong: American Consulate General, Consular Section, 1963. Reprint, Oakton, VA: Center for Chinese Research Materials, 1973.

Institute of Archaeology, Academy of Social Sciences, People's Republic of China. *Recent Archaeological Discoveries in the People's Republic of China*. Tokyo: Center for East Asian Cultural Studies, 1984.

Island of Maui: Cemetery (Map and History) Directory. Maui, HI: Government Printing Office, 1990.

Jablon, Robert. "Asians Reburying Ancestors in the U.S." *Torrance (CA) Daily Breeze*, August 19, 2002, sec. A, 5.

Jack, R. Ian. "Chinese Cemeteries outside China." In *Histories of the Chinese in Australasia and the South Pacific*, ed. Paul Macgregor, 299–306. Melbourne: Museum of Chinese Australian History, 1995.

Jackson, Beverley. *Splendid Slippers: A Thousand Years of an Erotic Tradition*. Berkeley, CA: Ten Speed, 1997.

Jankowiak, William R. *Sex, Death, and Hierarchy in a Chinese City: An Anthropological Account*. New York: Columbia University Press, 1993.

Jeong, Bessie, MD. Interviews by Suellen Cheng and Munson Kwok, December 17, 1981, and October 17, 1982. Tape recording and transcript. Southern California Chinese-American Oral History Project, vol. 7, interview 157, 3–4. Young Research Library, Special Collections, University of California, Los Angeles.

Jiao, Tianlong. "Gender Studies in Chinese Neolithic Archaeology." In *Gender and the Archaeology of Death*, ed. Bettina Arnold and Nancy L. Wicker, 51–64. Walnut Creek, CA: AltaMira, 2001.

Jochim, Christian. *Chinese Religions: A Cultural Perspective*. Englewood Cliffs, NJ: Prentice-Hall, 1986.

Jordan, David K. *Gods, Ghosts, and Ancestors: Folk Religion in a Taiwanese Village*. Berkeley: University of California Press, 1972.

Jung, Horatio (Look San Cemetery Committee member, CCBA). Interview by Linda Sun Crowder, March 1998.

Justice Court of Carlin, County of Elko (NV). Verdict of Coroner's Jury, no. 435, filed December 23, 1944.

Kallenberger, W. W., and R. M. Kallenberger. *Memories of a Gold Digger*. Garden Grove, CA: R. M. Kallenberger, 1980.

Katayama, Tsuyoshi. "Ritual Spaces for Soul Tablets." Noon Lecture Series, UCLA Center for Chinese Studies, December 6, 2001.

Katz, Paul. "Demon or Deities? The Wangye of Taiwan." *Asian Folklore Studies* 46 (1987): 197–215.

Keeler, Charles. *San Francisco and Thereabout*. San Francisco: California Promotion Committee of San Francisco, 1902.

Keightley, David N. "The Quest for Eternity in Ancient China: The Dead, Their Gifts, Their Names." In *Ancient Mortuary Traditions of China: Papers on Chinese Ceramic Funerary Sculptures*, ed. George Kuwayama, 12–25. Los Angeles: Far Eastern Art Council, 1991.

Kelly, James (manager of Armstrong Mortuary in Chinatown, Vancouver, BC). Interview by Linda Sun Crowder, July 1997.

Knapp, Ronald G. "The Changing Landscape of the Chinese Cemetery." *China Geographer* 8 (Fall 1977): 1–14.

Koppes, Herman. Interview by Terry Abraham and Priscilla Wegars, July 30, 1993. Centerville, ID.

———. Interview by Linda Morton-Keithley, August 4, 1994. Transcription of tape recording. Idaho State Historical Society, Boise.

———. Letter to Priscilla Wegars, December 4, 1996.

———. Telephone conversation with Priscilla Wegars, October 7, 1993.

Kraus, George. *High Road to Promontory: Building the Central Pacific (Now the Southern Pacific), across the High Sierra*. Palo Alto, CA: American West, 1969.

Kreinbrink, Jeannine. E-mail to HISTARCH mailing list. March 31, 1999. At http://lists.asu.edu/archives/histarch.html.

Ku Chieh-Kang. "Funeral Processions." In *Chinese Civilization and Society: A Source Book*, ed. Patricia Buckley Ebrey, 289–293. New York: Free Press, 1981.

Kutcher, Norman A. *Mourning in Late Imperial China: Filial Piety and the State*. Cambridge: Cambridge University Press, 1999.

Kwong, Henry (funeral director and owner of mortuaries in Monterey Park, CA, and Los Angeles Chinatown). Interview by Linda Sun Crowder, April 1998.

———. Interviews by Judith Rasson, PhD, Alhambra, CA, February 23 and June 11, 1999.

Lagerwey, John. *Taoist Ritual in Chinese Society and History*. New York: Macmillan, 1987.

Lai, Chuen-Yan David. "A Feng Shui Model as a Location Index." *Annals of the Association of American Geographers* 64, no. 4 (December 1974): 506–513.

Lai, David Chuenyan. "The Chinese Cemetery in Victoria." *BC Studies* 75 (1987): 24–42.

Lai, Him Mark. "Chinese Regional Solidarity: Case Study of the Hua Xian (Fah Yuen) Community in California." In *Chinese America: History and Perspectives, 1994*, ed. Marlon Hom and others, 19–60. San Francisco: Chinese Historical Society of America, 1994.

———. "Historical Development of the Chinese Consolidated Benevolent Association/Huiguan System." In *Chinese America: History and Perspectives, 1987* [ed. Him Mark Lai, Ruthanne Lum McCunn, and Judy Yung], 13–51. San Francisco: Chinese Historical Society of America, 1987.

Lai, T. C. *To the Yellow Springs: The Chinese View of Death*. Hong Kong: Joint Publishing, 1983.

Laney, Anita. "The Chinese in Our Area." *Yuba County–Sutter County Regional Arts Council* (newsletter), February–March 1987, n.p.

Lau, Camellia (funeral director at the Green Street Mortuary, San Francisco). Interview by Linda Sun Crowder, June 1997.

Lawton, Harry W. "Selected Newspaper Accounts of Riverside's Chinese Settlers." In *Wong Ho Leun, an American Chinatown*. Vol. 1, *History*, 267–286. San Diego: Great Basin Foundation, 1987.

Lee, Calvin. *Chinatown U.S.A.* Garden City, NY: Doubleday, 1965.

Lee, Erika. *At America's Gates: Chinese Immigration during the Exclusion Era, 1882–1943*. Chapel Hill: University of North Carolina Press, 2003.

Lee, George (Golden Hill Cemetery staff member). Interview by Linda Sun Crowder, June 1998.

Lee, Gorden. Letter to Priscilla Wegars, October 29, 1997.

Lee, Jessie Wong. *Rites of Passage in Death and Dying in the Chinese American Culture*. Master's thesis, California State University, Sacramento, 1975.

Lee, Murray (curator of Chinese American history, San Diego Chinese Historical Museum). "Grandfather's Bones: A Chinese American Family History." Working paper, n.d.

Lee, Sang Hae. *Feng Shui: Its Context and Meaning*. PhD diss., Cornell University, 1986.

Lee, Sky. *Disappearing Moon Cafe*. Seattle: Seal, 1990.

Lee, Steven J. (former national president of the Lee Family Association). Interview by Linda Sun Crowder, February 1996.

Legge, James, trans. *Li Chi Book of Rites*. Vol. 1. New Hyde Park, NY: University Books, 1967.

Lewis, Oscar. *San Francisco: Mission to Metropolis*. San Diego: Howell-North Books, 1980.

Li, Shuang, and Yongfang Li. "The Funeral and Chinese Culture." *Journal of Popular Culture* 27, no. 2 (Fall 1993): 113–121.

Li, Wei. "Los Angeles's Chinese Ethnoburb: From Ethnic Service Center to Global Economy Outpost." *Urban Geography* 19, no. 6 (1998): 502–517.

Library of Congress. "San Francisco Chinese Funeral." In *Library of Congress, American Memory: Historical Collections for the National Digital Library*, at http://www.sfmuseum.org/loc/chinfuner.htm.

Lin Yee Chung Association. "General Information Sheets." N.d. [ca. 1988]. University of Nevada, Las Vegas, Lied Library Special Collections, Asian American folder 93:13.

———. *The Story of the Manoa Chinese Cemetery: With a Discussion of Ancestor Worship*. Honolulu: Lin Yee Chung Association, 1988.

Loewe, Michael. *Chinese Ideas of Life and Death: Faith, Myth, and Reason in the Han Period (202 BC–AD 220)*. London: George Allen and Unwin, 1982.

Lopez, Herman. Interview by Wendy L. Rouse, September 26, 1996. Cypress Lawn Cemetery, Colma, CA.

Los Angeles Times. December 11, 1902, August 29, 1994, December 2, 1998.

———. "Remains to Rest Peacefully in Orient" (photograph), July 31, 1937. Young Research Library, Department of Special Collections, University of California, Los Angeles, collection no. 1429.

Louie, Emma Woo. "Chinese American Name Styles and Their Significance." In *Origins and Destinations: 41 Essays on Chinese America*, 407–416. Los Angeles: Chinese Historical Society of Southern California and UCLA Asian American Studies Center, 1994.

———. *Chinese American Names: Tradition and Transition*. Jefferson, NC: McFarland, 1998.

———. Letter to Priscilla Wegars, September 19, 2002.

———. "A New Perspective on Surnames among Chinese Americans." *Amerasia Journal* 12, no. 1 (1985–1986): 1–22.

———. "Surnames as Clues to Family History." In *Chinese America: History and Perspectives 1991*, ed. Marlon K. Hom and others, 101–108. San Francisco: Chinese Historical Society of America and Asian American Studies, San Francisco State University, 1991.

Lowe, Pardee. "Good Life in Chinatown." *Asia* (February 1937): 127–131.

Lu Cai. "The Errors of Geomancy." Trans. Chunyu Wang. In *Chinese Civilization: A Sourcebook*, 2nd ed., rev., ed. Patricia Buckley Ebrey, 120–124. New York: Free Press, 1993.

Lychee Garden Restaurant staff, San Francisco. Interview by Linda Sun Crowder, June 1997.

Lydon, Sandy. *Chinese Gold: The Chinese in the Monterey Bay Area*. Capitola, CA: Capitola Book Company, 1985.

Lyman, Stanford M[orris]. *Chinese Americans*. New York: Random House, 1974.

———. "Strangers in the Cities: The Chinese on the Urban Frontier." In *Ethnic Conflict in California History*, ed. C. Wollenberg, 61–100. Los Angeles: Tinnon-Brown, 1970.

Ma, L. Eve Armentrout. "Chinese Traditional Religion in North America and Hawaii." In *Chinese America: History and Perspectives 1988*, ed. Him Mark Lai, Ruthanne Lum McCunn, and Judy Yung, 131–147. San Francisco: Chinese Historical Society of America, 1988.

——. "The Social Organization of Chinatowns in North America and Hawaii in the 1890s." In *Early Chinese Immigrant Societies: Case Studies from North America and British Southeast Asia*, ed. Lee Lai Top, 159–185. Singapore: Heinemann Publishers Asia, 1988.

——. "Urban Chinese at the Sinitic Frontier: Social Organizations in United States' Chinatowns, 1849–1898." *Modern Asian Studies*, 17, no. 1 (1983): 107–135.

Maniery, Mary L., and Cindy L. Baker. "National Register of Historic Places Registration Form. Chung Wah Cemetery, Folsom, California." Sacramento, CA: PAR Environmental Services, 1995.

Mansfield, George C. *History of Butte County*. Los Angeles: Historic Record Company, 1918.

March, Andrew L. "An Appreciation of Chinese Geomancy." *Journal of Asian Studies* 27, no. 2 (February 1968): 253–267.

Marysville (CA) Appeal. May 11, 1893–March 4, 1927.

Marysville (CA) Appeal-Democrat. March 13, 1929–July 27, 1998.

Marysville (CA) Daily Appeal. January 24, 1860–March 4, 1919.

Marysville (CA) Daily Democrat. March 17, 1885–September 24, 1912.

Marysville (CA) Daily Herald. February 6, 1856–January 29, 1857.

Marysville (CA) Daily National Democrat. February 2, 1859.

Marysville (CA) Evening Democrat. December 27, 1911–February 27, 1922.

Marysville (CA) North Californian. February 5, 1867.

Marysville (CA) Times of Yuba-Sutter. May 10, 1996.

Marysville (CA) Weekly Appeal. March 6, 1869–February 22, 1895.

Marysville City Council. "Minutes." History Room, Yuba County Library, Marysville, CA. April 22, 1851–August 3, 1896.

Marysville Daily California Express. February 13, 1858–February 11, 1861.

McBride, Marla. "Chinese Funerals." In *Chinese Argonauts: An Anthology of the Chinese Contributions to the Historical Development of Santa Clara County*, ed. Gloria Sun Hom, 60–69. Los Altos, CA: Foothill Community College, 1971.

McCarthy, Justin. "Tales from the Empire City: Chinese Miners in the Pine Creek Region, Northern Territory, 1872–1915." In *Histories of the Chinese in Australasia and the South Pacific*, ed. Paul Macgregor, 191–202. Melbourne: Museum of Chinese Australian History, 1995.

McDannold, Thomas A. "Chinese Placenames and Their Significance." In *Origins and Destinations: 41 Essays on Chinese America*, 177–188. Los Angeles: Chinese Historical Society of Southern California and UCLA Asian American Studies Center, 1994.

McDermott, Joseph P. *State and Court Ritual in China*. Cambridge: Cambridge University Press, 1999.

McGowan, Joseph A. *History of the Sacramento Valley*. Vol. 1. New York: Lewis Historical Publishing, 1961.

McLeod, Alexander. *Pigtails and Gold Dust*. Caldwell, ID: Caxton, 1948.

McMurtrie, Mary Ellen. *Bricks and Boardwalks: A Walking-Tour Guide to Historic Idaho City*. Idaho City, ID: Idaho City Historic Foundation, 1995.

Meek, John. Telephone conversation with Priscilla Wegars, 1997.

Minnick, Sylvia Sun. Interview by Wendy L. Rouse, September 25, 1996.

———. *Samfow: The San Joaquin Chinese Legacy*. Fresno, CA: Panorama West, 1988.

Moore, Joseph M. *The Test Excavation of 26MN540, Acme Playa, Mineral County, Nevada*. NDOT Archaeological Technical Report Series 2. Carson City: Nevada Department of Transportation, 1986.

Moscow Cemetery Deed Book. "Addition to Blk. 5." Manuscript, Moscow City Cemetery, Moscow, ID, 1897–1930.

Motooka, Bobby. Interview by Reiko Neizman, 1999.

Mueller, Fred W., Jr. "Feng-Shui: Archaeological Evidence for Geomancy in Overseas Chinese Settlements." In *Wong Ho Leun, an American Chinatown*, vol. 2, *Archaeology*, 1–24. San Diego: Great Basin Foundation, 1987.

Muscatine, Doris. *Old San Francisco: The Biography of a City from Early Days to the Earthquake*. New York: G. P. Putnam's Sons, 1975.

Myrick, David F. *Railroads of Nevada and Eastern California*. 2 vols. Berkeley, CA: Howell-North Books, 1962–1963.

Naquin, Susan. "Funerals in North China: Uniformity and Variation." In *Death Ritual in Late Imperial and Modern China*, ed. James L. Watson and Evelyn S. Rawski, 37–70. Berkeley: University of California Press, 1988.

Neizman, Reiko. "Chinese Cemeteries in Maui." University of Nevada, Las Vegas, Lied Library Special Collections, Asian American folder 93:13.

Nelson, Judy. "The Chinese in Spokane, 1860–1915." Master's thesis, Eastern Washington State University, 1994.

———. "The Final Journey Home: Chinese Burial Practices in Spokane." In "The Chinese in the Frontier Northwest" (special issue), *Pacific Northwest Forum*, 2nd ser., 6, no. 1 (Winter–Spring 1993): 70–76.

Newmark, Harris. *Sixty Years in Southern California*. Boston: Houghton Mifflin, 1930.

Nez Perce County Leases. Book N. Nez Perce County Courthouse, Lewiston, ID, 1891.

Nielsen, Niels C., Jr., Norvin Hein, Samuel E. Karff, Grace G. Burford, and Alan L. Miller. *Religions of the World*. 3rd ed. New York: St. Martin's, 1993.

Nii, Esme. "Sons Fulfill Monumental Obligations." *Honolulu Advertiser*, April 3, 2000.

Nolte, Carl. "How Sweet the Sound." *San Francisco Examiner and Chronicle*, October 13, 1996, sec. 6, p. 1.

Nordyke, Eleanor C., and Richard K. C. Lee. "The Chinese in Hawai'i: A Historical and Demographic Perspective." *Hawaiian Journal of History* 23 (1989): 196–216.

Olney, Caroline M. "Mountains and Valleys of Yuba County." *Overland Monthly* 40 (December 1902): 569–588.

Oroville (CA) Mercury. August 3, 1912.

Osgood, Cornelius. *Village Life in Old China: A Community Study of Kao Yao, Yunnan*. New York: Ronald, 1963.

Owsley, Douglas, and others. "Osteology and Paleopathology of the Carlin Chinese Cemetery." Report dated November 1997, University of Nevada, Las Vegas, Special Collections Library, Asian American file #93.

Pacific Telephone and Telegraph Company. *Pacific Telephone Directory for San Francisco, Including Brisbane, Colma and Daly City.* [San Francisco]: Pacific Telephone and Telegraph Company, 1968.

———. *San Francisco, Including Daly City, Brisbane, and Colma Yellow Pages Directory.* [San Francisco]: Pacific Telephone and Telegraph Company, 1975.

———. *San Francisco, Including Daly City, Brisbane, and Colma Yellow Pages Directory.* [San Francisco]: Pacific Telephone and Telegraph Company, 1981.

Paden, Irene D., and Margaret E. Schlichtmann. *The Big Oak Flat Road: An Account of Freighting from Stockton to Yosemite Valley.* Oakland, CA: Holmes Book Company, 1959.

Pang, Duane. "The P'u-tu Ritual: A Celebration of the Chinese Community in Honolulu." In *Buddhist and Taoist Studies*, vol. 1, ed. Michael Saso and David W. Chappell, 95–122. Asia Studies at Hawai'i 18. Honolulu: University Press of Hawai'i, 1977.

Parish, William L., and Martin King Whyte. *Village and Family in Contemporary China.* Chicago: University of Chicago Press, 1978.

Patterson, Edna, Louise A. Ulph, and Victor Goodwin. *Nevada's Northeast Frontier.* Sparks, NV: Western Printing, 1969.

Peters, Larry. "Green Dragons and White Tigers on Gold Mountain: *Feng-Shui* in Barkerville." *B.C. Historical News* (Fall 1998): 17–20.

Pollard, A. M. "Dating the Time of Death." In *Studies in Crime: An Introduction to Forensic Archaeology*, ed. John Hunter, Charlotte Roberts, and Anthony Martin, 139–155. London: Batsford, 1996.

Pollard, Lisa (director and leader of the Green Street Brass Band). Interviews by Linda Sun Crowder, April 1996, May 1997, August 1998.

Porter, Kevin (musician for the Green Street Brass Band). Interview by Linda Sun Crowder, April 1998.

Prothero, Stephen. *Purified by Fire: A History of Cremation in America.* Berkeley: University of California Press, 2001.

Purnell, Nanette Napoleon. "Oriental and Polynesian Cemetery Traditions in the Hawaiian Islands." In *Ethnicity and the American Cemetery*, ed. Richard E. Meyer, 193–239. Bowling Green, OH: Bowling Green State University Popular Press, 1993.

Radin, Paul, ed. *The Golden Mountain: Chinese Tales Told in California.* Formosa, [Taiwan]: Orient Cultural Service, 1971.

Ramey, Earl. *The Beginnings of Marysville.* San Francisco: Lawton R. Kennedy, 1936.

Rawski, Evelyn S. "A Historian's Approach to Chinese Death Ritual." In *Death Ritual in Late Imperial and Modern China*, ed. James L. Watson and Evelyn S. Rawski, 20–34. Berkeley: University of California Press, 1988.

(Reno) Nevada State Journal. August 1, 1930.

Reno (NV) Evening Gazette. December 16, 1916–March 5, 1941.

Richards, Vern. "Boyhood Recollections of the Silver Creek Chinese." *Plumas Memories* 25 (June 4, 1967): 9–10. Plumas County Historical Society.

Riddle, Ronald. *Flying Dragons, Flowing Streams: Music in the Life of San Francisco's Chinese.* Westport, CT: Greenwood, 1983.

Rose, Jerome C., ed. *Gone to a Better Land: A Biohistory of a Rural Black Cemetery in the Post-Reconstruction South.* Arkansas Archeological Survey Research Series 25. Fayetteville: Arkansas Archeological Survey, 1985.

Rossbach, Sarah. *Feng Shui: The Chinese Art of Placement.* New York: E. P. Dutton, 1983.

Roy, William G., and Philip Bonacich. "Interlocking Directorates and Communities of Interest among American Railroad Companies, 1905." *American Sociological Review* 53, no. 3 (June 1988): 368–380.

Rusco, Mary. Photographs of the Chinese cemetery in Lovelock. University of Nevada, Las Vegas Library, Special Collections, Asian American photographs file.

Sacramento (CA) Bee. March 28, 1857–February 27, 1966.

Sacramento (CA) Daily Bee. November 13, 1885.

Sacramento (CA) Daily Record Union. February 24, 1877–January 1, 1878.

Sacramento (CA) Reporter. June 30, 1870.

Sacramento (CA) Union. January 21, 1858–September 16, 1885.

Salter, Christopher L. *San Francisco's Chinatown: How Chinese a Town?* San Francisco: R and E Research Associates, 1978.

Sam Yup Association. *A History of the Sam Yup Benevolent Association in the United States, 1850–1974.* San Francisco: Sam Yup Association, 1975.

Sanborn Map Company. *Map of the City of Marysville, Yuba County, California.* 1909, 1921. Copies at Paul G. Chace and Associates, Escondido, CA.

Sando, Ruth Ann, and David L. Felton. "Inventory Records of Ceramics and Opium from a Nineteenth Century Chinese Store in California." In *Hidden Heritage: Historical Archaeology of the Overseas Chinese*, ed. Priscilla Wegars, 151–176. Amityville, NY: Baywood, 1993.

San Francisco Alta. January 19, 1858–March 8, 1867.

San Francisco Bulletin. July 2, 1879.

San Francisco Call. January 20, 1883–January 27, 1897.

San Francisco Chronicle. January 27, 1897–September 24, 1903; October 26, 1947.

San Francisco Convention and Visitor Bureau staff. Interview by Linda Sun Crowder, November 2000.

San Francisco Herald. April 9, 1858–April 5, 1860.

San Francisco Morning Call. March 23, 1893.

San Francisco Post. September 21–28, 1877.

Santa Barbara (CA) Daily Independent. November 15, 1895.

Saso, Michael R. *Blue Dragon, White Tiger: Taoist Rites of Passage.* Washington, DC: Taoist Center, 1990.

———. "Orthodoxy and Heterodoxy in Taoist Ritual." In *Religion and Ritual in Chinese Society*, ed. Arthur P. Wolf, 325–336. Stanford, CA: Stanford University Press, 1974.

———. *Taoism and the Rite of Cosmic Renewal.* 2nd ed. Pullman: Washington State University Press, 1990.

———. *The Teachings of Taoist Master Chuang*. New Haven, CT: Yale University Press, 1978.

Schipper, Kristofer. *The Taoist Body*. Berkeley: University of California Press, 1993.

Schneider, Laurence A. *A Madman of Ch'u: The Chinese Myth of Loyalty and Dissent*. Berkeley: University of California Press, 1980.

Schumacher, Paul J. F. "Current Research: Pacific West; Shasta-Trinity National Forest." *Society for Historical Archaeology Newsletter* 12, no. 2 (June 1979): 20–21.

Schwartz, Steven J., and Kelly A. Rossbach. "A Preliminary Survey of Historic Sites on San Nicolas Island." In *Proceedings of the Society for California Archaeology* 6 (1993): 189–198.

Seuss, Dale. Interview by Wendy L. Rouse, September 25, 1996.

Shahar, Meir, and Robert P. Weller. "Introduction: Gods and Society in China." In *Unruly Gods, Divinity and Society in China*, ed. Meir Shahar and Robert P. Weller, 1–36. Honolulu: University of Hawai'i Press, 1996.

———, eds. *Unruly Gods, Divinity and Society in China*. Honolulu: University of Hawai'i Press, 1996.

Shan, Vivian Lim Tsui. "Specializing in Death: The Case of the Chinese in Singapore." *Southeast Asian Journal of Social Sciences* 23, no. 2 (October 1995): 63–88.

Sherwood, T. J. *The Resources of Yuba County, the Garden Spot of California*. Marysville, CA: Democrat, 1894.

Simmons, Trace. Interview by Judith Rasson, PhD, 1999. Rose Hills Cemetery, Whittier, CA.

Sing, Richard Tam. Interview by Reiko Neizman, 1999.

Sinn, Elizabeth. "Moving Bones: Hong Kong's Role as an 'In-between Place' in the Chinese Diaspora." Paper presented at the Association for Asian Studies Conference in Washington, DC, 2002.

Site Data Form. Maui, HI: Government Printing Office, 1990.

Smith, Dottie. *The History of the Chinese in Shasta County*. Redding, CA: Smith, 1995.

Speer, William. *The Oldest and the Newest Empire: China and the United States*. Vol. 2. Cincinnati, OH: National, 1870.

Spokane (WA) Spokesman-Review. May 25, 1902, September 24, 1905.

State of Nevada. *General Statutes of Nevada*. Carson City, NV: State Printing Office, 1879, 1885.

Steele, John, trans. The *I-Li, or Book of Etiquette and Ceremonial*. Vol. 2. London: Probsthain, 1917.

Steiner, Bill (assistant manager and funeral director at the Green Street Mortuary, San Francisco). Interviews by Linda Sun Crowder, April 1996, May 1997, August 1998.

Stepanchuk, Carol, and Charles Wong. *Mooncakes and Hungry Ghosts: Festivals of China*. San Francisco: China Books and Periodicals, 1991.

Stewart, Maggie. "Hawaii Cemetery Records Now Online." US GenWeb Archives: Hawaii Cemetery Project. At www.rootsweb.com/~usgenweb/hi/hicem.htm.

St. Louis (MO) Post-Dispatch. November 17, 1928.

Stuart, Jan, and Evelyn S. Rawski. *Worshipping the Ancestors: Chinese Commemorative Portraits*. Washington, DC: Freer Gallery of Art, 2001.

Sung, Betty Lee. *The Chinese in America*. New York: Macmillan, 1972.

Sung, Edgar (*fengshui* master). Interview by Wendy L. Rouse, October 24, 1996.

Swope, Sally. "Cathay Club: Chinatown's First Marching Band Celebrates 75th Year." *East-West*, September 11, 1986, 10–11.

Teather, Elizabeth Kenworthy. "Themes from Complex Landscapes: Chinese Cemeteries and Columbaria in Urban Hong Kong." *Australian Geographical Studies* 36, no. 1 (1998): 21– [37].

Teng, Wei. "Keeping the Public Clean Is Beneficial to You and Others." *Chinese Express,* May 1, 1996, 3.

Thiel, Homer. Letter to Roberta S. Greenwood, October 8, 1998.

Thompson and West. *History of Yuba County, California, with Illustrations Descriptive of Its Scenery, Residences, Public Buildings, Fine Blocks and Manufactories*. Oakland, CA: Thompson and West, 1879.

Thompson, Stuart E. "Death, Food, and Fertility." In *Death Ritual in Late Imperial and Modern China*, ed. James L. Watson and Evelyn S. Rawski, 71–108. Berkeley: University of California Press, 1988.

Thorp, Robert L. "The Qin and Han Imperial Tombs and the Development of Mortuary Architecture." In *The Quest for Eternity: Chinese Ceramic Sculptures from the People's Republic of China*, ed. Susan Caroselli, 16–37. San Francisco: Chronicle Books for the Los Angeles County Museum of Art, 1987.

Tihada, Alice. Interview by Reiko Neizman, 1999.

Tombstone (AZ) Epitaph, December 18, 1906.

Tong, Chee-Kiong. "Dangerous Blood, Refined Souls: Death Rituals among the Chinese in Singapore." PhD diss., Cornell University, 1987.

Tong, Yook Chew. Interview by Judith Rasson, PhD, Pasadena, CA, May 14, 1999.

———. "Tong Family Remembrance." Composition read at Rose Hills Memorial Park, Garden of Tranquility, August 22, 1998.

Tonopah (NV) Bonanza. February 1, 1921.

Towle, Russell, ed. *Artifacts from the Dutch Flat Forum, 1875–1878*. 3rd ed. Dutch Flat, CA: Giant Gap, 1993.

Traywick, Ben. "Tombstone's Dragon Lady." *True West* 46, no. 5 (May 1999): 26–31.

Tsai, Shih-shan Henry. *The Chinese Experience in America*. Bloomington: Indiana University Press, 1986.

Tu, Wei-ming. *Confucian Thought: Selfhood as Creative Transformation*. Albany: State University of New York, 1985.

———. "Soul: Chinese Concept." In *Encyclopedia of Religion*, vol. 13, ed. Mircea Eliade, 447–450. New York: Macmillan, 1986.

Tuscarora (NV) Times-Review. July 7, 1882.

United States Census. California, Yuba County, Marysville. 1850, 1852, 1860, 1870, 1880, 1890, 1900, 1910, 1920, 1930, 1940, 1950, 1960, 1970, 1980, 1990.

———. Nevada, Elko County, Carlin. 1870, 1880, 1900, 1910, 1920.

United States Immigration and Naturalization Service. Chinese Partnership Lists, San Francisco District. Record Group 85, boxes 58 and 59, folders 13525/1 through 13525/51. San Bruno, CA: National Archives, Pacific Sierra Region.

————. Partnership records of Quong Wing and Company, Carlin, Nevada, 1902. Record Group 85, file #13562/305. San Bruno, CA: National Archives, Pacific Sierra Region.

————. Partnership records of Sing Lee and Company, Carlin, Nevada, 1894 and 1902. Record Group 85, file #13562/304. San Bruno, CA: National Archives, Pacific Sierra Region.

United States Navy, Twelfth Naval District Commandant's Office. General Correspondence, Intelligence Office, 1945, formerly classified. NND Project 868156, Record Group 181, folder A8-5, National Archives, San Bruno, California, containing a detailed account, dated September 1868, of the histories, functions, and officers of the Chinese Six Companies.

Ventura (CA) Free Press. April 5, 1884.

Vierra, Anthony. Interview by Reiko Neizman, 1999.

Virginia City (NV) Territorial Enterprise. April 12, 1871.

Ward, Barbara E., and Joan Law. *Chinese Festivals in Hong Kong*. 3rd ed. [Hong Kong]: Guidebook, 1995.

————. "Funeral Specialists in Cantonese Society: Pollution, Performance, and Social Hierarchy." In *Death Ritual in Late Imperial and Modern China*, ed. James L. Watson and Evelyn S. Rawski, 109–134. Berkeley: University of California Press, 1988.

————. "Of Flesh and Bones: The Management of Death Pollution in Cantonese Society." In *Death and the Regeneration of Life,* ed. Maurice Bloch and Jonathan Parry, 155–186. Cambridge: Cambridge University Press, 1982.

————. "The Structure of Chinese Funerary Rites: Elementary Forms, Ritual Sequence, and the Primacy of Performance." In *Death Ritual in Late Imperial and Modern China*, ed. James L. Watson and Evelyn S. Rawski, 3–19. Berkeley: University of California Press, 1988.

Watson, James L., and Evelyn S. Rawski, eds. *Death Ritual in Late Imperial and Modern China*. Berkeley: University of California Press, 1988.

Watson, Rubie S. "Remembering the Dead: Graves and Politics in Southeastern China." In *Death Ritual in Late Imperial and Modern China*, ed. James L. Watson and Evelyn S. Rawski, 203–227. Berkeley: University of California Press, 1988.

Wechsler, Howard J. *Offerings of Jade and Silk: Ritual and Symbol in the Legitimation of the T'ang Dynasty*. New Haven, CT: Yale University Press, 1985.

Weekly Elko (NV) Independent. June 16, 1878–May 8, 1905.

Wegars, Priscilla. *The Ah Hee Diggings: Final Report of Archaeological Investigations at OR-GR-16, the Granite, Oregon "Chinese Walls" Site, 1992 through 1994*. University of Idaho Anthropological Reports 97. Moscow, ID: Alfred W. Bowers Laboratory of Anthropology, 1995.

————. "Chinese at the Confluence and Beyond: A Case Study of Asian Entrepreneurs and Other Pioneers in Early Pierce and Lewiston." Working paper, 1996.

————. "The History and Archaeology of the Chinese in Northern Idaho, 1880 through 1910." PhD diss., University of Idaho, 1991.

————. Interview by Wendy L. Rouse, October 12, 1996.

————. "Marjorie Fong, A Chinese American Pioneer of Baker City, Oregon." Working paper, 1996.

——. "Polly Bemis: Lurid Life or Literary Legend?" In *Wild Women of the Old West*, ed. Glenda Riley and Richard W. Etulain, 45–68, 200–203. Golden, CO: Fulcrum, 2003.

Weiss, Melford. *Valley City: A Chinese Community in America*. Cambridge, MA: Schenkman, 1974.

Weller, Robert P. "Bandits, Beggars, and Ghosts: The Failure of State Control over Religious Interpretation in Taiwan." *American Ethnologist* 12, no. 1 (1985): 46–61.

——. *Unities and Diversities in Chinese Religion*. Seattle: University of Washington Press, 1987.

Wells, Mariann Kaye. *Chinese Temples in California*. San Francisco: R and E Research Associates, 1971.

Wells Fargo and Company. *Directory of Principal Chinese Business Firms in San Francisco [Oakland, Sacramento, San Jose, Stockton, Marysville, Los Angeles, Portland, Virginia City, Victoria]*. San Francisco, Wells Fargo, 1882.

——. *Wells Fargo and Co.'s Express Directory of Chinese Business Houses, San Francisco, Sacramento, Marysville, Portland, Stockton, San Jose [and] Virginia City, Nev*. San Francisco, Wells Fargo, 1878.

Wey, Nancy, comp. "Chinese Sites in California." Photocopy in the Asian American Comparative Collection, University of Idaho, n.d.

Whyte, Martin K. "Death in the People's Republic of China." In *Death Ritual in Late Imperial and Modern China*, ed. James L. Watson and Evelyn S. Rawski, 289–316. Berkeley: University of California Press, 1988.

Williams, Charles A. S. *Encyclopedia of Chinese Symbolism and Art Motives*. New York: Julian Press, 1960.

Winnemucca (NV) Daily Silver State. June 8, 1878.

Winnemucca (NV) Humboldt Star. February 27, 1924–August 1, 1930.

Winnemucca (NV) Silver State. May 14, 1877–April 3, 1882.

Winterbotham, William. *An Historical, Geographical, and Philosophical View of the Chinese Empire*. London: Ridgway, 1795.

Wolf, Arthur P. "Chinese Kinship and Mourning Dress." In *Family and Kinship in Chinese Society*, ed. Maurice Freedman, 189–207. Stanford, CA: Stanford University Press, 1970.

——. "Gods, Ghosts, and Ancestors." In *Religion and Ritual in Chinese Society*, ed. Arthur P. Wolf, 131–182. Stanford, CA: Stanford University Press, 1974.

——, ed. *Religion and Ritual in Chinese Society*. Stanford, CA: Stanford University Press, 1974.

Wong, Bernard, PhD (professor of anthropology, San Francisco State University, and research expert on American Chinatowns and the Chinese in America). Interview by Linda Sun Crowder, June 1997.

Wong, Gerrye. "Golden Hill Memorial Park Helps Families Plan for the Future." *AsianWeek*, October 29, 1993, 8.

Wong, Wilson (owner-operator of Fat Ming Company, a stationery store on Grant Avenue, and former musician in the Cathay Band). Interviews by Linda Sun Crowder, April 1996, January 1997.

[Wong Kin, ed.]. *International Chinese Business Directory of the World for the Year 1913*. San Francisco: International Chinese Business Directory, 1913.

Wu, David Y. H. "'To Kill Three Birds with One Stone': The Rotating Credit Associations of the Papua New Guinea Chinese." *American Ethnologist* 1, no. 3 (August 1974): 565–575.

Wu, Ting-Fang. "China and the Chinese People." *Los Angeles Times*, July 15, 1900, 6.

Wu Hung. *Monumentality in Early Chinese Art and Architecture*. Stanford, CA: Stanford University Press, 1995.

Xu, Yixian, trans. "Translation Notes: Gravestone of 'Lee Mann.'" Asian American Comparative Collection, University of Idaho, Moscow, 1993.

Yang, C. K. *Religion in Chinese Society: A Study of Contemporary Social Functions of Religion and Some of Their Historical Factors*. Berkeley: University of California Press, 1961.

Yang, Jeannie K., and Virginia R. Hellmann. "What's in the Pot? An Emic Perspective on Chinese Brown Glazed Stoneware." Paper presented at the Twenty-ninth Conference on Historical and Underwater Archaeology, Cincinnati, OH, January 1996.

Yang, Martin C. *A Chinese Village: Taitou, Shantung Province*. New York: Columbia University Press, 1945.

Yang Fenggang. "Religious Conversions and Identity Construction: A Study of a Chinese Christian Church in the United States." PhD diss., Catholic University of America, 1996–1997.

Yao, Xiaoyun, trans. "Translation Notes: 'Burial Brick of Ru Chui Zhen'" (pinyin). Asian American Comparative Collection, University of Idaho, Moscow, 1999.

Yee, Clifford (manager and funeral director of the Green Street Mortuary, San Francisco). Interviews by Linda Sun Crowder, April 1996, May 1997, August 1998.

Yee Ah Chong. "Chinese Burial Customs," a chapter in "The Chinese in Vacaville," interview by Ron Limbaugh, February 4 and 12, 1977, transcript, 51–54, Vacaville Museum, Vacaville, California.

Yen, Tzy Kuei. *Chinese Workers and the First Transcontinental Railroad of the United States of America*. Ann Arbor, MI: Xerox University Microfilms, 1977.

Yick, Martha (owner-operator of the Wah Wing Sang, the oldest mortuary in New York Chinatown). Interviews by Linda Sun Crowder, June and September 1997.

Yoo, David K. *New Spiritual Homes: Religion and Asian Americans*. Honolulu: University of Hawai'i Press, 1999.

Young, Nellie May. *William Stewart Young, 1859–1937, Builder of California Institutions: An Intimate Biography*. Glendale, CA: Arthur H. Clark, 1967.

Yu, Ying-Shih. "'O Soul, Come Back!' A Study in the Changing Conceptions of the Soul and Afterlife in Pre-Buddhist China." *Harvard Journal of Asiatic Studies* 47, no. 2 (December 1987): 370–395.

Yuba City (CA) Independent-Herald. June 14, 1951.

Yuba City (CA) Weekly Sutter Banner. April 24, 1869.

Yuba County Deeds. "Deed Book," 29. Office of the Yuba County Recorder, Marysville, CA.

Yu Kuang-hong. "Making a Malefactor a Benefactor: Ghost Worship in Taiwan." *Bulletin of the Institute of Ethnology Academia Sinica* 70 (1990): 39–66.

Zhang, Zhiyuan, and Zunguan Huang. "A Brief Account of Traditional Chinese Festival Customs." *Journal of Popular Culture* 27, no. 2 (Fall 1993): 13–25.

Zhou, Yu. "How Do Places Matter? A Comparative Study of Chinese Ethnic Communities in Los Angeles and New York City." *Urban Geography* 19, no. 6 (1998): 531–553.

Zhu, Liping. "'A Chinaman's Chance' on the Rocky Mountain Frontier." *Montana: The Magazine of Western History* 45, no. 4 (Autumn/Winter 1995): 36–51.

———. *A Chinaman's Chance: The Chinese on the Rocky Mountain Mining Frontier.* Niwot: University Press of Colorado, 1997.

Zo, Kil Young. *Chinese Emigration into the United States, 1850–1880.* New York: Arno, 1978.

Index

acculturation, 2, 8, 9, 66–70, 115, 139, 147, 157, 162, 184–88, 191, 195–232, 255
adaptation:
of American customs, 5, 13, 17n37, 56, 67, 147
of Chinese traditions, 2, 40, 47, 67, 115
afterlife, 5, 6, 21–23, 28, 30, 256
agricultural workers, 176–91, 245
Ahern, Emily M., 4, 22, 24
Ah Hong Chee, 188
Ah Lee Sam (Mrs.) (Ah Loikeau), 188
Ah Lum, 17n45
Ah Quang or Quoy, 129
Ah Sam, 162–63
Aijmer, Goran, 4
altars, 114, 141n20, 158, 189, 243
at cemetery, 114, *244*
with coffin, 113
family, 246
Americanization, 2, 40, 69–70, 214
See also acculturation
American Canyon, Nevada, 142n44
ancestors, 186, 191
appeasing spirits of, 14, 21, 179, 246–47

care of, 9, 26, 40, 111, 139, 181, 248–49
reverence and respect for, 3–4, 13, 21, 23, 31, 181, 183, 201, 234, 242, *254*, 255–58
writers on, 1
ancestor worship. *See* ancestors: reverence and respect for
ancestral tablet. *See* spirit tablet
anti-Chinese sentiments and movements, 2–3, 7, 30–32, 35, 116, 118, 131, 147
against funeral customs and burial practices, 35, 38, 247
writers on, 1
See also Chinese Exclusion Acts; discrimination
archaeological excavations, 19, 21, 22, 41, 81–104, 107–39
assimilation, 1–2, 40, 67–68, 147, 154, 162, 195–232, 256
associations. *See* Chinese Consolidated Benevolent Association (CCBA); *huiguan* (district associations); *names* of individual associations
Auburn, California, 89, 159

About the Contributors

Terry Abraham is the head of the Special Collections and Archives at the University of Idaho Library in Moscow, Idaho. He has presented research papers on Chinese cemeteries at the Sixth Chinese American Conference, San Diego; at the Association for Asian American Studies meeting, Honolulu; and in the symposium "Temples and Tombstones: The Archaeology of the Overseas Chinese Dead," at the conference "Global and Local Dimensions of Asian America" in Sydney, Australia.

Paul G. Chace is a social anthropologist and archaeologist who received his PhD from the University of California, Riverside, in 1992. His dissertation presents a social history of the annual civic festivals for the Bok Kai Temple in Marysville, California, as a positive exemplar of interethnic community relations; the National Trust for Historic Preservation named this landmark temple, last renovated in 1880, to the trust's 2001 list of America's Eleven Most Endangered Historic Places. As proprietor of Paul G. Chace and Associates, a CRM/land planning consulting firm based in Escondido, California, Chace has served since 1976 as a principal archaeologist and historian for hundreds of planning projects. For more than two decades, he also has been an active member of the Chinese Historical Society of Southern California.

Sue Fawn Chung is an associate professor of history at the University of Nevada, Las Vegas. She received her BA from the University of California, Los Angeles; AM from Harvard University; and PhD from the University of California, Berkeley. She is an advisor to the National Trust for Historic Preservation, a member of the NTHP's Diversity Council, and an advisor to Preserve Nevada, the statewide preservation organization. She serves on the

Board of Museums and History for the state of Nevada. Her fields of specialization are late Qing history and Chinese American history. She has published numerous studies on Chinese Americans.

Linda Sun Crowder received her PhD in anthropology from the University of Hawai'i. Her research areas focus on death rituals, American Chinatowns, the Chinese diaspora, and public culture performances.

Fred P. Frampton received his BS and MA degrees in anthropology from Northern Arizona University. Since 1987 he has been the forest archaeologist for the Humboldt-Toiyabe National Forest. In this capacity Frampton has coordinated and conducted excavations at a number of nineteenth-century Chinese mining and logging camps across northern Nevada. An important aspect of this work has been public participation and interpretation.

Roberta S. Greenwood, RPA, is the president of Greenwood and Associates, a firm devoted to studies of both prehistoric and historical cultural resources. Among her distinctions is the J. C. Harrington Medal, the highest award of the Society for Historical Archaeology. Her publications include the award-winning book *Down by the Station: Los Angeles Chinatown, 1880–1933* (1996). She has conducted archaeological, historical, and collections research at Chinese sites in Los Angeles, Ventura, Napa, Santa Barbara, Cambria, El Paso, San Luis Obispo, San Diego, Phoenix, and California's gold rush counties.

Timothy W. Murphy received his BA from the University of Arizona in 1973. He has worked as an archaeologist for the Bureau of Land Management's Elko Field Office in Elko, Nevada, for the last twenty-three years. He is active in the Nevada Archaeological Association.

Reiko Neizman was born and raised in Lahaina, Maui, and graduated from the Kamehameha Schools as a boarding student. She received a BA in history from the University of Nevada, Las Vegas, and is currently working toward a master's degree in library and information sciences at the University of Hawai'i, Manoa. In addition to attending school full-time, Reiko works full-time for Kapalua Land Company as a help desk administrator.

Wendy L. Rouse has an MA in history and archaeology from California State University, Sacramento. Her research has focused primarily on the social history of the California gold rush, with a special emphasis on the history of Chinese Americans. She is currently a doctoral candidate at the University of California, Davis.

Priscilla Wegars, PhD, is the founder and volunteer curator of the University of Idaho's Asian American Comparative Collection, a repository of artifacts and documentary materials essential for the study of Asian American archaeological sites, economic contributions, and cultural history. She edited *Hidden Heritage: Historical Archaeology of the Overseas Chinese* (1993) and wrote *Polly Bemis: A Chinese American Pioneer* (2003) and "Polly Bemis: Lurid Life or Literary Legend?" in *Wild Women of the Old West*, edited by Glenda Riley and Richard W. Etulain (2003).